Praise for

Bonds: The Unbeaten Path to Secure Investment Growth
by Hildy Richelson and Stan Richelson

"Too many investors suffer from biting off more than they can chew. They would be better off financially if they would follow the keep-it-simple principle that the Richelsons meticulously de scribe in their new book."

Robert L. Freedman
Partner, Dechert LLP

"Standard advice says investors need to strike a comfortable bal ance between risk tolerance and return expectations. In *Bonds*, Stan and Hildy Richelson convincingly challenge conventional wisdom. Using a straightforward, repeatable approach, the au thors outline how to find safety without sacrifice by harnessing the unique risk-adjusted characteristics of bonds."

Bill D'Alonzo
Chief Executive and Chief Investment Officer, Friess Associates
Manager of the Brandywine Funds

"The unconventional wisdom in 'the unbeaten path' will soon be come the conventional wisdom for anyone nearing retirement and frightened by the stock market's volatility of the past dec ade. Hildy and Stan Richelson do all of us a big favor by outlin ing, step-by-step, how we can use bonds for growth and income in retirement."

Kevin Adler, MBA
Editor, *NAPFA Advisor: The Journal of the National Association of Personal Financial Advisors*

"Hildy and Stan Richelson demystify bond investing with this clearly written, comprehensive review of the fixed-income mar kets. In place of conventional, equity-based strategies, they con vincingly propose bonds as the preferred alternative for individ uals seeking attractive returns with low risk."

Andrew B. Williams, CFA
Chief Investment Officer, Philadelphia International Advisers

"All investment advisers and investors, particularly those who can't afford to see savings disappear, should read this book. It explains how the 100 percent bond portfolio strategy eliminates risk, can be superior to equity strategies, and can be imple mented by anyone. The book's summaries of bond basics, bond categories, and options for purchasing are important tools for everyone who invests. Don't miss them."

Paul H. Frankel
Partner, Morrison & Foerster LLP

"This is a highly provocative, entertaining, and thoroughly informative book. The first chapter sets the tone: Everything you thought you knew about portfolio management is probably wrong—especially about the alleged superiority of equities over bonds. A must-read!"

Sam Kirschner, PhD
Managing Director, MayerCap, LLC

BONDS

BONDS

The Unbeaten Path to Secure Investment Growth

HILDY RICHELSON
STAN RICHELSON

Foreword by

JOHN BRYNJOLFSSON
MANAGING DIRECTOR, PIMCO

Viva Books

New Delhi | Mumbai | Chennai | Kolkata | Bangalore | Hyderabad | Kochi | Guwahati

First Indian Edition 2009

VIVA BOOKS PRIVATE LIMITED

- 4737/23 Ansari Road, Daryaganj, New Delhi 110 002
  E-mail: vivadelhi@vivagroupindia.net, Tel. 42242200
- 76, Service Industries, Shirvane, Sector 1, Nerul, Navi Mumbai 400 706
  E-mail: vivamumbai@vivagroupindia.net, Tel. 27721273, 27721274
- Jamals Fazal Chambers, 26 Greams Road, Chennai 600 006
  E-mail: vivachennai@vivagroupindia.net, Tel. 28290304, 28294241
- B-103, Jindal Towers, 21/1A/3 Darga Road, Kolkata 700 017
  E-mail: vivakolkata@vivagroupindia.net, Tel. 22836381, 22816713
- 7, Sovereign Park Apartments, 56-58, K. R. Road, Basavanagudi, Bangalore 560 004
  E-mail: vivabangalore@vivagroupindia.net, Tel. 26607409, 26607410
- 101-102 Mughal Marc Apartments, 3-4-637 to 641, Narayanguda, Hyderabad 500 029
  E-mail: vivahyderabad@vivagroupindia.net, Tel. 27564481, 27564482
- First Floor, Beevi Towers, SRM Road, Kaloor, Kochi 682 018, Kerala
  E-mail: vivakochi@vivagroupindia.net, Tel: 0484-2403055, 2403056
- H. No. 12, P. B. Road, Rehabari, Near Arya Hospital, Guwahati 781 008
  E-mail: vivaguwahati@vivagroupindia.net, Tel: 0361-2735624

www.vivagroupindia.com

Published by arrangement with

Bloomberg Press
731 Lexington Avenue
New York, NY 10022

ISBN-10: 81-309-1120-5
ISBN-13: 978-81-309-1120-5

Published by Vinod Vasishtha for Viva Books Private Limited, 4737/23, Ansari Road, Daryaganj, New Delhi - 110 002.

Printed and bound by Raj Press, R-3, Inderpuri, New Delhi - 110 012.

To Mary Ann McGuigan, Jared Kieling, and Andrew Feldman, the visionaries at Bloomberg Press who trusted that the strategy of the 100 percent bond portfolio would illuminate a clear path for the individual investor and made this book a reality.

CONTENTS

FOREWORD

BY VIRTUE OF opening this book, you can count yourself among those who have chosen to explore the world of bonds and bond investing.

You won't see many books about bonds on the *New York Times* bestseller list. Bonds are after all the most predictable, and boring, of investments—we hope! You see, for bonds, boring is good. The principal and interest promised are fixed.

Not many people start out intending to focus on bonds. Even my boss, the "Bond King" Bill Gross, chief investment officer and founder of the $600 billion bond giant PIMCO, admits that in his early twenties his goal was to find a job as a "stock jock." Instead, his first job in the industry was as a bond analyst whose duties included literally clipping coupons in the basement vault of an insurance company. Who would have thought such a humble beginning would lead to a career as a media and investment giant? It is precisely because bonds are underestimated and underrated that they deliver the unexpected.

I crept my way into fixed income in a similar way, when I realized that my love for competition, math, and political economy intersected with the role of a fixed-income portfolio manager. The choice left my friends, parents, and professors perplexed. After all, the returns on safe bonds are modest and their upside capped. Still, PIMCO, the firm Bill Gross and I work for, has attracted $600 billion based on investors' need for cash flow and security.

And now here you are, book in hand, contemplating a dramatic change in your investment portfolio or simply hoping to secure your retirement by seeking a deeper understanding of bond investing. In *Bonds: The Unbeaten Path to Secure Investment Growth,* Hildy and Stan Richelson provide a road map for you. For years, they have worked with individual investors, helping them to decipher the unwritten "code" words put out by investment industry insiders. For their service, I applaud them.

I too have been trying to get the same message out: don't take needless investment risk.

I was first introduced to Hildy and Stan twelve years ago when they were doing research on bond funds. They wanted a better understanding of a small fund I was managing called the PIMCO Real Return Bond Fund. It invests primarily in U.S. Treasury inflation-protected securities (TIPS), and at the time, it had perhaps $200 million in assets under management.

The point of the fund, I explained to Stan and Hildy, was to provide a way for investors to protect their "grocery" money. TIPS, as you will learn in this book, have principal that is indexed to the Consumer Price Index (CPI). As such, TIPS, and funds owning them, allow investors to preserve the real purchasing power of their principal *and* earn interest on the principal. The grocery money people put aside for retirement will keep up with the generally rising cost of living—and grocery prices—regardless of the inflation rate. That small fund has since become a bit of a hit with investors and has grown to more than $12 billion.

Sure, I believe in some risk taking, sometimes even dramatic risk taking. Young athletes with skill, stamina, and steel nerves should single-mindedly devote themselves to training and competition. The scientist or entrepreneur should plunge into a career with both feet. But such virtues rarely serve professional or individual investors well. Plunging into risky investments may have disastrous outcomes. Unfortunately, professional advisers, and even some financial journalists, too often project virtues like boldness and risk taking onto the individual investor. Even Warren Buffet and Peter Lynch have been tempted to sing the siren's song of speculation, albeit couched in the robe of "prudent long-term" investing.

It is certainly easy to make straw men out of academic argu ments: "The Chicago professor didn't bother to pick up the $20 bill lying on the sidewalk because markets are efficient; if it was a real $20 bill, someone would have already picked it up." Other "pros" might point to the failure of the academics at Long-Term Capital Management in 1998 and thereby relegate the logic of modern financial theory to the dustbin.

Yet, in this book the Richelsons outline the wisdom and logic of a 100 percent bond portfolio. I buy their analysis. The zero-risk portfolio is on the efficient frontier as presented in academic research and is a starting point for any portfolio-construction effort. The prescriptions in this book are persuasive and compel ling. They are consistent with what I have learned in my years of study at the Massachusetts Institute of Technology and here at PIMCO. Reading this book should serve you well if you choose to hire a bond manager like PIMCO or advisers like the Richelsons or if you decide to try your hand at picking some bonds yourself. Enjoy!

—JOHN BRYNJOLFSSON
Managing Director, PIMCO

PREFACE

In *Bonds: The Unbeaten Path to Secure Investment Growth,* we take the complex world of financial investing and simplify it for you. The ancient Greek poet Archilochus said, "The fox knows many things, but the hedgehog knows one big thing." Jim Collins, author of the best-selling *Good to Great,* believes that hedgehogs, such as Freud, Darwin, Einstein, and Adam Smith, made a powerful impact because "they took a complex world and simplified it."

Like the hedgehog, we know one big thing that seems to remain undiscovered by the financial establishment: bonds are a better investment than stocks for individual investors. Viewed through objective eyes, stocks historically didn't outperform bonds when an individual investor's taxes, transaction fees, and bad timing are taken into consideration. Moreover, when stocks and bonds are viewed on a risk-adjusted basis (meaning how much of your principal is at risk), the case is clear that for individual investors, bonds were historically a better investment than stocks.

If stocks haven't outperformed bonds in the past, what is the basis for the argument that they are likely to outperform bonds in the future? Should you bet your financial future on the hope that stocks will rack up superior returns and that you will be able to realize those returns? We take the contrarian view and believe it's past time to trash the myth of stocks' superior investment returns. We propose instead an all-bond portfolio as a sure-footed strategy that will ensure real results.

Many investors want consistent success, but they pursue investments with the potential for spectacular *and* uncertain results. These investors believe they're capable of achieving such success, until they don't. And then they're greatly disappointed. Investing in stocks was all the rage in the late 1990s. However, when stocks tanked from 2000 to 2002, investors got reacquainted with the old Wall Street adage: trees do not grow to the sky. As stocks became scary, investors rediscovered the world of bonds and their benefits. Yet the reality is that bonds have always provided a secure place in the world of investments because of their enduring role in solving financial problems.

A wealth of data is available about investing, but most of what comes to the general public are story lines, dramatic events, and other fuel for enticement. What investors need to study instead is the investment process. Long-term investment success results from the strength of the investment strategy, rather than the individual wins and losses. Investing, like baseball, is a war of attrition, and what is being worn away—by fees, transaction costs, taxes, and poor timing—is your investment capital.[1]

A bond investor who is willing to take a measured approach to investing, scoring consistent and predictable returns without big losses, has the best possibility of winning. In the war against attrition, the bond investor hits no spectacular home runs. Instead, day in and day out he consistently gets on base, securing a predictable return while protecting his investment capital.

Warren Buffet is a great baseball fan and says investing is like being up at bat in baseball—only easier. When a player is up at bat in baseball, he has to swing, whereas the investor can stand at the plate indefinitely, until he gets the pitch he wants. But finding a good investment, like a good pitch, is difficult.

One reason we prefer purchasing individual bonds rather than bond funds is that you can decide when you want to swing. When you purchase most closed-end funds or open-end mutual funds, the fund managers must stay fully invested in a particular market sector as defined by the fund prospectus. That means a fund manager must swing whether the pitch is in the strike zone or not.

Unless you have the instincts of a Buffet or the skills of a quant searching under every rock to find an opportunity, there is considerable wisdom in settling on bonds with the aim of getting on base and scoring consistent runs. The fans may not cheer as much, but you will have the satisfaction of knowing you're financially secure. Bad pitches in the form of market hype will keep coming, but armed with the information we provide in this book, you'll have the discipline not to swing at a bad pitch.

Chapter Note

1. If you like baseball and want to understand our pitch, read Michael Lewis' book *Moneyball: The Art of Winning an Unfair Game* (New York: W. W. Norton & Company, 2003) about the success of the Oakland Athletics.

ACKNOWLEDGMENTS

Bonds: The Unbeaten Path to Secure Investment Growth is a major milestone in our careers because it has enabled us to clearly articulate our philosophy and deeply held beliefs about the importance of safe bonds—for both income *and* growth—in the portfolios of individual investors.

Our editor, Mary Ann McGuigan, made the most significant contribution to this book, and we are deeply grateful for her help. With a fine scalpel, she quickly and deftly sculpted our thoughts. Her insights into the book's structure, organization, and style shaped its form and content. We also want to express our appreciation to the staff at Bloomberg Press for their expert and very professional help in producing this book.

We particularly wish to thank and acknowledge the help of three special people: John B. Brynjolfsson, CFA, Managing Director, Pacific Investment Management Company (PIMCO), who took time from his incredibly busy schedule to write the foreword to the book; Victor F. Keen, Chair of the Tax Department, Duane Morris LLP, who reviewed some of the tax aspects of bonds; and our son-in-law, Evan B. Carpenter, who provided invaluable help in multiple reviews of Part 1 of the book, which focuses on the relationship of stocks and bonds. As you shall see, we were fortunate that he likes baseball as well as golf.

We would like to express our deep appreciation to the investment planners and investment professionals who generously stepped up to help us by reviewing chapters of the book and by sharing their wisdom with us. We take responsibility for any errors. We thank Jeffrey B. Broadhurst, George Connerat, Rick Dunphy, Joe Gaskey, Richard W. Kidd, Jeff Metz, and Arthur Sinkler. And we're grateful to our son Scott Richelson, an innovative young lawyer, who gave us many thoughtful comments on the chapter he reviewed.

We wish to acknowledge our friends in the investment community who teach us daily about bonds: Patrick Coyne, Jenny Ellis, Tim Hlavacek, Charles Ripley, Pete Rossi, and Debra Weiner.

Special thanks go to our dear friends and family, who have advised us and supported us throughout this project: Carole and Emilio Gravagno, Drs. Sam and Diana Kirschner, George Robinson and Dr. Abby Van Voorhees. Thanks also to Judy and Milton Moskowitz, who protected our time to write. We are grateful to our daughter, Jolie Carpenter, and our granddaughters, Maya and Emily, who bring the whys of saving into focus.

We learn about investments and the real world every day from our friends and fellow investors who provide the real-life context to our study and work. By asking questions and sharing aspects of their lives with us, they have enhanced and sharpened our skills. For this, we wish to acknowledge and thank Katharine Ayers, Dean Bress, Esq., John Clements, Jerry and Lois Cooper, Christopher Doyle, Esq., Mark Dresnick, Esq., Colleen Gordon, Ellen Greif, David Lihn, Esq., Drs. Gary and Elaine Liversidge, Ron and Holly Flaherty, Michael C. and Neeru Phillips, Dr. Linda Ripstein, Juliet Spitzer, Phil Wachs, Kevin West, and Dr. Stanley Wulf.

We were inspired by the love and encouragement offered us by our association with the Souls Network: Don Arnoudse, Peter Blake, Rich Constantine, Vince DiBianca, Jeffrey DiFrancesco, Tom D'Aquanni, Tony Freedley, Dr. Sam Kirschner, Anton T. Lahnston, Dave Laveman, and Jim Selman.

INTRODUCTION

BONDS ARE A misunderstood investment. In *Bonds: The Unbeaten Path to Secure Investment Growth,* we intend to rectify that by clearing up long-held misconceptions about bonds. We also explain an overlooked investment strategy for individual investors, the 100 percent bond portfolio, which enables investors to attain financial security while achieving a good return on their investment.

The bond market may at first seem complicated. However, its principles are straightforward, and anyone can master them. This book provides you with the tools to understand and successfully invest in the bond market so that you can build and protect your capital and effectively realize your financial and life goals.

For individual investors, that understanding is vital. The world has changed drastically in the past twenty years. The economic safety net is now frayed. Job security has sharply declined. Company-sponsored pension plans are becoming extinct, and many people worry about the health of the Social Security and Medicare systems. Given these concerns, we all must take responsibility for our own financial well-being.

If you want to take responsibility for your financial life, this book can be an indispensable guide to your decision making. *Bonds* is designed to educate novice and sophisticated investors alike and serve as a tool for financial advisers as well. We explain why bonds can be the right choice for you and how to use bonds to achieve your financial goals. We also present a broad spectrum of bond investment options, describe how to purchase bonds at the best prices, and most important, explain how to make money with bonds.

This book offers straightforward bond strategies that are used by the wealthiest investors and financial advisers to maximize the return on their bond portfolios while providing security of princi pal. These strategies can help you determine how to use bonds in your portfolio and investment program and take control of your own financial destiny. You'll be playing it smart while playing it safe.

Investments in bonds have grown significantly since the begin ning of the twenty-first century. Investors now understand that they can make money with bonds and that bonds are an essential part of every investment program. For the investor who is risk averse or who cannot afford to lose money, bonds are hugely important because basing a financial plan on stock appreciation is a very risky strategy.

A 2006 poll by the National Association of Variable Annuities found that many baby boomers were very concerned about retire ment and the risks of stock investing:[1]

- A majority of Americans between fifty and fifty-nine years old were concerned about having enough money to retire.
- 64 percent said that they would not put more than 30 percent of their money into stocks.
- 32 percent would not put any money in stocks at all.
- Among younger boomers, those forty to forty-nine years old, 53 percent would not put more than 30 percent of their money in stocks, and 23 percent would put no money at all in stocks.

These numbers are probably a surprise to many investors because investors are told that investing the bulk of their money in stocks is the key to financial success. However, many stock inves tors may share the same feelings expressed by this middle-aged woman named Ruth: "I am frightened and panicked to the point of paralysis about making decisions about my money and about whether to stay in the stock market or get out because of the current volatility. My future depends on being right."[2]

Bonds can free investors from any fear of investing. Safe bonds will protect your principal and generate substantial after-tax income without subjecting you to the substantial risk inherent in stocks. We believe that bonds will provide as good or better returns than stocks in the future and without substantial volatility. Bonds will also provide growth through the magic of compound interest if you reinvest the income that bonds provide. *Bonds* offers you a way to realize your financial goals and secure your financial future without taking a market risk.

Bonds is divided into five parts, namely, the rationale for the 100 percent bond portfolio, bond basics, descriptions of the major categories of bonds, how to buy bonds, and using bond strategies to structure your portfolio. Part One, "Clearing the Cobwebs," provides the rationale for our belief in the value of bonds. By focusing on the impact of taxes, fees, transaction costs, and bad timing, chapter 1 explains why the 100 percent bond portfolio is superior to diversifying into stocks and alternative investments. It explains why plain-vanilla bonds are the best investment for individual investors to use to achieve their life and financial goals. Chapter 2 explains how to structure and implement the all-bond portfolio. Chapter 3 presents a case study of how one stock investor turned to the all-bond portfolio to solve his financial problems and the implications for his personal and financial life.

Part Two, "Bond Basics," provides key information you need to know about bonds. Bond language, which is often arcane, is easier to understand when placed in its historical context. Chapter 4 provides that context and explains how bond structures are rooted in history. In chapter 5, we trace how a bond is created, issued, priced, and traded.

Part Three, "Bond Categories," introduces all the major types of bonds and compares them in detail in a uniform and useful format. There are descriptions of Treasuries, Treasury inflation-protected securities (TIPS), U.S. savings bonds, agency bonds, mortgage securities, municipal bonds, and corporate bonds (including junk bonds). Chapter 12 describes certain bond look-alikes, namely, CDs, immediate fixed annuities, deferred fixed annuities, and common and preferred stock. In Part Three, the advantages, disadvantages, tax implications, pricing, and special features become clear, allowing for easy comparison of one type of bond or bond look-alike to another.

Part Four, "Options for Purchasing Bonds," describes how an investor can buy bonds using a broker, online, or through mutual funds and similar vehicles. Included is thoroughly practical real-world advice on how to buy bonds without the use of an investment adviser, how to best use a broker, and how, through use of the Internet and other techniques, to evaluate the price of a bond. Drawing on our many years of experience representing clients in their purchase and sale of bonds, this chapter tells the secrets of the trade from the perspective of an experienced and expert bond investor.

If you prefer not to buy individual bonds on your own, you can rely on Part Four to learn how to buy bonds through mutual funds, unit investment trusts, closed-end funds, and exchange-traded funds. As an aid to our readers, we provide a comprehensive treatment of all the different types of bond funds and indicate the various categories available. We include income-producing funds containing no bonds for comparison.

Part Five, "Bond Investment Strategies," discusses financial planning and investment planning with bonds and bond strategies. Rich in detail, this section will enable you to determine how bonds can best fit into your portfolio. Chapter 17 tackles the vital subject of your financial and life needs and describes how to use bonds in your financial planning to achieve financial well-being. Chapter 18 contains case studies describing how bonds might be used to meet a variety of financial-planning goals, including socially conscious investing. Chapter 19 not only discusses techniques tailored to the individual investor but also offers a complete checklist of strategies useful as well to investment advisers and other professionals. Specific strategies address topics such as determining when to buy and sell, constructing and implementing a bond ladder, finding bargain bonds, keeping away from overvalued bonds, what to do when interest rates are rising or are falling, investing for tax advantages, investing by risk tolerance, and investing for income needs.

Finally, an appendix of useful Web sites annotating those mentioned throughout the text serves as an invaluable reference for finding bond information on the Internet. You will discover sites for bond calculators, yield curves, and other practical tools.

Whether you're a novice and want to read *Bonds* from cover to cover or a seasoned investor or adviser who wants to brush up on a long-neglected market, you'll find what you need here: an abundance of practical information about bonds, bond funds, and how to make them part of your portfolio.

Chapter Notes

1. Warren S. Hersch, "Boomers Fear for Their Nest Eggs, but Are Wary of Stocks," *National Underwriter*, December 18/25, 2006, 24.

2. Byron Katie, *Loving What Is* (New York: Three Rivers Press, 2002), 189.

BONDS

PART ONE

CLEARING THE COBWEBS

THE MAIN PURPOSE of this book is to debunk the many myths surrounding investing in stocks and bonds and to provide new thinking for you to consider when developing and carrying out your financial plan. In Part One, we take you on an unusual journey and encourage you to look at the financial world through our eyes and examine the proposition that for individual investors, bonds are a better investment than stocks or any other asset class.

In chapter 1 we compare stocks and bonds and describe the powerful case for investing in bonds. This case has always existed, but we believe we have a new way to explain it. If you find that bonds make sense for you, we describe in chapter 2 how to carry out the strategy of the all-bond portfolio, including the specific kinds of bonds to buy (we call them plain-vanilla bonds) and why. Plain-vanilla bonds are safe individual bonds, easy to buy and sell at low or no cost, and easy to understand. In chapter 3 we provide a case study illustrating why and how a family used the all-bond portfolio to support their life objectives and their financial goals using our four-step financial plan.

Come with us as we look at the financial world in an unbiased way, challenge the traditional thinking found in articles and books on investing, and offer evidence to support our belief in bond investments. Financial plans based on the traditional thinking and stock investing have not worked out well for many individual investors. They have taken substantial risks with their nest eggs and endured severe and upsetting market declines and financial uncertainty. Indeed, many individuals lost their retirement savings. We believe that the all-bond portfolio is a better way to plan and secure your financial future. This book will show you how to build one.

CHAPTER 1

BONDS

The Better Investment

Watching your stocks all day long is amusing up to a point, but income is the thing if you re shopping for anything from pajamas to pastrami sandwiches

—JOE MYSAK

Bloomberg columnist[1]

FOR GENERATIONS, STOCKS have gotten top billing over bonds. Stocks, many insist, have outperformed bonds in the past, will outperform bonds in the future, and are not risky if held for ten years or more. We believe these assertions are myths. This chapter makes the case that the stated historical return of 10 percent on stocks is merely theoretical because it does not take into account taxes, expenses, and investors' bad timing. It is uncertain that stocks will outperform bonds in the future, and the risk of a severe stock market decline increases as the investment period increases. Stocks are riskier and less predictable than bonds. Ultimately, they are not as good an investment as bonds.

In the holy name of diversification, investors are told to balance the bulk of their investment portfolio between stocks and bonds. We think that's a mistake. For individual investors, we believe that bonds are a better investment than stocks. Indeed, the ideal portfolio for individual investors would contain *only* plain-vanilla bonds. That's because after paying fees, expenses, taxes, and factorizing in the risk of bad timing, the return on stocks is not likely to exceed the return on bonds, particularly when the risks associated with stocks are taken into account. The bonds that we recommend are safe. If you can achieve your financial goals without taking a risk, why not do so?

We developed the 100 percent bond portfolio as a strategy that individuals can use to meet their financial goals, taking into account their capabilities and limitations. Individual investors can't use the advanced techniques or participate in big institutional deals, but they can and do invest in stocks and stock funds, and that puts them at risk. The 100 percent bond portfolio doesn't include investments in stock, stock funds, commodities, or real estate. It's a strategy that individuals can use to keep their assets safe and growing.

This chapter examines the historical returns on stocks and bonds—without equity-colored glasses—in a noninstitutional portfolio. The results will show you why we believe that the 100 percent bond portfolio is the best strategy for individual investors.

Individual and Institutional Investors: How They Differ

News stories abound on the outsized gains that certain large institutions, such as the Harvard Endowment, earn on their investment portfolios containing stocks and other investments. Naturally, you would want to emulate the Harvard Endowment and earn those large returns as well. In building a portfolio, an individual investor can't use an institutional model that might be used by the Harvard Endowment. That's because there are many significant differences between individual and institutional investors. Let's take Harvard as an example and consider what some of those differences are.

The Harvard Endowment was worth $29 billion in 2006. That enormous wealth enables the Harvard Endowment to hire the most experienced and competent money managers in the world.

These managers can evaluate and get access to the best and most complex investment opportunities available. Individual investors simply don't have enough assets to buy into such deals.

Because of the huge size of the Harvard Endowment, which grows larger each year, it can take significant risks. In addition, the Harvard Endowment has a limitless time horizon for its investments because it will be sustained indefinitely and can adjust the amount of money that is withdrawn each year.

Individual investors have a different time line and pockets that are not nearly as deep. They generally stop accumulating money when they stop working, at which point, they start to take distributions, which ultimately reduce the size of their nest egg. If their investment portfolio does not make a consistent return, they may run out of money. A bull market in one year may not undo the damage the bear market did the year before. What's more, individuals are subject to the inevitable emergencies, illnesses, and bumps in the road that require cash.

INSTITUTIONAL BOND INVESTORS

Although it is not the usual practice for U.S. pension managers, some now recognize that it is better to match their assets to their liabilities than to rely on hope to fund future liabilities. Instead of betting that stocks will achieve their historical average, the State of Maine Pension Fund,[2] the United Mine Workers of America 1950 Pension Plan, and the Texas Municipal Retirement System,[3] among others, match their assets (bonds) to their liabilities (the liabilities for pensions payable at worker's retirement dates). These pension funds do not want to be left to the mercy of good and bad years in the stock market and the uncertainty that there will be enough resources to pay all their retirees on time.

The Teacher's Retirement System of Texas in contrast, took a different path. The fund invested in stocks and lost its bet in the bear market of 2000 to 2002. Fund assets dropped to $79 billion in 2003 from a high of $90 billion in 2000. To make up the $16 billion budget gap, it decided to put its money into hedge funds and other higher yielding asset classes.[4] Unfortunately, it landed on the losing side of a hedge fund disaster. Amaranth Advisers revealed that in

September 2006 it had lost roughly $6 billion, or 65 percent of its assets, on misplaced bets in the natural gas market. When a $10 billion hedge fund drops by 65 percent in one month, its investors, which in this case included major pension funds across the United States, are shaken. What new risky investments will have to be made to make up for this and other shortfalls?

Many companies are shutting down their pension plans in favor of shifting the responsibility for pensions to their employees. Now employees are being asked to do what the pension fund managers, with all their education and expertise, are often unable to do. Although pension funds can receive a cash infusion from their sponsoring company or be terminated for all employees, what can individuals do in the face of underperforming retirement returns? How would you make up the shortfall if your investments did not achieve the expected return?

With all investments, except safe individual bonds, your chips are on the table until you sell. Either you make two right decisions, when to buy and when to sell, or you are just wrong and you lose. Until you close your position by selling, your money is at risk. Although stocks, real estate, and commodities might have performed well in the past during certain periods, there is no way to know whether they will have significant losses or gains in the future. Holding individual bonds, however, helps you to avoid this problem. With individual bonds, you do not need to make two right decisions—when to buy and when to sell. Bonds require only one decision: the decision to buy and hold until they come due. Your principal plus interest is returned to you without another decision.

Examining the Myths

To compare historical and potential returns from stocks and bonds, some important questions have to be addressed:

- Is it accurate to say that stocks had a historical return of 10 percent?
- If stocks outperformed bonds in the past, why can't we assume that stocks will outperform bonds in the future?
- Does the historical return on bonds compare favorably with the historical return on stocks?

- How can a portfolio of bonds provide both income and growth?
- Are bonds a better investment than stocks?

The answers to these questions cast doubt on the old assumptions on investing, which the media and most financial advisers accept as gospel. We've developed some new thinking that reflects decades of observing the financial markets. Let's evaluate stocks and bonds in light of the new thinking we propose and see if you're persuaded that bonds are a better investment than stocks. If you are and you're willing to change your approach to investing, the 100 percent bond portfolio can maximize your investment returns with the ultimate degree of safety.

HISTORICAL ANNUAL RETURN

OLD ASSUMPTION
The historical annual return of stocks is around 10 percent.[5]

NEW THINKING
The actual annual historical return on stocks is much less than 10 percent when taxes, transaction costs, and bad timing of the stock market are taken into account.

Ibbotson Associates, in its annually updated book *Stocks, Bonds, Bills, and Inflation, 2006 Yearbook,* provides one of the staples for obtaining historical data to compare the returns of stocks and bonds. However, the Ibbotson data do not prove that individual shareholders had an approximate annual 10 percent historical return. The Ibbotson data are merely theoretical because they do not take into account the actual frictions of real-life investing. You cannot measure the actual performance of a stock portfolio or stock fund for individual investors without taking into account the burden of income taxes, transaction costs, investment-management fees, and the possibility of an individual investor's poor timing when he buys and sells stock based on emotion. Because of these real life costs, it is impossible for individual investors to have realized the stock market returns reported by Ibbotson.

UNHAPPY RETURNS: UNCOVERING THE TRUE COST OF STOCK INVESTMENTS

To find the actual historical performance of stocks, we must reduce the theoretical Ibbotson stock returns by three elements: taxes, transaction costs, and bad timing.

1 Taxes. Individuals are subject to federal and often state and local taxes on income as well as on dividends and capital gains. If stock is held in a stock fund and the fund trades its stock a great deal, some or all of the reportable gains may be treated as short-term capital gains, which may be taxed at ordinary income rates. The outcome is the same if an individual holds his stock for one year or less before its sale.

2 Transaction Costs. Individuals must pay transaction costs to buy and sell stocks including commissions on individual stocks, managed account fees, and management fees and other expenses on stock funds. "It's fair to estimate that the all-in annual costs of equity fund ownership now run in the range of 2.5 percent to 3 percent of assets," says John Bogle, founder of the Vanguard Group of mutual funds.[6]

William Bernstein examined fund management fees and reported the following in the April 2001 issue of *Financial Planning*:[7]

- The average actively managed large-cap fund has annual fees and expenses of about 2 percent.
- The average small-cap and foreign fund has annual fees and expenses of about 4 percent.
- The average microcap and emerging market fund has annual fees and expenses of almost 10 percent.

3 Bad Timing. The most costly element of all is the buying and selling habits of individual investors. Investors are generally emotional in their investment choices and often have an atrocious sense of timing. They tend to buy into the stock market when it is hot after it has gone up a lot. They often lose their nerve and sell after a severe decline. Making money in stocks requires making two correct decisions: when to buy and when to sell. "From 1983 to 2003 index funds tracking the Standard & Poor's 500 index returned 12.8 percent and the average mutual fund gained 10 percent annually," says Michael J. Mauboussin, a strategist at Legg Mason Capital Management.

"Meanwhile, the average investor earned only 6.3 percent annual returns." Mauboussin attributes this seemingly impossible result to poor "market timing" and "the extraordinary proclivity for investors to invest in the wrong place at the wrong time."[8]

The buy-high, sell-low behavior pattern of individual investors observed by Mauboussin has been verified by research undertaken by Dalbar, Inc., in Boston, which tracked investor behavior for twenty years, beginning in 1986. Through all kinds of markets, "investors achieved an average annualized return of just under 4 percent, compared with a return of nearly 12 percent from a buy-and-hold strategy using the Standard & Poor's 500 index."[9]

Why is the actual performance of the dollar-weighted returns so much lower than the traditional reporting methods? "It says something about human nature," says Ilia Dichev, an accounting professor at the University of Michigan. "When things are going up, people get excited. That's when the money pours in."[10]

A buy-and-hold strategy may not solve the market-timing problem. Buying and holding works well for stocks in a bull market like the one from 1982 to 1999. But a buy-and-hold strategy results in serious losses and creates a great deal of wear and tear on individual investors in a bear market, such as the one from 2000 to 2002. The Nasdaq lost 77.9 percent of its value during the collapse of this market bubble. The success of a buy-and-hold strategy depends on the period in which the stock is held.

Consider, for example, the story of Boots, a drugstore chain in the United Kingdom. After making spectacular gains in the 1990s bull market in stocks, it fired its portfolio manager in 2001. Instead of watching its assets decline, the Boots pension plan sold all its stock and purchased high-grade bonds. This action enabled the chain's management to guarantee that there would be enough assets to satisfy its pension liabilities. The Boots pension fund ended up with a surplus, while many other pension funds had big losses as a result of the bear market in stocks.

Because individual investors have limited life spans, the holding period is of more than theoretical interest. For example, in the years 1965 to 1982, the Dow started out at about 1,000 and ended the period at pretty much the same place. If that happened to be the period during which you were saving for retirement, you would have been out of luck. It would be no help to you that the historical return was 10 percent.

TAXES, COSTS, AND RISKS OF INVESTING IN BONDS

By taking a savvy approach to bond buying, you can minimize your taxes, limit your expenses, reduce your risk, and increase your profit. But let's first examine the taxes, costs, and risks of investing in bonds.

1 Taxes. If you are in the 25 percent tax bracket or higher, the impact of federal and state income taxes is generally large enough to indicate that you should purchase tax-free municipal bonds for your taxable nonpension account. By purchasing municipals, you avoid paying federal income tax and possibly state and local income taxes as well on the interest income. Though the interest rate on municipals is lower than the taxable rates, after taxes you will come out ahead. Tax-free municipal bonds provide the best legal tax shelter available to individual investors.

Many taxpayers are now subject to the alternative minimum tax (AMT), which is pushing more taxpayers into paying higher federal income taxes. Municipal bond interest is not subject to the AMT, except for the interest income from the municipal bonds called AMT bonds. If you are in a lower federal income tax bracket in a high-tax state, consider purchasing Treasuries, home-state taxable munis, and certain agency bonds that are exempt from state and local income taxes, but not from federal income tax.

2 Transaction costs. The cost to purchase a bond is called the "spread," which is the difference between the price that the broker paid for the bond and the higher price at which he sells it to you. In addition to a spread, discount brokers may charge you a fee for service. Discount brokers don't save you money in the world of bonds. However, if you buy a bond on its initial public offering, you will receive an institutional price—the best possible price. If you hold an individual bond until it comes due, there are no further transaction costs.

3 Risk. With highly rated bonds, you have no significant loss of principal to worry about as long as you hold the bonds until they come due at their face value. We believe that in a comparison of stocks and bonds, highly rated bonds should be given a significant premium over stocks because these bonds are safe, dependable, and pay a steady rate of interest that can be counted on.

4 Bad timing. The risk of bad timing is small if you hold your bonds until they come due because every bond comes due at its face value, no matter what the price fluctuations might be before its due date. Keep records of your bond purchases so that they are recorded at face value, rather than adjusting their value every month as valued on your brokerage statement. If you keep your bonds recorded at face value, you will be less likely to sell your bonds before they come due and make a market timing mistake.

If you have a bond ladder (that is, you own bonds coming due each year or so), you may be able to meet your extraordinary financial needs out of your current cash flow and have funds to reinvest in the event of rising interest rates. How much is that worth to you in a comparison with volatile stocks and safe bonds? We'll discuss the strategy of a bond ladder in chapter 19.

PAST PERFORMANCE

OLD ASSUMPTION
Stocks will outperform bonds in the future.

NEW THINKING
It is uncertain that stocks will outperform bonds in the future.

There are two main reasons for the assumption that stocks will outperform bonds in the future: First, it's taken for granted that stocks have always outperformed bonds in the past. Therefore, the assumption is that they will continue to outperform bonds in the future. In fact, stocks have not always outperformed bonds. The leader depends on which span of years you choose to look at.

More important, as we'll discuss later in this chapter, the actual annual historical performance of stocks by our calculations is more like 6 percent to 7 percent rather than 10 percent.

Second, because stocks are riskier and more volatile than bonds, stocks should have a higher return than bonds to attract investors away from safe government bonds. We readily agree that stocks are riskier. However, that doesn't prove that stocks will outperform bonds in the future.

We are not suggesting that bonds will outperform stocks in the future. No one knows what will happen in the future. An open mind is essential on this important subject. But if you believe that stocks will always outperform bonds, why would you invest in bonds at all? If you're open to other eventualities, you'll understand the advantages of bonds and why we believe that bonds and the 100 percent bond portfolio are a better investment strategy for individual investors.

The present is significantly different from the past, so why should we expect that the past performance of the stock market or the bond market will be repeated in the present or the future? In the past, we had a depression, two world wars and other wars, a massive inflation followed by a deep recession, oil shortages and oil busts, high tax rates and low tax rates, and high unemployment and low unemployment. Which of these events will recur and with what consequences?

Dividends and stock appreciation. Influenced by the media, investors often assume that the major factor in stock appreciation is the increase in the value of the stock shares. Awesome bubbles and minibubbles form as stock prices in a particular sector rise. However, the classic explanation of stock appreciation is that it is principally driven by two factors:

- High dividend yields
- The growth of the dividends over time

Between 1926 and 1959, the dividend yield paid on large company stocks was higher than the interest paid on long-term Treasury bonds. This is because stocks were rightly considered risky at that time. From 1926 to 1954, the dividend yield on large company stocks was always above 5 percent, and in 1950, it hit its peak at 8.77 percent.[11] From as late as 1975 to 1985, the dividend yield on large company stocks was generally around 5 percent.[12] The dividend yield on large company stocks in 2006, however, was about 1.8 percent, and at least the majority of midsize and small-company stocks paid no dividends at all.

The reinvestment of dividends has been the major driver of large stock appreciation. When stock performance includes the reinvestment of all dividends paid on stocks, $1 invested in 1824 grew to $3.2 million in 2005 (see **Figure 1.1**). However, if dividends are left out of the calculation and not reinvested, $1 invested in 1824 grew to only $374 in 2005.[13] That's right, $374, not $374,000, or $3.2 million. Since high dividends were the main driver of stock appreciation in the past, why would we expect high appreciation in the future when dividends are much lower?

FIGURE 1.1

Effect of Dividends on Stock Performance, 1824 to 2005

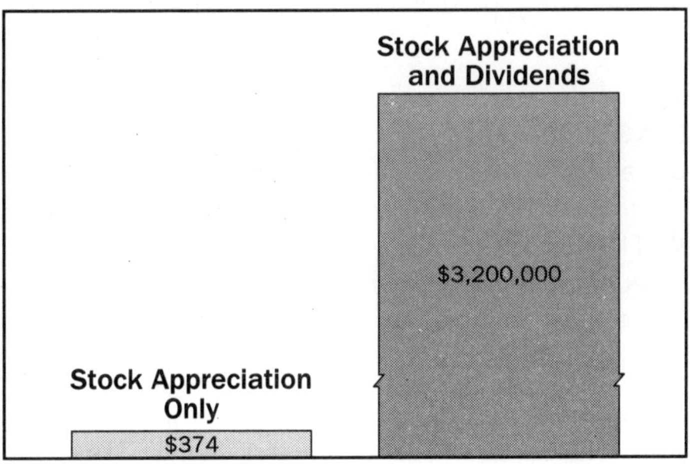

Source: Data from Roger G. Ibbotson, *Stocks, Bonds, Bills and Inflation: Historical Returns (1926–1987)* (Chicago: Irwin Professional Publishing, (1989), 201.

Consider the following questions:

- Without substantial dividends, will stocks appreciate by the historical 10 percent per year?
- Are you willing to bet your retirement on the hope that past performance will be repeated without significant dividends?
- Is it significant that a great deal of stock appreciation came from the period 1982 to 1999, when the yield on long-term Treasuries declined from a record rate of 13.34 percent on December 31, 1981, to 6.82 percent on December 31, 1999?[14]

Every financial product provides a disclaimer that past performance may not be repeated. Why don't investors believe this? It seems to be a matter of faith for investors that stocks *must* outperform bonds. We think it's unwise for investors to bet their financial life on this hope. That's because the answer to the question of whether stocks will always outperform bonds is simply not knowable. Our purpose is to call into question the paradigm that stocks will always outperform bonds and to open investors' minds to another way of measuring performance. If investors saw the validity of such measurement, would their asset allocation to bonds increase because of the greater safety, predictability, and cash flow they provide?

RISK

OLD ASSUMPTION

Stocks are not risky if you hold them for ten years.

NEW THINKING

The risk of a severe stock market decline increases as the investment period increases. Stocks are riskier and less predictable than bonds.

Investors love to believe in the possibility of easy gains. Gains, however, must be measured against the risks taken. This concept is known as "risk adjusting" the return on an investment. For example, if you buy a high-tech start-up company, you might make a gain of 20 percent or more over a short time. However, this upside possibility must be balanced against a total loss of your investment since high-tech start-up companies have a high failure rate. In this case the risk-adjusted return would be much less than 20 percent even if the stock appreciated by that much.

Stocks are risky. Over certain periods of time, stock markets declined and even crashed. The crash of 1929, for example, is infamous. Less well known is that on October 19, 1987, the Dow Jones Industrial Average declined 508 points in one day, a 22.6 percent loss.[15] More recent was the bear market of 2000 to 2002, when the Nasdaq lost 77.9 percent of its value. Consider also the huge decline in Japanese stocks from 1989 to 2003, when stocks declined by about 78 percent.[16]

Investors who take on a lot of risk can never be confident that they have succeeded until they sell their investments. In the financial markets, when a trader makes big money for many years and then dramatically loses it all and a lot more, he is considered to have "blown up." Yogi Berra, the famous baseball player and common man's philosopher, summed this up in the expression, "It ain't over till it's over."

The longer investors go without encountering a rare event, the more vulnerable they will be to it. This is how bubbles form in stocks, real estate, and commodities. Investors get comfortable and are very happy with the appreciation of their assets and invest more at or near the top. It looks like a sure thing. Despite the message endlessly repeated by the media that stocks are safe in the long run, stocks have been risky in the past and they will likely be risky in the future.

Risk has two dimensions, explains Zvi Bodie, professor of finance at Boston University School of Management and world-renowned investment consultant. "There's the probability of a bad thing happening. But the other dimension is the severity of the bad thing happening." The risk of a stock market crash happening increases as the investment period increases, says Bodie. To prove his point, he reminds us that the longer the life of a put option, the greater its cost. A put option gives an investor the right, but not the obligation, to sell securities at a fixed price within a specified period of time. If a put option for one year costs about $8,000, the same option for twenty-five years would cost about $40,000. Bodie concludes that if stocks are really less risky the longer you hold them, then the cost of the put option should go down and not up when the option period increases.[17]

In his book *Worry-Free Investing*,[18] Bodie tells readers that conventional wisdom is wrong. Stocks don't always produce the highest return, diversification doesn't always protect you against loss, and the risk of owning stocks does not always decline the longer you hold them. Stocks are risky and will remain risky, no matter how long you own them.[19]

When a market goes up dramatically, the media quotes the financial services industry, which periodically insists, "This time it's different." The analysts will then backfit the current data to a new theory. This partly explains why investors wind up buying when asset prices are rising, often buying at or near the top. When the market declines, they can't stand the pain and often sell at the bleakest bottom. This predictable behavior is why there are so few investors who actually reap the reported gains from a long-term rising market in stocks, commodities, or real estate.

A review of the actual year-by-year historical returns of stocks shows that they are unpredictable. They are random. Random movements of stock in the past make for highly unreliable predictors of future stock prices. If stock prices are random, it follows that stocks retain substantial risk no matter how long you hold them; and you should not build a financial plan around them.

GROWTH AND INCOME

OLD ASSUMPTION

Bonds are for income and stocks are for growth.

NEW THINKING

Bonds can provide both growth and income.

Advisers tell investors that stocks should form the major part of their investment portfolio because stocks always provide so much more growth than bonds provide income. Stock appreciation, however, is not predictable, whereas bond income is. When you invest in stocks, you should do so counting on your dividends and hope for stock appreciation only as icing on the cake. But the dividend cake has been below 2 percent since 1998, while bond interest remains more attractive.

Zero-coupon bonds. Investors who hold the old assumption that bonds provide only income have never heard of zero-coupon bonds. A zero-coupon bond pays no interest currently and sells for a price that is significantly below its face value. For example, in 2006, we purchased a U.S. Agency zero-coupon bond that comes due in twelve years. The bond is also noncallable, which means that the agency can't buy the bond back from the investor before its due date. The unit price for the bond was 50, and it will come due at a price of 100 in twelve years. Therefore, in twelve years these bonds will double in value. There is no question that the bonds will double if held to maturity because a U.S. Agency bond is essentially risk free. Is this doubling in value income or growth? Would you be interested in a guaranteed 100 percent return in twelve years without the possibility of a loss? Zero-coupon bonds show the power of compounding, Einstein's eighth wonder of the world. We'll discuss zero-coupon bonds in detail in chapter 6.

Instead of investing in a zero-coupon bond, you might purchase a coupon bond paying current interest and reinvest the interest in additional bonds rather than spending the interest income. In this strategy, you would have the cash flow as well as the growth. Should the gain be considered income or growth?

A Second Look at Risks and Returns

The media makes finding undervalued assets seem easy. Volatile markets, whether in stocks, commodities, or real estate, always attract a lot of media attention. Investors want to get rich quick, and the media are happy to tell them how.

There is another, more subtle reason why the markets seem to be going up more than they actually are. Consider two examples in which the movement of the markets is described in percentages (see **Figure 1.2**).

What is happening here? The investment is going up and down by 50 percent, but in both cases you lost 25 percent. If you translate the percentages into cash, you started with $100 and ended up with $75 in both cases. It is not much consolation to know

FIGURE 1.2

Why the Stock Market Always Seems to Be Going Up

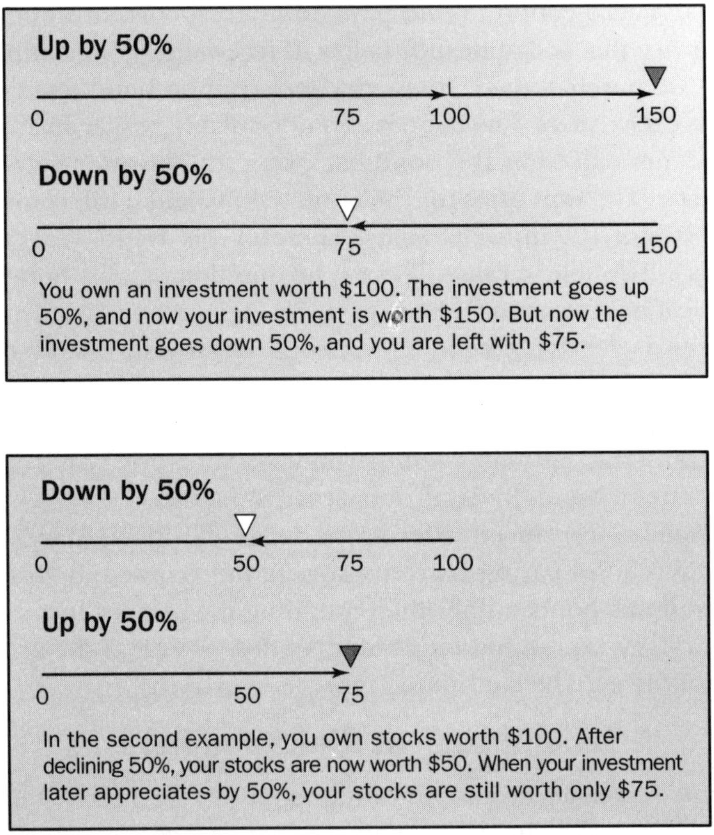

that you are up 50 percent in the second case if you still have an overall loss.

Let's take a real-life example. The Nasdaq hit a high of 5,048 on March 10, 2000, before it declined to 1,114 on October 9, 2002, in the bear market. To get back to its all-time high of about 5,048, from 1,114, the Nasdaq would have to appreciate by almost 400 percent. The media, however, were happy to report that the

Nasdaq doubled when it went from 1,114 to over 2,000. That sounds great, except that at around the 2,000 level it is still down almost 60 percent from its high of 5,048. If you had invested $100 at the high point, you would have only $40 after the double. If you had invested in bonds, you would still have your $100 and the accumulated interest paid on that investment. We can learn from these examples that recovering from a stock loss is quite difficult, and some investors will ride their winners down and not recover.

The evaluation of risk and return can be quite elusive. Stock, commodity, and real estate funds can appear to go up more than they actually are because of what's called survivorship bias. For example, many losing funds are no longer visible because they were terminated or merged into other, better-performing funds so that the losing funds don't show up in the databases anymore. Funds may also appear to be doing better than they actually are because there are more than 6,000 mutual funds. At any point in time, some of them will be doing very well. The best performing of these winning funds are the ones advertised heavily to the public.

We value a large and safe cash flow more than the possibility of inflated assets. In the high-tech bull market of the 1990s, some stocks increased dramatically in value only to crash some years later. The increase and decrease in asset values of these stocks looked random to us, and the gains looked to be brought about by luck. We don't depend on the rising asset values produced by a bull market for our success with bonds; we have no fear of a bear market collapse. In fact, bonds generally increase in value when there is a bear market in stocks, commodities, or real estate because of the so-called flight to quality that generally follows a market collapse.

Stock Market Volatility: The Impact on Retirement Planning

Let's assume for the moment that stocks do outperform bonds over every ten-year period. Let's further assume that when you retire you are depending on withdrawals from your nest egg of stocks to fund your retirement, and you have significant losses in your early retirement years. In this case, you may run out of money even if there are good returns in future years and they average 10 percent per year. Consider what would have happened if you retired in one of the following years:[20]

- 1973: market loss of 14.6 percent
- 1974: market loss of 26.5 percent
- 2000: market loss of 9.1 percent
- 2001: market loss of 11.9 percent
- 2002: market loss of 22.1 percent

If you had the misfortune to retire in one of those years, you might have a problem meeting your retirement goals. Let's take a simplified example of what might happen if you had losses in the year or years immediately after your retirement. Bob Goodtiming had $1 million in stocks at the date of his retirement. Bob believed that he would receive the historical return of 10 percent per year on stocks and could withdraw 10 percent, or $100,000 per year, from his $1 million nest egg. In the first year of his retirement, Bob's stocks declined 10 percent, and he withdrew $100,000 to live on. In the next year, stocks also declined 10 percent, and Bob took out another $100,000 with the understanding that there was bound to be a recovery in the third year. However, at the beginning of Bob's third year of retirement, his nest egg was worth only $620,000, and that Wal-Mart job was looking very attractive because he concluded that his retirement fund was now inadequate.

Why Bonds Are a Better Investment Than Stocks

We've seen that Ibbotson data indicate that the historical return is 10 percent on stocks and 5 percent on bonds. But after paying fees, expenses, and taxes, the return on stocks in the real world is more likely to be 6 percent to 7 percent rather than the widely believed figure of 10 percent or 11 percent.[21] Furthermore, when you adjust for the possibility of significant losses on stocks, the risk of bad timing, and the stomach-churning volatility, we conclude that bonds are a better investment vehicle to save for your education expenses, retirement, and other financial goals.

Think about this: if you knew that after taxes and transaction costs you could get only a 6 percent to 7 percent return on stocks, how much of your money would you move from stocks to highly rated bonds? And if the return on stocks before taxes and transaction costs is actually likely to be less than 10 percent, as predicted by many commentators, the return on stocks might be even lower than the return on bonds. How much is it worth to you to know that your nest egg is not at risk and will be there if and when you need it?

QUESTIONS TO PONDER

What risks are you prepared to take in the stock market? How much are you willing to lose? Can you afford to sit out a bad stock market? If you have invested in stock, have you gotten the published return or the return you expected? What stories do you tell your friends about your successes in the financial markets? After a loss, what are your "yeah, but" rationalizations that you don't share with friends? Are you playing in someone else's game? How much time do you have to allocate to investment management?

Chapter Notes

1. Joe Mysak, "How to Make $500,000 a Year and Pay No Taxes," Bloomberg .com, August 31, 2001.

2. Mary Williams Walsh, "Maine Takes a Cautious Path on Its Pensions," *New York Times*, April 23, 2004, C1.

3. Mary Williams Walsh, "The Nation: Undone by Market Risk: A Premature Sunset for Pensions," *New York Times*, sec. 4, November 28, 2004, 5.

4. Elizabeth Albanese, "Alternative Assets," *Bond Buyer* Online, October 27, 2003.

5. Ibbotson Associates, *Stocks, Bonds, Bills, and Inflation, 2006 Yearbook*, 61. The precise return with dividends reinvested between 1925 and 2005 was 10.4 percent.

6. John Bogle, "What Went Wrong in Mutual Fund America?" *Journal of Indexes* (July/August 2006): 30.

7. William Bernstein, "Sucker's Bet," *Financial Planning* (April 2001): 183–184.

8. Michael J. Mauboussin, as reported in the Legg Mason Capital Management publication, *Mauboussin on Strategy*, May 18, 2006, 9.

9. Charles A. Jaffee, "New Way to Gauge Fund Performance," *Philadelphia Inquirer*, October 15, 2006, E7.

10. Johnathan Clements, "Curb Your Enthusiasim: Why Investors Often Lag behind the Market Indexes," *Wall Street Journal*, October 18, 2006, D1.

11. Ibbotson, 228.

12. Ibid., 229.

13. Ibid., 201

14. Ibid., 39.

15. Zvi Bodie and Michael J. Clowes, *Worry-Free Investing* (New York: FT Prentice Hall, 2003), 83.

16. Ibid., 103.

17. Raymond Fazzi, "Stocks Not For the Long Run?" *Financial Adviser*, January 2004, 51.

18. Bodie and Clowes, 83–103.

19. Fazzi, 57.

20. Ibbotson, 39, for each of these dates reflecting the S&P 500.

21. Bernstein, 184.

CHAPTER 2

THE ALL-BOND PORTFOLIO

When the market goes up, risk tolerance is infinite, but when it goes down, risk tolerance is often at zero.

—HAROLD R. EVENSKY

Chairman, Evensky & Katz

OUR POSITION THAT investments in safe bonds is the key to your financial success is a controversial one—especially among brokers. Many investors believe that all diversification results in a reduction of their investment risk. Our concern is that in the name of diversification, these individual investors place a substantial amount of their nest egg in risky investments that they may not understand and ultimately take on more risk than they can actually sustain. Individual forays into risky investments either exhilarate us with their gains or leave us in a puddle of miseries.

It's easy to be misled if one looks only at the historical return of an investment or asset class instead of focusing on the risks involved to realize that return. A higher return means more risk, and more risk means that losses—yes, losses—are more likely. Overlooked tax consequences may severely reduce the expected return of an investment. Up-front, yearly, and back-end fees substantially reduce returns, whether you win or lose.

We believe that individual investors should match their investment assets with their financial needs (for example, retirement and education expenses), rather than speculate in the markets. If safe bonds are the core of your investment assets, you will be able to align your investments with your financial and life goals. This book will show you why you should do this, and how it can be done.

The old guarantees of job security, adequate Social Security benefits, and a company pension plan have been revised if not rescinded and the long-term values of our homes are in question. Despite these uncertainties, bonds can be the unbeaten path to secure investment growth and a way to limit the risk of investment loss without losing out on substantial income and gains.

Advantages of the All-Bond Portfolio

Simply stated, the 100 percent bond portfolio is a portfolio of safe bonds that will result in a secure cash flow while minimizing your investment risks. The 100 percent bond portfolio is a tried-and-true method that savvy individual investors have been using for generations.

The 100 percent bond portfolio investment strategy can enhance and enrich your life in a number of ways. We struggled for years with how to best satisfy the financial needs of our clients before we developed the 100 percent bond portfolio.

The portfolio is designed to provide the following advantages:

- It delivers better returns than other asset classes if you take into consideration the risks, taxes, fees, transaction costs, and the general bad timing of individual investors.
- It can be customized to your goals and needs.
- It provides a very low-risk investment. We've never lost a cent and you're not likely to either if you buy plain-vanilla bonds, safe

individual bonds denominated in U.S. dollars, and hold them until they come due.

◆ It provides income and growth. Come what may, you will have a safe and predictable return on your money.

◆ Execution costs are low. There is generally no commission payable when you buy a bond. There is, however, a cost to you called a "spread," which is the difference between the price the broker paid for the bond and the higher price at which he sells the bond. Spreads on plain-vanilla bonds are generally small. If you buy bonds at their initial offering, the spread will generally be zero.

◆ You need to make only one right decision because bonds repay their face value on their due date. With all other investments, you have to make two right decisions: when to buy and when to sell.

◆ Constructing the portfolio is a simple process to understand, and you can do it yourself.

Investing in the 100 percent bond portfolio has a number of life-enhancing characteristics. Investing your money in plain-vanilla bonds reduces your exposure to market volatility and decreases your investment risk, which will reduce the anxiety level in your life. Life has enough problems and concerns without worrying about the ups and downs of your investments every day.

A plain-vanilla bond portfolio represents an economical and safe alternative for your investment needs and diversifies some of the risk of other investments you may own, such as a business, real estate, and collectibles. Bonds give you core stability and enable you to be more adventurous in other areas of your life. For example, when your bond portfolio is large enough, you may decide to change your life by changing jobs or taking other chances in life. When your assets are safe and liquid, you're better able to deal with the bumps in the road of life.

FINANCIAL PLANNING

The concept of the 100 percent bond portfolio is now a new and better way for individual investors to deal with their anticipated and unanticipated transitions and deal with their financial problems. Investors can plan for unanticipated transitions and emergencies, such as an accident, disability, medical issues, or support for children and parents, by owning bonds that are easy and inexpensive to sell or to use as collateral for a loan. Investors can also plan for anticipated expenses, such as college costs, a first or second home, or retirement and a second career, by having bonds come due at the time they will need cash for these expenses.

Streams of income. When drafting a financial plan, financial advisers generally track two streams of income: the client's earned income and the client's total return on financial investments. Generally, a client's earned income is viewed as fixed and stable, and the investment income is considered variable and separate from the earned income. We believe that the concepts should be reversed. Your cash flow from a portfolio of plain-vanilla bonds should be your fixed base and will keep you safe; and your earned income should be the variable because it may vary and may cease altogether for a time or forever if you quit your job, retire early, get laid off, or become disabled.

For example, if you are self-employed, the earned income from your business may vary greatly from year to year. These days even an individual working on straight salary may find himself out of work at any time due to the rapid changes in an employer's business. How do you smooth out your cash flow? If your funds are invested in a portfolio of safe plain-vanilla bonds, you will know how much interest income is coming in for sure each year. Your earned income will be your variable. You will be more financially secure as your interest income increases.

Figure 2.1 is a diagram that outlines how your cash flow would support you in good times and bad. If you needed regular monthly payments, the funds would be there for you. If you did not need the income, you could reinvest the funds and have your portfolio grow. That is how bonds provide growth as well as income.

If you were beginning your investment program, you might buy U.S. savings bonds or certificates of deposit (CDs) because of their safety and low cash minimums. With $1,000, you could purchase corporate bonds or Treasury bonds. If you had $5,000, you could

FIGURE 2.1

Cash Flow From a Bond Portfolio

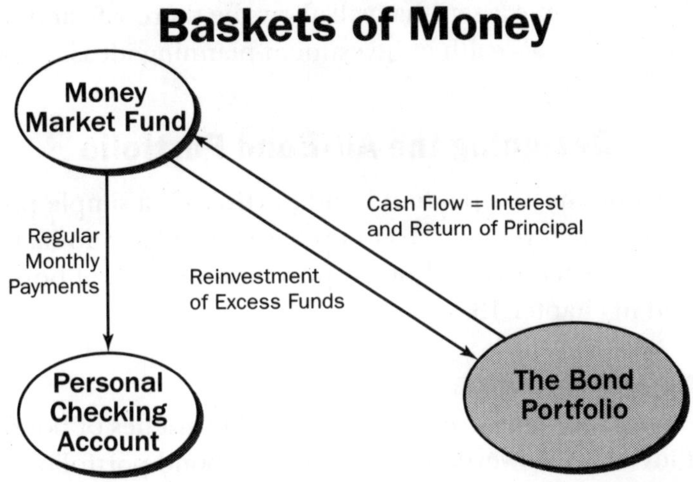

purchase a tax-free municipal bond. You pick the year you want the bond to come due.

The hard facts. There are at least three ways for you to secure your financial future:

1 Increase your wealth so that you have the option of early retirement.

2 Decrease your expenses.

3 Continue to work forever.

Decreasing expenses and increasing your interest income from bonds is a safe and sound way to achieve a less stressful financial life. It also may enable you to accept a job that you love even though it pays less. The 100 percent bond portfolio is your passport to a richer, more flexible, less stressful life.

Although we know that getting aggressive with your investments may create great wealth, it may also result in a financial disaster. If you decide not to invest all your money in bonds, we recommend that you keep at least a portion of your portfolio in plain-vanilla bonds. This will enable you to keep at least some assets safe for emergencies, changing jobs, or starting a business. You'll know that there are some assets that will always be there safe and sound. See Part Five for a wealth of investment-planning ideas.

Designing the All-Bond Portfolio

Constructing the 100 percent bond portfolio is a simple process, and you can do it yourself. You purchase only plain-vanilla bonds. Detailed instructions on how to purchase individual bonds are provided in chapter 13.

PLAIN-VANILLA BONDS

We describe in Part Three all the different varieties of bonds you might invest in. However, the 100 percent bond portfolio focuses on what we refer to as plain-vanilla bonds. Plain-vanilla bonds are the most suitable bonds for individual investors because they have the following characteristics in common:

◆ They are individual bonds that come due on a specific date.

◆ Their principal is essentially risk free. For example, a Treasury bond or a U.S. Agency bond will not default. The default rate on municipal bonds is historically less than 1 percent, and those defaults are generally in predictable sectors.

◆ They are easy to buy at a fair price.

◆ They can be sold easily and quickly (this is called liquidity).

◆ The cost of buying them is little or nothing.

◆ They are denominated in U.S. dollars, rather than foreign currency.

◆ They are easy to understand and evaluate.

Examples of plain-vanilla bonds include:

◆ Safe cash equivalents, such as short-term Treasury bills and CDs.

◆ U.S. Treasury bonds and Treasury inflation-protected securities (TIPS) (see chapter 6).

- ◆ U.S. savings bonds (see chapter 7).
- ◆ U.S. Agency bonds (see chapter 8).
- ◆ Highly rated municipal bonds and insured municipal bonds (see chapter 10).
- ◆ Corporate bonds AA-rated or better (see chapter 11).
- ◆ Foreign bonds AA-rated or better, are denominated in U.S. dollars that are called "Yankee" bonds (see chapter 11).

PLAIN-VANILLA EXCLUSIONS

The 100 percent bond portfolio does not include risky bonds. Our reason for this is the "sleep factor": We don't buy any bonds that will prevent a good night's sleep. Investments in risky bonds create the same kind of anxiety as investments in gyrating stocks. If you buy a portfolio of risky bonds, there is a risk that one or more of them may default. And you may not make enough on the risky bonds to compensate for that loss. For those reasons, the definition of plain-vanilla bonds excludes the following types of bonds and securities:

- ◆ Low-rated bonds such as high-yield bonds (also called "junk" bonds) and emerging-market bonds, which generally have a significant risk of default (see chapter 11). In the early 1990s, 30 percent of so-called high-yield bonds defaulted.
- ◆ Any bonds denominated in a foreign currency, such as euros, which have significant currency risk. The foreign currency may decline against the U.S. dollar and result in a loss because the buyers in this case spend their money in U.S. dollars.
- ◆ Many types of mortgage-backed securities, which carry high risks that are hard to define because of the complexity of their structures (see chapter 9).
- ◆ Entities that hold bonds, such as bond funds, exchange-traded funds (ETFs), closed-end funds, and unit investment trusts (UITs), which generally don't come due on a specific date. As a consequence, you may take a loss when you sell them. In addition, when you buy these entities, they may have up-front fees, annual management charges, other fees, and/or back-end fees when you sell them. We believe that these entities are a different animal from individual bonds (see chapter 14).

Alhough you may come to appreciate the world of bonds as much as we do, learning about bonds may seem overwhelming. It is, after all, a business that has developed over centuries. Focusing on plain-vanilla bonds will help you learn about the bonds that are the most important investments for you. However, even with plain-vanilla bonds, there are new terms to learn so you won't stand out as a greenhorn. All the terms you need to know are clearly explained in chapter 5.

A Word About Other Bonds

Although our preference is for plain-vanilla bonds, there is a vast landscape of possible bond investments, all of which we describe in Part Three, including a full discussion of mortgage-backed securities, junk bonds, and entities that hold bonds (bond aggregators). You should understand all the different varieties of bonds so that you don't come to the conclusion that all bonds are similar and buy only the highest yielding. Bonds are generally aligned in accordance with their risks and due dates. If high returns are promised, you can be sure of high risks. There are very few undervalued bonds. If a bond looks like a bargain to you, that probably means that you're missing one or more significant facts known to the bond traders and dealers. The 100 percent bond portfolio is risk averse. Don't reach for yield and think you're safe because you invested in bonds. What you don't know or don't understand may hurt you.

HIGH-YIELD DEBT

There are times when risky bonds may be profitable for those willing to take the plunge. "Yesterday's weeds are being priced as today's flowers," Warren Buffett observed in 2004.[1] He was referring to the junk bond sector. In 2006, the returns from junk bonds were still not worth the risk of investing in them[2] because the interest rates on Treasury bonds rose while the interest rate on risky high-yield bonds and other risky debt including emerging-market debt continued to fall.

Since the mid-1980s, the extra yield received for investing in junk bonds over Treasury bonds has ranged between 3 percent and 10 percent on a seven-year bond. In May of 2006, junk bonds yielded about 3 percent more than similar Treasury bonds. If the spread between Treasury bonds and junk bonds is only at 3 percent, you may actually earn a lower return on a portfolio of junk bonds if one or more of them defaults, even though they pay more current interest.

If you reach for a higher yield by investing in junk bonds or emerging-market bonds, you will need substantial diversification in these asset classes to reduce the risk of a major loss to your portfolio. Chapter 16 describes how to buy bond funds to achieve the required diversification of risk. If you do invest in junk bonds, consider them as part of your risky investment category because they have characteristics more similar to equities than to the plain-vanilla bonds we recommend.

The All-Bond Antidote to Greed and Fear

An old saw on Wall Street goes "All investors walk the line between greed and fear." Greed is ignited in part by media saturation that trumpets the news that investors who bet on the bull and give their money to the loudest advertisers in the financial services industry will become rich. Risks and fees are often understated or minimized if they're described at all. Many of today's so-called leading-edge new financial products are examples of what's called "black box" technology. Investors are not told what is in the box. Even if someone described the technology to them, they probably would not understand it. It is unclear what risks are imbedded in these new financial products and the total of the up-front, annual, and back-end fees is also cloudy. This is what happens when investors "play in someone else's game." It is understandable that investors get fearful when they contemplate these black-box investments. But even if investors, drawn by greed, overcome their fear, should they be willing to get into a game if they don't understand the rules, the degree and amount of risk, or the total cost to play?

In the complex world of new financial products, you face the conundrum: What do you do if you know that you don't know? With new financial products multiplying faster than rabbits, it's easy to conclude that you don't know enough. The real question is what to do about it? Should you just walk away from the latest financial technology purported to have the highest return? Investors struggle to decide how to sort out the unknowable financial products and decide which investment strategy is best for them. As financial advisers, we struggled with this problem for many years before we settled on the solution of the 100 percent bond portfolio invested in plain-vanilla bonds. We are fully convinced it is the best choice.

Chapter Notes

1. Dr. Steve Sjuggerud, "High Yield Bond Funds," *Investment U E-Letter*, January 31, 2005.
2. Jennifer Ablan, "The Fed's Done Diddly," *Barron's* (April 24, 2006): M18.

CHAPTER 3

ADOPTING THE ALL-BOND PORTFOLIO

A Case Study

FOR MANY INVESTORS, the unfortunate outcome of following the accepted wisdom of having a diversified portfolio is to realize that they cannot be sure that their investment portfolio will adequately fund their financial objectives and life goals. In addition, they may not realize that they're taking on a great deal of additional risk. A client we'll call Peter is a typical example. He came to us well into his career but early enough for a change in his investments to make a difference.

A Poor-Fitting Portfolio

Peter is forty years old and in the prime of his life. He is married to Jane, and they have two beautiful children ages eight and ten. Jane looks after the children, and Peter works at Bigco, a major international consulting firm. Peter is well regarded at Bigco and was promoted to the position of senior consultant last year. Peter has worked his entire career at Bigco and is well compensated.

Peter and Jane live the American dream. They have a huge house, expensive German cars, a single-engine airplane, and a Harley motorcycle. But all is not well with Peter and Jane despite their lavish lifestyle. Although Peter's work is challenging and exciting, he has become a road warrior and is away from home all week. Peter's absence and out-of-town travel is having an adverse effect on him and on his relationship with Jane and his children. To save his marriage and his relationship with his children, Peter has decided that he must leave Bigco and set up his own consultancy, even though he will take a big cut in pay, at least initially.

In addition to his distress about his family situation, Peter had become very concerned about his financial well-being. At work he found himself checking the movements of the stock market several times a day. He was especially concerned about the safety of his investment portfolio, particularly since he was leaving Bigco and his large monthly paycheck.

PETER'S FINANCIAL OBJECTIVES

Peter has three financial objectives, which he explained to us:

1 To have enough liquid and easily salable assets to launch and support his new consulting business.

2 To provide for his children's college education.

3 To provide a savings program for his retirement.

Before becoming our client, Peter had a traditional financial adviser who worked at a large brokerage house. The adviser allocated Peter's $400,000 of financial assets into the investment portfolio, as set forth below. The only investment asset held in a tax-sheltered retirement account was the stock fund in the 401(k) plan. All other assets were held outside of tax-sheltered retirement accounts.

20 percent in stock mutual funds—in a 401(k) plan
30 percent in stock mutual funds
10 percent in a variable annuity that holds stock funds
20 percent in bond funds
10 percent in a real estate partnership
10 percent in a commodity partnership

Peter's financial adviser told him that this diversified portfolio would maximize his returns while minimizing his risks. The series of mutual funds, partnerships, and an annuity that the adviser bought for Peter were designed to provide a balance of large-cap stocks, mid-cap stocks, small-cap stocks, foreign stocks, and emerging-market stocks. He also bought Peter an annuity and investment partnerships in commodities and real estate to provide an allocation to alternative investments.

Peter's financial adviser told him that based on past performance this portfolio would generally appreciate at the 10 percent historical rate for stocks and would always outperform bonds. He advised Peter that it was best to ignore the daily and even yearly performance of the stock market and other markets; all would be well, eventually. He assured Peter that his children would have enough money for college in ten years and that he would retire rich in twenty-five years because his $400,000 nest egg would be worth more than $4,000,000 when it compounded at 10 percent per year, the historic rate of return on stocks, even if he added no more savings to it. Peter's adviser never factored in the need for liquid assets for the new start-up consulting business because the adviser generally used the same asset allocation for all his clients. A one-size-fits-all approach like this one is not uncommon at large brokerage firms.

PETER'S CONCERNS ABOUT HIS PORTFOLIO

Although this investment portfolio is not unusual, Peter's initial concern was that it did not support or align with his financial and life objectives. He had no idea what these investments would be worth in the future, how much income they would produce from year to year, or what their tax consequences would be each year.

As a result of these unanswered questions, he could not get comfortable with or understand how the investment portfolio selected by his adviser would be worth enough for him to fund his new business start-up, his children's college expenses, and his scheduled retirement. He read articles about the many pension funds that bet on stocks to fund retirees' benefits and later found themselves with huge budget gaps between the value of the pension funds and the amount needed to pay retirees.

Peter had other concerns about his investment portfolio as well. He noticed that when the stock market went down, all his stock funds and the variable annuity went down as well despite the portfolio's diversification. He didn't see how these investments, although diversified, would protect him in hard financial times. Even when his stock investments were doing well, he worried about the market's unpredictable changes. He knew about the 1929 stock market crash and the 1987 crash, when the market dropped by 22.6 percent in one day. And he witnessed the bear market, when the S&P 500 declined by 47.5 percent—from 1,527 on March 23, 2000, to 801 on March 11, 2003. The Nasdaq did even worse, declining by 77.9 percent—from 5,048 on March 10, 2000, to 1,114 on October 9, 2002.[1] Peter's adviser told him that quick movements in the market were called "volatility" and that even if the market was inconsistent day to day, it would ultimately achieve the 10 percent growth rate based on past history. This assurance did not make Peter feel any more secure. He took an analytical approach to his investments, but the stock market moves seemed to him to be without rhyme or reason.

Another of Peter's major concerns was the high fees embedded in his stock funds and other investments. The stock funds had high front-end fees, high management and maintenance fees, and some had back-end fees. To add insult to injury, he was paying hefty fees for funds that often did not outperform stock index funds. The annuity and the partnerships—which also had high front-end fees, high management fees, and other fees—were difficult if not impossible to value. They also had long lockup periods, when they could not be sold at all, and penalties for early withdrawal. The partnerships were illiquid, in that they were hard to sell at a fair price.

Peter's stock mutual funds traded frequently, which generated a lot of short-term capital gains (when there were gains at all), which were taxable at ordinary income rates, creating a very tax-inefficient investment. Peter detested the idea of risking his hard-earned principal and paying high taxes. His concern was magnified in light of his view that the economy was vulnerable to a decline in these highly unstable times.

In the late 1990s, Peter thought that his investments in the stock market would fund his children's college education. After the losses from the dramatic stock market decline in 2000 to 2002, however, he no longer knew where the money would come from to fully fund their college expenses. Peter decided that he could not bet his and his family's financial well-being on what the stock market might be worth in the future. He also wondered what would happen to him and his family if the stock market declined significantly either at the point when he needed cash for his business or before his retirement. He didn't know how he could rely on the historical past performance of the stock market, commodities market, or real estate market when he knew that the world of the past was different from the present, let alone the future.

Peter terminated his engagement with his financial adviser because despite his portfolio's diversification he found that his investments were volatile, unpredictable, and expensive. But worst of all, he didn't believe that his investments supported his financial or life goals or that he would reach those goals safely.

A Consultation With Stan Richelson

Peter came to my office to investigate whether the strategy of the 100 percent bond portfolio might address his concerns. Peter wanted help. As we shook hands and sat down for an initial consultation, Peter was uptight and sat anxiously in his chair. He told me about his plan to leave Bigco and start his own consultancy. He also shared his fear that his investment portfolio might not be adequate to provide for his children's college education or his own retirement.

Peter asked if I could create a predictable financial plan that aligned with his financial life objectives and was not dependent on the unpredictable future performance of the stock market, real estate market, or commodities market. Peter no longer had any interest in listening to the "noise" of these markets and struggling to detect a signal that would indicate when to buy or sell these investments. These markets seemed to him to be driven more by luck and randomness than by skill, knowledge, and certainty.

I introduced Peter to the strategy of the 100 percent bond portfolio as a key part of his financial plan. It would work better than stocks, commodities, or real estate to secure his family's financial future. I explained that although stocks, real estate, and commodities might have performed well during certain periods in the past, there was no way of knowing whether they would have significant losses or gains in the future.

With investments in stocks, real estate, and commodities, the investor must make two right decisions—when to buy and when to sell. Those decisions are either right or wrong. There's no middle ground. Until an investor closes the position by selling, the money is at risk. In other words, with all investments, except safe bonds, the "chips are on the table" until the sale. Safe bonds are the only asset class in which an investor's chips are not on the table because a bond automatically pays off at its face value if the buyer holds it until its due date. For example, a stock investor in the 1990s made big money only if he purchased stocks early in the 1990s and then sold before March of 2000, before the bear market wiped out most of their gains.

I told Peter that a key question in financial planning is whether an investor has enough financial resources so that he can withstand the consequences of being wrong. If not, we tell him he should not play. Relying on an optimistic reading of financial history to plan your financial future may end badly. To be safe, place your savings in safe investments like plain-vanilla bonds rather than rely on risky investments to do the heavy lifting.

I explained the strategy of the 100 percent bond portfolio and how it would reduce his anxiety and allow him to focus his energy on his new business and on his family and life interests. Because of the safety and predictability of bonds, we could prepare a conservative and comprehensive financial plan.

A Financial Plan Aligned With Objectives

I described the four-step procedure that we use to create a financial plan based on the 100 percent bond solution:

1 The client determines his life objectives and financial needs with the help of some coaching.

2 The client divides his investment portfolio into two categories:

◆ **Assets to be invested in plain-vanilla bonds.** We call this category "investments" because they are safe and we can determine the return on these investments.

◆ **All other investment assets such as stocks, real estate, and commodities.** We call this category of assets "speculative" because it is not clear what the value of these assets will be in the future or how much cash flow they will provide each year.

3 Determine the tax consequences of existing and proposed investments taking into account the client's overall tax position.

4 Determine which selection of bonds and other investments will align with and support the client's life objectives and financial needs taking into account the tax consequences.

STEP 1: PETER'S OBJECTIVES AND FINANCIAL NEEDS

Peter's major objectives are clear:

◆ Preserve his marriage and continue his good relationship with his children.

◆ Launch his new consulting business, allowing him to be self-employed and in control of his life.

◆ Have enough assets available to pay for his children's tuition.

◆ Provide for his retirement.

Peter's decision to leave his job at Bigco and set up an independent consultancy is a major objective and creates the need for a substantial amount of liquid assets. He will no longer have a monthly paycheck and may need additional assets to launch his business while supporting his family's personal expenses.

STEP 2: ALLOCATION BETWEEN SAFE BONDS AND ALL OTHER ASSETS

Peter decided to invest his financial assets in plain-vanilla bonds and money market funds to support his new business. He understood from my explanation that he must, at this time, keep all his investment assets safe because he could not take the risk of a decline in his stocks, commodity, or real estate investments (other than his house). Thus, he decided to sell his stock mutual funds, real estate partnership, and commodity partnership. In addition, he could not take the risk of continuing in his bond fund because bond funds don't come due at a fixed date and if interest rates went up, his bond fund would decline substantially in value.

Peter understood that the 100 percent bond portfolio was not in reality an extreme position because he had other assets, such as his house, which is a real estate investment. In addition he had cars, an airplane, a motorcycle, and collectibles. Even when he put all his investment assets in bonds, he had a substantial allocation to real estate and other assets.

STEP 3: TAX REVIEW

Peter sold his investments in the year after he resigned from Bigco so that he was in a low tax bracket to minimize the taxes to be paid on his investment gains.

After his tax review, Peter was able to decide which investments would give him the best after-tax return. Because Peter was just starting a new business, it was prudent for him to invest a great deal of his financial assets in taxable cash equivalents, such as money market accounts and Treasury bills, to fund his start-up needs. These taxable investments yield more than tax-free investments, and Peter will initially be in a low tax bracket because of his start-up business.

Once his business becomes profitable, Peter's financial plan is to extend the maturities of his bonds to get a higher return and invest some of his assets in tax-free municipal bonds.

STEP 4: A GOAL-DIRECTED PORTFOLIO

After Peter sold his stock funds, cashed in his annuity, and sold his real estate and commodity partnerships, he decided to invest his

$400,000 as follows in plain-vanilla bonds:

◆ **$50,000 in taxable money-market funds.** Money market funds will not go up or down in value no matter what interest rates are doing. However, the interest rate will vary. Peter will first draw from the money market fund as a substitute for his salary from Bigco. See chapters 14 and 15 for a discussion of money market bond funds.

◆ **$100,000 in taxable Treasury bills.** Of these, $50,000 will come due in three months, $25,000 in six months, and $25,000 in one year. These Treasury bills may yield more than the money market fund and will be free of any state or local income taxes. The Treasury bills will be drawn on to fund business expenses as needed and to fund Peter's living expenses. Treasury bills can be sold easily before they come due and at a very small spread (that is, the fee to sell is small). See chapter 6 for a discussion of Treasury bills and bonds.

◆ **$50,000 in one-year CDs.** The CDs will yield somewhat more than the money market funds and Treasury bills. If purchased directly from a bank, they will not decline in value whether interest rates go up or down. However, if they are cashed in early, there may be a penalty. Peter found a bank that has only a three-month penalty. See chapter 12 for a discussion of CDs.

◆ **$100,000 in taxable agency bonds.** These bonds will come due in two years. Agency bonds are essentially low risk and the interest from some varieties is exempt from state and local income taxes, although subject to federal income tax. Peter may even be able to reinvest the proceeds of these bonds in tax-free municipal bonds if his business is successful and he finds himself in a higher tax bracket at the end of the two-year life of the bonds. If not, he can buy more agency bonds. Agency bonds yield somewhat more than Treasury bills and bonds of the same maturity. See chapter 8 for a discussion of agency bonds.

◆ **$50,000 in TIPS bonds.** These bonds will be part of Peter's tax-sheltered retirement account where they won't be subject to income tax until he withdraws cash from the account. Treasury inflation-protected securities(TIPS) provide a hedge against inflation and will serve as a first building block of his pension savings. The value of a TIPS bond increases if there is inflation. This increase results in taxable income even though no cash is currently paid to the bondholder. Thus, TIPS are generally suitable only for retirement accounts. If Peter's business goes well, he will add cash to his retirement account, which he will use to buy additional plain-vanilla bonds. See chapter 6 for a discussion of TIPS bonds.

◆ **$50,000 in zero-coupon municipal bonds.** These bonds will come due eight, nine, ten, eleven, and twelve years from the purchase date to help pay his children's college tuition. If Peter invests $10,000 in bonds maturing in each of these years, none of the increase in value of these bonds will be subject to federal income tax at any time, and the face value of the bonds will be available on their due dates. (See chapter 17 for more on portfolio construction.) If Peter gets into a financial jam and needs these bonds for living expenses, he can sell them at their fair market value at that time and use the proceeds for his family's needs. If all goes well, he will keep the bonds until they come due and use the proceeds to help pay tuition each year. If Peter's business goes well, he will add bonds earmarked for his children's education but keep them in his and Jane's names. Another possibility for funding education expenses is U.S. savings bonds. (See chapter 7 for more on funding education expenses and why this makes sense tax-wise. See chapter 10 for more on municipal bonds.)

REACHING A COMFORT LEVEL

The 100 percent bond portfolio changed Peter's life. The bulk of his investment portfolio is now in safe plain-vanilla bonds, which are essentially risk free. His bonds pay predictable interest income each year, and they align with his financial and life goals. As a consequence, he no longer worries about stock market fluctuations or stock market performance. He now has a realistic, tax-efficient, low-cost, and predictable financial plan. Peter knows that if he can maintain his savings rate, his plain-vanilla bonds will create adequate cash flow and growth so that he will have enough money to fund his retirement and meet his other financial obligations. And, best of all, he understands how his bond portfolio supports his financial and life objectives and the reason why he purchased each bond.

Chapter Note

1. See the tables set forth on the Yahoo Web site at http://finance.yahoo.com for the S&P 500 and Nasdaq past performance data. Click on the following links: Investing, Stocks, Research Tools, Historical Quotes.

PART TWO

BOND BASICS

POPULAR THINKING TODAY holds that you can never be too thin or too rich. We guarantee that this book will not make you thin. However, we do believe it will help you to increase your wealth. These pages present detailed information on all types of bonds and also offer financial planning and investment advice that teaches you how to conservatively preserve your capital and make money with bonds.

This section explains the history, language, and basics of bonds. Once you've read and digested this material, you'll be better equipped to evaluate the information and strategies we present in the remainder of the book. You may think that this is too much work. Why should you bother learning all this? After all, you can take the easy way out and invest in stocks or diversify in bond funds without too much thought. Here's why. If you believe such a stock- or fund-based investment approach affords safety, you may be missing out on an important fundamental concept. Here's one way to explain it: Bonds come due. You know when you'll get your principal back. You'll get it if you invest in high-grade bonds. Neither stock nor bond funds—nor any other investments—come due as do bonds and automatically return your principal.

In addition, every moment of every day, whether you're awake or sleeping, the interest on your bond is compounding and accumulating. When the bond pays interest, the money will flow into a money market account, if you so direct your broker, earning interest there until you're ready to reinvest it. If the great bugaboo of inflation raises its head, that should be no concern of yours unless you purchased long-term bonds. In fact, rising interest rates are an opportunity to invest at higher returns. With each rising sun, your bond comes one day closer to maturity. The passing of each year brings it closer to redemption, when it will repay at face value.

When inflation lights a fire under the yields, driving down the price of your individual bond, that's no reason to despair. Your bonds will pay out their face value at maturity. Meanwhile, you can reinvest your interest at the higher rates, giving you an overall higher yield-to-maturity than you might otherwise have had if rates had not risen. You'll get your invested dollars back and get a higher yield than you had expected. If you reinvest the interest, your assets will grow through the geometric magic of compound interest. You will earn interest on interest as well as interest on your principal with every day that passes.

You earn interest on interest plus interest an your principal, which grows with every day that passes. You have the opportunity for better yields if there's inflation, you're protected from the worst returns in a deflation, and you get your money back. Sounds like a pretty good deal to us.

CHAPTER 4

THE EVOLUTION OF A BOND

From Verbal IOU to Electronic Entry

BONDS ARE NEGOTIABLE or salable loans, and there is a ready marketplace in which to trade them—a big advantage for investors. In 1704, England passed a law making loans negotiable. Today, bonds can be traded like wheat and pork in the commodity markets. The bond markets are called the credit markets, the place where governments and corporations come to gather money to create their dreams. Formerly the province of bankers and kings, these markets are now open to everyone.

Learning the Language

To fully understand these markets, it helps to know why they exist as they do. And while it is true that bond brokers speak English, they use expressions that act as shorthand, creating an often inscrutable language in the process. To make learning their lingo and the forms it describes interesting, we trace the development of the words through bond history.

Financial language derives from a vocabulary created over the centuries. This vocabulary is particularly puzzling to those new to marketable securities based on debt: namely, bonds, notes, bills, and other fixed-income investments. Based on U.S. case law, a bond, according to *Black's Law Dictionary*, is "a long-term, interest-bearing debt instrument issued by a corporation or governmental entity, usually to provide for a particular financial need; especially, such an instrument in which the debt is secured by a lien on the issuer's property."[1] This is the definition we'll use in this book. All the following terms can be subsumed under the general heading of debt:

◆ A bill, as in dollar bill or Treasury bill, is also a promise to pay. It is a "promissory note."[2] In financial usage, a bill is a short-term obligation of the U.S. Treasury.

◆ A note is "a written promise by one party (the maker) to pay money to another party (the payee or bearer)."[3] In current usage, a note refers to intermediate corporate bonds that were issued with maturities of around twelve years or less, or issues of the U.S. Treasury with an issuance life between one and ten years.

◆ Another term you might hear is paper. Paper is "an instrument other than cash, for the payment of money…typically existing in the form of a draft (such as a check) or a note (such as a certificate of deposit)."[4] Commercial paper is short-term unsecured debt issued by a corporation. Although as an individual investor you probably will not buy commercial paper directly, you likely own it through your money market fund. When you call a broker and ask to purchase a bond, the broker might respond, "What kind of paper do you want?" As such, it could refer to any of the above financial instruments or others described later.

Bonds: The Early Years

Most of the earliest legal codes sought to limit the use of credit or to prevent it altogether. The biblical Israelites did not permit lending at interest. Ancient South Indian literature reviled usurers and set interest limits. However, merchant activity requires the use of loans. The earliest use of loans in trade was in the form of bills of credit. Merchants financed their trade with written promissory notes entitling them to get money in distant ports. That way they didn't have to carry hard currency with them.

During the Dark Ages, merchant activity for all intents and purposes ceased. In addition, Charlemagne became the first ruler to prohibit all usury. If the result of lending was considered usury, the punishment was death. The Catholic Church effectively prevented all above-board acts of lending and borrowing, except as conducted by the Church itself.[5] The Church had liquid capital that it lent to nobles and secured the debt with their land. The loan was called a "land gage." It was a live gage when the land's revenue repaid the debt and a mort gage (mortgage) when it did not.

By the fifteenth century, the pressure to allow borrowing was intense. With credit scarce and tax revenues falling short, as usual, kings and popes resorted to creative money-raising schemes to finance their armies, wars, luxuries, and political ambitions. To finance the monarchs' needs, they created merchant banks. In lieu of interest, the banks compensated the lenders by participating in the kings' monopolies and by franchises, special privileges granted to them[6]—much as with venture capitalists today in their role as financiers to emerging enterprises.

After the Protestant Reformation in 1517, interest became an acceptable form of payment in Europe, making lending and borrowing easier. Interest was then accepted as compensation for risking the loss of borrowed funds and the possibility that the funds could be put to better use elsewhere. Catholic countries resisted the acceptance of interest. It wasn't until the early nineteenth century that the Holy Office decreed that anyone could take interest at rates defined by law. As recently as 1950, Pope Pius XII attempted to eradicate the stigma of the past in formally declaring that bankers "earn their livelihood honestly."[7]

Islam's Shari'a law still does not permit the use of interest. Despite that, however, Muhammad Yunus established the Grameen Bank in Bangladesh in 1976 to provide microcredit to the impoverished. For this work, he won the Noble Peace Prize in 2006.

Today, negotiable loans pay interest. *Black's Law Dictionary* defines interest for money as "the compensation fixed by agreement or allowed by law…especially, the amount owed to a lender in return for the use of borrowed money."[8] From Roman times, a distinction has been drawn between usury (the price paid for borrowed capital) and interest. Usury was considered to be profit. It included being paid more than the legal limit and/or with the purpose in mind to get more. Interest, on the other hand, was associated not with profit, but with loss. It was compensation for the loss of the use of money. At first, it was levied only if the loan was not repaid on time. Later, there were other qualifying reasons. For example, if it was viewed as a wage, compensation for the time and effort in making the loan, then it became acceptable to levy interest from the beginning.

Today, usury is defined as "an illegally high rate of interest."[9] You are compensated through the payment of interest when you lend money by buying a bond. You find out at the time of purchase whether you will receive interest monthly, semiannually, or only when the bond comes due. In the United States, state law defines usury; however, the parameters defining usury are not the same in all states.

By the time Europe's age of exploration began in the sixteenth century, many of the concepts underlying today's bonds were already in place. The term *bond*, for example, is not used when a loan is made to an individual. Bonds are negotiable—they can be bought and sold. Central governments and their agencies, supranational governmental agencies such as the World Bank, state and municipal governments, and corporations are the only entities that issue bonds.

Our large-scale bond markets were based on patterns developed in Venice and other merchant towns in Italy and later on the financial success of the Dutch cities of Antwerp and Amsterdam, where a popular government was able to pledge the resources of a town, province, or nation. In the eighteenth century the English made two improvements to the Dutch systems of finance. First, the English clearly stated on each issue how much money was being borrowed, when the bonds would come due, and if there were any special terms that were part of the loan. For example, a special feature might be the issuer having the right to call in the bonds before the redemption, or due date. Second, they did not change the terms or features of the bonds from one issue to another. Once you understood the nature of the bond, you could buy any subsequent bond without having to consider the terms of the loan. Furthermore, the issues were for large amounts of money, enabling large-scale investors to purchase blocks of bonds to meet their investment needs instead of buying many little issues that each required analysis.[10] Today, the Treasury and Euro markets most reflect these advances. Issues of bonds by large corporations can also approximate this ideal.

A Colonial Debut

Since colonial times, bonds have been part of American history. Although the colonists lived in relatively basic conditions, they had the heritage of English law and finance to help shape the nation. England, whose bonds were primarily issued to pay for wars, laid the debt for the Anglo-French War on the doorsteps of the colonies. Massachusetts was the first colony to offer bonds to cover its costs. In 1690, Massachusetts issued paper to help pay for its share of the debts incurred by all the colonies while helping the British fight a war with the French Canadians. The attitude of the English was that it was a war to protect the colonies, so the citizens of the New World should bear the responsibility of the debt.

Massachusetts's first issue was successfully repaid from tax payments. (Today we call municipal bonds backed by property and other tax receipts "general obligation bonds," in that they are the obligation of everyone in the political entity that issued them.) Seeking other ways to raise revenue, in 1744 Massachusetts became the first colony to use a lottery to help pay off the war debt. The English Act of 1709 prohibited the use of lotteries in England, but this law did not apply to the colonies. They passed their own laws limiting or prohibiting its use later on. If the lottery was a revenue stream guaranteed for the repayment of bonds, we would call those bonds "revenue bonds" today. However, the lottery was just a means for the government to raise more funds. Massachusetts had a successful lottery; the one in New York two years later failed.

In keeping with the informal character of business in the colonies, a group of savvy Boston merchants decided to issue their own paper money in 1733. A set amount of silver, which could be redeemed after ten years, backed these bonds. When the price of silver increased by almost 50 percent above the redemption price, these notes appreciated in value. In this case, the issuer (the borrower) bore the risk of inflation. If there is inflation, it is usually the lenders (the bond buyer) who suffer, because they are repaid in depreciated currency.

Between 1751 and 1764, England put a stop to the issuance of paper money by the colonial governments. Unable to issue paper money, colonial governments issued Treasury bills instead, which were redeemable in gold and silver after two to three years. Like modern municipal bonds that are the general obligation of the state, actual tax payments rather than lotteries backed the bills. With the solid financial guarantee of the government, these Treasury bills did not depreciate.

After the American Revolution

The states still issue bonds today, but the term Treasury bond is restricted to bonds issued by the U.S. Treasury. After the American Revolution, one of the first acts of the U.S. Treasury in 1789 was the assumption of all war debts incurred by the states. Although the federal government agreed to pay, it did not have the money. In 1795, the Secretary of the Treasury Alexander Hamilton decided to adopt a method borrowed from the British: the use of a so-called sinking fund. In essence, the fund consisted of money set aside and invested to pay off a debt through the accumulation of interest. Sinking funds are still a feature of some revenue bonds today, although the money might not actually be set aside for the periodic debt recall. The funds usually kick in after fifteen years.

Hamilton's successor, Albert Gallatin, quickly figured out that the scheme was not working: interest on the debt was growing faster than the sinking fund interest that was supposed to pay off the debt.

His solution was to reduce the debt by buying bonds in the marketplace if they were selling at or below face value. In so doing, he created the U.S. government's first open market operations. The Federal Reserve periodically engages in such activity today, buying and selling bonds in the open markets to expand or contract credit.

Gallatin also supported and planned the construction of roads and canals in the new republic. Direct federal funding for these plans ended, however, with the election of Andrew Jackson in 1830. The job of completing them fell to state and local governments, which had little experience and money to complete the costly projects.

Lack of experience, however, did not deter state governments from freely issuing debt for railroads, turnpikes, and other public improvements. It was commonplace in the early 1800s for banks also to issue notes to finance such projects. There were soon so many notes in circulation that they did not retain their value.

To create some clarity as to the strength of the issuer, John Thompson started the Thompson Financial and Rating Agency in 1842. He rated bank notes by sending his sons to banks to redeem notes for gold. If the bank refused, Thompson would condemn the note to death by writing about it unfavorably. From this beginning came today's financial tabloid *American Banker.*

At the time Thompson started his agency, a depression had hit the U.S. economy, and state revenues declined sharply. Payment of interest and principal was postponed, in some cases for as long as seven years, until all debts were repaid. (Principal is the face value of a bond, as opposed to the interest it pays.) Only two states, Mississippi and Florida, repudiated their debt at that time. Lest anyone think that lenders have short memories when they've been stiffed, it's reported that when officials from Mississippi went to London to sell a taxable Eurobond issue in 1987, they were told, to their surprise, that "the state's credit was no good. The state of Mississippi, the bankers explained, still owed London banks principal and interest on $7 million of defaulted state debt—sold 156 years earlier and repudiated in 1857!"[11]

During the Civil War, the federal and confederate governments financed the war by selling bonds bought by the banks and sold to the general public. As the lines of credit evaporated, they issued fiat money—that is, paper money not backed by gold or silver. The Yankees issued greenbacks, the predecessors of modern U.S. currency.

Following the Civil War, economic life was harsh for the southern states. The difficulties were aggravated by the nationwide panic of 1873. Reeling under its impact and from the heavy load of bonds issued for railroads and so-called carpetbagger debt incurred after the Civil War, many states simply refused to pay a substantial portion of what was owed. The states relied on Section 4 of the Constitution's Fourteenth Amendment, prohibiting any state from paying debt incurred to fund a rebellion against the federal government. The *Bond Buyer,* a financial newspaper, reported that by 1873 a total of ten states had repudiated $300 million of principal and interest, with Virginia leading the pack, owing $72,220,000.[12] The federal government refused to bail the states out.

Four outcomes of the profligacy of the states define the bond markets today.

1 First, as a result of these problems, state legislatures limited the amount of debt states could issue, although each did so in a different way. The controls placed on the issuance of state general-obligation debt created strong state credits that are still respected in the marketplace.

2 Second, states encouraged local governments to issue debt for their own developmental needs, and this they continue to do.

3 Third, the troubled period established precedence for the repudiation of debt and the long-lasting consequences of doing so.

4 Fourth, events established that the federal government would not always bail out state and local governments when they encountered problems.

It is important to note that in the present day as well, repudiation of debt is much more likely to occur when the populace does not specifically vote to incur the debt in the first place. Government officials always have visions of projects they wish to fund, some of which are basic improvements and others reflect special interests. Tax-averse citizens try to limit their local government's ability to issue bonds by writing laws placed on the ballot and approved by vote. As we'll explain later, creative financing methods circumvent those restrictions. California is at the forefront of these conflicting interests.

Entering the Twentieth Century

Perhaps the most significant event in the beginning of the twentieth century to affect bonds was the founding of the Federal Reserve in 1913. The Federal Reserve is a central banking system much like the one long used in Europe to pool bank reserves and create a lender of last resort. The initial effect of the Federal Reserve was to smooth out the fluctuation of short-term interest rates by making short-term money nearly always available. With the advent of World War I, the Federal Reserve took on the additional responsibility to manage the issuance of Treasury bonds, which were absorbed by banks, and the Federal Reserve System. Low interest rates soon became a government objective.[13]

Corporate bonds became a major factor in the U.S. economy with the advent of World War I because of their high returns. By law, national banks had to hold Treasury debt in order to issue bank notes. In 1917, Treasury bonds yielded 2 percent, and corporate bonds, under no restraining regulations, were yielding up to 5 percent. Not surprisingly, the general public preferred the more lucrative returns of the corporate debt.

The Treasury needed to entice the public to buy its bonds, so that the federal government could finance the looming war. It came up with a creative solution, called Liberty Bonds, and sold them through banks. If patriotic Americans did not have the money to pay for the bonds they wished to buy, the banks lent it to them, charging the interest that the bonds paid. The American public bought the bonds on what is called margin, borrowing money to finance the purchase of securities. The call to patriotism led people to purchase Liberty Bonds, which in 1917 yielded 3.5 percent for fifteen-year bonds and 4 percent for the ten-year. Banks could use the bonds as collateral for loans, and credit flowed freely as the banks lent liberally for the time.

In 1920, fearful of inflation, the Federal Reserve used its powers to control this rapid expansion of credit by raising the discount rate. Subject to the vagaries of the market, the yield in 1920 on twelve-month Treasury certificates rose to 7.75 percent. Corporate bonds declined in value by 11 percent as interest rates rose from 4.95 percent to 5.56 percent, rates not seen again until 1967.[14] Against such competition, Liberty Bonds issued in 1918, with a coupon rate of 4.5 percent, declined by 17 percent. Of Liberty Bonds' 18 million owners, an estimated 14 million liquidated their holdings due to rapid fluctuations in value.[15] However, if they kept those bonds instead of selling them, they would have seen their value appreciate. The year 1920 marked the peak of prime bond yields, not seen for close to five decades before or five decades after that date. The holders of noncallable 100-year railroad bonds issued in the late 1890s with interest rates between 4 and 4.5 percent likewise saw their value plummet in 1920, but by 1946 those same bonds were worth 25 to 50 percent more than face value.

In the 1920s, nobody imagined bonds backed by mortgages, but in 1938 the creation of Fannie Mae, a government agency dedicated to the refinancing of unpopular long, fixed-rate mortgages, sowed the seeds. The creators could not have possibly realized that they were inaugurating an exciting new debt form that would evolve into the multitrillion-dollar mortgage-backed securities market.

During World War II, interest rates remained low for Treasury bonds, with fixed rates ranging from 2 percent to 2.5 percent for the 25- to 30-year bonds. Despite the low returns, when the highest federal income tax rate hit 94 percent between 1944 and 1945, the tax-exempt appeal of municipal bonds became magnetic.[16] With 1945 came the end of the war and a suspension of long-term Treasury bond issuance for eight years. The so-called long bonds were eagerly bought in 1945 and again in 1999, when the government announced that it was going to pay down the government debt and reduce the supply of these 30-year bonds. Traders expected to see rapid price appreciation as their supply diminished.

Changes in the Twentieth Century

The year 1946 marked the beginning of a bear market in bonds that ultimately ended in 1981, when interest rates peaked. The yield on prime corporate bonds rose from 2.46 percent in 1946 to a whopping 15.49 percent in 1981.[17] The yields were even higher on sectors deemed riskier. The bond market experienced seven major price declines interspersed with six price rallies until yields on Treasury bonds peaked at 14 percent in 1982.

In the 1960s, Treasury bond sales to the general public were in the form of U.S. Savings Bonds, series E, F, and G. The Treasury was able to sell a 25-year bond at 4.25 percent interest, while the yield on a 25-month note brought 4 percent, a much better deal. The legal interest limit was 4.5 percent. By 1965, a wage-price spiral had begun, accompanied by ballooning inflation. Borrowers focused on the short-term markets because the Treasury could not sell long-term debt beyond the legal debt yield, and corporations did not want to borrow for high, long-term fixed costs.

By the late 1960s, holders of savings bonds began to cash them in at such a rapid rate that federal government bond sales netted less than the redemptions. The savings bonds had a fixed rate of 4.5 percent interest, while corporate and muni bonds yielded much more. To staunch the flow, the Treasury allowed the holders of low-yielding Victory Savings Bonds to exchange them for higher-interest H Bonds in January 1972. In 1980, still trying to stem the flow of funds, the Treasury introduced a new series of higher-yielding savings bonds with more limited liquidity. These are the well-known EE and HH Bonds.

Stand-alone mutual funds were beginning to attract investors' cash, and the money market funds competed with all the banks and savings and loans for ordinary deposits. The process, known as disintermediation, whereby assets are invested outside of the traditional financial institutions, was well under way. Another major change was the appearance in 1970 of the first mortgage-backed security in the United States, which was guaranteed by the federal agency Ginnie Mae. (For more on mortgage-backed securities, see chapter 9.)

The 1970s also marked the first appearance of so-called junk bonds. Before their first issuance in 1977, bonds of low quality that provided high yields were called "fallen angels." Viable corporations with investment-grade ratings that simply had fallen on hard times issued these bonds. Junk bonds, by contrast, were bonds of companies that had succumbed to hostile takeovers and were loaded with debt.

Trading in junk bonds was largely the work of Michael Milken, partner in the firm of Drexel Burnham Lambert Group. Milken figured that the savings and loans that invested in mortgages were failing because they locked in long-term debt in the face of rising interest rates. Their depositors were leaving for more lucrative returns elsewhere. The savings and loan associations (S&Ls) needed the quick infusion of income that junk bonds could supply.

In addition, junk issues offered corporations a lower-cost financing alternative than borrowing from banks. In the 1980s, leveraged buyouts and hostile takeover attempts used junk bonds as financing vehicles. Milken found that large, cash-rich conglomerates like RJR Nabisco could be bought using high-yield debt. The companies were then chopped into pieces that were sold to pay off the debt.

Milken created unusual debt forms to achieve his objectives. Increasing-rate notes, which were developed for the RJR deal, were one such innovation for short-term financing. These are notes that increased in yield the longer they remained unpaid. CDs and some corporate bonds now carry this feature. Similarly, step-up notes are temporary notes that cover a bridge loan until more permanent financing can be arranged.

Milken and Drexel were implicated in the insider-trading scandals of the late 1980s. Milken went to jail for ten years and paid a fine of $600 million; Drexel paid a $650 million fine.[18] The high-yield market tumbled in 1989, and Drexel declared bankruptcy. The junk bond market nearly dried up. However, today there is again an active market for such debt, which prefers the name high-yield to junk. (For more on high-yield debt, see chapter 11.)

In the 1970s, high inflation, soaring interest rates, and heavy investments in junk bonds resulted in the bankruptcy of many banks and S&Ls. During the period 1979 to 1982, inflation reached double digits in three of those years, and interest rates were in the teens. Thereafter, however, following their peak in 1982, interest rates began a more than twenty-year decline. In that same year, the stock market began to rise with great price gyrations not seen before in the post–World War II world.

The peaking of inflation in that unprecedented 1979 to 1982 period, with resulting high interest rates and declining bond prices, imprinted the riskiness of bonds in the minds of investors and financial advisers alike. Bonds now had to pay more to compensate for this market risk. They were avoided, and the declining interest rates that eventually followed provided a big boost to the stock market. Yet a lot of money could be made in the bond markets as well. The dramatically falling interest rates that made stocks look attractive also created huge capital gains on bonds.

Had you bought bonds in the early 1980s, you would have made double-digit returns. As high interest rates later declined, prices of bonds bounded higher as investors sought to grab the yields before they sank further. According to a study by Salomon Brothers entitled "What a Difference a Decade Makes," bonds were the most profitable place to store wealth in the 1980s, averaging a return of 20.9 percent. Stocks were second best, averaging 16.5 percent. In the inflationary 1970s, real assets, such as real estate, natural resources, and precious metals, were king, and both stocks and bonds suffered negative returns.

A Modern Metamorphosis

The emergence of the information age profoundly affected the bond world. In 1969, the firm of Cantor Fitzgerald introduced the Telerate machine, which later became the electronic marketplace for Treasury bonds. In 1981, Michael Bloomberg developed the Bloomberg electronic information service that gave bond traders instant access to information about bonds and interest rates. That same year, J.J. Kenny Company established the first bond index as a yield benchmark for variable-rate bonds.

The information age also revolutionized the tracking of bond ownership. So-called bearer bonds were the equivalent of money. They had coupons attached for the payment of interest that was deposited in a bank account when the interest came due. The coupon rate was literally the value of the coupon when it was deposited in the bank.

After July 1983, all new issues of bonds had to be registered. This change coincided with establishment of electronic clearing among banks in 1983. When you own a registered bond, you receive a paper certificate, called a "bond," and a check in the mail, instead of clipping a coupon, on each interest payment date. (The rate of interest on a bond is still called the "coupon" even though they are no longer issued.) So-called book-entry bonds—bonds that can be held only in the custody of a financial institution—soon crowded out the registered bonds, as the clearinghouses rapidly transferred the ownership of securities without actually transferring paper. Registered bonds are still sometimes available, but only to humor those investors who must be dragged kicking and screaming into the electronic age.

New forms of bonds developed as well as techniques for risk management. From the junk bond arena and from corporations with better resources came high-yield zero-coupon bonds, pay-in-kind securities, extendable reset notes, convertible bonds, and different forms of preferred stock. The federal government developed inflation-protection TIPS for the broader market and I Savings Bonds for the general public. Federal agency paper in the form of Ginnie Maes and later forms of federally sponsored paper exploded as Fannie Mae and Freddie Mac created a secondary market in mortgages, thereby enabling you to invest in them. Staid, conservative municipal bond issuers looked for new sources of revenue to back their bond issues. They created moral-obligation bonds, which were soon displaced, first by lease-backed bonds and later by certificates of participation (COPs) to expand debt issuance. (For more on these bonds, see chapter 10.)

More novel still, financial innovators at the major financial firms created new trading instruments that depend on the value of other assets such as stocks, bonds, or market indexes. These so-called derivative assets, or contingent claims, are classified as futures or options. Bonds that had a given life, or maturity, paid a certain interest, and were of a certain quality were now sliced and diced in myriad ways. Interest payments were stripped from a bond and sold separately as zero-coupon (deferred payment) bonds. Bond portfolios were managed for their total return, and individual bonds were analyzed based on their various attributes in ways not done before.

This groundbreaking approach began around 1980 with the idea of selling the principal and interest of a bond separately, a technique called "stripping." The notion that existing illiquid assets could be transformed revolutionized the bond markets. Banks sitting on mortgage bonds, for example, realized that they could package them and sell them to the public, a process called "securitization," and make them tradable. This spawned the synthetic mortgage market (collateralized mortgage obligations, or CMOs), where mortgage principal payments were sold separately from the interest payments, and both those payments were sorted into tranches based on the likelihood that they would be repaid. (For more on CMOs, see chapter 9.) Car loans, credit card loans, home equity loans, manufactured house loans, church loans, and loans based on the sale of recordings by your favorite rock star later appeared. Instead of buying and selling bonds, traders began selling options to streams of income as a way to manage interest rate risk. Salomon Brothers engineered the first such swap between the World Bank and IBM in 1981. An interest rate swap involves an exchange between two parties of interest-rate exposures from floating to fixed rate or vice versa.

In one example of a swap, one party sells the flow of fixed-rate interest payments on the bonds they hold in exchange for payments tied to a short-term variable rate of interest. Each party to the exchange is protecting a different financial position. Instead of buying and selling the physical security, traders sell options and futures they created based on, or derived from, holdings of bonds, stocks, or commodities. Nonexistent in 1980, this business has become a trillion-dollar leveraged market that trades over the counter. In times of financial crisis, derivative trading can roil the bond markets in ways never seen before.

In the late 1990s, the Internet took off, opening up even more new possibilities affecting bonds. Although best known for all the new companies and stock that it spawned, the online revolution created possibilities for price transparency that did not exist before. Brokers started posting their offerings on Web sites; buyers had more up-to-date information on bond prices. In 2002, issuers electronically transmitted offering statements for newly issued bonds to national depositories; many also posted the statements on the Web for information transparency to support bond sales. Mutual funds took advantage of the medium by posting their prospectuses on their Web sites to provide easy access to buyers and reduce distribution costs. Information was available immediately in a quantity hitherto unimaginable. The effect was to make the sale and purchase of bonds quicker, easier, and simpler.

Inflation-indexed bonds, zero-coupon bonds, and many other bond types noted previously are described in detail in the rest of this book. So traumatic was the inflation of the 1970s that it led to the creation of these all-new bond types and ways to manage the risks associated with them. This book is going to tell you not only how to understand but also how to profit from all this creative turmoil. First, however, it's necessary to understand the basics of a bond—how it's created, issued, priced, and traded—and that's what the next chapter describes.

Chapter Notes

1. Bryan A. Garner, ed., *Black's Law Dictionary*, 8th ed., (St. Paul, MN: West Group, 2004), 187.

2. Ibid., 175–176.

3. Ibid., 1088.

4. Ibid., 1142.

5. Sidney Homer and Richard Sylla, *A History of Interest Rates* (New Brunswick, NJ: Rutgers University Press, 1991), 88.

6. Cynthia Crossen, *The Rich and How They Got That Way* (New York: Dow Jones and Company, 2000), 98.

7. Homer and Sylla, 81.

8. Garner, 829–830.

9. Ibid., 1580.

10. Homer and Sylla, 154–155.

11. Steven Dickson, "Civil War, Railroads and 'Road Bonds': Bond Repudiation in the Days of Yore," *The Bond Buyer Centennial Edition* (New York: The Bond Buyer, 1991), 36.

12. Ibid., 30.

13. Homer and Sylla, 333.

14. Ibid., 346.

15. Ibid., 356.

16. Matthew Kreps, "Ups and Downs of Municipal Bonds: Volume and Yield in the Past Century," *The Bond Buyer 100 Anniversary Edition: A Salute to the Municipal Bond Industry* (New York: The Bond Buyer, 1991), 18.

17. Homer and Sylla, 367.

18. Edward Chancellor, *The Devil Take the Hindmost: A History of Financial Speculation* (New York: Farrar, Straus & Giroux, 1999), 278.

CHAPTER 5

THE LIFE OF A BOND

How It's Created, Issued, Priced, and Traded

THIS CHAPTER PROVIDES the information you need to become an educated bond buyer. Although it may be tempting to skip this material and flip to the chapter on buying bonds, consider this: it will be much harder to profit from the money-making strategies we outline if you don't understand bond basics. Read this chapter to get an overview and refer back to it when you need a refresher to help you understand a particular investment. When we first identify a word or term, we highlight it in boldface to make it easier for you to relocate it.

To induce you to read further, remember that bond returns can be quite lucrative. Consider that when stocks collectively took a hit during the market downturn that began in March 2000 and continued into 2002, the 10-year Treasury bond gained 22 percent in value between May 15 and November 7, 2001.[1] At the same time, tax-exempt municipal bonds provided yields of 5 percent for bonds maturing between fifteen and nineteen years, and 30-year

Treasuries were yielding 5.35 percent. That 5 percent return on municipal bonds is a taxable equivalent yield of better than 7.7 percent for someone in the highest tax bracket, a return that comes with little risk. Trust us. The more you know about bonds, the better off you'll be.

By Way of Background

Let's start at the beginning. Every bond has two components: (1) a time span and (2) a face value. The **face value** is the term used to describe the amount of money or principal you will receive at the end of the specified time span when the bond comes due.

There are two basic ways to earn income from this arrangement (see **Figure 5.1**). In the first, you receive regular interest payments over the life of the bond. As briefly noted in chapter 4, people who received such income were once known as coupon clippers. That's because interest payments were printed on coupons that were attached to the bond. When they clipped the coupon and turned it in, they received their payment. The practice was gradually replaced by automatic, direct payment and it officially ended in July 1983, when municipal bond issuers finally did away with the paper coupons.

In today's more technologically sophisticated society, interest payments are automatically sent to whatever address you

FIGURE 5.1

Two Ways to Earn Bond Income

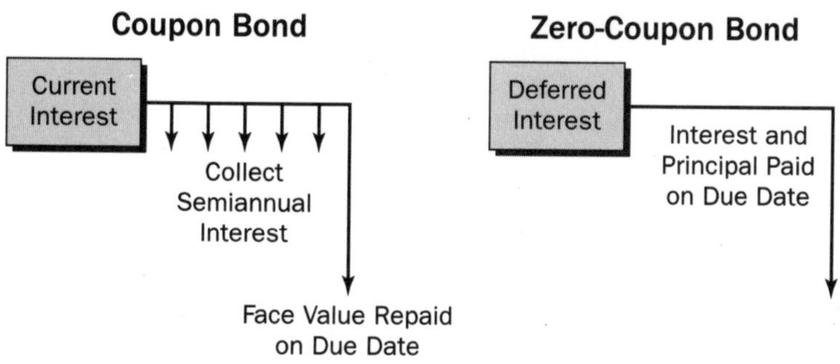

designate—be it a brokerage account or your home—and there is no need to physically present a coupon to the bank teller to get your income. However, the idea of a coupon lingers in bond terminology because a bond's interest rate is referred to as its **coupon rate**, or just plain **coupon**. The coupon rate is set as a percentage of the face value when the bond is issued. Thus, a $10,000 10-year bond with a coupon rate of 5 percent will annually pay $500, which is 5 percent of $10,000.

The second way of earning bond income involves buying a bond at less than, or at a discount to, its face value. For example, you may pay only $5,000 for a $10,000 10-year bond. This does not necessarily mean that you are getting a bargain. Sometimes the discount is deliberate and includes no interest payments whatsoever. This kind of bond is called a **zero-coupon bond** (which makes sense, because it has no coupons). The difference between your purchase price and the face value represents the income you receive. At other times, the discount reflects the fact that the bond is out of favor, and investors believe it's not worthwhile to hold the instrument until they can redeem it at full value, or they just might need the cash and must sell into an unfavorable market. As we see in **Figure 5.2**, if interest rates rise, the yield offered increases and bond prices fall. When interest rates fall, the yield offered on a bond is less and the price of purchase is higher.

FIGURE 5.2

Bond Price/Yield Relationship

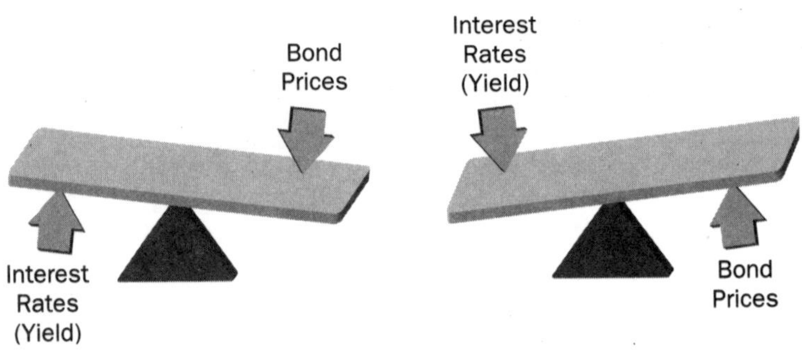

For the buy-and-hold investor, these two basic bond structures provide financial peace of mind because they will either enjoy a steady stream of income until—or receive a lump sum at—the time the face value of the bond is returned to them. This is called **redemption at maturity**. People can also receive a mix of money now and money later. In other words, you buy a bond, get regular income over a period of time, a lump sum all at once, or some mix of the two, and then get all your money back when the bond comes due. For this reason, countless investors, particularly those who seek to triple and quadruple their money by speculating in the exciting stratospheres of high-risk stocks, frequently regard bonds as stodgy investments. In times when the price of those stocks sink out of sight, the so-called stodginess of bonds becomes a little less problematic.

Bonds are neither simple nor stodgy. They are, rather, very rewarding. In contrast to stocks, which represent part ownership of a company, bonds are debt—pure but not always simple. As described in chapter 4, companies, municipalities, states, and the federal government issue bonds for either short-term or long-term funding needs.

Preparing a Bond Issue

Let's look at the roles of various individuals and entities in creating and bringing a bond to market and how they shape its ultimate form. At the very beginning of the bond-issuance process, a financial adviser is called in. The adviser is a consultant who helps the issuer decide if bond debt is the best and most appropriate means of raising money for a project or need. The federal government and its agencies have internal financial advisers that perform these services. Corporations often rely on their investment banks to act as financial advisers. With regard to municipal bonds, an outside consultant frequently works with the municipality's finance director and lawyers to organize, collect, and represent the financial data to prospective buyers of the debt, including the underwriters. Most municipalities come to market infrequently and do not have an in-house staff.

After the need for bond debt has been established and a preliminary draft completed, a bond counsel reviews the contract, called the **bond indenture**, and gives a legal opinion that the debt is being appropriately issued. In the early twentieth century, many bonds did not have legal opinions. As investors discovered that bonds with legal opinions were less likely to default, they began to demand opinions on all issues. Bond counsel also determines where in the receiving line the bondholders stand when cash is distributed in troubled times. With regard to tax-free municipal bonds, bond counsel provides a legal opinion certifying that the bonds are, in fact, tax-exempt for federal income tax purposes.

Next, underwriters appear on the scene. They are necessary because bonds are generally not bought directly from the issuing entity. (Those issued by the U.S. government, as described in chapters 6 and 7, are conspicuous exceptions to this practice.) An underwriter is the bank or brokerage house that initially buys the bonds from the issuer and then resells them to investors. Since buying a large block of debt and then reselling it into a constantly shifting market can be financially hazardous, underwriters spread their risk by having similar organizations join in the sale of the bond to investors. The resulting grouping is called an **underwriting syndicate**.

Lawyers are crucial to the process of creating and issuing bonds. They next appear in the form of underwriters' counsel. In this position, they represent the brokerage house that will buy the bonds from the issuer. In today's marketplace, issuers may bypass the underwriter and sell the issue for the highest price to brokers, pension funds, bond funds, banks, hedge funds, or insurance companies.

At some point in this process, the issuer decides whether or not the bond will be callable. A **call** is a kind of option that gives an issuer the right, but not the obligation, to redeem a bond issue before its maturity (due date). Many bond issues have a fixed call prior to maturity. Municipal bonds may also have extraordinary calls that certain situations trigger. Bonds are called when it is advantageous to the issuer, leaving the buyer to scratch around to find another bond investment, often at a lower yield. If the possibility of an early redemption (call) worries you, the most desirable bonds for you would provide at least ten years of call protection.

Call protection is always desirable for you since the ability to call a bond is always in the interest of the issuer.

In the event of a bankruptcy, not all of an issuer's bondholders are treated equally. Some bonds have senior liens, meaning that they come first in line before other creditors if there is a financial problem. Other bond issues from the same company may have only subordinated or junior lien positions.

When a single issue consists of bonds with different redemption dates, the bonds are called **serial bonds**. These types of bonds give the issuer the flexibility of not having to pay off everything in one lump sum. Many municipal bond issues are commonly offered this way. A term bond is a longer-term bond with a final maturity date. Many corporate and U.S. government bonds are issued this way.

Once the issuer assembles all the necessary information, writers specializing in obscure prose prepare an **offering statement (OS)**, or **prospectus**. As a friend of ours once described it, only half facetiously, "[The offering statement] is written about matters that few understand and for people who will never read it." This document, produced under the issuer's aegis, sums up all the work of the professionals who created the bond and details its type, structure, special features (if any), and the strength and weaknesses of the issuer. It also describes any liabilities that might exist and the participants in the deal. If you take time to peruse it, you will learn a great deal.

It appears that the municipalities and corporations that produce offering statements feel they are not necessary to read prior to purchase since sometimes the OS is sent only after the buyer purchases a new issue bond. This situation is changing, however, since Web sites such as www.emuni.com, www.directnotes.com, and www.internotes.com post offering statements in advance of new bond issues. Individual issuers, such as the state of Utah, at www.finance.state.ut.us, are also posting prospectuses on their Web sites. We hope this trend will continue.

RATING A BOND

Having been primed and primped through many legal hands, the now dressed-up bond is ready to meet the rating analysts. These are the people who evaluate the risk of bonds as evidenced by the probability of buyers being repaid their principal and interest in a timely manner. As described in chapter 4, rating agencies came into being as a service to describe risks associated with a bond. Because there is a chance that an investor could suffer substantial losses if a bond defaults, bond issuers have to pay more to induce buyers to assume any extra risk.

Credit analysts do ratings work for bond insurers, underwriters and other large institutions, and rating agencies. Each organization relies on its analysts to review a bond's structure and its issuer's financial strength. Rating agency analysts are best known because their ratings are widely publicized and provide a recognized guide to bond purchasers. With this recognition, these analysts have become powerful players in the bond markets because their ratings strongly influence how much an issuer will have to pay to borrow money. If a bond, for example, receives the highest rating, it has almost no risk of default. Thus, under similar time spans, an issuer with a bond boasting the highest AAA rating might have to pay only 60 percent of the interest offered by an issuer with a bond rated double-B. All things being equal, bonds of the same rating and maturity are sold with similar yields if sold at the same time. When there are sharp yield disparities among similarly rated bonds, you should investigate why this is so before you invest.

Rating agencies may place bonds on credit watch if the financial condition of the issuer deteriorates. Usually the adjustments in ratings are minor. Downgrades that bring a bond rating below the investment grade of triple-B are more serious. Some institutions holding those bonds may be forced to sell them, depending on the covenants under which they operate, resulting in a general decline in the bond's price and value. Alternatively, going from double-B to triple-B can result in a nice pop-up in price.

When the changes in a bond rating are gradual and the issuer comes to market frequently, the ratings are more apt to be up to date and accurate than when an issuer only infrequently comes to market. When you purchase bonds that are not newly issued, the rating attached to the bond might not be current and in that sense is less reliable.

Rating agencies are in a delicate position because they are paid by issuers to rate their bonds. Such a situation may imply that an agency would give the most positive possible rating. On the other hand, if the public does not trust an agency's judgment, the value of its rating is useless and issuers will no longer hire the firm. Rating agencies protect their reputations by continually pointing out that their ratings are not meant to advise you to buy or sell. They also monitor the performance of their major clients, those whose bonds are actively traded in the market, and, often without being specifically paid to do so, will either downgrade or upgrade the debt of an issuer when financial conditions markedly change. This type of unsolicited rating also may occur on occasion when an issuer elects not to request a rating from one agency because they expect a different agency might be more generous.

As evident in precipitous defaults, such as Kmart, the rating agencies often play catch-up. Conseco, Xerox, and the Finova Group are other formerly blue-chip companies that have watched the sun quickly set on their company's prospects.[2] Rating agencies constantly ponder how they can provide better public notice without pulling the rug out from under an ailing company. "How volatile does the marketplace want ratings to be?" they ask. Market sentiment always precedes any downgrade. Thus, ratings are broadly viewed as lagging indicators, especially in the high-yield market.

With regard to the publicity surrounding the bankruptcy of Enron, rating agencies are not responsible for uncovering fraud. Although cooked books ultimately make rotten financial stews and result in precipitous downgrades, they are supposed to be part of accounting firms' oversight. Market prices may tell you what the ratings do not.

The three primary bond-rating agencies are Moody's Investors Service (Moody's), Standard & Poor's (S&P), and Fitch Ratings (Fitch). Federal regulators granted official status in 2003 to relatively small Dominion Bond Rating Service, of Canada. The first such move in decades, the recognition resulted from the fallout

FIGURE 5.3

The Agencies and Their Ratings

Credit quality	Moody's	S&P	Fitch
Solid as a rock	Aaa	AAA	AAA
Very fine quality	Aa1	AA+	AA+
	Aa2	AA	AA
	Aa3	AA–	AA–
Strong capacity to pay	A1	A+	A+
	A2	A	A
	A3	A–	A–
Adequate ability to pay;	Baa1	BBB+	BBB+
lowest investment grade	Baa2	BBB	BBB
for banks	Baa3	BBB–	BBB–
Somewhat speculative;	Ba1	BB+	BB+
risk exposure	Ba2	BB	BB
	Ba3	BB–	BB–
More speculative;	B1	B+	B+
risk exposure	B2	B	B
	B3	B–	B–
Major risk exposure;	Caa1	CCC+	CCC+
on verge of default	Caa2	CCC	CCC
	Caa3	CCC–	CCC–
Crucial risk exposure;	Ca1	CC+	CC+
may have defaulted	Ca2	CC	CC
on interest payments	Ca3	CC–	CC–
Default or Imminent Default	C	C	C
General default	D	D	D
No rating requested	NR	NR	NR

from massive accounting failure at Enron for which the rating agencies were allocated part of the blame. (See **Figure 5.3** for rating agencies and their ratings.)

The agencies readily admit that their ratings contain subjective judgments. All of life's experiences cannot be boiled down into numbers, and the value of "hard numbers" is often questionable. This, plus the fact that the agencies also can disagree on exactly how new circumstances will affect cash flow for particular loan payments, sometimes leads to dissimilar conclusions. When agencies do not agree on a rating, the result is known as a **split rating**. The split rating may vary by an entire category (for example, AA to a high A) or reflect only variations within a category (for example, high A to a lower-grade A).

Although information that might affect the ratings is on the Internet, you have to search a bit to find relevant data. For example, you can obtain a free prospectus but no material event information that describes current changes for corporate issues by going to www.sec.gov/edgar/quickedgar.htm. The opposite is true with regard to municipal bonds. You can get free material event information from www.nrmsir.org or www.bloomberg.com, but you will have to pay to obtain a prospectus. The latter Web sites are two of four approved by the Municipal Securities Rulemaking Board (MSRB) as private repositories for offering statements. Since they are private, the sites look to make money from the sale of bond information.

SETTING A COUPON RATE

The next step in the bond-debut process is setting the coupon rate, or the stated amount of interest. At all times, the issuer seeks to set a rate at which the largest buyers, mutual fund companies, banks, and insurance companies are eager to buy the bond.

Sometimes issuers sell zero-coupon bonds. As explained at the beginning of this chapter, these bonds do not pay current interest. However, the issuers have to determine the extent of the discount to face value at which the bond will be offered. These bonds are also called accrual bonds because the interest accumulates and is not paid out. It is deferred until the bond comes due.

Most bonds have a fixed rate. That means that the coupon rate is set at the time of issuance and will remain the same for the life of the bonds. That is why they are called fixed-income securities.

Once the bond is issued, its selling price may rise or fall, but its stream of interest payments, at the established coupon rate, continues unabated.

Other bonds are known as floaters or variable-rate bonds. As the names of these bonds indicate, their rates float, or are variable, and are reset periodically, generally in relation to some measure of current market rates on specified dates. Some of these bonds may have their interest rate fluctuation limited by a cap (maximum rate) and/or a floor (minimum rate). The floaters may move in the same direction as the rate to which they are tied (reference rate), or in the opposite direction, in which case they're called inverse-floaters.

LAUNCHING A BOND

Having been structured, described, and rated, a bond then makes its market debut, where it is bought and frequently resold in what is known as the **over-the-counter market**. There is no organized exchange where buyers and sellers meet. There is no bond ticker showing the changes in prices for bonds, except for certain Treasury issues that the entire bond industry uses as benchmarks.

In a competitive new issue, the highest bidder buys the bonds; in a negotiated issue, negotiation between the issuer and a selected brokerage syndicate may predetermine sales prices. In a competitive deal, there may be three or four underwriting syndicates competing for the bonds. The bonds are then remarketed to institutional and retail buyers at the set prices. Once the order period is over, the bonds are free to trade at market rates.

At its first appearance, a bond is said to be in the primary, or new, bond market. Within the primary market, Treasury bonds are sold by auction at announced times. Some large corporate bond issuers have so-called shelf registrations and allow brokers to sell bonds over time. In this case, the offering rate adjusts with the fluctuation of interest rates. Other corporate issuers, federal agencies, or municipal issuers arrange for the sale of their bonds all at once.

When a purchaser buys a new issue bond and it remains in a purchaser's portfolio until the day it comes due, it never reenters the marketplace. The issuer simply redeems it without cost. If, however, a purchaser resells a bond before its redemption date, the bond automatically enters the secondary, or previously owned, bond market. There, powerful forces come into play and determine what the actual yield will be.

Understanding Risk

Four key forces affecting a bond's yield are the credit quality of the issuer; market supply of the bond and similar issues; market demand; and overall economic conditions, including inflation. These forces either drive up or push down the amount of money buyers are willing to shell out to purchase a bond. They are all associated with risk, and, thus, it is important to differentiate among the kinds of risk.

There are nine types of risks commonly associated with buying and holding bonds:

1 Default risk. The risk that the issuer is unable to meet the interest and principal payments when due.

2 Market risk. The risk that interest rates will rise, reducing the value of bonds. We know for certain that interest rates fluctuate and that there are long-term trends. What we cannot predict is whether a shift in interest rates is only short-term volatility or whether it is reflective of a longer-term trend.

3 Liquidity risk. The risk that bonds cannot be sold quickly at an attractive price.

4 Early call risk. The risk that high-yielding bonds will be called away early, with the result that the proceeds may be reinvested at a lower interest rate.

5 Reinvestment risk. The risk that the interest payments and principal you receive may have to be reinvested at a lower rate. Only zero-coupon bonds do not have interest payment reinvestment risk.

6 Event risk. The uncertainty created by the unfolding of unexpected events.

7 Tax risk. The possibility that changes in the tax code or in an individual's tax position might adversely affect the tax advantages of bonds.

8 Political risk. The likelihood that an issuer will exercise its legal right to terminate appropriations for municipal issues and that changes in the law will adversely affect the credit quality of existing issues.

9 Inflation risk. The possibility that the fixed value might erode with an increased cost of living. In the United States, this is a long-term risk that is best judged in hindsight.

Where appropriate, we discuss the implications of these risks in this book, under each individual bond's description. When you are choosing investments, keep in mind the saying by Bob Farrell, a retired chief market analyst at Merrill Lynch: "Where money goes the quickest, the risk goes even faster."

That amorphous creature called the market is at all times seeking to create equilibrium, a state in which all yields are in an approximately equal state, once risk and maturity have been factored in. Because the market cannot change the fixed-coupon rate, which is set in stone when the bond is issued, it affects the price at which the bond is sold. As the price changes, so does the yield (see **Figure 5.4**).

FIGURE 5.4

Effect of Market Yield on Price for Fixed-Income Securities

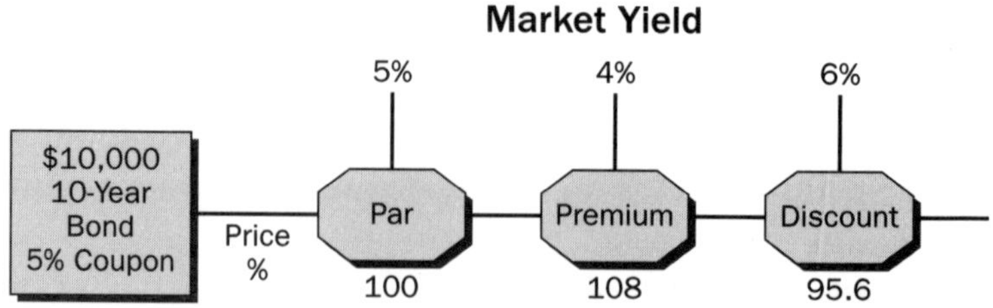

This connection between yield and price is important to grasp. For example, when a bond carries a 5 percent coupon rate and the prevailing interest rates are 4 percent, buyers will pay more than the face value of the bond to receive the benefit of a higher coupon rate. Then, the bond sells at a premium to face value. On the other hand, when that same 5 percent bond is selling at a time when prevailing interest rates are 6 percent, it can tempt buyers to purchase only at a price much lower than the bond's face value (thus, buying at a discount to face value). Occasionally, a bond will sell at its face value, and at such times it is said to be at par. Price changes reflect changes in the bond's yield. These changes can occur throughout the life of a bond, but it affects you only if you choose to purchase a bond or sell a bond you already own.

A Bond's Cost and Yield

Bond costs are always quoted in "points," not in dollars. A bond selling at 101 really costs $1,010. Simply move the decimal point one place to the right to find the dollar equivalent. Thus, a par bond quoted at 100 has a face value of $1,000. To find out what your total cost would be, multiply the dollar amount by the number of bonds. Thus, 10 bonds at the 101 price would cost $1,010 × 10, or $10,100.

DETERMINING A BOND'S YIELD

The concept of yield creates the equilibrium between bonds sold at different prices. This concept is so important that we highlight it here: *Bonds are bought and sold based on yield, not on price.* This represents a key distinction between these financial instruments and stocks, which are always bought and sold in terms of price. **Yield** is the general term for the percentage return on a security investment. It is often called the **rate of return**. In bond language, it is very different from the stated coupon rate. It is critical to understand these concepts in order to understand how bonds are valued. (See **Figure 5.5**.)

Keep in mind that the value of bonds declines when interest rates rise, and the value increases when interest rates decline. In short, we say that yield moves inversely to price.

FIGURE 5.5

Bond Price/Yield Relationship

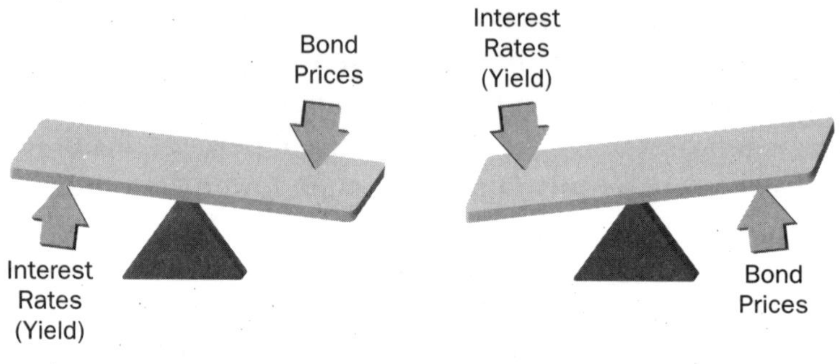

Your monthly brokerage statement reflects the market valuation of your bond. It does not show concurrent changes in yield. This is called **marking to market**. This is of interest to you if you plan to sell your bonds. Otherwise, sit back and relax, because if we know nothing else, we know that interest rates and, therefore, the price of your bonds will fluctuate. We also know that bonds come due at their face value, and you will get your money back.

Sellers of individual bonds as well as bond funds use a variety of yield terms. Understanding them will enable you to buy bonds and invest wisely in bond funds. While many of the yields require a financial calculator to compute them accurately, the following discussion of six fundamental terms gives a general description of their use and value. Brokers will calculate bond yields for you, and funds are required to post the yields in their prospectuses. Sites that offer yield calculators include http://investinginbonds.com, www.bloomberg.com, and www.kiplinger.com.

Yield can and does mean many things to many people. Bond professionals in particular have come up with a bewildering array of meanings. Here are just a few: current yield, yield-to-maturity, yield-to-call, yield-to-worst, and yield-to-average life. Bond funds have their own terms, described in chapter 14, because bond funds do not have a fixed maturity. Each term, in its own way, seeks to create equivalency among bonds with different characteristics.

CURRENT YIELD

Current yield (CY) is the only simple calculation among the lot and is used for comparing cash flows.

$$\text{Current yield} = \frac{\text{Annual interest from the bond}}{\text{Amount paid for the bond}}$$

Simply speaking, the more money you pay for a bond above its face value (par), the lower the current yield. Conversely, the bigger the discount from par, the higher the current yield. When you purchase bond mutual funds, which pay dividends, you are quoted a current yield because these securities have no maturity. The dividends from bond mutual funds are a combination of bond interest and capital gains from bond sales. Therefore, they are not directly comparable to compounding bond yields, which are quoted as a yield-to-maturity or yield-to-call.

Preferred and common stock use current yield to compare their dividends as well. However, the board of directors must approve these dividends each quarter, and there is no requirement that they pay them. By comparison, bonds must pay scheduled interest payments, or they are in default.

SIMPLE AND COMPOUND INTEREST

With the exception of current yield, all bond yield calculations take compound interest into account. Thus, this is as good a place as any to review the differences between simple and compound interest. Compound interest is called the eighth wonder of the world. It can work *for* you by creating wealth when you buy bonds, or it can work *against* you when you pay interest on your debts. It has great impartial power.

Simple interest is simple because it's calculated only on your initial investment or principal. **Compound interest** is complex—and rewarding—because it adds the interest to your principal and then compounds the new total; in effect, interest earns interest. **Figure 5.6**, which shows a $1,000 bond that pays an annual 5 percent interest once a year, illustrates the different returns from the two kinds of interest.

FIGURE 5.6

Comparing Simple Interest to Compound Interest

Year	Principal + Simple Interest	Principal + Compound Interest
1	$1,050	$1,050
5	$1,250	$1,276
10	$1,500	$1,629
20	$2,000	$2,653
30	$2,500	$4,322

Compounding—interest earning interest—makes a dramatic difference over many years. Unlike bank certificates of deposit, which are sold with simple interest, bond interest is compound interest and, thus, grows at a much faster rate over the long term. The more frequently interest is compounded on the total amount, the more dramatic the difference. If you need to compare two investments, ask how much you will receive at the end of the investment. No matter what the calculation, it still boils down to your final dollars and cents.

The Rule of 72. The Rule of 72 tells you approximately how many years it takes money to double when it compounds at a particular rate of annual interest. For example, if the rate of return is 10 percent, you divide 72 by 10 and learn that it takes approximately 7.2 years for the money to double at a 10 percent compounded rate. Similarly, if the rate of return were 5 percent, it would take 14.4 years to double your money ($72 \div 5 = 14.4$ years).

YIELD-TO-MATURITY

Yield-to-maturity (YTM) is the benchmark against which individual bonds are traded and quoted. YTM and the following two yield calculations all use the concept of compound interest. In the bond world, calculations assume that money never lies fallow or hidden away in a mattress. Rather, it is constantly reinvested to generate further income. Although YTM is not a perfect calculation, it is widely used because it is the unifying standard for all bond pricing.

YTM makes the following assumptions: (1) You retain ownership for the remaining life of the bond and (2) all interest payments are reinvested at the same prevailing rate (YTM). However, since interest rates change over time, your actual return on a bond does, too, unless you own a zero-coupon bond. If rates rise, for example, and you are able to reinvest the semiannual interest payments at a better rate, your actual return will be higher than quoted. If interest rates decline over the life of the bond, and you reinvest the interest at a lower rate, your actual return will be lower. Note that the key concept underpinning all this is compound interest. The YTM calculation assumes reinvestment of every interest payment, whether monthly or semiannually, at the YTM rate.

Whether or not you understand the dense calculations involved in determining YTM and the assumptions on which these calculations are based is irrelevant. For better or for worse, YTM is the calculation used in the bond market as the great leveler, the calculation that helps you to determine the value of one bond compared with another.

YIELD-TO-CALL AND YIELD-TO-WORST

Sometimes the call date instead of the maturity date determines the bond price, and as a result the yield is calculated in terms of yield-to-call (YTC) instead of YTM. YTC is particularly important when interest rates have been falling because there is a good likelihood that the issuer may decide to exercise its right to call (redeem or repurchase) the bond early. This is especially likely if the coupon rate of the bond is higher than the prevailing rate of interest. If there is more than one call, the bond price is set by the yield-to-worst (YTW), the worst possible yield you could receive for the bond as a result of an early call. Request a YTC and a YTW calculation from your broker because you don't know what direction interest rates will take (see **Figure 5.7**). The worst call yield determines the bond price just in case the bond is called. That way you are not surprised by the possibility that you will get a lower yield.

FIGURE 5.7

YTC and YTW Calculations

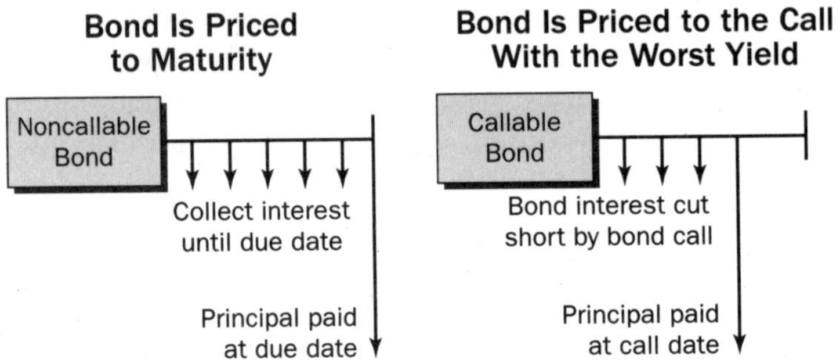

YIELD-TO-AVERAGE LIFE

The term **yield-to-average life** is used in a number of different ways. It comes into play in situations in which the actual maturity is not known and is estimated instead. For example, when an individual bond has a sinking fund, a lottery determines which bonds are called, with a rising proportion of bonds called each year. It's possible that only some of your bonds will be called. Even though a bond has a call feature, it doesn't necessarily mean it will be called. Since you can't tell if your particular bonds will be called away, your broker will provide you with the yield-to-average life (also called the yield to the intermediate point), the point when half the bonds can be called away.

Municipal bonds often have sinking funds. Mortgage-backed securities also use this term. In both instances, yield-to-average life uses the anticipated compound rate of return and presumes the reinvestment of the cash flows as received. For municipal bonds, the cash flow consists of the interest payments; for the mortgage-backed securities, it includes both principal and interest.

DURATION

Introduced as a concept in 1938, duration is a popular analytical tool to evaluate how much the price of a bond will increase or decrease as a result of an increase or decrease in interest rates. The duration of a bond fluctuates daily. Thus, duration serves as one measure of risk. You can use it to compare one bond to another or one bond fund to another.

In general, the longer the life of the bond, the longer its duration. The longer the duration of a bond, the greater the loss you will take if interest rates go up and you sell the bond before its due date. Similarly, the longer the duration of the bond the more of a gain you'll realize if interest rates decline and you sell the bond before its due date. If you plan to hold your bond until its due date and you actually do that, you can ignore all changes in the price of the bond because it will come due at its face value.

In general, the lower the current interest payment or coupon of the bond, the longer the duration; the higher the coupon, the shorter the duration. The duration of a zero-coupon bond is the same as its maturity. Thus, the price of zero-coupon bonds changes the most with a change in interest rates.

Let's consider a simplified example. Assume that a bond has a duration of four years, and you sell it soon after its purchase. In this case, if interest rates go up by 1 percent, the price of the bond will go down by approximately 4 percent. Similarly, if interest rates go down by 1 percent, the price of the bond will go up by approximately 4 percent.

You don't need to know how to calculate duration. You can ask your broker for this measure. Think of it as a measure to explain any interest risk. Duration is neither bad nor good. It is a measure of risk that applies if you don't hold your bond until its due date. Since bond funds never come due, it is frequently used to describe them.

Total Return

Bond traders all look at their bond returns on a total-return basis. Because we recommend a buy-and-hold approach for individual investors, we are not in favor of looking at bonds in this way. In this, we're in the minority, so you ought to know what the majority is talking about. Total return takes into account both the interest you receive plus the change in value of the bond. In addition, you should take into account any transaction costs, fees, and taxes you might have to pay, which are frequently left out of the calculation.

Total return = Interest + or − (Change in value)
− (Transaction costs, fees, and taxes)

The concept of total return is the same for individual bonds as it is for stock or any other investment. The only difference is that bonds have a better cash flow and generally less price fluctuation than most other investments. By marking to market your investments every day, brokerage houses encourage you to think about bonds in terms of total return. One outcome of total-return thinking is that you may impulsively sell your bonds when you have a gain or a loss without thinking through the advantages of the buy-and-hold strategy. Keep in mind that in showing market movements, brokers do not show the effects of the transaction costs, fees, or taxes.

Funds always use the concept of total return because funds generally don't liquidate at a defined date. Instead, they mark to market daily with the fluctuation of interest rates and the purchase or sale of bonds within the fund. The interest received as well as the capital appreciation of the bonds in the fund determine the dividends. Funds can pay out interest and capital gains monthly, and they must pay out all the interest at least annually. If there are losses, they are not passed through to the shareholder, but may be retained to offset capital gains that the fund makes from the sale of the bonds.

Income from bond funds = Interest + Capital gains − (Losses, transaction costs, fees, and taxes)

Figure 5.8 offers a sample of what interest payments might look like, from a portfolio of bonds that you create for yourself or one created by a bond fund. It also shows a semiannual interest payment from one individual bond.

FIGURE 5.8

Comparing Interest From a Bond Portfolio and an Individual Bond

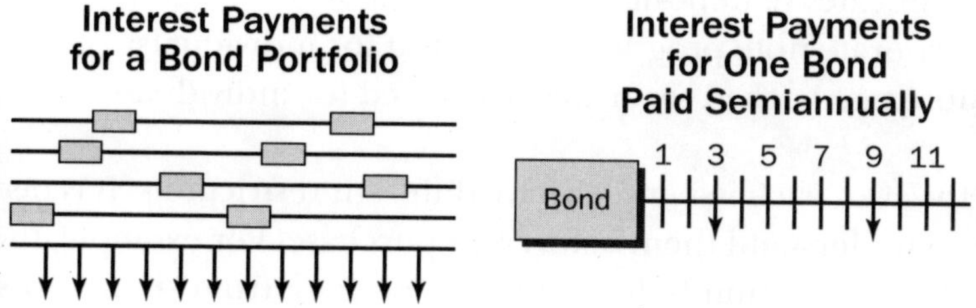

Each bond pays interest semiannually. They are like packets of energy, usually bursting every six months. A collection of bonds, whether purchased through a fund or created on your own, pays interest spread over the year. Your cash flow from a fund might contain capital gains as well as interest so it would not flow in even amounts, though you could request an even distribution. You could sell some shares if the dividend payments from your fund were not sufficient to cover your costs. You could sell a bond, but it would be more costly. However, if you purchase bonds that mature at regular intervals, the bonds will return principal and maintain good cash flow.

Cash Flow Upon Death: The Estate Feature

To ease concern about selling bonds in the secondary market, some issuers add a put feature to their bonds to make them more attractive to individual buyers. In the event of death of the bondholder, the estate can receive the face value of the bonds even if the bond is selling at a discount. The advantage of this feature is that you can purchase longer-dated bonds without concern for the market value of the bonds beyond the natural life of the holder. Theoretically, your bonds would become liquid upon your death.

It is important to inquire if the securities you're considering purchasing have a survivor's option. It is generally available on the following types of securities:

- U.S. Agency Freddie Mac weekly notes
- Certificates of deposit
- Corporate note programs structured for individuals
- Mortgage-backed securities structured for individuals

However, each issuer may have different restrictions. It is necessary to understand them before you purchase. For example, there may be a minimum holding period, ranging from six months to one year. The owner might be required to have lived for a defined period of time before a claim is submitted. There may be limits on the amount redeemed in any one year, or at any one time. Claims may be paid only on specified dates. There may be limitations if the account is not held in the individual's name or in a joint account with rights of survivorship.

Although there is a market for discounted bonds with this feature, it's important to consider the taxes you may have to pay on the gain between the purchase and redemption prices when calculating your yield.

PRICING A SECONDARY MARKET BOND

When you purchase secondary market bonds, the bond may have been outstanding for some time. The bond may have little or no call protection. In this situation, the yield at the par call determines your purchase price.

Pricing becomes tricky within the secondary, or used, bond market. Corporate and agency bond pricing changes in relation to the price of Treasuries, although the actual spreads over Treasuries vary because they are based on the market's view of the particular bond being sold. This kind of spread is sometimes called a **credit spread**, distinguishing it from the spread that refers to the difference between the broker's buy and sell price. A broker asks a customer to buy a bond (ask price) and offers to buy bonds by placing a bid in to purchase bonds (bid price). The spread between the bid and the ask is generally tiny for Treasury bonds, while widening for less frequently traded securities. If you want to determine the spread on the bond you're considering purchasing, you can ask the broker to give you a hypothetical bid as well as his selling price. If you ask him to drop the jargon, you're less likely to be confused.

The spread is measured in basis points (bp). One basis point equals one hundredth of 1 percent (.01 percent). There are 100 basis points in 1 percent. The difference between a yield of 5 percent and 6 percent, for example, is 100 basis points. If a Treasury bond is yielding 5 percent and the spread over Treasuries was 125 basis points, the yield on a corporate bond would be 6.25 percent.

The yields on Treasury bonds are benchmarks for all bonds, although as noted above, they are particularly useful for corporate and agency securities. Treasury yields are in constant flux. The latest, most liquid 10-year and 30-year Treasury bonds are the benchmarks for evaluating the interest rate payable by other bonds with similar maturities. These are called **on-the-run Treasuries**, compared to other off-the-run Treasuries, or those that are not actively traded.

To illustrate how spreads are used in pricing corporate bonds that are not in alignment with their ratings, we present their value quoted in basis points compared to the 10-year Treasury on February 13, 2002:

- AAA-rated General Electric Corporation 7.375 percent of January 19, 2010, was priced +85 basis points to the 10-year Treasury.
- A2/A+ Target Corporation, the retail department store, 6.35 percent of January 15, 2011, was only +80.
- WorldCom Inc., the telecommunications company, 7.5 percent coupon due May 15, 2011, still rated A3/BBB+, was +320.

The numbers above reflect the marketplace's estimation of risk despite the ratings. The marketplace determined that General Electric's balance sheet had too much debt despite its AAA rating, while lower-rated Target's reputation was not in jeopardy. WorldCom had already been judged risky, and the spread over Treasuries reflected that. The market's evaluation of WorldCom was prescient because the accounting scandal announced in June 2002 sent the value of WorldCom bonds to the deep sea.

Municipal traders in the secondary market use price matrixes showing ratings and due dates to determine what a bond is worth, since most muni bonds trade infrequently. Traders see where other similar bonds are trading and price the bonds accordingly. You can check for yourself at www.investinginbonds.com by inserting the CUSIP number of your bond and finding out what the trading history is. This is like pricing a used car. In an unstable market, those prices can be very misleading; however, you will have a framework for understanding what is being offered to you.

The scale for muni bonds is different from the scale for corporate bonds or Treasury bonds. Each is a separate though related market. Municipal bond prices are not adjusted as quickly as Treasuries, although they also move in relation to Treasuries. This difference exists because muni bonds serve a different market, namely, buyers interested in a tax-exempt product. Demand and supply differences skew the prices.

Why bother with the concept of basis points and yield? Why not just look at the cash you invested and the cash return you are getting on your money—so-called cash on cash? The answer is that by simply counting the actual dollars earned, you are looking at interest as a "naturally barren commodity,"[3] like an ear of corn. If you refer to Figure 5.6 comparing simple interest to compound interest, it will help you to understand why cash on cash is not sufficient. Figure 5.6 shows that if you invest $1,000 at 5 percent interest, you will have an extra $50 after one year. A yield-to-maturity calculation cannot improve on that. However, by the thirtieth year, you would have $2,500 ($1,500 of interest plus the return of your $1,000 principal), a little more than double, using simple interest and cash on cash. With compound interest, you would have more than a fourfold increase to $4,322. As you can see, for longer periods of time, cash on cash is inaccurate because unlike an ear of corn, interest can reproduce itself. That is the magic of compound interest reflected in the yield-to-maturity and yield-to-call calculations. If you want to have some fun, visit

Google and type in "compound interest calculator" to find one. If you take the time to fully understand these concepts, your investment tree will grow many green leaves.

Chapter Notes

1. James A. Klotz, "A Short-Term Outlook Leads to Long-Term Misery," www.fmsbonds.com, November 27, 2001, Commentary.

2. Riva D. Atlas, "Enron Spurs Debt Agencies to Consider Some Changes," *New York Times,* January 22, 2002, C6.

3. Aristotle, *Politics,* I, 10:5. According to Aristotle, money was incapable of reproducing itself, and therefore interest.

PART THREE

BOND CATEGORIES

IN THIS SECTION, we describe what may seem like a dizzying array of bond choices. It is your guide through the maze so that you can increase your wealth. We want your money to work as hard as you do, to put in overtime chugging out interest while you sleep. We want you to rest easy, knowing that you have invested wisely and that your funds will be there to take care of you and the people you love.

The United States has the largest debt market in the world, with more than $8 trillion in outstanding government debt alone. Through the credit markets, loans are sold in the form of Treasury debt and inflation-protected securities, while government agencies package housing loans into bite-size securities. The agencies add liquidity to those markets and finance themselves as well by selling bonds. Those bonds can also add liquidity to your portfolio.

The federal government sells EE and I savings bonds directly to you. You can purchase these bonds over the Internet and through bank branches in small denominations. They're accessible to every person, enabling even those with small sums of money to put their dollars to work earning interest. These bonds are complex, however, and we show how you can use them to your advantage.

Subsidized by anticipated federal revenue or using solely their own sources, municipalities sell bonds to finance sewers, transportation, health care, education, energy, economic development, and other projects. This borrowing ability of state and local governments enables them to build an infrastructure so that businesses and individuals may grow and prosper. Most of these bonds are superb investments, although some can be hazardous to your financial health. You'll understand why when you read chapter 10.

Corporations sell bonds to provide liquidity for the development of new ideas and projects and for refurbishing the old ones. Banks, brokerage firms, airlines, chemical companies, retail clothing chains, computer companies—you name it—access the credit markets to build factories and offices and to explore new markets. Corporations also borrow using medium-term notes and convertible bonds. In chapter 11, we describe how these bonds may start out as high-yield bonds or be transformed along the way.

Finally, there are bond look-alikes that use banks, brokers, and insurance companies to tap your funds for income-producing investments. Included in this category are the ubiquitous CDs issued by banks; preferred stock sold by corporations; fixed-immediate and deferred annuities sold by insurance companies; and stock dividends, sometimes a by-product of stock ownership. We warn you of some of the pitfalls associated with these financial instruments and highlight their usefulness.

For the sake of clarity, we used the same format to describe all the bonds in this part of the book. For each one, you'll find information on its advantages, risks, and tax implications as well as on any special features. This format should make it easy for you to compare one bond with another and to see which ones will best suit your needs and enrich your portfolio.

CHAPTER 6

U.S. TREASURY SECURITIES

THIS CHAPTER DESCRIBES marketable bonds and other securities issued by the U.S. Department of the Treasury. Popularly known as Treasuries, these securities are all backed by the full faith and credit of the U.S. government. With the United States rise to world economic dominance, such backing represents the strongest safety guarantee available. Accordingly, these securities have less default, event, liquidity, and political risk than any other investment. That backing does not mean that they're without risk. Longer-term Treasuries still have substantial market risk.

The Big Picture

Marketable securities, as the name implies, can be sold to other individuals or entities. Thus, if you buy a 5-year Treasury note on a Monday morning, you can sell it that Monday afternoon. However, you can never have physical possession of a marketable Treasury bill, note, or bond. In other words, you never receive a certificate from the government with your name on it. Rather, all Treasuries are available in what is known as book-entry form. These entries, with your name, are recorded in the books (or, in today's more modern terms, the accounting records) of commercial firms, such as banks or brokerage houses or in the records of the U.S. government itself if you participate in the TreasuryDirect Program. However, you do receive a statement confirming your ownership of a Treasury.

Before 1985, the government issued 30-year Treasury bonds that it could call—that is, buy back—should it choose to do so. The Treasury could demand redemption of these bonds five years prior to their maturity date. In 2000 and 2001, when the government was running budget surpluses, many of these older bonds were called and, thus, retired from public circulation. Owners of 30-year Treasuries that were bought in 1976 with an annual 14 percent interest rate were not happy in 2001 when they were told by the government that the party was over and that they had to part with those bonds at a time when other Treasuries were yielding about 4.5 percent.

All Treasuries issued since 1985, however, are noncallable prior to their maturity date. The last callable bonds issued were the 30-year bonds that came to market in November 1984. These bonds have a guaranteed coupon of 11.75 percent, and the government can recall them on November 15, 2009, rather than waiting until November 15, 2014, to do so.

The interest rate on Treasury securities is initially set at public auction. Auction bids for Treasury securities may be submitted as noncompetitive or competitive bids. If you make a noncompetitive bid, you agree to accept the interest rate determined at auction. In that case, you are guaranteed to receive the full amount of the Treasuries that you bid on. Most individuals make noncompetitive bids when they buy Treasury securities. If you make a competitive bid, you specify the interest rate that's acceptable to you. This bid may be accepted in the full amount of your bid if the rate specified is less than the interest rate set by the auction. However, the bid may be accepted in part or rejected if the rate specified is higher than the interest rate set at the auction. To place a competitive bid, you must use a broker or financial institution. The bid may not be made from TreasuryDirect.

All Treasuries are issued with a minimum face value of $1,000 and in increments of $1,000 above that. You can purchase them at auction by using the TreasuryDirect system. TreasuryDirect is a book-entry securities system, operated by the U.S. Bureau of the Public Debt, which allows you to maintain accounts directly with the U.S. Treasury. Alternatively, you can purchase all Treasury securities from a bank or a brokerage firm, either in the open market or at a Treasury auction. You can transfer most types of Treasury securities you buy from your bank or broker to your TreasuryDirect account. Upon your instructions, TreasuryDirect will get three bids for you if you want to sell in the secondary market any Treasury securities you hold in your TreasuryDirect account.

There are two principal advantages of using TreasuryDirect. First, you pay no fee and no spread (the difference between the broker's buy and sell prices) to purchase Treasuries. Second, the custodian of your Treasury securities is the federal government. Thus, the possible risks associated with a failed brokerage firm holding your securities do not exist. The two principal disadvantages of using TreasuryDirect are that you can purchase Treasury securities only at the time of an auction and that TreasuryDirect will not make a margin loan. A more detailed discussion regarding TreasuryDirect and the purchase of bonds is found in chapter 13. You can find good information on all U.S. Treasuries at www.treasurydirect.gov.

U.S. Treasury Notes and Bonds

Treasury notes and bonds both pay interest every six months and are initially sold at auction. Although both Treasury notes and bonds are issued to finance the longer-term needs of the U.S. government, they are distinguished by the terms of their maturities. The maturity of Treasury notes is set at a minimum of one year and does not exceed ten years. The government currently issues notes in 2-, 5-, and 10-year maturities. Auctions for the 2-year and 5-year notes are held monthly. The auction for the 10-year notes are held quarterly, and auctions for the 30-year bond are held quarterly beginning in 2007.

Although the maturity time frame makes it easy to distinguish between Treasury notes and bonds when they are first issued, it can be confusing when they are sold in what is known as the secondary market, or aftermarket. As noted, these issues can be freely traded much the way stocks are. You can buy Treasuries currently outstanding that will come due in any year. For example, a Treasury bond that was originally issued as a 30-year bond in 1993 would in effect be a 20-year bond in 2003 because it has been outstanding for ten years. It would still be known as the 1993 30-year bond.

All fixed-income investors should at least consider ownership of Treasury notes or bonds because of their safety and liquidity. Their rates are widely quoted on Web sites such as www.bloomberg.com, in the financial pages, and on television as an indicator of the rate and direction of all interest rates. The 10-year and the 30-year bond are quoted as major benchmarks for all fixed-income securities.

ADVANTAGES

Treasury notes and bonds are the most liquid securities in the world. This means that you can easily buy or sell them, and the cost to purchase or sell is extremely low. When you sell, the cash proceeds of your sale post to your account the next day. This is called a one-day settlement. Generally, it takes longer to receive cash when you sell other types of securities.

RISKS

Treasury notes and bonds are not immune to the market risks that affect all bonds. The interest rate volatility in the period from August 11, 2001, to January 10, 2002 (a period that included the tragic events of September 11), provides a clear example of how Treasuries can be affected by such swings. On August 11, 2001, the 10-year, 5 percent Treasury sold at par; on October 31, this Treasury sold at 103.5, reducing its yield to 4.25 percent; and on January 10, it again sold at par, to yield 5 percent. Those who bought this Treasury in October and sold it in January suffered a capital loss. Certainly the September 11 tragedy added to the market's volatility, but severe interest rate swings on long-term bonds are not unusual.

TAX IMPLICATIONS

Interest income from Treasury notes and bonds is subject to federal income tax but not to state and local taxes. The interest paid at six-month intervals is taxable in the year received. In addition, if a Treasury bond is purchased for less than its face amount, in certain cases, the difference between the amount paid and its face value may be taxable as interest income over the period between the date of acquisition and the earlier of the maturity date or the date you sell the bond. If you pay more than the face amount for the bond, you may be entitled to deduct the difference between the amount paid and the face amount over the same period.

The fact that interest earned on Treasury securities is not subject to state and local taxes can provide significant after-tax advantages for those living in high-tax states, such as California or New York. For example, assume that you buy a $1,000 bank CD and a $1,000 Treasury that both pay 5 percent interest and that your state income tax rate is 10 percent. You would receive $50 in interest, pretax, on both investments. However, with a state income tax of 10 percent, you would have to pay $5 in state taxes on the CD and only net $45 on an after-tax basis. Since you would pay no state tax on the Treasury, you would net the full $50 and quickly appreciate the tax advantages of Treasury securities. Interest income from Treasuries and CDs are both subject to federal income tax. In addition, sellers of Treasury notes and bonds must report the interest accrued to the date of sale on their federal income tax return.

PRICING INFORMATION

Unlike stocks and most bonds, which are priced in decimals, Treasury notes and bonds are priced in fractions as low as 1/32. Thus, a Treasury might be quoted as selling at 99 20/32. To convert 20/32 to a decimal, you divide 20 by 32 to get .625. Thus, 99 20/32 would be 99.625 when converted to a decimal.

Although Treasury notes and bonds are issued with face values at or in multiples of $1,000, the price you pay is subject to market conditions at the time. Thus, a $10,000 5-year note that was issued two years ago with a 7 percent coupon would be worth more than a $10,000 5-year note issued two months ago with a 3 percent coupon. Both bonds have the same face value, but investors will pay more than face value for the bond with the higher coupon rate because it will pay them more interest income.

SPECIAL FEATURES AND TIPS

Investors love that they can convert Treasuries so quickly to cash. In addition, there is always a market in which to sell them at a fair price, no matter what disasters are going on in the world. This cannot be said for many other securities. You can sell or transfer Treasuries as one lot or in part. For example, if you own a $10,000 bond, you can sell only $5,000 of it if you choose. You must, however, always sell in $1,000 multiples.

You can also use Treasuries as collateral (that is, security) for a loan from your broker. Depending on your brokerage firm, you may be able to borrow as much as 96 percent of the value at your broker's loan rate. For example, assume you have $10,000 of Treasuries in your brokerage account and need cash either for another investment or for a personal expense. Your brokerage firm might lend you up to $9,600 and use the Treasuries as collateral (security) for the loan. The interest rate charged on the loan would be a floating rate that would be much lower than a credit card loan because marketable Treasuries are considered such good security.

U.S. Treasury Bills

Treasury bills, popularly known as T-bills, are used to finance the short-term needs of the U.S. government. The 4-week bills, 13-week bills, and 26-week bills are each offered weekly and are available in commercial markets.

T-bills also differ from Treasury notes and bonds in that they do not pay interest every six months. Rather, they are sold at a discount to their face value. The difference between the discounted price you pay and the face value you receive at maturity is treated as interest income, rather than as a capital gain. Thus, T-bills pay interest only at maturity. In addition, although T-bills can be sold at any time without a penalty, you might realize a gain or a loss on the sale.

ADVANTAGES

Very short-term T-bills are a cash equivalent. As with Treasury notes and bonds, you can easily buy and sell them at extremely low transaction costs.

RISKS

Of all Treasuries, T-bills have the least market risk because of their short-term maturities. The 4-week T-bills, which the government first started selling on July 23, 2001, are the safest investment we know of.

TAX IMPLICATIONS

As with Treasury notes and bonds, income from T-bills is subject to federal income tax but not to state and local income taxes. As discussed previously, this feature can provide significant advantages for those living in high-tax states. The interest income from T-bills is taxable in the year in which the T-bill is redeemed or sold.

Unlike Treasury notes and bonds, you can use T-bill purchases as a short-term tax planning strategy. This is done by taking advantage of the fact that you report interest income from T-bills only in the year in which the bill comes due. To move interest income from one year to the next, buy a T-bill that has a maturity date in the next year. For example, if you bought a 26-week bill on August 1, 2006, you would report your interest income as having been received on February 1, 2007. That interest income would not be subject to tax in your 2006 federal income tax return but would be subject to tax in your 2007 return.

PRICING INFORMATION

T-bills also differ from Treasury notes and bonds in that the prices are quoted in decimals rather than in fractions.

STRIPS

STRIPS is the popularly used acronym for the U.S. Treasury's Separate Trading of Registered Interest and Principal of Securities Program. In many ways, the approach is similar to that of T-bills in that STRIPS are zero-coupon securities sold at a discount to their face value, with interest payments made only at maturity. As with T-bills, the difference between the purchase price of STRIPS and their face value provides the return.

The STRIPS program represents a unique partnership between the government and the private sector. In August 1982, Merrill Lynch became the first government dealer to create its own brand of zero-coupon government bond and gave it the catchy acronym of TIGRs (Treasury investment growth receipts). Salomon Brothers produced CATS (certificates of accrual on Treasury securities). LIONS (Lehman investment opportunity notes) and other acronyms soon jumped into the fray. There were two major drawbacks to these financial instruments: (1) Even though they were based on U.S. Treasury securities, the U.S. government did not guarantee them; and (2) their sponsoring firm determined their trading, thus, curtailing their liquidity.

In 1985, the U.S. Treasury announced STRIPS. In addition to more accurately describing the different types of zero coupons offered, the Treasury program also registered each one traded. With this registration, all STRIPS securities are the direct obligation of the U.S. government even though brokerage firms and other financial institutions create them.

STRIPS are constructed by taking a Treasury note or bond and stripping off the interest coupons. This process creates two different kinds of zeros: coupon strips, consisting of the interest coupons, and a principal payment strip, consisting of the principal payment. These are then sold separately. The number of interest payments determines the number of coupon strips created from any one Treasury security.

For example, assume that a brokerage firm buys a $1 million Treasury note with a 6 percent coupon rate that comes due in ten years. Over the lifetime of that bond it will annually yield $60,000, which is 6 percent of $1 million. Since interest payments are made semiannually, each coupon will be a strip with a face value of $30,000. When the coupons are stripped off, there will be twenty interest strips and one principal strip. Each $30,000 interest strip then becomes a separate $30,000 zero-coupon security, and the one principal strip becomes a separate ten-year zero-coupon security in the amount of $1 million. These strips may each be sold separately, with the price of each interest strip dependent on the time remaining to its maturity and the market interest rates at the date of sale.

ADVANTAGES

Although STRIPS have the same backing of the U.S. government as other Treasuries, they may yield somewhat more than a note or bond with the same due date because the STRIPS are more thinly traded and, thus, harder to sell. This is an advantage for those who like to buy and hold their bonds. STRIPS are useful for investors who want to receive a known payment on a specific future date.

Another advantage is that the total return on STRIPS is known precisely at the date of purchase if you hold the STRIPS to their due date. In interest-paying bonds, such as Treasury bonds, the total return depends in part on the rate at which you reinvest your interest payments every six months. In addition, you can buy STRIPS to come due in any year that would be desirable for your retirement or college education program.

Since STRIPS are more volatile (they move up or down more) than other Treasuries, you can use STRIPS to speculate on interest rate movements. For example, if you want to place a bet that interest rates will go down, you might buy long-term STRIPS. Since STRIPS are more volatile than Treasury bonds, you would have a larger gain if you guessed correctly.

RISKS

STRIPS have market risk. The longer the maturity of the STRIPS, the greater the risk of market volatility compared to equivalent interest-paying Treasuries. In addition, since STRIPS are traded less frequently than Treasuries, STRIPS will be slightly more expensive to buy and sell because the broker has a larger risk of a price decline.

TAX IMPLICATIONS

Even though interest from STRIPS is exempt from state and local taxes, you should consider the advantages of holding these bonds in a tax-sheltered retirement account, such as an IRA, as opposed to a taxable account. Interest on STRIPS held in a tax-sheltered retirement account is not subject to federal income tax until there is a distribution of cash from the account. However, if you hold the STRIPS outside of a tax-sheltered retirement account, you must report interest on STRIPS annually on your federal income tax return as ordinary interest income, even though you receive no cash until you redeem or sell the STRIPS. Such interest is referred to as imputed interest or phantom income. As a result, most people purchase STRIPS in tax-sheltered retirement accounts.

PRICING INFORMATION

You can buy STRIPS at discounts to their face value and in a wide variety of denominations, including small amounts. There is no limit on the size of your purchase.

TIPS

With great fanfare and even more debate, the U.S. Treasury introduced a brand new security concept on January 29, 1997. It appears that the name of this security, Treasury inflation-indexed securities, escaped scrutiny by acronym coiners. The marketplace quickly corrected what could have been an awkward name of TIIS by dubbing the newcomers TIPS (Treasury inflation-protected securities). Five-year, ten-year and twenty-year TIPS are each auctioned twice a year.

Again, Treasury notes and bonds pay out a fixed amount of cash, based on the coupon rate, every six months. In contrast, every six months, TIPS pay out a variable amount of cash that is initially lower than the amount paid by Treasury notes and bonds. As described next, this generally more modest coupon is designed to allow for the substantial principal accrual that is supposed to match the variability of the future cost of living. In this way, TIPS are designed to provide a guaranteed return over and above the inflation rate. Although the value of the principal varies over time, all TIPS are initially sold at auction in minimum amounts of $1,000.

The return on TIPS, then, consists of two parts:

1 The dollar amount of the semiannual cash interest payment changes every six months and is computed as follows: Multiply the coupon interest rate that is fixed at the time of auction by the sum of (a) the original principal of the bond plus (b) any inflation adjustment to the bond's value.

2 The value of the TIPS principal increases daily at a rate of inflation based on the consumer price index for all urban consumers (CPI-U): The TIPS' accrual during any month is based on the difference between the two most recent monthly nonseasonally adjusted U.S. city average consumer price indexes for all urban consumer figures. There is a three-month lag in the application of the consumer price index (CPI-U) to the Treasury calculation of the TIPS principal amount.

If you hold the TIPS until it comes due, the Treasury will pay you the sum of (a) the face amount of the security plus (b) an amount equal to the inflation (as measured by the CPI-U) that has occurred over the life of the security. Think of the semiannual inflation adjustment as a bonus that is added to the face amount of the bond. These inflation adjustments are not paid out until the security comes due. If you sell your TIPS before its due date, you will get a price that is set by the bond market. This price may be higher or lower than the bond's face value plus the inflation adjustment.

The inflation adjustment works in reverse if there is deflation rather than inflation. Deflation is when the CPI-U basket literally drops in price each month, as it did for much of the 1930s. In contrast, the more common term *disinflation* refers to the situation where inflation, the increase in the price of the basket, becomes smaller over time. For example, in 1990, the basket increased in price by about 5 percent; by 1998, that increase dropped to 2 percent, which meant that there was disinflation, not deflation.

If there is deflation rather than inflation or disinflation, the value of the TIPS is adjusted downward, and the coupon interest payments that are paid in cash semiannually are calculated using the reduced principal value. However, in the case of deflation, all is not lost, because the Treasury guarantees that upon maturity, when the bond comes due, the minimum price that you will receive is the face value of the TIPS. This eliminates the risk that a severe deflation will substantially reduce the value of your TIPS.

These payment calculations sound more complicated than they actually are. Let's see how it works by using a simplified example. Assume that you bought a $1,000 TIPS on January 1 that has a fixed coupon rate of 4 percent. Further assume that the CPI-U increased by 1 percent for the period January 1 to June 30 (that is, about a 2 percent per annum inflation rate). As we said, the 4 percent coupon rate will stay the same for the life of the bond, while the amount of the semiannual interest payments to you will vary with inflation.

With the above assumptions, the calculation of the interest payment for the first six months that you own the bond is as follows: the value of the principal of your TIPS increases $10 from $1,000 to $1,010 because of the 1 percent inflation increase ($1,000 × .01). The actual amount of cash interest that you receive would be calculated as follows: multiply the adjusted principal amount of your bond ($1,010) by 2 percent (or, one-half the annual rate), because the calculation is for six months (or, one-half of the year). Thus, the amount of the first cash interest payment to you is $20.20 ($1,010 × .02).

If for the second six months of the year inflation remains the same, the inflation-adjusted principal amount of the TIPS rises to $1,020 and the interest payment for that period is $20.40 ($1,020 × .02). Therefore, if there were inflation every six months as measured by the CPI-U, the principal amount of your bond would increase, and the amount of interest paid to you in cash would also increase. If the bond was a 10-year TIPS and you held it until it came due, the Treasury would pay you the principal amount of the security as adjusted upward for inflation. In this case, the bond you paid $1,000 for would be worth about $1,344 if the rate of inflation increased and averaged 3 percent and about $1,790 if the rate of inflation increased further and averaged 6 percent. In addition, the interest payment paid to you semiannually would rise every six months in proportion to the CPI-U.

The market value of the TIPS fluctuates with the rise and fall of other interest rates, the inflation rate, and the supply and demand for the security.

ADVANTAGES

TIPS provide a way to diversify your portfolio, as well as three levels of protection. First, interest payments rise with inflation. Second, the principal amount increases with inflation. Third, the Treasury guarantees that when the bond comes due, the minimum price that you will receive is the face value of the bond. Thus, the risk of a severe deflation reducing the value of the bond below its face value is eliminated. As a result, TIPS should be less volatile than other bonds with the same maturity. All primary dealers trade TIPS, though not as much as they trade other Treasuries.

RISKS

What you gain in inflation protection, you lose in current cash flow. A TIPS coupon rate is typically lower than what you would receive from other interest-paying Treasury notes and bonds because the TIPS provide inflation protection. Furthermore, if inflation is low over the life of your TIPS, you would receive a lower overall return on this bond investment than if you purchased other Treasury securities. And, as mentioned, should deflation occur, the amount of your semiannual interest payment would decrease along with the security's principal value, although not below the face value. If you purchased TIPS in the secondary market at a price above its face value (say at 110) and there were a severe deflation, your TIPS might come due at 100 (its original face value) resulting in a loss of 10 (110 − 100). This is a reason to buy TIPS at the Treasury auction if they sell at face value.

Although TIPS protect you against inflation, they do not guard against market risk, the risk of selling at a loss. General increases in interest rates that are not accompanied by inflation may result in a decline in the value of your TIPS if you need to sell it before it comes due. In 1997, the first year the bonds were issued, they declined in value.

There is also the tax risk of phantom income (see "Tax Implications").

TAX IMPLICATIONS

TIPS have tax consequences similar to those applicable to STRIPS. The upward adjustments to the principal of your TIPS will result in no current cash distributions to you until you either sell the bond or it comes due. However, unless you hold the TIPS in a tax-sheltered retirement account, such as an IRA, you must report this upward adjustment each year on your federal income tax return as taxable income even though you do not currently receive the value of the upward adjustment in cash. Correspondingly, a downward adjustment in the principal amount (in a period of deflation) will give rise to a deduction against the interest income paid to you. If you are in a low tax bracket, you might own these bonds in any account. However, if you are in a high tax bracket, you should consider owning TIPS only in a tax-sheltered retirement account.

There are different consequences if you own your TIPS through mutual funds. Please see chapter 15 for a discussion of TIPS owned in a mutual fund.

TIPS are not subject to state or local income tax.

SPECIAL FEATURES AND TIPS

Investors can use TIPS as collateral for a loan, and they allow investors the opportunity to benefit from inflation. TIPS also have a low correlation to other financial assets and, thus, may help investors reduce risk as part of their asset allocation.

Since 1926 inflation in the United States has averaged about 3 percent per year. For this same period, U.S. government bonds have yielded about 5 percent. Thus, the so-called real yield on U.S. government bonds has been about 2 percent. If you can get a real return on TIPS that exceeds 2 percent, you might consider TIPS favorably compared to other Treasuries of the same maturity.

Some advisers believe that TIPS are good for retirees, who can be hurt if their purchasing power starts to erode with inflation. Thirty-year-olds, by contrast, do not need as much inflation protection because their salaries are expected to go up over time, and the bulk of their earnings are ahead of them.

Jeff Metz, a financial *adviser* located in Marlton, New Jersey, says that his strategy in buying TIPS is to compare them to Treasuries of comparable maturity and to buy TIPS only at a Treasury auction. That way it is easier to compare the rate of return on the Treasury to the rate of return on TIPS, and you also save transaction fees because there is no cost to buy TIPS at a Treasury auction. Metz compares the coupon on the TIPS to the yield-to-maturity on the Treasuries and then makes an estimate for inflation. For example, if the yield-to-maturity on a 10-year Treasury bond is 4.5 percent and the coupon on the TIPS is 2 percent, it makes sense to buy the TIPS if you estimate that yearly inflation over the 10-year term of the TIPS will exceed 2.5 percent (4.5 percent minus 2 percent).

Key Questions to Ask About All Treasury Securities

◆ When is the next Treasury auction for the bond maturity I want?

◆ What bond maturity makes sense for me?

◆ What is my after-tax return on Treasuries?

◆ Does it make more sense to purchase Treasury bonds or TIPS for me?

◆ How much is the imputed income on which I will have to pay taxes annually if I purchase Treasury STRIPS or TIPS outside of a tax-sheltered retirement account?

CHAPTER 7

U.S. SAVINGS BONDS

U.S. SAVINGS BONDS are sold in two forms: EE bonds and I bonds. The U.S. Treasury Department issues them and markets them as a patriotic and profitable investment for the so-called little guy. Not surprisingly, they're the most widely held security in the world. The paper version of the series EE savings bond is named the Patriot Bond.

Simple Investments, With a Few Complexities

Although U.S. savings bonds have the reputation of being simple and straightforward, nothing could be further from the truth. Therefore, we start this chapter with the following warning: the structure of savings bonds is not only complex but has changed many times over the years. For example, the calculation of the yield on EE bonds has changed four times since 1990. Until May 2005, you could not predict what your return would be on EE savings bonds because it had a floating rate. I bonds still have a floating rate. Their tax consequences are even more complex.

The way you register ownership of savings bonds has important tax consequences.

Because of these complexities, we describe the best way to capitalize on the advantages of the EE and I savings bonds under each individual description. Despite their complexity, savings bonds may be great investments. There are no fees, loads, or commissions to buy them. They are fully guaranteed by the U.S. government, will not decline in value over the years, and are not callable. They are free of state and local income tax and may be free of federal income tax if used for certain educational expenses by qualified taxpayers.

All savings bonds are nonmarketable, which means that you cannot sell them to anyone other than a paying agent authorized by the Treasury Department. You may not use them as collateral for a loan. However, after you own them for a minimum of twelve months, you can sell (redeem) your savings bonds back to the Treasury Department at any time. You simply take them to your financial institution with proper identification, and you'll be assisted through the redemption process. However, if you redeem your EE or I savings bond earlier than five years from the issue date, you must pay an early redemption penalty equal to the last three months of earned interest.

PURCHASING A SAVINGS BOND

You can buy EE and I savings bonds in two ways: You can buy and hold savings bonds in electronic form in a direct electronic account with the Treasury Department at TreasuryDirect. Go to www.TreasuryDirect.gov. This Web site is an excellent source of information on all savings bonds. Alternatively, you can buy paper savings bonds at any of the approximately 40,000 financial institutions that the Treasury Department authorizes as issuing and paying agents.

You must choose one of three ways to register savings bonds:

1 Single ownership. With single ownership registration, only the registered owner, such as "John Doe," can cash or make a gift of the bond. On John Doe's death, the bond will become part of his estate and will go through probate.

2 Co-ownership. With co-ownership registration, such as "John Doe or Robert Smith," either co-owner may cash the bond without the knowledge or approval of the other. When the first co-owner dies, the second becomes the sole owner of the bond. This is similar to a joint account at a bank and avoids probate. You should determine whether there may be gift tax consequence of registering a bond in the name of someone who has not provided the cash to purchase the bond.

3 Beneficiary. With beneficiary registration, such as "John Doe, payable on death to Mary Doe," only the owner, John Doe in this case, may cash the bond. The beneficiary, Mary Doe, if she survives John, automatically becomes the sole owner of the bond when John dies. This type of ownership avoids probate, unless Mary predeceases John.

If you own paper EE or I savings bonds, you can trade them in for electronic bonds at TreasuryDirect, using a program called SmartExchange.

Series EE Savings Bonds

The TreasuryDirect Web site, www.TreasuryDirect.gov, has a description of the rules relating to all the EE savings bonds issued to date. Different rules apply depending upon what date you purchased your EE bonds. The description that follows applies only to EE bonds sold (a) between May 1997 and April 2005 (called here "old EE bonds") and (b) EE bonds sold beginning May 2005 (called here "EE bonds").

EE BONDS PURCHASED ON OR AFTER MAY 1, 2005

Interest on EE bonds purchased on or after May 1, 2005, accrues monthly and is compounded semiannually. However, no cash is paid out until the bonds are redeemed. EE bonds stop earning interest thirty years from their issue date.

A fixed interest rate for EE bonds is announced for new issues each May 1 and November 1. The fixed rates have ranged from a low of 3.2 percent to a high of 3.7 percent from May 2005 to April 2007, depending on the date that the EE bonds were purchased.

EE bonds earn a rate of return that is fixed at the date of purchase for the first twenty years of the bond, and this rate will be extended automatically for ten more years unless the Treasury announces different terms for the final ten-year period. Thus, you can calculate what the EE bonds will be worth for their first twenty years. You can buy EE bonds either electronically or as paper EE bonds.

If you buy your EE bonds electronically, they go to your designated account at TreasuryDirect. You can buy these electronic bonds at face value in any amount for $25 or more. Any individual can purchase a maximum of $30,000 in any one calendar year. Thus, you and your spouse can each buy $30,000 of EE bonds per year. (See "Recommendations and Tips" under I bonds for a way to buy more EE bonds than $30,000 if you're married.)

If you buy paper EE bonds, they are issued as paper bond certificates, and you can buy them at half their face value. For example, you pay $25 for a $50 bond, but it won't be worth its face value of $50 until it matures. You can buy the paper EE bonds in denominations of $50, $75, $100, $200, $500, $1,000, $5,000, and $10,000.

SPECIAL RULES FOR OLD EE BONDS

Old EE bonds, those purchased between May 1997 and April 30, 2005, earn a variable rate of return that is set at 90 percent of the average yield on 5-year Treasury securities for the preceding six months. The interest rate on old EE bonds changes every May 1 and November 1. If you own old EE bonds, you never know what long-term return you will get. These bonds do, however, provide two very important guarantees: (1) they reach their face value in a maximum of seventeen years, and (2) they will not yield less than 4.2 percent for that seventeen-year period. Thus, no matter how low the 90 percent average falls, holders of old EE bonds are guaranteed a minimum 4.2 percent compounded interest rate of return at the end of seventeen years. Should the 90 percent average turn out to be greater than 4.2 percent, the holders of old EE bonds will benefit by receiving a correspondingly greater return than 4.2 percent. Between May 1997 and

May 2002, for example, the six-month returns on old EE bonds varied from a low of 3.96 percent to a high of 5.68 percent. Each time the interest is added, the redemption value of the bond increases.

ADVANTAGES

EE bonds have numerous attractions. Most important, they provide protection against inflation and deflation, plus a guaranteed lump-sum distribution at any time after you hold them for twelve months. EE bonds will never decline in value. At a minimum, the U.S. Treasury guarantees that after twenty years, an EE bond will at least double in value. If an EE bond does not double in value as the result of applying the fixed rate for twenty years, the U.S. Treasury will make a one-time adjustment at original maturity to make up the difference. EE bonds earn interest for thirty years. EE bonds purchased before June 2003 are guaranteed to double in less than twenty years. What's more, an EE bond initial investment is as low as $25, rather than $1,000 for a Treasury security. As discussed later, these bonds can provide several tax advantages, particularly with regard to higher-education expenses.

RISKS

EE bonds have a small reduction in liquidity in that you cannot redeem them for the first twelve months that you hold them. If you redeem them in the first five years from your purchase date, you will lose the last three months of interest.

TAX IMPLICATIONS

EE bonds are subject to estate, inheritance, and gift taxes whether federal or state. Before September 1, 2004, exchanging old E bonds or EE bonds for HH bonds enabled you to defer reporting the taxable income of these bonds. Since September 1, 2004, you can no longer do this. We'll discuss HH bonds later in this chapter.

The difference between the purchase price and the amount you receive when you cash in your EE bonds or I bonds is reported as taxable interest income, which is subject to federal income tax but not state or local income tax. The interest income earned on EE bonds may be reported on your federal income tax return in one of two ways:

- The first and usual way is to report all the income earned in the year in which you redeemed the bonds. If the taxpayer is your child, is over eighteen, and elects to cash in the bonds, he or she may pay a lower tax on the postponed interest income if in a lower tax bracket than you. But keep in mind the possible exclusion of taxes on all EE bond interest if you (but not your child) are the owner of the EE bonds and you use the cash from the redeemed bonds for college tuition (see "Special Features" later in this chapter).
- The second way is to report the increase in redemption value as interest income each year even though you do not receive any cash. This approach may have advantages. For example, when a low-income taxpayer who has no other taxable income owns an EE bond, it might be advantageous to report the interest income yearly. This may enable the low-income taxpayer to reduce paying tax when he or she later redeems the bond.

If you want to change your method of reporting savings bond interest from the first way to the second way, you can do so without notifying or getting permission from the IRS. However, when filing your federal income tax return for the year you change, you must include on that return all savings bond interest accumulated to date that you have not previously reported.

If you want to do the opposite, change your method of reporting savings bond interest from the second way to the first way, you can do so by requesting permission from the IRS. The IRS automatically grants permission for the change if you send it a statement that meets a number of requirements set forth in IRS Publication 550, *Investment Income and Expenses.* You can find this publication at www.irs.gov.

If you are a surviving co-owner and the decedent (for example, your deceased husband or wife) had postponed reporting the interest income while he or she was alive, there are two choices for reporting the deferred interest income:

1 You can report all the postponed interest income on the decedent's final federal income tax return. In this case, you will not have to include any of this income in your federal income tax return. You would include only interest earned after the date of death.

2 You can report all the interest income earned before and after the decedent's death on your federal income tax return.

SPECIAL FEATURES

The Education Savings Bond Program, which applies to both EE bonds and I bonds, offers significant tax advantages to qualifying individuals. The Treasury Department introduced this program in 1990 as a response to the soaring costs of higher education.

If you qualify, this program allows you to exclude from your income all or part of the taxable interest income you receive on the redemption of your EE or I bonds. This exclusion applies to qualified higher-education expenses that you pay for yourself, your spouse, or any dependent for whom you are allowed a dependency exemption on your federal income tax return. The exclusion only applies for tuition paid to an eligible institution or state tuition plan.

To exclude some or all of the taxable interest income from your savings bonds, you must meet all the following requirements:

Year of purchase. You must have purchased EE bonds in January 1990 or later. All I bonds are eligible for this program. You are not required to indicate that you intend to use the bonds for educational purposes when you buy them.

Age. You must be at least twenty-four years old on the first day of the month in which you bought the savings bonds.

Registration. When using the bonds for your child's education, the bonds must be registered in your name and/or your spouse's name using one of your Social Security numbers. You can list your child as a beneficiary on the bond but not as a co-owner. If you list your child as a co-owner, the bond does not qualify for the income exclusion. When using bonds for your own education, you must register the bonds in your name. If you are married, you must file a joint return to qualify for the exclusion.

Year of redemption. You must redeem the bonds in the year you pay the tuition. You must use both the principal and interest from the bonds to pay qualified expenses in order to exclude the interest from your gross income.

Qualified institutions. You must pay the tuition to post-secondary institutions, including colleges, universities, and vocational schools that are eligible to participate in a student aid program administered by the U.S. Department of Education.

Qualified expenses. Qualified educational expenses include tuition and fees (such as lab fees and other required course expenses) at an eligible educational institution. The expenses may be for the benefit of you, your spouse, or a dependent for whom you are eligible to claim an exemption on your federal income tax return. Expenses paid for any course or other education involving sports, games, or hobbies qualify only if required as part of a degree or certificate-granting program. The costs of books and room and board are not qualified expenses.

Income limits. The full interest exclusion is available only if your income is under a certain limit in the year you use EE or I bonds for educational purposes, not the year in which you buy the bonds. In tax year 2006, for example, the IRS eliminated the exclusion for single taxpayers with modified adjusted gross incomes of $78,100 and above and for married taxpayers filing jointly with modified adjusted gross incomes of $124,700 and above. Married couples must file jointly to be eligible for the exclusion.

If you meet all these requirements, and certain additional qualifications, and you cash in your EE or I bonds and use them for college tuition, some or all of the interest earned on the bonds will be tax free. IRS Form 8815, the instructions for this form, and IRS Publication 970 explain all the technical requirements. You can find these documents at www.irs.gov. Thus, if you satisfy all the requirements, EE or I savings bonds may be as tax-efficient as investing in tax-free municipal bonds. Moreover, in certain cases you might receive a higher return on savings bonds than on municipal bonds.

RECOMMENDATIONS AND TIPS

EE bonds provide a tax deferral for up to thirty years, whereas other bonds (except for tax-free municipal bonds) are subject to annual federal income taxes.

EE bonds have no market risk and will never decline in value—a very helpful feature in your financial planning. At a time of low interest rates, you might purchase EE bonds and hold them until the interest rates on other bonds go up and then cash in your EE bonds and buy the higher-yielding bonds. Keep in mind there is a restriction on this strategy: You must hold your EE bonds for at least twelve months, and if you sell them before five years, you will have to pay a penalty of three months' interest.

EE bonds increase in value on the first day of each month. Thus, if it is near the end of the month when you plan to redeem your bonds, you may want to wait until the first day of the next month to earn a full month's interest. For example, if you planned to cash your bonds on March 28, you would lose interest for the entire month of March. If you can wait until April 1 to redeem your bonds, you would earn interest for the entire month of March.

When held for a long time, EE bonds may result in a large tax liability in the year you redeem them. One tax-planning technique is to gift your EE bonds to an individual over eighteen who is in a tax bracket lower than yours before you cash in the bonds. The person who cashes in the EE bonds must report the interest income on their federal income tax return.

Series HH Savings Bonds

As of September 1, 2004, the U.S. Treasury is no longer issuing HH savings bonds. Thus, investors are no longer able to reinvest their EE bonds in new HH bonds as they could before September 1, 2004. The description of HH bonds that follows applies only to HH bonds issued before September 1, 2004.

HH bonds pay out interest every six months at a fixed rate set on the day you bought the bond. HH bonds do not increase in value. Instead, every six months you receive a payment in cash by a direct deposit to your checking or savings account equal to six months of interest on your HH bond. When you purchase an HH bond, you lock in this rate for the first ten years. Interest rates are reset on the tenth anniversary of the HH bond's issue date. Bonds issued on January 1, 2003, through August 2004 earn 1.5 percent interest for their initial ten-year maturity period. Bonds entering an extended maturity period beginning January 2003 or later earn interest at 1.5 percent each year. Bonds issued March 1993 through December 2002 earn interest at 4 percent each year until they enter extended maturity after the first ten years. After that, they start earning interest at 1.5 percent each year. HH bonds reach final maturity and stop earning interest twenty years from their issue date.

ADVANTAGES

HH bonds are free of default risk because the U.S. government guarantees them. They have no liquidity risk because you can redeem them at face value at any time. If you exchanged EE bonds for HH bonds before September 1, 2004, you can continue to defer paying federal income taxes on the interest accrued on your EE bonds until the end of the extended due date. This may be of value if you exchanged your EE bonds for HH bonds before January 1, 2003, and are earning 4 percent while continuing your deferral. However, with the interest rate set at 1.5 percent for exchanges made after December 31, 2002, you may want to cash in your HH bonds (see "Tax Implications").

RISKS

Cashing in HH bonds may result in a large tax liability in the year you redeem them. The reason is that if you held the EE bonds for a long time before exchanging them for HH bonds, there may be a bunching of income in one year at a high federal income tax rate.

TAX IMPLICATIONS

You must report the payments you receive from HH bonds as interest income on your federal income tax return for the year you earn it. This income is not subject to state or local income taxes.

You must report any deferred interest from savings bonds that you exchanged to buy HH bonds as taxable income on your federal income tax return at the earlier of the year in which (1) your HH bonds reach final maturity or (2) you cash your HH bonds prior to final maturity.

Let's look at an example of the tax treatment of deferred interest. Assume that you bought an EE bond twelve years ago for $500 and it was worth $1,000 on August 1, 2004 (before the September 1, 2004, deadline). If on August 1, 2004, you traded your EE bond for an HH bond worth $1,000, you would continue to postpone reporting the $500 of interest income you earned on your EE bond until you cash in your HH bond or until the HH bond reached final maturity. However, the interest income you earn on your $1,000 HH bond every six months will be subject to federal income tax each year.

Series I Savings Bonds

The I bond was first issued in September 1998. It is more complex than the EE bond. Interest is accrued and added to the I bond monthly and compounded semiannually. However, you do not pay tax on the accrued interest until you redeem the bond.

The I bond's earnings rate is composed of two separate rates: a fixed rate of return and a variable semiannual inflation rate. When these two rates are combined, they produce the composite earnings rate on the I bond. The Treasury Department sets the fixed rate of return twice a year, each May 1 and November 1. The announced fixed rate applies only to bonds purchased during the six months following its announcement. The fixed rate that's in effect for the six-month period during which you buy your I bond remains your fixed rate for the thirty-year life of your bond. Between September 1, 1998 (when I bonds were first introduced), and May 1, 2006, for example, the fixed rate ranged from a low of 1 percent in November 2005 to a high of 3.6 percent per year in May 2000.

The semiannual inflation rate changes every six months, and the Treasury Department announces it each May 1 and November 1. The inflation rate is computed using the consumer price index for all urban consumers, published by the Bureau of Labor

Statistics. The semiannual inflation rate announced in May is a measure of inflation over the preceding October through March; the inflation rate announced in November is a measure of inflation over the preceding April through September. From September 1, 1998, to May 1, 2006, the inflation rate ranged from a low of 0.28 percent in May 2002 to a high of 2.85 percent in November 2005.

As we've noted, the composite earnings rate on your I bond is computed by combining the fixed rate and the inflation rate according to a set formula. An I bond's composite earnings rate changes every six months after its issue date. For example, the earnings rate for an I bond issued in August 2002 changes every August and February. However, the formula used to calculate the composite rate is more complicated than simply adding together the fixed rate and the semiannual inflation rate (see **Figure 7.1**).

The composite rate of 4.4 percent applies for the first six months after the issue. This composite rate combines the 2 percent fixed rate of return with the 1.19 percent semiannual inflation rate as

FIGURE 7.1

The Formula for the Composite Earnings Rate for I Bonds Issued from November 1, 2001, to April 30, 2002

Fixed rate for I bonds issued from November 1, 2001, to April 30, 2002 = 2 percent

Inflation rate for I bonds issued from November 1, 2001, to April 30, 2002 = 1.19 percent

Composite rate = [Fixed rate + (2 × Semiannual inflation rate) + (Semiannual inflation rate × Fixed rate)] × 100

Composite rate = [.02 + (2 × .0119) + (.0119 × .02)] × 100

Composite rate = [.02 + .0238 + .000238] × 100

Composite rate = [.044038] × 100

Composite rate = .044 × 100

Composite rate = 4.4 percent

measured by the consumer price index. In effect, if you purchased I bonds issued between May 1, 2001, and October 30, 2001, you would earn a 2 percent fixed rate of return over and above inflation for the thirty-year life of the bond.

The example provided in Figure 7.1 assumes that each year there will be at least some inflation. However, it is possible that there may be deflation in one or more years you hold your I bond. In the case of deflation, your I bond's composite rate will be lower than its fixed rate. That's because instead of an inflation rate being added to your fixed rate, the deflation rate will be subtracted from your fixed rate. Deflation will cause an I bond to increase in value slowly or not at all during the period of deflation.

A safety guarantee is built into the I bond to protect you in case the deflation rate exceeds your fixed rate. The terms of the I bond provide that no matter how bad deflation gets, the composite rate will never be reduced below zero. In the case in which the deflation rate exceeds the fixed rate, the redemption value of your I bonds will remain the same until the composite rate becomes greater than zero. For example, if your fixed rate is 2 percent and the deflation rate is 1 percent for the year, your composite rate for the year will be 1 percent (2 percent minus 1 percent). If your fixed rate for the year is 2 percent and the deflation rate is 3 percent, your composite rate for the year would be 0, because the composite rate cannot be reduced below zero.

The Treasury Department provides all the rates and detailed calculators on its Web site, www.TreasuryDirect.gov. Go to the Savings Bond Calculator to find the value of your bonds and what they are earning currently.

ADVANTAGES

I bonds are guaranteed to protect the holder against the risks of inflation and are also guaranteed to keep their value even if there is deflation. I bonds have no market risk because you can redeem them at their computed value from the Treasury Department at any time after twelve months. In addition, I bonds generally have all the same advantages we've noted for EE bonds.

RISKS

Unlike EE bonds, which guarantee a minimum rate of return, I bonds do not guarantee a minimum level of earnings. In addition, although I bonds generally increase in value monthly, they can stop accumulating interest in periods of deflation.

I bonds have a small reduction in liquidity in that you cannot redeem I bonds for the first twelve months you hold them, and if you redeem them in the first five years from your purchase date, you will lose the last three months of interest.

I bonds stop earning interest thirty years from the issue date. When your I bonds reach final maturity in thirty years, you must redeem them and report all the interest in the year of redemption.

TAX IMPLICATIONS

The taxation of I bonds is generally the same as noted for EE bonds. The Education Savings Bond Program applies to I bonds just as it does to EE bonds.

RECOMMENDATIONS AND TIPS

I bonds and EE bonds are an effective tax-deferral vehicle if you have contributed fully to all your tax-sheltered retirement accounts—such as your 401(k), 403(b), IRA—and you still want an investment that will provide a tax deferral.

The amount of EE bonds you buy does not limit the amount of I bonds you can purchase. If you're single, you can buy $30,000 per year in I bonds. If you're married and want to buy more, you and your spouse can each buy another $60,000 per year of I bonds. You could accomplish this by registering $30,000 of these bonds in separate names as individual owners. In addition, another way to register the bonds as a couple is to put your name as the first co-owner together with your Social Security number and list your spouse's name (without Social Security number) as the second co-owner on the first bond. On the other bond, do the opposite: put your spouse's name and Social Security number as the first co-owner and list your name (without Social Security number) as the other co-owner.

Keep in mind that the EE bond rate will be fixed for at least twenty years; nevertheless, you can redeem your bond after twelve months with only a three-month interest penalty if the redemption takes place within five years of your purchase. In comparison, only part of the I bond rate is fixed for the thirty-year life of the bond, but the added inflation rate will change every six months. If you're just starting out your investing career and don't have much money to invest, these bonds are a good starting place.

Key Questions to Ask About Savings Bonds

- What is the current interest rate on EE bonds?
- What is the current fixed rate on I bonds, including the current inflation rate?
- Will the interest-rate deferral that EE and I bonds provide be offset by a bunching of income in the year you redeem your bonds, making these bonds less attractive?
- If you, your spouse, or a dependent will be paying college tuition in the future, will you be in a low enough tax bracket to use the exclusion from income for education expenses?

CHAPTER 8

U.S. AGENCY DEBT

ONE OF THE lasting legacies of the Great Depression is the increased use of U.S. federal agencies to aid a wide variety of consumers including homeowners, farmers, agricultural interests, and students. One way that the agencies assist consumers is by reducing borrowing costs. Since 2000, there has been a tremendous increase in the issuance of agency debt. Fannie Mae, Freddie Mac, and the Federal Home Loan Banks have issued most of the new agency debt.

The agencies issue debt securities in the form of discount notes, which come due in less than one year; notes, which come due between one year and ten years; and bonds, which come due in more than ten years. If this sounds familiar, it's because Treasuries are issued in the same way. For clarity, we'll call all the debt securities issued by the agencies "agency bonds." This chapter discusses only agency bonds. The agencies also issue mortgage pass-through securities, which we'll discuss in the next chapter. The major agencies we'll discuss in this chapter are federal government owned or government-sponsored enterprises, popularly know as GSEs. GSEs are shareholder-owned corporations that the U.S. government regulates.

Agency bonds are extremely safe because they are either owned by the federal government, by agencies financially supported by the federal government, or agencies engaged in financial activities vital to the health of the country. Agency bonds are the safest bond investment after Treasury bonds. The Bond Market Association Web site, www.investinginbonds.com, has an excellent summary regarding the safety of agency bonds under the heading "About Government Bonds".

> Most agency and GSE debt is not backed by the "full faith and credit" of the federal government, but investors generally treat the securities as if they had negligible credit risk. The markets believe the federal government would prevent an agency or GSE from defaulting on its debt because of its role in promoting public policy and because of the sheer size of the largest of the agencies. As a result, agency securities have an "implicit guarantee" and trade in a narrow spread to Treasuries. (Their yields are usually slightly higher than Treasuries with comparable maturities but move in similar patterns.) However, both the agencies themselves and the federal government continually emphasize that there is no legal obligation for the federal government to support the debt of the agencies in the event of an insolvency or default.

Although most agency bonds carry an AAA rating, you must still check the rating of the bond you're considering buying because there are exceptions. For example, although Fannie Mae's senior unsecured bonds have a rating of AAA, Standard & Poor's rates Fannie Mae's subordinated benchmark notes AA– and Moody's rates them as Aa2. And as of September 23, 2004, Standard & Poor's placed Fannie Mae's subordinated benchmark notes on negative credit watch.

Major Debt-Issuing Agencies

The four largest issuers of agency bonds are:

- Fannie Mae (formerly the Federal National Mortgage Association)

◆ Freddie Mac (formerly the Federal Home Loan Mortgage Corporation)
◆ Farm Credit System (sometimes referred to by its acronym of FCS)
◆ Federal Home Loan Bank System (an agency that has yet to acquire an acronym, let alone a popular name)

Other agencies that issue or previously issued debt are Financing Corporation (FICO), Resolution Funding Corporation (REFCORP), Student Loan Marketing Association (Sallie Mae), Tennessee Valley Authority (TVA), and Federal Agricultural Mortgage Corporation (Farmer Mac).

FANNIE MAE AND FREDDIE MAC

Fannie Mae and Freddie Mac are GSEs regulated by the federal government. Fannie Mae was chartered in 1938, and Freddie Mac was chartered in 1970. Both of these GSEs assist low- and moderate-income families in buying homes by providing support and liquidity to the U.S. mortgage market. They do that by borrowing in the capital market (by selling bonds discussed in this chapter) and using the funds raised to purchase mortgages, mortgage securities, and other home loans from banks and other lenders. Fannie Mae and Freddie Mac are two of the largest issuers of bonds in the United States.

Fannie Mae. Fannie Mae sells a large variety of bonds. It generally issues bonds in a minimum purchase amount of $1,000 and in increments of $1,000. It issues a large number of its bonds pursuant to its global and benchmark notes programs. These programs are huge and international in scope and, as a result, the bonds are very liquid and trade easily at small spreads. In addition, Fannie Mae issues bonds called investment notes designed for the retail market and small investor. The investment notes are continuously issued and have a put feature that allows the estate of a holder of these notes to sell them back to Fannie Mae at face value. Despite the put feature, we prefer the global notes and benchmark notes to the investment notes because the benchmark notes and the global notes are more liquid so you get a better price if you sell them. In addition, the investment notes have shorter and more call provisions than either the global or the benchmark notes.

The Fannie Mae global notes and benchmark notes generally sell at a yield that is 20 to 25 basis points (one-fifth to one-quarter of 1 percent) above similar Treasury bonds for 2-year bonds, 25 to 30 basis points for 5-year bonds, and 30 to 35 basis points for 10-year bonds. These spreads can widen or tighten depending on market conditions.

Freddie Mac. Freddie Mac sells a large variety of bonds. It generally issues bonds in minimum purchase amounts of $1,000 or $2,000 and in increments of $1,000. It issues a particularly large amount of them pursuant to its reference notes and global bonds programs. The bonds issued pursuant to these programs are very liquid and, thus, trade easily at small spreads. Freddie Mac also issues Freddie notes. These are similar to the Fannie Mae investment notes in that they are designed for the retail investor and have a put feature. We prefer the reference notes and the global bonds to the Freddie notes for the same reasons we prefer the Fannie Mae benchmark notes and global bonds to the Fannie Mae investment notes. The Freddie Mac reference notes and global bonds generally sell at a yield that is 20 to 35 basis points above similar Treasury bonds (see the discussion of Fannie Mae global notes and benchmark notes).

FEDERAL FARM CREDIT SYSTEM

The FCS was established in 1971. It is a nationwide system of borrower-owned banks that sell bonds to raise funds and then lend directly and indirectly to ranchers, farmers, and certain farm-related businesses. Banks in the system generally issue a variety of bonds with a minimum denomination of $5,000 and in $1,000 increments.

FEDERAL HOME LOAN BANK SYSTEM

The Federal Home Loan Bank System (FHLB) was established in 1932 to revitalize the thrift industry during the Depression. The

FHLB includes the twelve regional Federal Home Loan banks. The system's membership consists of private savings and loan banks, and they in turn own the twelve regional Federal Home Loan banks. These banks sell bonds in the capital market and lend the money raised to thrifts, commercial banks and credit unions, and savings and loan banks, which in turn lend it to home buyers as mortgage loans. The Federal Home Loan banks issue a variety of bonds generally in minimum amounts of $10,000, with increments of $5,000. Any bond issued in the system is a joint obligation of all twelve Federal Home Loan banks; thus, if there is default by one, the others are legally liable to cover it.

FINANCING CORPORATION

FICO is a government corporation of mixed ownership chartered by the Federal Home Loan Bank Board. It began in 1987 to finance the recapitalization of the Federal Savings and Loan Insurance Corporation (FSLIC) and to help create liquidity for it after insolvency threatened many savings and loan banks. Although FICO's borrowing authority was terminated in 1991, many of its $8 billion of bonds are still outstanding. To ensure payment of principal on FICO bonds, the agency has purchased enough zero-coupon U.S. government-guaranteed securities to make total principal payable maturities approximately equal to the face value on FICO obligations.

All the FICO and REFCORP bonds that we see in the market are zero-coupon bonds. We purchased them in small and large pieces. We buy these bonds for our tax-sheltered retirement accounts so that the phantom taxable income they throw off will not affect us.

RESOLUTION FUNDING CORPORATION

REFCORP is another mixed-ownership GSE. It was established in 1989 to fund the Resolution Trust Corporation. It provided financing to bail out the large number of thrifts that failed in the 1980s. Although the bonds issued by REFCORP are not direct obligations of the U.S. government, the U.S. Treasury guarantees the interest, and Treasury bonds secure the principal. Thus, there is little if any default risk on these bonds. REFCORP originally brought to market 30- and 40-year bond issues. Many of these bonds were stripped to create zero-coupon bonds. These zero-coupon bonds are what are generally available in the secondary market to retail investors. They are sometimes found in pieces as small as $1,000.

TENNESSEE VALLEY AUTHORITY

The TVA was created in 1933 to develop the resources of the Tennessee Valley and its adjacent areas. The TVA is both wholly owned and an agency of the U.S. government. Despite this ownership, the U.S. government does not back TVA bonds. The TVA pays the principal and interest of the bonds only from the proceeds of its power program. The TVA issues a variety of bonds. Many are called "globals," which are retail-oriented electro notes. Both are available in the secondary market. It issues these bonds in minimum amounts of $1,000 and in $1,000 increments.

FEDERAL AGRICULTURAL MORTGAGE CORPORATION

Farmer Mac is a GSE established in 1988 to promote liquidity for agricultural real estate and rural housing loans. It does this by buying loans from lenders and creating pools of these loans, against which it issues bonds that investors purchase. Farmer Mac issues a variety of bonds in minimum amounts of $1,000 and in $1,000 increments.

STUDENT LOAN MARKETING ASSOCIATION

Sallie Mae was created by Congress in 1972. It was a federally chartered GSE established to provide liquidity for banks and other lenders that originate guaranteed student loans. As a result of the federal government becoming more involved in issuing student loans, Sallie Mae was restructured in 1997 and phased out its GSE status by the end of 2004, ending its ties to the federal government.

ADVANTAGES

Although most agency bonds are not well known, they are very attractive investments because of their high credit rating and yields, which are higher than Treasuries. Agency bonds are extremely safe and have negligible credit risk because the federal government is unlikely to let one of its sponsored enterprises default. Investors can use agency bonds as collateral for loans.

RISKS

Although there is no significant liquidity or tax risk associated with agency bonds, they are subject to possible event and political risk. In terms of political risk, Congress has periodically become concerned about the mushrooming amount of agency bonds and has sought to curtail the amount of agency lending.

After an accounting scandel in 2005 rocked Freddie Mac and Fannie Mae, both agencies came under close ongoing scrutiny.

Most agency coupon bonds have call provisions. However, agency zero-coupon bonds generally don't have call provisions. These call provisions for the agency coupon bonds constitute the major risk of agency bonds. Many of these calls are extremely short; for example, a three-month call is not unusual. Thus, even if your agency bond has a good return, it can be called away before you have a chance to fully benefit from it. A short call subjects you to reinvestment risk because agencies will call in the bonds at times when interest rates are declining. Reinvestment risk means that if your bond gets called and you get your money back, you may have to reinvest at lower interest rates. If you buy a 20-year or 30-year agency bond with a one-year call, you're subject to market risk (that is, inflation) should interest rates go up (that's because the value of your long-term bond will go down) and reinvestment risk if interest rates go down, because your bond may be called. You can avoid this risk by not buying long-term agency bonds with short calls. However, you might buy shorter maturity issues with longer call protection. For example, you might buy 5-year agency bonds with two-year call protection.

TAX IMPLICATIONS

All agency bonds are subject to federal income taxation. However, the following agency bonds may not be subject to state and local income taxation:

- Farm Credit System
- Federal Home Loan Banks
- Financing Corporation (FICO)
- Resolution Funding Corporation (REFCORP)
- Tennessee Valley Authority (TVA)

The following agency securities are subject to state and local income taxation:

- Fannie Mae
- Freddie Mac

SPECIAL FEATURES AND TIPS

Bonds issued by Fannie Mae, Freddie Mac, Federal Home Loan Banks, and Farm Credit System are quite liquid and, as such, are easy to buy and sell, which results in lower trading transaction costs. We particularly like noncallable agency zero-coupon bonds for your tax-sheltered retirement accounts. For example, in 1997, the yield on 15-year agency zeros was 7.5 percent while the overall stock market was racking up 20 percent per year gains. Bond aficionados that we are, we ignored the techs and tucked into our IRAs an assortment of noncallable agency zeros with a 7.5 percent yield. These bonds doubled in less than ten years without any further action or monitoring on our part as well as without any need to reinvest the coupons. In essence, we bought a risk-free investment that was guaranteed to double in less than ten years while the stock market boomed and then busted. It doesn't sound as sexy as a new, high-tech IPO, but it sure has proved rewarding for our clients and for us.

Although early call features are a risk, agency bonds of five years or less can also present an opportunity, especially in an atmosphere of rising interest rates. If agency bonds with short calls have a higher yield, consider buying them. **Figure 8.1** presents the interest rates in September 2001 and the plan that a major brokerage firm presented to us.

"Even if the agency bond is called away in two years," the firm wrote, "it will have yielded 5.1 percent, which is 160 basis points

FIGURE 8.1

Callable Agency Bonds Compared to Treasuries

	Yield-to-Maturity
Money markets	3.1%
1-year CD	3.2%
2-year U.S. noncallable Treasury	3.5%
5-year U.S. noncallable Treasury	4.2%
10-year U.S. noncallable Treasury	4.8%
5-year noncallable Fannie Mae	4.8%
5-year Fannie Mae with first call	5.5% (if not called in 2 years; 5.1% if called in 2 years)

(1.6 percent) higher than a comparable U.S. Treasury, which yields 3.5 percent. If the agency bond is not called and is held to maturity, it will yield 5.5 percent, versus 4.2 percent for a comparable U.S. Treasury."

We believe that if the yield difference between an agency and a Treasury is only 20 basis points (0.2 percent), you should consider buying the Treasury for your taxable account because of its greater call protection, liquidity, and safety—particularly if you can advantageously use the state tax exemption. If you can earn more than 50 basis points (0.5 percent) on an agency bond compared to a Treasury of similar maturity, we believe the agency may be more attractive if it has adequate call protection.

Sources of additional information. Excellent bond-specific Web sites are www.fhlb.com, www.freddiemac.com, www.fanniemae.com, and www.tva.com.

Key Questions to Ask About Agency Bonds

- What are the calls on this bond?
- How much more yield, if any, am I getting on this callable bond versus a noncallable bond?

◆ What is the reinvestment risk on this bond if it is called?
◆ What is this bond rated? (An issuer may put out subordinated debt that has a rating below AAA.)
◆ Does this bond have the state-tax exemption? (If you live in a high-tax state, this is critical.)
◆ How does this bond compare in terms of after-tax yield to an equivalent Treasury bond in my tax bracket?

CHAPTER 9

U.S. AGENCY and Other MORTGAGE-BACKED SECURITIES

THIS CHAPTER DESCRIBES two types of mortgage securities. We first start with mortgage pass-through securities that are guaranteed by an agency. They're called "agency mortgage securities." We then describe the more complex "collateralized mortgage securities" that may or may not have an agency guarantee.

In its basic form, a mortgage pass-through security (generally known as a mortgage-backed security) represents an ownership interest in a number of similar mortgage loans made by financial institutions such as savings and loans, commercial banks, and mortgage companies. When these mortgage loans are combined or pooled, they become mortgage-backed securities. U.S. government agencies issue and/or guarantee many of these mortgage-backed securities. For simplicity's sake we'll refer to mortgage-backed securities as mortgage securities. The cash flow, consisting of both principal and interest payments, from the pool of mortgage loans, reduced by fees, is passed through to holders of the mortgage securities.

A Complex Structure

Although there's a lot of money to be made from these financial instruments, their complex structure makes them more difficult to understand than other investments. It helps first to understand how a mortgage security's underlying asset, a simple mortgage loan, is created. Mortgages came into being because most people have only enough money for a down payment when purchasing a house. They require help in the form of a mortgage loan to pay the balance. Banks provide this sort of help. For example, let's say you borrow $100,000 for thirty years to finance the purchase of your house. Your loan agreement is documented by a mortgage, and it stipulates how much and how frequently you will make payments. The bank might charge a series of fees for making the loan.

After receiving your $100,000 mortgage document, your bank—without your knowledge—will probably turn around and sell it to another entity. If the bank agrees to collect your mortgage payments and provide you with payment records even though it no longer owns your mortgage, it receives a fee from the buying entity for doing so. The bank now has its $100,000 back and can lend that money to another borrower.

In its turn, the purchasing entity creates a mortgage pool by combining your mortgage with other, similar mortgages. The purchasing entity then may either guarantee the creditworthiness of that mortgage pool or obtain a guarantee from another institution. The resulting financial package, highly desirable because of the value of the underlying mortgages and the credit guarantees, is divided into units that are sold to investors as mortgage securities. Many of these mortgage securities are agency mortgage securities, and one of three government agencies—Fannie Mae (originally named Federal National Mortgage Association), Freddie Mac (originally named Federal Home Loan Mortgage Corporation), and the Government National Mortgage Association (which is widely known as Ginnie Mae)—either issues or guarantees them. When we refer to agencies, we mean these three companies.

The creation of mortgage securities can benefit all parties.

◆ The homeowner is able to borrow money at the lowest rate available because a financially strong agency guarantees the payment of principal and interest of the mortgage loan.

◆ The bank earns its fees and may sell the mortgages, reducing its risk. The investors in the mortgage securities are happy they have an easily traded (liquid) security that an agency collateralizes and guarantees. In addition, the mortgage security may yield more than an equivalent Treasury bond.

◆ Finally, the agencies are fulfilling their mandate, which is to increase home mortgage liquidity while enabling banks and other lenders to finance mortgages for low-income and middle-income families.

It is important to note that the agencies are barred by their charters from originating mortgages. A network of lenders, which includes mortgage bankers, savings and loan associations, and commercial banks, originates the mortgages in the pools. After ensuring that the mortgage loans meet established credit quality guidelines, the agencies either directly or indirectly convert the loans into mortgage securities—a process known as securitization. The resulting mortgage securities may carry an agency's guarantee of timely payment of principal and interest to the investor, whether or not there is sufficient cash flow from the mortgage pool. Agency mortgage securities provide investors with an investment that offers liquidity, safety of principal, and attractive yield. They are one of the most widely held and safest securities in the world.

The Agencies

A little history will be useful in understanding why the agencies that guarantee mortgage-backed securities were created and how they differ. Until the late 1930s, affording a home was difficult for most people because a prospective homeowner had to make a down payment of 40 percent and then pay the mortgage off in three to five years. During the three- to five-year period, the mortgage holder paid only interest on the mortgage. At the end of that time, the principal had to be paid in one lump sum, called a "balloon payment." As the boom of the 1920s turned into first a stock market crash and then a depression, more people defaulted on their mortgages because they could not meet the final balloon payment. Thus, while prospective homeowners preferred long-term, fixed-rate mortgages, banks and other mortgage lenders were reluctant to offer them because of the risk of default on the mortgages.

The government stepped in and created the Federal National Mortgage Association as part of the Federal Housing Administration (FHA) on February 10, 1938, charging the association with bolstering the housing industry by expanding the flow of mortgage money. Throughout its first years of operation, the Federal National Mortgage Association primarily bought mortgages issued to lower-income people; banks held on to the lucrative returns from mortgages issued to more prosperous customers. This situation changed during a credit squeeze in which banks and savings and loan institutions were receiving 6 or 7 percent annual interest on 30-year fixed-rate mortgages and paying out 9 percent to 12 percent interest on bank deposits. By the late 1960s, banks found the idea of selling a greater number of mortgages more attractive because of their realization that holding them could be risky.

Once again the government stepped in. In 1968, it split the Federal National Mortgage Association into two separate legal entities. One became a shareholder-owned, privately managed public corporation supporting the secondary market for conventional loans. This corporation became popularly known as Fannie Mae, a nickname legally sanctioned in 1997. Although a shareholder-owned public corporation, it didn't completely sever its ties with the government because it operates under a congressional charter and is subject to oversight from the U.S. Department of Housing and Urban Development (HUD) and the U.S. Department of the Treasury. The association with HUD and the Treasury gives Fannie Mae a powerful backing in the event of any financial problems; the aura of the association with the U.S. government extends to its securities, which, as noted previously, carry an implicit AAA rating.

Fannie Mae has two primary business activities: (1) portfolio investment, in which it buys mortgages and mortgage securities (the debt securities it issues, which were described in the last chapter, fund this activity); and (2) credit guarantees, in which it charges fees to guarantee the credit performance of single-family and multifamily loans.

The second entity resulting from the government's 1968 split of the original Fannie Mae is the Government National Mortgage Association, known as Ginnie Mae. Ginnie Mae differs from Fannie Mae in four important respects:

1 It is a government corporation located within HUD;

2 Its obligations are fully rather than implicitly backed by the full faith and credit of the United States;

3 Its purpose is to serve low-income to moderate-income home buyers as opposed to all home buyers; and

4 It does not form mortgage pools but rather guarantees the timely payment of principal and interest on qualified pools of mortgages, which are known as Ginnie Mae pools. There are hundreds of issuers of qualified pools, and they administer more than 400,000 Ginnie Mae mortgage pools. All mortgages in a Ginnie Mae pool are insured by the FHA, the Veterans Administration (VA), or other governmental entities.

In 1970, Congress further increased mortgage activity by chartering the Federal Home Loan Mortgage Corporation as an active participant in the secondary mortgage market. In 1989, this agency followed in Fannie Mae's footsteps and became a shareholder-owned, privately managed public corporation subject to oversight from HUD and the Treasury. In 1997, it once again copied Fannie Mae's example and legally changed its name to the popularly known Freddie Mac. Although there is little discernable difference between Fannie Mae and Freddie Mac, competition between the two ensures that the benefits of the secondary market are passed on to home buyers and renters in the form of lower housing costs.

Each agency has a Web site that provides helpful information: www.fanniemae.com, www.freddiemac.com, and www.ginniemae.gov.

Mortgage-Backed Securities

Let's take a closer look at mortgage pools and how securities are created from them. In our example at the beginning of this chapter, we noted that your mortgage might be combined with many other similar mortgages to form a mortgage pool. Assume that your mortgage is in the amount of $100,000 and that there are nine other similar mortgages also in the amount of $100,000 each. In this case the value of the mortgages in the pool is $1 million (100,000 × 10). This mortgage pool will receive cash flow from three sources:

◆ First, the homeowners pay interest on their mortgages.

◆ Second, the homeowners pay scheduled principal payments on their mortgages.

◆ Third, and most important to understand, the homeowners may make nonscheduled prepayments on their mortgages, creating additional cash flow. These nonscheduled prepayments are the result of homeowners refinancing or prepaying their mortgages, selling their homes, or defaulting on their mortgages. Refinancing is particularly prevalent when interest rates go down and homeowners pay off existing mortgages to obtain new, cheaper ones. As a result, a pool of 30-year mortgages might be paid off in twelve to fourteen years. Thus, while debt securities such as bonds are traded in terms of their due dates, mortgage securities are traded in terms of their assumed "average life."

When any nonscheduled prepayments take place, additional cash comes into the mortgage pool. The originator/servicer of the mortgage pool collects all the cash flow and charges a fee of about

0.5 percent for this work. Each month the originator/servicer distributes all the cash collected minus its fee pro rata to the owners of the mortgage securities.

Put another way, when you hold a mortgage security, you may receive a monthly, quarterly, or semiannual cash flow from three sources: interest on the mortgages; principal payments on the mortgages; and nonscheduled payments resulting from homeowner refinancing, prepayments, home sales, and defaults.

Keep in mind that not all this cash flow is income. The principal payments and nonscheduled prepayments are an early return of your principal. When you invest in a mortgage security, you're in the position of a bank lending money on a mortgage to a homeowner. When you are repaid, you receive back mostly interest in the early years and mostly principal in the later years.

ADVANTAGES

Agency mortgage securities are very attractive because they often yield more than Treasuries of comparable maturity. Although there is a difference in the underlying credit of each agency, all agency mortgage securities are very safe and have AAA ratings. The U.S. government directly guarantees the Ginnie Mae mortgage securities as to timely payment of interest and principal. Fannie Mae and Freddie Mac can borrow directly from the U.S. Treasury if conditions so warrant. However, in 2006, some members of Congress expressed opposition to this borrowing power.

Even though the U.S. government does not directly guarantee the Fannie Mae and Freddie Mac mortgage securities, they have an implied AAA rating because the assumption is that the federal government will stand behind the debt. It is unlikely that the U.S. government would let one of its government-sponsored enterprises, such as Fannie Mae or Freddie Mac, default. It is interesting to note, however, that in 2001 Standard & Poor's issued a credit rating report for Fannie Mae and Freddie Mac stating that if the agencies were viewed on their own without the support of the U.S. government, their credit rating would be AA–, rather than AAA.

Finally, keep in mind that in practice there has been no difference in the safety record of the three agencies' securities. None has ever defaulted or missed a payment of interest or principal to an investor.

RISKS

Mortgage securities have a number of significant disadvantages when compared to Treasuries, most notably their uneven and unpredictable cash flow, which results from prepayments. These prepayments are a wild card in analyzing mortgage securities because they make it impossible to predict the overall cash flow. If you can't predict cash flow, you can't predict current return, and you certainly can't compute a yield-to-maturity. Thus, it is difficult to compare the yield on a mortgage security to the yield on a Treasury or corporate bond. This unpredictability of cash flow causes the mortgage securities to often yield more than Treasuries.

The prepayment assumptions used to evaluate mortgage securities are based on complicated statistical models. Usually, the payment history of the mortgage securities is compared to prepayment patterns prepared by the FHA. If interest rates change markedly, the FHA may issue new prepayment guidelines. Unless you purchase mortgage securities through a fund, the relatively small blocks that an individual can purchase might actually be statistical aberrations from the norm. Another concern that individual investors have is that they might get an unfavorable price on the mortgage security that they buy because of the difficulty in evaluating the price.

Unpredictable prepayments may cause other problems. If you base the estimated yield on the mortgage security on the mortgage pool remaining in existence for, say, twelve years, prepayments may result in a pool coming to an end in only nine years. This might result in a lower yield on the mortgage security. Under these circumstances, if you purchased a mortgage security at a premium, you could lose money.

Capital depletion is a potential problem for the inexperienced investor in mortgage securities. The large cash flows look like manna from heaven. But if you spend all the cash flow that you receive from the mortgage security as it comes in, you will deplete your capital and have nothing to reinvest when the cash flow stops. Thus, a mortgage security is similar to an investment in an oil well: large cash payments in the early years but declining payments in the future as the oil is depleted. By comparison, a debt security, such as a Treasury bond, pays you the principal at its maturity date as well as interest payments twice a year.

Mortgage securities also have interest rate risk. If interest rates rise, homeowners will generally not refinance their mortgages, thereby causing the average life of the mortgage pool to extend. This will result in a yield lower than originally estimated because it will take longer for you to get your capital back. Mortgage securities perform best when interest rates remain within a narrow range.

Finally, there is not much daily pricing information available to investors about mortgage securities. Even the *Wall Street Journal* provides little information on mortgage securities.

TAX IMPLICATIONS

All agency mortgage securities are subject to federal income tax and state income tax on all interest income and original issue discount (OID). OID exists if a mortgage security is issued at a discount from its face value. Your broker will report the amount of interest income and original issue discount to you on Forms 1099-INT and 1099-OID. The portion of any payment from a mortgage security that represents a return of the principal that you originally invested is tax free.

SPECIAL FEATURES AND TIPS

It's difficult for individual investors to evaluate information about specific mortgage securities offered by brokers and to commit enough cash to properly diversify a portfolio of mortgage securities. For these reasons, mortgage securities may not be suitable for individuals to purchase on their own. Some investors, however, may find buying individual Ginnie Mae certificates to be attractive if they want a large cash flow and do not care if their principal is returned unpredictably.

For most investors, the best way to invest in mortgage securities is through buying a Ginnie Mae open-end mutual fund. This approach uses the expertise of the fund's investment adviser and provides diversification among different Ginnie Mae securities. You might wish to consider the following Ginnie Mae funds: Vanguard GNMA Fund (877-662-7447), Fidelity Ginnie Mae Fund (800-544-6666), and USAA Invest-GNMA Trust (800-382-8722).

Key Questions to Ask About Mortgage-Backed Securities

- ◆ How do I evaluate the price I receive on these securities?
- ◆ Do you have research you can share on the prepayment speed of the particular lot you are selling?
- ◆ How do I know if the funds I receive from a prepayment are interest or the return of my principal?
- ◆ How has trading affected my yield?

Collateralized Mortgage Obligations

Collateralized mortgage obligations (CMOs) are similar to mortgage securities in that they are based on underlying mortgages. A CMO is a package of mortgage securities and/or mortgage loans that an issuer assembles as a multiclass security offering.

Financial engineers in the investment-banking world created CMOs in 1983 to alleviate the problem of how to deal with the prepayment uncertainties associated with mortgage pools. The CMO solved the prepayment problem, at least in part, by allowing a greater certainty of return for those willing to accept a lower yield, while rewarding those who assume a much more unpredictable return and maturity with a higher yield. CMOs created a whole new range of profitable financial products for Wall Street. They have become a big business. There are more than $1 trillion in CMOs outstanding.

Mortgage-backed securities may seem complicated, but CMOs are much more complex. They consist of endless variations of combined cash flows originating from mortgage pools. Michael

Vranos, the former head of mortgage securities at Kidder Peabody, once boasted to the *Wall Street Journal* that his job is to sell securities to the dumb guys. Some of his clients understandably resented the assessment. Grudgingly, however, many investors concede that Vranos's tactless remark contained a kernel of truth. The following simplified explanation captures the basics: although holders of mortgage securities receive cash through pro rata monthly distributions, owners of CMO securities receive cash from a mortgage pool on a prioritized basis. That prioritization is called a class or a *tranche,* a word derived from the French word for slice.

CMO: A CLOSER LOOK

Let's consider a simple example of a CMO with three classes of securities and see how it works. In practice, there may be as many as fifty different classes, the thought of which can induce nightmares for people trying to understand this product. We'll call our three classes the A Class, the B Class, and the Z Class. The term Z Class originally referred to the last class to be paid; today, it often describes an accrual bond that may or may not be the last in the CMO to be paid. This class is also known as an accrual tranche, or a Z bond.

In our example assume that $1 million has been invested in the three classes as follows:

◆ **A Class.** The face value of the securities in the A Class is $600,000. Interest at the annual rate of 6 percent is paid monthly on the face value of the securities until they are paid off. All scheduled principal payments and all prepayments are paid monthly to the A Class until $600,000, representing the full face value of the A Class, is paid off. No principal payments or prepayments are paid to the B Class or Z Class until all the A Class securities are paid off.

◆ **B Class.** The face value of the securities in the B Class is $300,000. Interest at the annual rate of 8 percent is paid monthly on the face value of the securities even when the A Class is still outstanding. All scheduled principal payments and all prepayments are made monthly to the B Class, but only after all the A Class is paid off. No principal payments or prepayments are made to the Z Class until $900,000, representing the full face value of the A Class and B Class securities, is paid off.

◆ **Z Class.** The face value of the securities in the Z Class is $100,000. Interest at the annual rate of 10 percent is accrued but not paid on the face value of the securities until $900,000, representing the full face value of the A Class and B Class, is completely paid off. Such interest as well as scheduled principal payments and all prepayments are made monthly to the Z Class only after all the A Class and B Class are both paid off. Thus, the Z Class gets the remainder of the payments from the mortgage pool. The Z Class bears some similarity to a zero-coupon bond in that interest is accrued but not paid. The Z Class may have a very long life and no definite maturity. It may also be difficult to determine the tax consequences of the Z Class.

Note the higher interest rates for the B Class and Z Class to make up for the longer life and higher risks in these classes as compared to the A Class.

The A Class security is similar to a short-term bond. Since the A Class receives a share of the interest and all the prepayments initially, it will turn out to be a shorter-term security and will have a more predictable return than the B Class or the Z Class securities. It might be possible to predict with a high degree of reliability that the A Class will retire in, say, three years. The life of and thus the return on the B Class will be more difficult to predict than the A Class, and, thus, the B Class should earn a higher return.

As noted, the last class, the Z Class, will receive no interest or principal payments until all the other classes are repaid in full. Although the A Class may have an expected life of three years, the Z Class may not retire for twenty or thirty years. The return on the Z Class is the most difficult to predict and value. It should have the highest yield because of its uncertainties. It will lose value quickly when interest rates rise because prepayments decline and lengthen the life of the Z Class. Many CMO investors have lost money when their estimates were not met with respect to Z Class securities.

There are two major types of CMO structures. One, as in our example, provides that only principal payments be redirected, and interest goes pro rata. In the other type, principal as well as interest payments are redirected. The pattern for the latter, while Byzantine, is similar to that described previously and makes later tranches even more volatile.

CMOs can be, and often are, categorized by type of issuer. The term agency CMOs refers to those issued by the agencies. The mortgages in the agency CMOs are already pooled mortgages and in securitized pass-through form. They are of similar size, age, and quality. Investors in agency CMOs have only prepayment risk, but no credit risk.

The terms private-label CMO, nonagency CMO, and whole-loan CMO refer to investments comprising mortgages that do not have an agency guarantee. Some private institutions, such as subsidiaries of investment banks and other financial institutions, issue nonagency CMOs, usually consisting of jumbo loans. Agency CMOs do not use jumbo loans. Nonagency CMOs often carry an AA or AAA rating due to credit enhancements. Within the same issue, individual tranches may carry different ratings.

ADVANTAGES

Agency CMOs have minimal credit risk, and they may offer a higher return than Treasuries because of the market risk relating to the uncertainty of the CMO's maturity. In the absence of a government or other guarantee, nonagency CMOs may provide a potentially higher return than agency CMOs or agency debt bonds of comparable maturity, reflecting the greater credit risk on the nonagency CMOs.

If you buy the A or B classes in a CMO (that is, the top classes), the cash flow should be more predictable than with other agency mortgage securities. This is the purpose of CMOs. If you buy the A Class, it should resemble a short-term bond, although with a less predictable maturity. The A or B Class CMOs will provide high monthly cash flows. You can buy CMOs in $1,000 pieces, rather than the $25,000 minimum required for a Ginnie Mae security.

RISKS

The attractiveness of CMO securities varies considerably because of repayment unpredictability. The safest are the A Class and B

Class agency CMOs. Predictions relating to the life of the CMO and, thus, the yield predictions may be very far from the actual outcome. What may appear to be a short-term investment could lengthen by many years if interest rates later rise sharply (resulting in smaller prepayments). Even the shortest classes are not immune to maturity extensions.

The Z Class nonagency CMO is generally the riskiest and should not be approached unless you or your financial adviser can do a careful analysis of the risks. Any Z Class security may be hard to analyze. Called "toxic waste" in the trade, the Z Class will also be more volatile than other mortgage securities, particularly when interest rates are moving rapidly. The Z Class has poor liquidity. Finally, the Z Class may have accounting and tax aspects that are difficult to understand.

It is very difficult to find information about CMOs. Neither the *New York Times* nor the *Wall Street Journal* provides price quotes on these securities.

TAX IMPLICATIONS

The tax treatment of CMOs is complex, and you must consult your tax adviser for specific advice. The portion of the payment treated as interest is subject to federal and state income tax, whereas the portion treated as return of principal or original cost is not subject to tax. However, if you purchase the CMO securities at a discount from their original issue price, part of the discount (the OID) may be taxed as interest income, and some may be taxed as capital gain.

For CMOs held in a brokerage account, your broker will report the tax consequence to you. However, there is a risk that the outside source that's reporting to your brokerage firm may not report the tax consequence of the CMO before March 15, and that might delay you in preparing your income taxes.

PRICING INFORMATION

You can buy CMO securities in minimum amounts of $1,000. Many CMOs are created for institutions, however, and their minimum purchase price is much higher. You might also buy CMO securities by buying a mutual fund or unit trust that invests in CMO securities. Many of these entities have minimum investments of $1,000.

Key Questions to Ask About CMOs

Because of the inherent disadvantages in CMOs, particularly nonagency CMOs, you should proceed with caution and seek answers to the following questions:

◆ Is the CMO an agency CMO? If not, what is its credit rating? Can I lose some of my principal?

◆ Can I get a full prospectus for the CMO? If not, where can I get detailed information on the CMO?

◆ Am I buying the CMO at original issuance or on the secondary market? If on the secondary market, how can I be sure that the price is appropriate?

◆ If the CMO has a trading history in the secondary market, has it met its original assumptions? If not, why not?

◆ What is the exact class of CMO that I'm buying, and what are the exact terms of the payout?

◆ Is the return the CMO will yield compared to that of a comparable Treasury or agency debt security high enough to merit the additional risk of the investment?

◆ What are the tax consequences of the CMO?

◆ Is there an active market in this CMO if I want to sell it?

Keep in mind that what looks like a high yield might be a high return of your principal. Don't make the mistake of spending that principal because you think it's income.

◆ Are these CMOs proprietary products, that is, products that are created by a particular brokerage house? If so, you might receive a relatively low price if you need to sell your securities because the broker that originally sold you the CMO might be the only interested buyer.

CHAPTER 10

MUNICIPAL BONDS

WHEN IT COMES to tax-advantaged investments, it's hard to beat municipal bonds, or munis, as they're popularly called. The American public, particularly those in income tax brackets over 25 percent, has been quick to capitalize on these investments, so much so that the municipal bond sector is the only bond category in which individuals, as opposed to institutions, exert a significant force. However, their strength has been diluted by the activities of hedge funds and arbitrage accounts that have been attracted to the market by the comparatively steep yield curve.[1] It's interesting to note that European institutional investors now see the value of U.S. municipal bonds and are vigorous participants in this $2.1 trillion market.[2] In 2006, munis outperformed taxable bonds. "Not only were the absolute returns strong, but on a risk-adjusted and tax-adjusted basis, they are compelling,"[3] says Paul Disdier, director of municipal securities at Dreyfus.

Munis: The Opaque Market

Despite their popularity and significant tax advantages, municipal bonds remain a mystery to most people. In large part, this is because munis encompass such a broad universe of bonds of varying quality and returns. In other words, if you've seen one muni, you haven't seen them all.

Our goal in this chapter is to render any seemingly mysterious features both intelligible and manageable for investors. We have been buying and selling many millions of dollars worth of munis for our own personal needs and for our clients for the past twenty-five years, and in the process we've made a lot of money for both our bank accounts and theirs. We hope the information in this chapter will help you do the same.

We'll begin with some basics.

◆ **Issuers.** A key feature to understand about munis is that they are issued by states, local governments, or special public entities, such as school districts and sewer authorities. In large part, the creditworthiness and revenue sources of these various issuers determine the financial attractiveness of their bonds.

◆ **Taxes.** Tax free is a relative term when applied to munis. Although most munis are exempt from federal income taxes, some are taxable and some are subject to the alternative minimum tax. Many munis find it impossible to escape the clutches of state or city tax departments. Fortunately, the Bond Market Association has taken a giant step in clarifying this situation by creating the Web site www.investinginbonds.com, which provides helpful information to compare a tax-free yield to the taxable yield. For example, this site can help you determine if a 4.5 percent muni or a 6.5 percent corporate yield is more attractive in tax terms. Later in this chapter you will find a simple formula you can use to help make the comparison yourself. However, the tax law is so complicated that you should seek definitive advice on the precise value of municipal bonds in your particular situation from your personal adviser.

◆ **Redemption dates.** Munis are generally issued in serial form. This practice protects the issuer from paying out a huge lump sum. For example, when issuing $10 million worth of construction bonds, a school district will sell them all at once but have blocks with different redemption dates. In this case, you could buy two blocks of bonds from the same issue, yet each would be redeemed at a different time. This allows you to target the bonds to mature at a time that suits your needs.

◆ **Interest.** Municipal bonds pay interest either semiannually or only when the bond matures. The issuer, in conjunction with the underwriters, decides whether the bonds are issued as paying current interest or as capital-appreciation zero-coupon bonds. If the bonds pay current interest, they can be issued at a discount, at a premium, or at face value.

◆ **Pricing.** Municipal bond pricing is a bit like what goes on in an "Asian bazaar." Although muni bonds all start with a minimum $5,000 face value and are quoted in decimals, market forces quickly take over and raise or lower the purchase price. These prices are no longer difficult to track because muni trades are reported, with a fifteen-minute delay, at www.investinginbonds.com.

◆ **Call features.** Here's a big catch: Some municipal bonds have fixed call options, with a first call usually between five and ten years from their date of issue, after which they're callable with a thirty-day notice. Others are noncallable for their entire lives. Some have a sinking fund. Some revenue bonds have extraordinary calls that are only exercised in specified catastrophic situations. Housing bonds generally can be called at any time due to mortgage prepayment. Any call exposes you to reinvestment risk.

◆ **Form.** Most issues are in book-entry form, and a brokerage house or other custodian must hold them. Some appear as registered bonds with certificates you can hold in your hands.

Risks

We find municipal bonds are not only profitable but also a comparatively low-risk investment. Periodically, the rating agencies issue statements reevaluating the health of various market sectors. Since rated municipal bonds are extremely stable, these reevaluations do not have much impact for the buy-and-hold investor. Fitch Ratings examined data from 1979 to 1999 and found that the overall default rate was less than 1.5 percent on its sample. In a 2003 update of default risks, Fitch's analysts said that the additional data revealed "no meaningful changes" overall. One exception is the higher default rate for environmental facilities as a result of the deregulation of that sector, which had been expected.[4] The ten-year cumulative default rate from 1970 to 2005 for Moody's investment-grade municipals, excluding the safest sectors of general obligation and water and sewer bonds is .2883 percent.[5] Moody's points out that the default rate is so low because municipalities receive extraordinary assistance from federal and state governments, as exhibited in the bailout of Gulf Coast communities in the wake of Hurricane Katrina in 2006. In addition, Moody's notes that the government instituted reforms—such as oversight of troubled municipalities, the implementation of generally accepted accounting principles (GAAP), and tighter controls on investment funds—in response to default risk. No reforms have yet dealt with increasing defaults in health care or affordable housing.[6]

The spectrum of risk for municipal bonds is wide. Some categories are extremely safe: that group includes general obligation bonds, because they require voter approval, and revenue bonds, which have substantial and multiple sources of funds. You can be comfortable buying these categories if they have an A rating or better or if one of the major muni bond insurance companies insures them.

Some munis, however, are extremely risky, with narrow streams of revenue that may not be secure. These bonds will have a low rating or none at all. A nonrated bank may guarantee them. Through the media, you'll learn about problems in an industry, although they may not mention bonds being at risk specifically. For example, note the regular drumbeat of articles on the problems of hospital reimbursements and tobacco settlements. Such "big picture" information tells you that those market sectors represent a weaker area in the muni market. Tread cautiously. In good times, lower-grade bonds may yield only slightly more than better quality paper—maybe 15 or 20 basis points—but the spreads open up in bad times. That means that buyers lower the price they're willing to pay when there is negative economic news, whereas sellers maintain the price at which they're willing to sell.

RISKS IN COMMON

Municipal bonds are subject not only to specific risks particular to certain classes of bonds but also to risks that all muni bonds have in common. Risks common to all munis include the following:

- **Fluctuations in state and federal aid.** Fluctuations in aid have destabilizing effects on municipal budgets and can impair their ability to repay fixed debt. Federal programs often provide only start-up costs or a portion of capital costs. Relying on the traditional last-minute state appropriation to fund its ailing schools and city, Buffalo, for example, was devastated to find the state's cupboard empty at the close of 2001 because money had been diverted to disaster activities as a result of the September 11 attacks. Having already spent the $54 million they were seeking, the city and school district had to drastically cut services to cover the shortfall.[7]

The devastation caused by Hurricane Katrina to New Orleans and surrounding areas, however, did not cause a blip in the municipal credit world because not a single issuer missed interest or principal payment on debt sold by local governments. The federal and state governments stepped in to provide much needed liquidity to the badly damaged area.

◆ **Lack of diversified tax base.** Dependence on a restricted revenue source increases the vulnerability of both general obligation (GO) and revenue bonds. Airline terminals, for example, saw their revenue decline after the September 11 attacks, and as a result, many of the bonds backed by this revenue were downgraded.[8] What's more, bonds issued for limited geographic areas, like specified assessment districts, such as the Los Osos, CA, Community Services District Wastewater Assessment District No.1, can default when politics and mismanagement impede the completion of a project.[9]

◆ **Fiscal imprudence.** Putting political decisions before fiscal responsibility has frequently resulted in rating downgrades or worse. The news in 2006 was that municipalities' pension funds were only 84 percent funded on average, but those deficits were dwarfed by the roughly $700 billion and $1 trillion in unfunded health care and other postemployee benefits that had previously been paid on a pay-as-you-go basis. For the first time, new 2006 Government Accounting Standards Board requirements for pension funds were implemented, requiring municipalities to report both the accrued liabilities and their annual costs for items such as health care.[10] Unfunded pension obligations have burgeoned as our feel-good politicians try to defer the pension fund reckoning until after they've left office. Unions make demands and cities and states cave into the requests, figuring that they can pay salary increases now and defer contributions to the pension plans. In 2006, the San Diego pension fund fiasco resulted in indictments of the mayor and five former pension officials, and that sad story has been repeated in some form nationwide. Pension funds have begun issuing bonds and investing the money in stock in the hope that a rising stock market would bail them out. As of 2006, this strategy was not working. Whether we pay now or pay later, the only source of revenue is the taxpayer.

◆ **Excessive debt.** Debt mountains soaring over the tax base or revenue source is not a good sign. Indications of possible problems include increases in the amount of debt, the requirement of paying off sizable issues in one year, and increases in the amount of annual interest. New York City is a case in point. Following the September 11 attack, the city was put on credit watch after its revenues from taxes throughout the city plunged while its need for money for rebuilding and essential services skyrocketed.

Ratings and Other Security Enhancements

Ratings are a key guide to understanding the creditworthiness of bonds. Ratings enable the most inexperienced to purchase bonds; such investors rely on ratings to protect them from loss. Although the rating companies do not want investors to base their purchase solely on the judgment reflected in the ratings, they are, nevertheless, a very important consideration in the decision-making process. During the period of 1986 to 2006, for example, Standard & Poor's found the AAA-grade bonds quite stable even if they lack enhancements, with 96 percent remaining the same one year later. For bonds rated BBB or lower, the likelihood of their remaining stable one year later was 88 percent.[11]

> All of Standard & Poor's default studies, the present update included, have found a clear correlation between credit quality and default remoteness: the higher the rating the lower the

historical average of default, and vice versa. Over each time span, lower ratings correspond to higher default rates.[12]

The investment attractiveness of munis is frequently gussied up with the addition of insurance. An insured bond, which means the face value and interest payments are guaranteed, is given a higher rating than one that is not insured. This extra coverage that guarantees payment makes munis especially attractive. Sometimes only specific maturities of a bond issue are insured. Insurance, however, costs money, and issuers often seek to do without it if they can obtain an AA rating or better on their own. For example, in December 1994, the Wissahickon School District in Pennsylvania issued $5 million of bonds. The district received an AA rating that made it possible to save the $60,000 that would have been required to purchase bond insurance had it received a lower rating.

However, insurance can be very comforting when disaster strikes. After Hurricane Katrina, investors feared that bonds would default and the insurers would fail to meet their obligations. According to Chip Peebles, a senior vice president at Morgan Keegan & Co. in Memphis, "Bond insurance has proven its worth through this whole thing. It's what we've been telling our customers: if you're insured, rest easy. They are going to pay."[13]

The insurance firms are rated, and their ratings are automatically transferred to the bonds they insure. Thus, a firm receiving an AAA designation from a major rating agency bestows that designation on all the bonds it insures. The firms do not insure bonds willy-nilly. They carefully scrutinize the creditworthiness of each and insure only those they deem likely not to default. These are private and public companies with no government backing—no relation to FDIC, which insures your bank deposits (see **Figure 10.1**). Naturally, the insurance does not cover any premium over face value that you pay for a bond.

Sophisticated buyers always ask what the rating on an insured bond would be without any insurance. It is better to have insured bonds that are of better credit quality than insured weaker credits. If the underlying rating is strong, you can rely on the underlying

FIGURE 10.1

Bond Insurance Companies

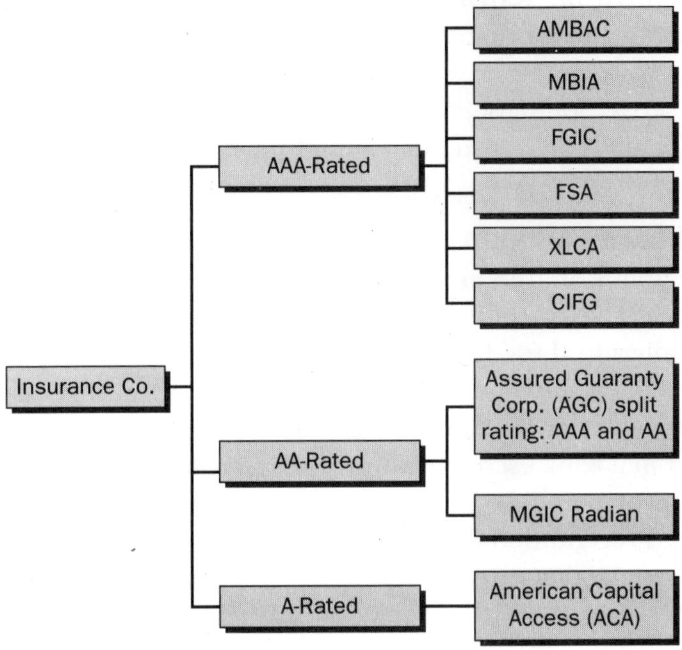

These insurance companies insure more than half of all municipal bonds issued annually. They pay interest and principal on time and when due. The companies have few problems because they insure mostly investment-grade credits, and defaults are very infrequent.

strength of the bond as well as on the insurance for protection. This is called belt-and-suspenders protection.

This is as good a place as any to note that insurance guarantees return of interest and principal, but it does not necessarily protect against a falling price for trading purposes—market risk. When Wall Street heard that a nonprofit bond issuer for student apartment complexes was withdrawing money from operating expenses to build up its reserve fund, the rumor mill cranked into high gear on the fear there might be a technical default. The price of the actively traded bonds plummeted 8 percent in a day.[14] Because these were insured bonds, if there had been a default, the bond insurers would have continued to pay interest and principal when due. Despite this assurance, if you sold the bonds in the bad news market, you would have suffered a loss. For example, after Hurricane Katrina, even some insured bonds sold for 50 basis points more than those outside the region.[15] As they say in the marketplace, there's a moral to the story: Insurance does not make a bad bond good, but it's surely much better than not having it at all. It helps you sleep at night.

SECONDARY MARKET

Some bonds offered in the secondary market are enhanced after issuance. They are either escrowed or prerefunded. Municipalities generally add these features as an approved accounting method for reducing the debt on their balance sheets. In this case, U.S. government bonds, U.S. Agency bonds, or other obligations are placed in a bank escrow account created solely to meet the interest and principal requirements of the outstanding municipal bonds. Prerefunded bonds—popularly dubbed "pre-rees"—are priced to the first call date when they will be redeemed. Although many traders assume escrowed bonds are protected from early calls, several loopholes allow the occasional early recall of these bonds.

INFLATION-LINKED BONDS

A recent addition to municipal bond offerings is an inflation-linked bond that began its infancy in a 1997 sewer revenue deal. Like their cousins Treasury TIPS and corporate inflation-linked bonds, they are linked to the Consumer Price Index. Since they are not well-known, there is not much demand for them if you decide to sell. For a description of how they work, refer to the description of TIPS in chapter 6.

Purchasing Municipal Bonds

You can purchase munis from large all-purpose brokers or through bond boutique houses. The buyer must pay for the bonds three days after the date of purchase, unless they are new issues. A buyer may have a week to a month to pay for the bonds once the sale has been confirmed. The approximate settlement date of the trade is established at the time of sale.

Since most municipals trade infrequently, municipal traders in the secondary market use price matrixes to determine what a bond is worth. Traders see where other similar bonds are trading and price the bonds accordingly. Brokerage houses use the price matrix to evaluate a bond portfolio. This approach is like pricing an existing house for sale by looking at what comparable houses have sold for recently. In an unstable market, those prices can be very misleading.

Taxes on Municipal Bonds

In this book, we broadly group municipal bonds by their taxable status: taxable munis, which are completely taxable even though municipalities issue them; private activity bonds, which are subject to the alternative minimum tax; tax-exempt municipal bonds, which are not subject to federal income tax, and sometimes not to state income tax as well. Included in the tax-exempt group are the major categories of general obligation bonds and revenue bonds.

Because there are taxable munis as well as tax-exempt munis, it's important to be aware of the differences so that you can benefit the most. Taxable munis are just that—fully taxable. Some munis are subject to the alternative minimum tax. If you're not subject to that tax, then you can benefit from the higher yield on these bonds.

But even tax-exempt munis may be subject to some tax, which you should take into account in your financial planning. For example, many states subject bonds issued by other states to state and local taxes. If you live in a high-tax state like New York, it probably would not be tax efficient to purchase bonds issued by another state. This is especially true if you live in New York City, where New York State bonds give you "triple-tax-exemption," and bonds of any other state would give you an exemption only from federal taxes. Some taxpayers are challenging these laws, insisting that they are unconstitutional. We will have to wait for the Supreme Court to decide the ultimate outcome.

Tax-exempt munis can also be subject to some tax if you purchase them in the used bond market at a market discount, meaning for less than face value. According to the The Bond Market Association's Web site, bonds bought at a discount may be subject to capital gain or ordinary income tax depending on whether they are subject to the de minimus rule. Since this explanation is very technical, please visit www.investinginbonds.com, choose the tab on the top labeled "Learn More," then choose "Municipals," and finally "Taxes and Market Discount on Tax-Exempts." You may also want to look at "Taxation of Municipal Bonds." If you are not computer savvy, you can write to us and we will send them to you. Be aware that even your adviser may not fully understand these very complicated rules.

All municipal bonds may be subject to a capital gain or a capital loss when you sell or redeem them. You should consult with your tax adviser to determine whether it might be advantageous for you to sell your bonds before redemption. When the purpose of a sale is to get a tax benefit, this is called a "tax swap," discussed in chapter 19.

Tax-Exempt or Taxable Bonds: How to Decide

How do you determine whether to purchase tax-exempt municipal bonds or taxable bonds for your cash account? The greater your taxable income and the higher your tax bracket, the more likely you will seek shelter in the municipal bond market. The general rule is that when computing the tax benefit, it's assumed that any state and local income tax paid will reduce the amount of federal tax because the state tax is deductible on your federal tax return. There is an exception to this rule: If you're subject to the AMT, you will not receive the benefit of the state taxes as a deduction on your federal income tax return.

If you earned $100,000 in taxable income in 2006 and filed a joint federal income tax return, your 5 percent yield would be equal to a 6.67 percent pretax equivalent return in Florida, where there is no state income tax, and a 7.45 percent pretax equivalent return in New York City, where there are high state and city taxes. If you are subject to the AMT, this calculation would be different.

You need to determine if it is more advantageous for you to purchase taxable bonds or tax-exempt bonds. On the Web site www.investinginbonds.com, you can enter your taxable income from your tax return. The calculator will compute your federal income and state income tax rate, and your total effective rate. Note that the Web site does not take into account any local taxes you might pay nor AMT. Based on those tax rates, the calculator will provide you taxable equivalents for tax-exempt yields beginning at 1 percent for taxpayers filing single or jointly. When you use these rates to compare a tax-exempt bond to a taxable one, be sure to compare apples to apples. The rating quality and call structure should be similar for the comparison to be justified.

You can also use the calculation in **Figure 10.2** to determine your taxable equivalent yield, but the calculator on the Web site is so much easier.

Assume that you were offered a 4 percent tax-exempt bond return and wanted to know how that would compare to a taxable bond return. Convert the yield to a decimal by dividing 4 by 100, thus 4 percent is expressed as .04. Assume that your effective tax rate is 25 percent. Change that to a decimal and subtract it from the number 1 to get the reciprocal of your tax bracket ($1 - .25 = .75$). As indicated in Figure 10.2, divide .04 by .75 and the result is .0533. Turn the decimal back into a percent by multiplying by 100 and you will find that your 4 percent tax-exempt yield is equal to a 5.3 percent taxable return. This is called your tax-equivalent yield. If you were offered a taxable bond of the same quality, with a yield higher than 5.3 percent, you might purchase that in lieu of the tax-exempt bond yielding 4 percent.

FIGURE 10.2

Tax-Exempt Yield = Taxable Yield Equivalency Calculation

$$\text{Taxable equivalent yield} = \frac{\text{Tax-exempt yield}}{(1 - \text{Tax-bracket})}$$

In most states if you purchase bonds sold by an issuer within that state, the interest income is exempt from federal, state, and local income taxes. In those states that have income taxes and an exemption for in-state municipal bond interest, it's usually better to purchase in-state bonds, as in the high-tax states of New York and California.

Some states do not tax the interest income from bonds sold by an out-of-state issuer. In those states, it does not matter whether the issuer is in state or not. The same would apply if your home state taxed all tax-exempt municipal bonds equally, no matter what the state of the issuer.

Taxable Municipal Bonds

Municipalities have issued a large amount—about $60 billion worth—of taxable muni bonds that are subject to federal income tax. These bonds have been on the scene since 1986 and are the result of the federal government's attempt to limit the use of the municipal tax exemption. These bonds are issued for private purposes that are not eligible for tax exemption, such as stadiums funded by gate receipts, investor-led housing, privately operated toll roads, and pension funds. Lease-revenue bonds can also be taxable if the private sector is occupying public space.

ADVANTAGES

Municipal debt subject to federal income tax may be free of taxes in the state of issuance. Pennsylvania residents, for example, don't have to pay state taxes on the interest derived from taxable munis issued in their state. This feature gives taxable municipal debt a leg up when compared to corporate debt or CDs. In addition, taxable munis may be insured, unlike most corporate bonds.

RISKS

Although they're not really a risk, you'll find that taxable munis are not widely available because insurance companies and banks usually buy up the issues. Many brokers do not sell them at all—which leads to the next problem, namely liquidity. Because they are not plentiful, they do not trade well. Do not plan on buying them to resell.

TAX IMPLICATIONS

Taxable munis are subject to federal and, for nonresidents, state and local income taxes. If you purchase bonds issued in your state of residence, they may be exempt from state income taxes.

SPECIAL FEATURES AND TIPS

Insured! That's what a majority of taxable municipal debt is, and that's always a great comfort. Most other taxable bonds are not insured. Like other municipal debt, taxable munis can be prerefunded to their earliest call date. Taxable municipal debt may have fixed calls. When we compare taxable munis to corporate bonds, the risk/reward ratio says buy insured taxable munis whenever possible.

Private Activity Bonds

Private activity is a relatively new designation, describing bonds that are subject to the AMT. One of two aspects of a bond will trigger this designation: (1) more than 10 percent of the proceeds will be directly used for private trade or business, or (2) more than five percent of the proceeds will be loaned to private entities.

Since January 2002, school districts became free to issue private activity bonds for school construction purposes. Unlike general obligation or revenue school bonds, discussed later, these bonds are subject to the AMT. This development reflects the takeover of public schools by private companies, such as Edison Schools, and the addition of charter schools operating within public school districts.

ADVANTAGES

Private activity bonds provide a real benefit to you if you are not subject to the AMT. They provide a higher return because so many muni buyers do not find it advantageous, in tax terms, to purchase them.

RISKS

One very risky category of private activity bond goes by the name of the industrial development bond (IDB). These bonds are issued for economic development and pollution control, including solid waste and resource recovery issues in which private entities are responsible for debt service. Of all the types of bonds issued, these have had the highest default rate in recent history, representing 29 percent of the defaulted debt during the 1990s, according to a Standard & Poor's 2001 study. Along with health care, this sector continued to be risky in 2007.

In a 2003 update of its default study, Fitch found that the cumulative default rate for IDBs between 1980 and 2002 was 14.62 percent, by far the largest category of municipal defaults. However, the report notes that although single-family and multifamily housing have higher-than-average default rates, they also have higher-than-average recovery rates (68.33 percent based on the number of defaults) because of the collateral backing of most of these transactions. This rate is higher than for public corporate bonds, which have a recovery rate of 40 percent.[16] Most of those bonds were unrated. Muni bonds subject to the AMT are less liquid than other tax-exempt munis.

TAX IMPLICATIONS

As noted, private activity bonds may be subject to the AMT.

Tax-Exempt Bonds

The most compelling feature of tax-exempt bonds is their immunity from federal income taxes. However, although tax-exempt bonds are exempt from federal income taxes, they are not uniformly exempt from state and local taxes. Only bonds issued by U.S. territories, namely Guam, the Virgin Islands, and Puerto Rico, are tax-exempt in all states. That's the good news. Unfortunately, they are weak credits, with Puerto Rico the strongest of the three. Using the services of a knowledgeable bond broker or a financial adviser may be the best way to take advantage of the tax breaks inherent in munis.

There are two categories of bonds that finance traditional government responsibilities: general obligation (GO), which are supported by the taxing power of the issuing entity, and revenue bonds, which are supported by specified revenue streams, generally consisting of fees paid by users of the project being financed. Sometimes they are jointly financed.

Until the late twentieth century, GO bonds constituted the majority of issued munis. Then they slowly began to fall out of favor as governments found it politically more acceptable to issue debt backed by dedicated streams of revenues rather than general tax receipts. Furthermore, GO bonds have to be approved by public referendum whereas revenue bonds do not.

It's important to know the kind of tax-exempt bond you may be purchasing. The following are capsule descriptions highlighting the advantages and risks of the many choices offered among GO and revenue bonds. As with all bonds, it's essential to check the rating before you commit to buying these types of munis.

GENERAL OBLIGATION BONDS

Unless specifically limited by law, the full faith and credit and all the financial resources of the issuer back these GO bonds.

Municipalities of any kind and size may issue GO bonds, from the largest state to the smallest township. Bonds backed by the broadest taxing power are called unlimited tax GO bonds (UTGO bonds). Sometimes a specific taxing power supports munis. These are called limited tax GO bonds (LTGO bonds). Voters might support a limited tax designated for the construction of a prison, for example.

An issuer's strength is based on the breadth of its tax base—a diversified economy drawing from many revenue sources—and a low level of debt. States, as opposed to counties and municipalities such as towns and cities, generally feature the broadest tax base and the most flexibility, and this is reflected in the ratings assigned to their bonds. As a result, they tend to be rated AA or better.

School district (SD) bonds, issued for school construction and other educational requirements, employ a variety of revenue sources and may be classified as GO, revenue, or private activity bonds. School district bonds are GO bonds that are generally backed by real estate taxes and frequently state support as well. Pennsylvania and Arkansas, for example, have state intercept programs that direct state aid to bond payments in the event the school district cannot meet its obligations. Texas has a Permanent School Fund based on oil revenues, real estate, stocks, and other investments to back the debt of its schools.

General obligation SD bonds are similar but distinct from Public School Building Authority bonds. The latter are revenue bonds. The authority represents many schools at one time; however, the bonds are usually the responsibility of the specific school for which the debt is issued. They pay the authority, and the authority pays the trustee who directs the paying agent to pay you. The quality of the schools and the price determine whether these bonds are a good buy.

Advantages. Fitch ranked GO bonds among the safest in a 2003 study, with a cumulative default rate of .25 percent during a sixteen- to twenty-three-year period. Moody's has had no material payment default since 1970 on the bonds it has rated.[17] Since these bonds require voter approval, they come with a broad commitment for debt repayment.

State debt sells well because of its sterling track record, no matter what the rating. This means that should you need cash, you should be able to quickly sell a state GO at a reasonable price. State legislatures limit the amount of school district GO bonds that can be issued by raising the bar regulating the percentage of voters who must approve a bond issue. As such, these bonds are generally viewed as very safe debt because they are voter approved and supported by real estate taxes.

Risks. The advent of a recession and the consequent drop in tax revenues from all sources pose one of the greatest risks to GO bonds. In addition, serious restrictions can be put on the ability of legislatures to raise taxes. An issue raised by Hurricane Katrina's devastation of New Orleans and the surrounding area was what happens to GO bonds when there are no longer as many residents to pay taxes and support the debt services. The actual outcome was that a massive influx of funds from all levels of government and private sources supported all the debts. None of the bonds defaulted.

Special Features and Tips. GO bonds tend to be very "clean." That means they do not have many special provisions, and there are no long stories required to describe them. GO bonds generally do not have extraordinary calls. Buy state GO bonds whenever possible unless state politics take the bloom off the rose.

State GO bonds are generally more liquid because they are known quantities and very safe. Given this reputation, there is generally a smaller spread between the asking and selling price. The next best buys are GO school district bonds and those issued by counties, cities, and local governments.

School district GO bonds may be small, bank-qualified (BQ) deals meaning that banks may legally purchase the bonds. The BQ deals are issued for less than $10 million, usually with five-year calls, or they may be larger deals with ten-year call protection.

REVENUE BONDS

Specified revenue streams support revenue bonds. Their rise in popularity over the past few decades has led to the creation of several variations and twists on how entities can package and sell bonds. The issuing entity is the key distinguishing factor among municipal revenue bonds. As such, knowledge about this entity should help you distinguish, for example, among three AAA-rated insured bonds with one supporting a housing development, another a stadium, and the third an electric utility. In good times, it probably won't matter what you buy. However, when unemployment is rising, sales are dropping, and mortgages are defaulting, how you allocate your assets makes a difference. Remember, traders consider the underlying ratings of insured bonds and value them accordingly.

What follows are the various bond packaging approaches now used.

Authorities. These are political entities, originally thought to be above the influence of politics, which are conduits for the issuance of bonds. Huge governmental conglomerates, known as authorities, issue revenue bonds for transportation, water and sewer, housing, and other purposes.

The word *authorities* originated in England, when the creators of the Port of London sought a way to differentiate it from other entities. In the enabling legislation where the powers of the port were granted, the document repeatedly referred to the word *authority*, as in "Authority is hereby given."[18] In the United States, the use of authorities to issue debt began in 1921 with the formation of the Port of New York Authority (later renamed the Port Authority of New York and New Jersey). After 1960, when revenue bonds began to replace GO bonds, authorities became more prevalent.

Bond banks. Bond banks are entities structured by states to lower the cost and to improve the marketability of debt issued by small municipalities. The banks purchase bonds from the municipalities with funds raised through the sale of their own bonds. The local municipalities then repay the bond bank.

Leases. Leases back bonds when a municipality or its agency issues bonds to build a facility and then leases it to a state agency. The rent paid is sufficient to pay off the bonds, at which time the lessee is usually granted the right to purchase the facility for a nominal sum. A possible hitch in this scheme is that the rent payments usually depend on the vagaries of annual appropriations in the state's budget, although facility usage fees may also support the debt. If the money is not appropriated, the bonds will be called. The investor is at risk if the money is not appropriated.

When issued by the state, lease debt is usually rated one notch below that given to the sponsoring state's general-obligation debt. In some states, leaseholders may not have priority status as creditors in bankruptcy situations without taking action in court.[19]

On a cautionary note, in 2002 Kmart filed for bankruptcy, and $215.2 million worth of lease-backed and mortgage-revenue bonds originally issued in 1981 went into default. Although the bonds backed by mortgages were expected to fare better, those backed by leases of closed stores had no value. Since 1986, municipal issuers are no longer permitted to sell bonds backed by retail stores.

In an interesting twist, investment bankers have found the lease structure to be acceptable to some segments of the Muslim community as backing for a bond issue. Under Shari'a law, interest payments are unacceptable. To float a $600 million Malaysian government global bond issue, HSBC holding company structured the deal as follows: Malaysia's federal land commission was to sell the property (including the building housing the Ministry of Finance) to a special-purpose company, which would then lease the property back to the government. Investors in the bond would buy the land from the special-purpose company and were to be paid the lease proceeds every six months. The lease payment was to correspond to the interest rate that London banks use to lend each other money. Upon the bond's maturity, the bond investors would sell the land back to the special-purpose company and get back their principal, while the special-purpose company would sell the land back to the government. Although there was some concern about the interest component of this deal, the structure received approval from Islamic scholars in Malaysia, Dubai, and Bahrain who were "very pragmatic" because they did not want to throttle Islamic Finance at birth.'[20] Large U.S. banks want to be enthusiastic participants in issuing this type of bond, which may result in their being included in the foreign bond category.

Certificates of participation. COPs are debt instruments that are typically backed by lease payments, although they are legally different from bonds. Like leases, COPs require annual appropriations by the state legislature. There have been rare attempts by issuers to renege on these obligations. The most infamous was in AA-rated Orange County, California, when citizens voted down a sales tax increase to pay for losses in an investment portfolio and the county filed for bankruptcy in 1994. In 1989, citizens of Brevard County, Florida, tried to walk away from COPs backing a municipal building because they did not like its location. Eventually, the pressure of the bond market rating and insurance companies led to the refinancing of these bonds.

Special tax districts. These districts provide infrastructure improvements for residential and/or commercial real estate development. In Colorado, they are called special improvement districts. Florida calls them community development districts. In Texas, special sewer districts are called municipal utility districts (MUDs). These districts are based on the idea, "Build it and they will come." Alas, they don't always come. Problems arise more frequently with these kinds of loans than with more traditional munis. Frequent defaults in Texas brought stringent requirements for debt issuance in 1997, resulting in investment-grade ratings for some of these projects and more oversight overall.[21]

TYPES OF REVENUE BONDS

Let's look now at the major types of revenue bonds issued by various entities and consider their advantages and risks.

Airport bonds. See transportation bonds.

Charter school bonds. See education bonds.

Convention and casino bonds. See entertainment industry bonds.

Education bonds. Charter schools are private schools that receive funding from the existing school districts and federal funds through the Department of Education. Each state must separately authorize the establishment of charter schools, and the terms of the charters vary. As of September 2006, forty states and the District of Columbia had authorized charter schools.[22] Unlike public schools, charter schools can go out of business, although such failures are generally the result of poor management or financial disorder.[23]

School construction may be financed through the establishment of a lease issued by an authority or a building corporation. Grants from the federal government, as well as from the school district in which the charter was granted, and student fees provide funding. Charter school bonds may be more likely to attract an investment-grade rating if their main purpose is to relieve overcrowding. Some charter schools have secured insurance for their bond issues as well.

Bonds for colleges and universities are usually issued under the auspices of state authorities. The authorities are pass-through entities enabling the debt to be issued. The security for college and university bonds is based on a variety of income sources. They include government grants and private endowments, revenue from student housing rents, private and federal research contracts, and entertainment, such as sporting events and theatrical productions. The bonds that receive the highest ratings are those issued by larger, well-known institutions that are better endowed and more financially secure than smaller, less influential schools. State-supported schools get funding from state appropriations, student enrollment fees, and other sources.

Advantages. School district bonds are considered the backbone of any conservative portfolio. Buying college and university debt adds diversity to your portfolio. Public higher-education debt was deemed to be the least risky class of debt in this category by Fitch in its 1999 study and confirmed by Moody's own sources in 2006.[24]

Risks. The downside of charter school bonds is that, for the most part, they have no track record. Their survival could be threatened if existing school districts are able to restructure and reform. Fitch points out that the waiting lists at charter schools could evaporate if students were attracted to a public school with a strong athletic program or some other special features. Poor community relations, publicity, governance, leadership, or a negative demographic change could affect the charter school's viability.[25] For these reasons, existing charter school debt is mostly classified as high risk.

For higher-education bonds, in addition to the usual risks such as poor fiscal management and declining enrollment, the primary risk is that the cost of education will outweigh the perceived benefits. In an economic downturn, private colleges with small endowments may have difficulties staying afloat.

Special features and tips. Do not confuse junior college debt with community college debt. The former is private; the latter public. A junior college may or may not be well endowed. Privately funded junior college debt, therefore, may not be as strong a credit as publicly funded community college debt.

Entertainment industry bonds. Municipalities, particularly those in urban areas, find it beneficial to attract tourists and suburban residents to downtown hotels, restaurants, and stores. They do so by sponsoring the construction of convention centers, cultural centers, and sports arenas to draw these outside spenders. Entertainment debt supports such construction activities, and dedicated tax revenues and usage fees fund them.

Advantages. Municipal officials view stadiums, hotels, golf courses, and convention centers as ways to jump-start a depressed area. As such, municipalities are committed to their establishment. For example, in 2006 the Internal Revenue Service approved the financing for two stadiums in New York City issued by the Industrial Development Agency (IDA), wherein payments in lieu of taxes (PILOTs) would back the bonds.[26] Typically, PILOTs are used to help otherwise exempt entities, such as governments, schools, and hospitals, by purchasing land and then allowing the entity to use it at below current tax rates. The New York Mets and Yankees were allowed to issue PILOTs because their payments to the city were to be considered the equivalent of taxes.[27]

Risks. Declines in economic activity can adversely affect both dedicated taxes (such as hotel occupancy taxes) and usage-fee revenues. The problem may be that the revenue projections were overly optimistic. The Sheraton Grand Hotel in Sacramento had an above-average industry occupancy rate and room rate. However, the actual room rate was $122.86, whereas the projected room rate was $145, so the city did not have enough funds to pay for the first debt-obligation payment due in 2006. [28] Furthermore, this hotel was supposed to spur use of the adjacent convention center, which it did not. According to Heywood Sanders, a professor in the department of public administration at the University of Texas at San Antonio, the convention center business is declining, and adjacent hotels are not a catalyst for greater use.[29] Yet public officials still follow the motto: "Build it and they will come."

Tribal casino debt has its own unique issues. Since Native American tribes are sovereign countries that exist within the United States, it is not clear if a debt can be collected if there is a dispute. Many tribal governments are in disarray, and the reservations are economically impoverished. Not all tribal debt is of the same caliber. Many states have been crafting agreements with tribal governments to permit the opening of casinos.[30]

Special features and tips. We don't like to purchase bonds that are issued to fund anything not essential to a community. Although you may consider attending a sporting event or playing golf essential when times are good, in hard times that may not be the case. Insurance is highly advisable when considering investing in entertainment deals because you can't judge the likelihood of their ongoing success.

Health care and hospital bonds. Hospitals have a continual need to upgrade facilities and buy new equipment. Bonds to finance many of these improvements are issued through state health authorities, which act as financing conduits for hospitals as well as for nursing homes and the relatively new continuing-care retirement communities (CCRCs). Bonds for the latter, which are residences for elderly citizens who require some assistance, are frequently not rated. According to Fitch, it is expected that the financial stability of this sector will remain stable as the baby boomers purchase these services. The older CCRCs will have to upgrade and expand to meet the competition, placing a drag on profits.[31] Nursing home bonds also are frequently nonrated. Whether or not the bonds are rated, the issuing authorities assume no responsibility for the repayment of their issues. The responsibility rests with the health care facilities for which the bonds were issued.

Advantages. Comparatively higher yield is the advantage of purchasing CCRCs and nursing home bonds, especially when they are unrated. Typically, hospital bonds yield more than similarly rated GO bonds.

Risks. The financial health of hospitals has stabilized after reeling under the onslaught of rising costs and restricted managed-care payments. However, health care bonds are viewed as risky. In the event of a default, hospitals are likely to be liquidated or sold, resulting in a 75 percent to a 100 percent loss in bond value.[32] In Standard & Poor's study of defaults in the 1990s, it was primarily the nonrated bonds in this sector that defaulted, with nursing home bonds defaulting more frequently than any other type. Insurance companies paid if the bonds were insured. If you're considering buying nonrated bonds, it is essential to know a good deal about the issuer.

Special features and tips. Hospital bonds are subject to extraordinary calls in addition to regular calls. They also may have sinking funds. The higher yields resulting from downgrades can make hospital bonds attractive for junk bond buyers. Insurance may reduce some of their characteristic risk, but remember: insurance does not make a bad bond good.

The long-term financial viability of CCRCs remains to be proven, and bonds for their purposes are relegated to the high-yield market. CCRCs supported by financially solvent religious and nonprofit institutions are more attractive than those without such backing.

Highway bonds. See transportation bonds.

Housing bonds. Municipal housing bonds support the creation of multifamily or individual housing units for the poor and elderly. There are three kinds, each having a different purpose and special security provisions. All are managed through state and local housing finance agencies.

◆ State housing agencies float bonds for builders of multiunit apartment buildings for the elderly. Some of these have federal insurance and are very creditworthy. The others are difficult to evaluate.
◆ State housing finance agencies sell bonds to secure funds for the purchase of mostly single-family mortgages from banking institutions. The mortgage revenue and a variety of insurance policies back these bonds.
◆ Local housing authority bonds support the development of multiunit apartment buildings and are secured by comprehensive rent subsidy packages.

Underlying mortgages fund housing bonds, and the federal government may insure or subsidize these bonds. Federally insured housing bonds are rated AA or AAA, depending on the extent of the coverage provided by the FHA or the VA. HUD subsidizes rent payments for qualified individuals. Some housing bonds also carry a moral obligation pledge from the state that issues them. In addition, there may be insurance on the properties in case they are damaged or destroyed and insurance on the contractors for proper performance in construction.

Although single-family mortgage bonds are quite safe from default, they have a very high probability of being called away early. "Supersinkers" are single-family mortgage-revenue bonds with maturities between twenty and thirty years that will probably be redeemed within ten years. A sharp drop in interest rates could result in bond calls after a year. In extreme cases, this could result in a cash shortfall if the revenue fund did not appreciate sufficiently to pay the costs of bond issuance.

Advantages. Housing bonds for single-family homes tend to have higher yields than other munis. Default risk is minimized on housing bonds that carry federal support and other kinds of insurance. State housing authorities have rigorous underwriting standards. Many multifamily housing deals are backed by federal insurance, carry an A to AA rating, and have additional private insurance as well.

Risks. Although federal rent subsidies provide a reliable stream of income supporting multifamily housing bonds, HUD reserves the right to stop paying if the rental unit is vacant for more than a year or if the housing administration does not follow HUD rules. Public Housing Authority bonds issued in anticipation of federal payments from HUD run the risk that the funds to pay the debt service will not be appropriated in sufficient amounts. However, expecting that this might be a problem, the issuer can build in safeguards. The rating should reflect them.

Housing bonds are subject to unpredictable, so-called extraordinary calls that can occur any time after the bonds are issued. Some bonds might be called from unexpended proceeds. In this case, the issuer would be unable to use all the money that the bond issue raised. Bonds can also be called because the mortgages backing the bonds have been retired. When interest rates are declining, calls tend to increase with home refinancing activity.

Special features and tips. Cautious buyers should purchase single-family mortgage revenue bonds at or near par due to the likelihood that they will be called away early through an extraordinary call. For this reason, they have limited upside price potential. However, if you purchase them at a discount and they are called early, you may have an unexpected gain. Your gain may be subject to ordinary income tax. Multifamily bonds have a much lower prepayment risk than single-family housing bonds.

Along with tax-exempt bonds, housing agencies may issue some taxable debt that is subject to the AMT. These bonds have higher yields than bonds not subject to this tax.

Supersinkers and high-coupon housing bonds are attractive to investors who prefer the high yield of long-term bonds and are willing to deal with unpredictable early calls. When prepayments slow because of rising interest rates, housing bonds with high coupons can be good performers as the ample cash flow continues for a longer period of time. In the first half of 2005, prepayments varied from one state to another, with the West having the highest rate of prepayment, followed by the Mid-Atlantic and New England regions. Florida was the fourth fastest of all states in the nation, while the South in general had the slowest prepayment speed.[33]

Nursing home bonds. See health care and hospital bonds.

Public power bonds. Public power bonds were initially floated to subsidize electrification of underdeveloped rural areas of the country. The use of municipal bonds for this purpose began in the 1930s in California, Nebraska, and the Northwest. The first authority that grew out of federal legislation aimed to harness the Columbia River to produce hydroelectric power.[34] One of the major bond defaults of the twentieth century occurred when the Washington Public Power Supply System undertook the construction of five nuclear power plants to supplement that power. Municipal electric utilities have thrived since the turbulence of deregulation derailed some of the investor-owned utilities in 2002.

Advantages. Formerly included in every widow and orphan portfolio, electric utility bonds fund a basic need to supply heat, cooling, and light for homes and businesses. Some very well-managed utilities issue debt; however, one needs to pick and choose carefully today to find a power bond with both an attractive yield and protection against default.

Risks. A power provider must comply with federal and state regulations, restricting its flexibility. Deregulation of the power industry in California, for example, led to runaway costs for the utilities while limiting the prices charged to consumers. California Edison teetered on the brink, and Pacific Gas and Electric declared bankruptcy. Although all muni bonds are subject to changes in political climates, the years 2000 and 2001 highlighted the particular vulnerability of investor-owned public power bonds to this risk factor.

Special features and tips. Like other revenue bonds, utility bonds are subject to extraordinary calls that could result in their being called away early.

Tobacco bonds. An arrangement between R.J. Reynolds Tobacco Co., Philip Morris Inc., and Brown and Williamson Tobacco Corp. and forty-six states established by a master settlement agreement has given those states the right to payments from tobacco profits for twenty-five years. The process of issuing bonds to access the use of the anticipated revenue is called securitization. States depend on the revenues produced by this arrangement, forming uneasy bedfellows.

In August 2006, a federal judge found that the tobacco companies violated federal racketeering laws, ordered them to admit that they had lied about the hazards of smoking, and ruled that they must warn consumers that cigarettes are addictive. The judge did not penalize the tobacco companies for past actions, thus, protecting the outstanding municipal bonds backed by tobacco revenues.

Tobacco bonds typically have a Baa3/BBB rating. Their value has fluctuated widely as suits against the tobacco companies have alternatively been won and lost. But not all tobacco bonds are the same. Only tobacco proceeds or tobacco proceeds mixed with other revenue sources may secure the debt service. Arkansas, for example, has issued revenue bonds with only 5 percent of the proceeds coming from tobacco.[35]

Advantages. There are two advantages of purchasing tobacco bonds: They tend to offer higher yields than other munis, and they also provide an element of diversification to a bond portfolio. According to the Government Accountability Office, forty-six states that were part of the tobacco settlement received $5.8 billion in 2005, about a third of which supported health-related programs. The remainder supported debt repayment or was added to the general fund of the states.

Risks. Although the current stream of income from tobacco is quite good, revenue will decline if and when people stop smoking. The revenue could also be undermined if huge punitive damages are awarded to plaintiffs in malpractice suits. Given the special nature of these bonds, they are not as liquid as other types of munis. If you are a buy-and-hold investor, that is not a problem.

Special features and tips. Authorities were created specifically to issue the large deals backed only by the tobacco revenue, passing on the risk and the reward to you. You have to decide if you're being compensated well enough for that transfer of risk with the extra 30 to 40 basis points you're paid for buying tobacco bonds. Tobacco bonds may be structured more like mortgage bonds, rather than straight debt. Some bonds have "turbocharged" redemption provisions so they are best purchased at par or at a discount.

Transportation bonds. Transportation authorities engage in just about every aspect of bringing goods and services into and out of a region. Some even include real estate activities among their portfolios. Transportation bonds include bonds issued for ports, roads, trains and buses, and airports. A key factor in considering transportation bonds is not the name of the authority issuing them but rather what entity is paying for them. Highway revenue bonds, for example, are of two types: toll road bonds and public highway improvement bonds. Earmarked funds from gasoline taxes, automobile registration payments, and driver license fees finance public highway improvement bonds. However, as fuel efficiency reduces the amount of gasoline used, the taxes collected for the sale of fuel are reduced. In addition, the historical reluctance to increase taxes or to have the tax keep pace with inflation has put pressure on highway trust funds to meet ever-burgeoning needs, according to Standard & Poor's.[36]

As a result, the transportation arena has been forming public/private partnerships to finance the construction, operation, and maintenance of our nation's crumbling infrastructure. These partnerships will change the way future revenues are predicted and will add the complication of payment to equity investors as well as debt repayment.[37] For the states, it is a way of "outsourcing political will," said Representative Peter DeFazio (D-Oregon) in June 2006, expressing concern about the Indiana toll road privatization. However, in its defense, Governor Mitch Daniels said that tolls had not been raised since 1985 and that the privatization would enable Indiana to finance road improvements that it otherwise could not afford.[38] The road was privatized later in 2006, and other states are considering following suit.

A recent source of funds available to states for accelerating road and bridge construction is from grant revenue anticipation notes, an expectation of payments from federal grants. These so-called "Garvees" are used in conjunction with other sources of bond payments because federal transportation funds used to back such debt are subject to reauthorization by Congress every six years. As a result, the shorter maturity debt in such issues is viewed more favorably from a credit perspective.[39]

Trains and buses rely on usage fees to fund their bonds, although federal grants are occasionally available for such purposes. One current federal program, dubbed Bus Rapid Transit, supports the construction of bus-only lanes, traffic lights that stay green as a bus approaches, and bus-boarding platforms, among other ideas.

Three different sources of revenue finance airport bonds: (1) ticket fees paid by passengers, (2) a wide number of airport usage fees (including flight fees paid by airlines for air travel; concession fees paid by shops, stands, and restaurants; parking fees; and fueling fees), and (3) lease income from the use of hangars or terminals. The wave of airline bankruptcies has tested the structure of the leases in the bond covenants. At the Denver airport, the bonds were tied to a true lease, while at three other airports the leases were recharacterized as loans or financings, letting the airlines off the hook for their special-facility revenue debt in 2006.[40] This is expected to increase the cost of financing and raise the yields on such debt.

Advantages. Transportation bonds represent the full range of credit quality, from established, broad-based issuers and solid debt coverage at one end to some of the more vulnerable issuers with lower collateralization and coverage on the other. Investors can pick up some high yields here, but you always have to balance the yields with their risk.

Risks. Downgrade and default are possible for transportation bonds funded by revenues. For example, in 2007 bankrupt Delta Airlines planned to eliminate "at least $1.2 billion of its $1.7 billion of tax-exempt debt. Holders of unsecured claims, the category that some special facilities revenue bonds will fall into, would receive a payout of between 63 and 80 percent under the plan."[41]

Although reliable streams of income support most revenue bonds, the issuers may be overtaken by adverse political actions and events beyond their control. Since the destruction of the World Trade Center on September 11, 2001, the realization that the United States may be a target of Islamic terrorists has cast a cloud on all transportation issues. Security has been added to protect our ports, airports, and other transportation conduits, but the possibility of terrorist acts, which always existed, has become more immediate.

Special features and tips. Owners of struggling toll road bonds can see the value of their holdings rebound if the toll road is leased to a private entity. This was the case in the Richmond, Virginia, area. "Pocahontas Parkway Association senior bonds traded as low as 64 cents on the dollar, rebounding to 104, as investors anticipated the possible defeasance of the bonds," said Philip Villaluz, vice president for municipal research at Merrill Lynch & Co.[42] The low bond price can be ex*plain*ed by a 2002 study by Robert Muller of J.P. Morgan Securities, which examined toll road issuance and concluded that "more than half of all 'project finance type' [start-up toll road] feasibility studies overestimate their [revenue] forecasts by a substantial margin."[43]

Transportation bonds usually have extraordinary calls that can be exercised in the event of a catastrophe. Sometimes they have stated calls and sinking funds. When considering transportation issues, ask yourself if you would use the services being provided by the issuer and backed by the bonds. Ask also if there are any alternative providers of the same service in the same area.

Water and sewer bonds. Water and sewers are essential to civilized living, and the entities that provide these services have little trouble collecting bills. In addition to usage fees, water and sewer districts charge assessment fees to determine the placement of the sewers and connecting fees that are collected before the sewers are built. The water and sewer bonds issued to support these activities are generally regarded as being among the safest municipal investments, a finding confirmed by Fitch in its 1999 study and reaffirmed in 2003. Moody's also affirmed this finding in 2006.[44] Standard & Poor's notes that "the general governmental sectors of tax-secured [bonds] and utilities are the most stable of all [municipal bond] sectors."[45] A municipality, or in the case of the wastewater bonds municipalities within a given area, generally issues these bonds. An authority, a water conservancy district, or a state bond bank may also issue bonds. Bonds issued through a state bond bank may carry a moral obligation pledge protecting cash flow against loan defaults. When the funding source is the federal government, the money is channeled into a state infrastructure bank, and the municipal project is subject to state and federal guidelines.

Advantages. Considered, as was noted, among the safest of municipal investments, water and sewer bonds are often double-barreled. The payment sources for the bonds are twofold: the revenue from water usage and a pledge of the municipality's tax revenue. Such double-barreled bonds may be sold as general-obligation bonds or, with a more restricted revenue source, as limited-tax general-obligation bonds.

Risks. These bonds come with a wide range of ratings, each determined by how established an area is and the solvency of customers who will pay for the bonds. As with other types of bonds, start-up situations tend to be riskier than bonds floated for repairs of established systems. Texas MUDs are special taxing districts that often sell nonrated debt in order to jump-start a development project.

Default potential is higher in areas where utilities are not allowed to discontinue service even in the event of nonpayment of bills. Problems might also arise if bonds financed an existing antiquated system, in that more money than initially projected might be required to repair it. Furthermore, utilities must provide for water even in the face of prolonged drought conditions.

Note that the introduction of conservation programs can cause a decline in revenue. Changes in legislation can also negatively affect water revenue if payments for purchased water are somehow restricted. For example, a Utah state senator proposed legislation in 2001 that would prevent the use of property tax revenue for the repayment of water and sewer bonds, reasoning that the tax lowered the cost of water, thus, encouraging careless consumption. If that legislation had passed, it would have undermined the credit quality of future water and sewer bond issues in the state. Sometimes legislation undermining rates causes problems. A 2006 decision in California agreed that Proposition 218 passed in 1996 gave voters the right to petition for a ballot initiative to lower the rates of a public water district. However, the water agency had the right to raise other fees or create new fees so they are not particularly concerned it will be a problem.

Special tips and features. Traders value water bonds more than sewer bonds, and sewer bonds more than wastewater bonds, although they may be offered to you at the same yield. MUDs with investment-grade ratings must compete with other similarly rated bonds, but buyers are wary because of the unsavory history of defaults on unrated paper. That results in higher yields for those willing to take the risk.[46]

Checking Prices on Municipal Bonds

Using www.investinginbonds.com for municipals bonds is fairly easy once you know your way around. Click on "Municipal Markets-at-a-Glance" and choose either today's or yesterday's prices. You can choose a state of issuance and then sort the bonds by maturity, issuer, CUSIP, trade time, price, or yield. This is helpful if you are seeking general market conditions. **Figure 10.3** presents a view of a municipal bond screen with only one bond included.

In Figure 10.3, the column on the left gives you the Standard & Poor's, Moody's, and Fitch ratings. "N/R" means the bond is not rated. In the next column, you're given the issuer, then the CUSIP, and finally for revenue bonds you're given a sector, like hospitals or

FIGURE 10.3

Municipal Bond Screen

1 2 3 4 5 6 7 8 9 ...

Ratings ins.	Issuer CUSIP Sector/ Subsector	ST	Coupon Maturity	Call dates
N/R S AAA M AAA F Insured	WEST HEMPSTEAD NY UN FREE SCH DIST 953259EV6	NY	4.375 03/01/2019	03/01/2015

Source: www.investing in bonds.com. Courtesy of SIFMA.

transportation, so you'll know the purpose for which the bonds were issued. Click on the highlighted CUSIP, and you'll get more information about the bonds. ST tells you the issuing state. Coupon and maturity are next, followed by the call date and price. The site gives you the high and low trade for the day, although it's not unusual for there to be no trades or only one. Then you see the high and low yield, in this case 4 percent. In this example, there was one trade for $150,000. Then you are told that this security is nontaxable, a bond and book-entry only. If there is any more information, it would appear in the next column. You can see the history of yesterday's trades only or a full history. You can also view the prospectus by clicking on "Statement" which appears in blue, like the other links do.

If you want to check out a specific offering, it's most helpful to put in the CUSIP at the bottom of the screen under bond history. When you enter the CUSIP, the name of the bond will appear, and you can click on the number of trades in the right corner and see a complete trading history for that particular bond. This screen will tell you the trade date and time, price, yield, amount traded, and the type of trade. This site conveys much more information than you'll find about corporate bonds. The information in **Figure 10.4** shows trade data for one bond issue. Like most munis, this bond trades infrequently. There was one sale to a customer in May and no other trades until August. On August 25, there were two interdealer trades

Call prices	Price: High Low	Yield: High Low	Volume # of trades	Notes	More info
100.000	102.651	4.000	150K	Nontaxable	Yesterday
	102.651	4.000	1 trade	Bond	Full history
				Book-entry only	Statement

FIGURE 10.4

Municipal Bond Trade Data

Trade Date Time	Price	Yield	Amount	Type of Trade
09/07/2006 15:08:24	100.000	3.999	10K	Sale to customer
08/25/2006 14:47:16	97.780	4.242	10K	Purchase from customer
08/25/2006 14:46:26	97.780		10K	Interdealer
08/25/2006 14:45:26	98.280		10K	Interdealer
05/05/2006 16:15:29	93.625	4.700	5K	Sale to customer

Source: www.investing in bonds.com. Courtesy of SIFMA.

(trades between dealers) and one dealer purchase from a customer. (Yields are not shown for interdealer trades.) About two weeks later, there was a sale to a customer. Assuming that one of these represented dealers sold the ten bonds, there was about a 2 percent spread between the dealer's purchase and sale prices. When the trades are current, it gives you an idea of what might be a reasonable price and yield if the market has not moved dramatically.

Key Questions to Ask About Municipal Bonds

- What is the rating?
- Who is the insurer? What is the underlying rating?
- Is there any negative information about the bonds I should consider?
- If the bonds are premium bonds, what is the yield-to-worst?
- If the bonds are discount bonds, what is the after-tax yield?
- If the issue is outside your home state, what is the after-tax yield?
- Are these bonds subject to the AMT?

Chapter Notes

1. Matthew Posner, "Households Keep Muni Holdings Lead With Hedge Funds' Help," *The Bond Buyer* online, December 13, 2006.

2. Jacob Fine, "Achtung, Munis: Fitch Ratings," *The Bond Buyer* online, October 14, 2003.

3. Virginia Munger Kahn, "Good Times Keep Rolling for Municipal Bonds," *New York Times,* October 8, 2006, BU 28.

4. David T. Litvack and Mike McDermott, "Municipal Default Risk Revisited," FitchRatings.com, June 23, 2003, 1.

5. Naomi Richman and Bart Ossterveld, Moody's Public Finance Credit Committee, "Mapping of Moody's U.S. Municipal Bond Rating Scale to Moody's Corporate Rating Scale and Assignment of Corporate Equivalent Ratings to Municipal Obligations," Moody's Investors Service, June 2006, 4.

6. Ibid., 2.

7. Ryan McKaig, "Desperation Rears Head in New York," *The Bond Buyer,* October 12, 2001, 1, 39.

8. "Moody's Downgrades JFK Terminal Debt," *The Bond Buyer,* October 8, 2001, 37.

9. Jackie Cohen, "California Water District Downgraded after Declaring Bankruptcy," *The Bond Buyer* online, September 1, 2006.

10. Lynn Hume, "Panelists Warn of 'OPEB Tsunami,' Urge Early Liability Disclosure." *The Bond Buyer* online, July 1, 2006. OPEB stands for other postemployee benefits.

11. Colleen Woodell and James Weimken, "U.S. Rating Transitions and Defaults, 1986–2006," 3. Retrieved from www.standardandpoors.com/ratingsdirect.

12. Ibid., 3.

13. Jacob Fine, "Munis Hold Their Ground," *The Bond Buyer* Online, September 1, 2006.

14. Shelly Sigo, "Florida Issuer Details Cash-Flow Trouble of $158m Deal," Thomson Financial, December 14, 2001. Retrieved from www.TM3.com.

15. Fine., Note 13.

16. Litvack and McDermott, 8.

17. Richman and Ossterveld, 4.

18. Robert Lamb and Stephen P. Rappaport, *Municipal Bonds* (New York: McGraw-Hill, 1987), 85.

19. Lynn Hume, "NFMA Releases Final GO Disclosure Guidelines for Issuers," *The Bond Buyer* online, December 7, 2001.

20. Philip Day and S. Jayasankaran, "Learning Islamic Finance," *Wall Street Journal,* March 12, 2003, C5.

21. "Rating Guidelines for Texas Municipal Utility Districts," Fitch Research, August 21, 1997, 1.

22. Elizabeth Genco, Program Support Manager, National Association of Charter School Authorizers, e-mail, January 10, 2007.

23. David G. Hitchcock, "Public Finance Criteria: Charter Schools," Standard & Poor's, November 13, 2002, 2.

24. Moody's U.S. Municipal Bond Rating Scale, November 2002, 5.

25. Elizabeth Albanese, "Fitch Calls Its Charter School Ratings More 'Attentive' Than Others," *The Bond Buyer,* May 31, 2001, 3.

26. No Author, "N.Y.C. Ballpark PILOTs Look, Act Like Taxes," *The Bond Buyer* online, August 7, 2006.

27. Ibid.

28. Joe Mysak, "Hotels Now Part of Convention Center Space Race," Bloomberg .com, April 13, 2005.

29. Ibid.

30. Rochelle Williams, "Looking beyond Gambling: California Tribes Get Boost from Judge's Ruling," *The Bond Buyer* online, August 2, 2002.

31. Christine Albano, "Fitch: Despite Challenges, Prognosis for CCRCs Looks Positive," *The Bond Buyer* online, March 29, 2006.

32. Helen Chang, "Heavy Health Care Exposure Means Rating Risk, S&P Says," *The Bond Buyer* online, February 4, 2005.

33. Matthew Vodum, "Report: For High-Premium Single Family Revenue Bonds, Now Is the Time to Buy," *The Bond Buyer* online, August 22, 2005.

34. Lamb and Rappaport, 91.

35. Elizabeth Albanese, "Arkansas to Sell $60 Million Tobacco Deal Next Week," *The Bond Buyer,* August 30, 2001, 4.

36. Humberto Sanchez, "Public-Private Deals Testing Traditional Credit Issues, S&P Says," *The Bond Buyer* online, April 8, 2005.

37. Ibid.

38. Humberto Sanchez, "Corporate Road Warriors on the Move," *The Bond Buyer* online, June 19, 2006.

39. Tedra DeSue, "Georgia Eyes $4.5B of Debt for Highways," *The Bond Buyer* online, April 4, 2004.

40. Yvette Shields, "Judge Rules in United's Favor in O'Hare Case," *The Bond Buyer* online, July 26, 2006.

41. Yvette Shields, "Delta, Trustee Continue to Negotiate Dropping Leases," *The Bond Buyer* online, January 12, 2007.

42. Rich Saskal, "Toll Road Public-Private Partnerships Could Be Good Play for Muni Investors," *The Bond Buyer* online, May 8, 2006.

43. Joe Mysak, "Experts Aren't Paid to Write Infeasibility Studies," Bloomberg News online, May 23, 2002.

44. Moody's Public Finance Credit Committee, 3.

45. Standard & Poor's, "U.S. Rating Transitions and Defaults, 1986–2006," 3.

46. Richard Williamson, "Investors, Analysts Warm to a Texas Specialty: MUD Bonds," *The Bond Buyer* online, May 31, 2004.

CHAPTER 11

CORPORATE BONDS

AT $2.2 TRILLION in outstanding debt, the corporate bond market is huge. Bought by institutions and individuals because of their high yield, corporate bonds span the spectrum of maturities and finance just about every aspect of the economy. As such, their credit ratings range from good-as-gold AAA to down-and-out junk. Corporate bonds are generally sold to institutions in very large quantities, although there are certain kinds that are targeted for retail.

The Big Picture

Good-as-gold corporate bonds are hard to find. According to Kamalesh Rao of Moody's Investors Service, the number of AAA-rated companies has shrunk over the past thirty years.[1] In the late 1970s, fifty-eight companies had AAA ratings and accounted for 25 percent of corporate debt. In 2001, only nine had the AAA rating, and those companies accounted for only 6.2 percent of corporate debt. The stellar nine are now the stellar five, consisting of two corporate descendants of 1970s AAA-rated companies—General Electric and ExxonMobil—and three newcomers rated AAA by both Moody's and Standard & Poors—Johnson & Johnson, Pfizer, and United Parcel Service (UPS). This list keeps changing.

RATINGS

The higher a bond's rating, the less you're supposed to worry about a corporate bankruptcy and vice versa. With the collapse of Enron in 2001, the ratings assigned by agencies came under increased scrutiny. Moody's Investors Service responded to the critical nature of the government scrutiny by sending out a request for information about off-balance-sheet financial arrangements to about 4,200 companies in January 2002. The last time Moody's Investors Service took this action was in 1994, when Orange County, California, filed for bankruptcy.

With a dearth of AAA-rated companies, credit protections have become increasingly important. Secured bonds offer such protections because they have a first claim on specific assets if the corporation is unable to pay. Examples of secured bonds are mortgage bonds, collateral trust bonds, and equipment trust certificates. If you see one of these names in the title of a bond, you know that you have a secured bond. For example, a description might read: "Duke Power, First Mortgage Bonds." This means that the issuer, utility company Duke Power, issued a bond that is secured by a first mortgage on certain of its property. Collateral trust bonds are secured by securities of other companies (usually subsidiaries) owned by the company issuing the bonds. Equipment trust certificates are liens against the rolling stock of railroads or the airplanes owned by an airline company.

Guarantees are also a form of credit protection. Although usually featured on munis, they are sometimes on corporate bonds as well. The guarantees often appear as letters of credit (LOC), which are credit guarantees issued by banks. LOCs provide funds to pay off the corporate bond issue should the corporation default. Another form of a guarantee is when a parent company guarantees the bonds of one of its subsidiaries. Some corporate bonds are insured by the companies that also insure municipal bonds.

Unsecured bonds are known as debentures and are protected only by the full faith and credit of the company. Debentures can receive high bond ratings if the issuing company is financially strong. Bonds with a lesser claim on assets are called "subordinated debentures."

To protect their creditability and to inform investors, rating agencies have developed "watch lists" that indicate when a company's rating might be either raised or lowered. Moody's Investors Service provides its list on its Web site, www.moodys.com. You can enter the name of the bond, or identify it by CUSIP. The Securities and Exchange Commission has the most current information from company filings on its Web site, www.sec.gov/edgar/quickedgar.htm.

INTEREST RATES

Although the overwhelming majority of corporate bonds feature a fixed interest rate, some are offered with variable rates. Long featured in European bonds, variable rates have been attached to U.S. securities only since the 1970s. The rates are tied to some other measure, usually a Treasury bond rate or the London interbank offered rate (Libor) and are adjusted at specified intervals. They're called floating-rate notes (FRNs). As with other debt instruments, corporate bonds may be sold as zero-coupon bonds, which means they pay no interest until maturity.

TAXATION

The taxation of corporate bonds is very complicated, and you should consult your tax adviser on the specifics. However, some general points apply if the bonds are not held in a tax-sheltered retirement account:

◆ The interest you receive on corporate bonds is generally subject to federal and state income tax at ordinary income tax rates. If you own zero-coupon bonds, you may have to report phantom income each year even if you receive no current interest.

◆ If you sell your bonds or redeem them at their due date, usually you must report either a short-term or long-term capital gain or loss on your federal and state income tax returns.

◆ If you buy a corporate bond at a premium (that is, more than face value), you can generally amortize the premium over the life of the bond. This means that you can deduct a piece of the premium each year as an interest deduction on your income tax returns.

Key Categories of Corporate Bonds

There are two major indexes, one compiled by Dow Jones and the other by Lehman Brothers, that track corporate bonds, and each has its own variation on how to categorize the bonds. The categories help to clarify the type of risk you take when you buy corporate bonds. Bond sectors are of more than theoretical interest to bond buyers because bad news affecting one issuer in a sector can affect all other bonds within the sector.

Following Lehman's example, we cut the corporate universe into financials, industrials (under which transportation falls), utilities, Yankee bonds, and emerging-market bonds.

◆ **Financial institutions.** Included here are banks, finance companies, brokerage houses, insurance companies, real estate investment trusts (REITs), and other related firms. In some classifications, banks are separated from other financial companies because they do not always move in tandem.

◆ **Industrials.** This is a catchall category, including manufacturing, mining, retail, and service-related companies. Transportation companies are also included. Their creditworthiness has been negatively affected by deregulation and new technologies. Railroad bonds were at one time some of the safest bonds, but their attractiveness has increasingly eroded. Airlines are one of the latest industries to suffer the effects of government deregulation, and the new freedom provides management the opportunity to make horrendous mistakes. Many airlines passed through bankruptcy between 2002 and 2006.

◆ **Utilities.** This category, which includes telephone and communications companies, gas distribution and transmission companies, water companies, and electric power companies, is reeling under the effects of deregulation. Historically considered stable investments, utilities have been forced from cozy, monopolistic arenas into free-market environments that are not always conducive to their well-being. Under the Telecom Act of 1996, for example, AT&T was left with the long-distance business and the Baby Bells were given aegis over local telephone calling. A combination of increased competition in the long-distance business and imprudent investments in cable, wireless, and Internet businesses resulted in AT&T assuming a staggering $36.5 billion of debt.[2] By 2006, AT&T was dismembered and sold. We still see the AT&T name because it's used by one of the purchasing companies.

◆ **Yankee bonds.** These are investment-grade foreign bonds that are dollar denominated, thereby eliminating the currency risk. Yankee bonds are registered with the SEC and issued and traded in the United States. Included in this category are bonds issued by Canadian provinces and utilities; supranational agencies, like the World Bank; sovereign bonds, such as bonds issued by Australia and Sweden; and, to a lesser extent, corporate bonds.

Yankee bonds may yield more than similarly rated U.S. corporate bonds due to investors' lack of familiarity with the credit. They may also be issued with shorter maturities and better call protection, making them particularly attractive to U.S. and foreign buyers of dollar-denominated bonds.

◆ **Emerging-market bonds.** Bonds under this rubric are bonds issued by foreign companies and countries that may have more limited financial structures and assets. They are international junk bonds, affected by political instability and shaky economies. Sovereign debt crises include "cases where the sovereign debt has been semicoercively restructured or rescheduled under the threat of default (Pakistan, Ukraine, Uruguay) and cases in which sovereign debt service distress has been avoided only through very large International Monetary Fund (IMF) loan packages (Mexico [1982], twice in Brazil in 1999 and 2001–2003, Turkey, Uruguay."[3]

The emerging markets are no stranger to defaults. In 1998, Russia defaulted on its sovereign debt, which was triggered by an attack on its currency. Argentina defaulted in 2001, with most spectacular consequences. Before the Argentinean default, an expected loss of principal—otherwise known as the haircut—was between 30 and 50 percent on the dollar. Argentina's loss is estimated to be 70 percent or more and sets a disturbing example for other third-world countries because it demonstrates that declaring bankruptcy can be one way to escape crushing debt loads. The lesson investors learned from the Argentinean default: "Lend to deadbeats at your own risk."[4]

With the advent of high oil prices in 2006, oil-producing nations like Russia, Mexico, Venezuela, and even Ecuador are able to pay off some of the devastating debt. Investors must be assuming that oil prices will not go down because the JPMorgan Emerging Market Bond Index plus additions (EMBI+) was yielding 6.6 percent in 2006, only 2 percentage points more than Treasuries, the safest world credit.

Some, like Brady bonds, are dollar denominated. Named after Treasury Secretary Nicholas Brady, these bonds were introduced in 1980 as a way for commercial banks to repackage their nonperforming emerging-market loans.[5] Some of the debt backed by the Brady name is collateralized. U.S. zero-coupon bonds back the principal, and eighteen months of interest is guaranteed on a rolling basis. In 1999, Ecuador became the first country to default on its Brady payments. In 2003, Mexico became the first country to retire its Brady bonds.

Most emerging-market bonds are not dollar denominated, making them subject to currency risk as well as default risk. Investors in these bonds are betting that the dollar will weaken against the foreign currency. The differences between dollar-denominated debt and foreign-currency debt of the same nation are quite revealing. For example, in 2006, the bonds denominated in Turkish lira due in 2007 yielded about 14.7 percent, while the dollar-denominated debt yielded 5.2 percent. The higher yield did not guarantee that you would earn more because the Turkish lira devalued 6.1 percent against the dollar. The exit doors to these exotic investments are very narrow. Because of these issues, institutional investors often hedge against loss by purchasing credit swaps or they hedge against currency. To do so, however, is to incur a significant cost and give up the possible upside on the currency exchange.

ADVANTAGES

Corporate bonds provide a predictable stream of income. Interest is usually paid semiannually, although some bonds, if they're notes, pay interest quarterly or monthly. Corporates yield more than Treasury and agency bonds and usually more than other taxable fixed-income investments. They're suitable investments for tax-sheltered retirement accounts and for those in low tax brackets.

RISKS

The corporate bond is no stranger to event risk. They may be subjected to leveraged buyouts (LBOs) or takeovers. In an LBO, the employer or a purchaser takes the company private, often creating a windfall for the stockholders. However, an LBO may result in great uncertainty for the bondholders because their bonds may be downgraded. LBOs have turned investment-grade bonds to junk overnight, in the process smearing the bonds of similar companies identified as potential acquisition candidates. In 1988, for example, when RJR Nabisco was taken over, prices of many large corporate bonds plummeted across the board as traders reacted to the realization that even large companies were not safe from such hostile actions.[6]

The credit quality of bonds is often downgraded when corporations try to boost their stock prices. In 2000, for example, scores of companies raised the reported per share earnings by the simple expedient action of buying back their shares even though their earnings did not increase. After all, when you have four shares outstanding and you earn $1.00, your per-share earnings are $0.25. This earning report is doubled to $0.50 when you buy back two shares and, thus, have only two shares outstanding. While the companies were beefing up their per-share earnings, however, they were acquiring boatloads of debt to buy back their shares. Stock buybacks are now a familiar part of the debt landscape. This heavy debt led Moody's Investors Service to downgrade three times as many bonds as it upgraded in that year, a ratio not seen since the recession of the early 1990s.[7] To discover whether the bonds you own were issued by a company buying back its stock, call your broker and ask if the bonds are on the stock buyback list. Then evaluate your risk. On a cautionary note, never equate a company's rising stock price with good financial health or a willingness to support its outstanding debt.

Floating-rate notes have their own specialized risks. Although the coupon payments adjust to the changes in the marketplace interest rates, they do not adjust to changes in the credit quality of the issuer. Thus, the interest rate being paid is based on the credit quality of the issuer when the floating rate was established.

PRICING INFORMATION

Although generally issued with a minimum face value of $1,000, corporate bonds are frequently sold in lots of $5,000. Prices for frequently traded issues are currently reported on the Web site www.investinginbonds.com after a lag; however, the market is moving toward greater price transparency.

Although companies generally have only one class of common stock, they usually have many distinct bond issues because some have a better claim on the company's assets in the event of a default than others. Bonds that trade often are easy to evaluate, whereas bonds that seldom trade are more difficult to price.

SPECIAL FEATURES AND TIPS

Basic features. Corporate bonds come with one of three alternative features. You can pick the feature that suits you best.

- **Callable.** The call feature can vary from every thirty days to several years or be known as extraordinary, which is triggered by the sale of assets or other special provisions.
- **Noncallable.** This provision covers the life of the bond.
- **Convertible.** This feature means the bond can be exchanged for shares, the number of which is stipulated by the indenture.

Sinking funds. These funds are a frequent provision of some types of corporate bonds. They are frequently found in the indentures of industrial bonds and public utilities but not in bonds issued by telecommunications and finance companies.[8] Although sinking funds might redeem your bonds at an unwanted time, they provide for the orderly repayment of debt. With zero-coupon bonds, however, no debt is repaid at all until the bonds come due. In that case, you place your faith in the issuer's ability to pay all the debt at once.

Make-whole calls. These calls were introduced in 1995, but they are now frequently found in addition to fixed calls. A make-whole call allows the issuer to call a bond whenever it wants at par plus a premium, usually expressed as *X* basis points over the equivalent Treasury bond. High interest rates, poor ratings, and long maturities produce more "room" for an issuer's borrowing costs to decline if the following happens: interest rates decline, company ratings improve, and the maturity of the bonds shorten. But is this call attractive to the bond buyer? You should still require a price premium for the uncertainty that the bond might be called early and that the price of the bond may not appreciate much over par due to the call possibility. Advantageous circumstances for you would include falling interest rates and rising Treasury bond prices. You would have a higher call price than if there were a fixed call, although you would still have to reinvest at lower rates. It is very expensive for an issuer to exercise this call so it is not exercised frequently.

Puts. Puts are a relatively recent feature in corporate retail notes. They are the opposite of calls in that they allow buyers to redeem their bonds before maturity at face value and without penalty. One variant is the death put. If the bondholder dies, his or her estate can redeem the bond at face value. By its very nature, the death put increases the attractiveness of long-term bonds, especially those selling at a discount to their face value. However, the increase in value may be offset by the taxes due on the gain.

Unadorned puts are often used as an added inducement when an issuer is on credit watch. Another provision is the "step-up," which increases the size of the coupon by a fraction of a percentage point for a stated reason, like a rating agency downgrade. AT&T used both these inducements, plus a juicy yield, to attract buyers for its November 2001 issue.[9]

Corporate Medium-Term Notes

Having read about the complexities of bonds, it should not be too surprising to learn that medium-term notes (MTNs) are not always medium term. Once upon a time, when they first appeared in the

1980s, they did have maturities that fell between short-term commercial paper and long-term bonds and deserved their medium-term designation. They were noncallable, unsecured, senior debt securities with fixed coupon rates and investment-grade ratings with maturities of five years or less.

Now, however, their maturities range from nine months to thirty years. In 1993, the Walt Disney Company even issued a medium-term note with a 100-year maturity. Starting as small niche offerings of the automobile industry, MTNs are now issued by hundreds of corporations both within the United States and in Europe. Not only are they not necessarily medium term, they may be callable, variable-rate, asset-backed, or debentures.

An aspect of MTNs that has remained constant since their inception is their distribution process. Under the traditional system, underwriters buy the bonds themselves and take on ownership risk. With MTNs, brokers don't need to do this. They act simply as middlemen in selling the bonds directly from the company to an investor, in the process pocketing a fee from the company for their services.

A second constant feature of MTNs is that they are offered on a continuous basis, rather than as one lump sum. This was made possible through SEC Rule 415, which went into effect in March 1982. The ruling allows a corporation to register at one time all bonds it plans to sell over a two-year period. This is called a shelf registration. It gives corporations great flexibility in issuing bonds and is especially useful in allowing them to take immediate advantage of drops in interest rates. The value of each shelf registration generally ranges from $100 million to $1 billion. Once all bonds in a registration have been sold, the company can "reload" by filing for more debt in another registration.

ADVANTAGES

Unlike corporate bond offerings that are issued all at once, MTNs are available continuously so you can purchase them at a time that's convenient for you. In addition, coupon rates can be quite attractive for maturities that are beneficial to the issuer.

RISKS

Because of their flexibility, MTNs are issued both privately and publicly, which allows corporations to conceal some of their debt. MTN offerings are often issued simultaneously with derivatives to hedge company risks. They are then called "structured notes." They may appear to be regular bonds, but they may have exotic derivatives embedded in them. These notes can cause an investor to lose invested principal because the risks are not obvious.

PRICING INFORMATION

Investors in MTN offerings must have deep pockets because these offerings are usually in the range of $1 million to $25 million. Many brokers step in and buy them for trading purposes. They sometimes slice the MTNs into bonds with much smaller face values, generally in the $1,000 to $5,000 range. These bonds are then sold in packages, with an investor's needs determining the package's total size.

SPECIAL FEATURES AND TIPS

Medium-term notes are issued intermittently when the time is most propitious. Institutional buyers of corporate notes purchase them in blocks of $1 million or more. The small investor will usually not have access to this market except as we've noted.

Corporate Retail Notes

Corporate retail notes are shelf-registered notes that are the equivalent of MTNs for little guys. These notes are posted on the Internet and purportedly sold directly to you as original issue securities through a broker. The issuer adjusts the coupon so you will always buy them at or near par in the initial offering. Whether you purchase them through a "discount" broker or a full-service broker, the price will be the same when they are newly issued, unless the broker tacks on a fee.

Corporate retail notes are also distinguished from MTNs in that you always know when they are going to be issued. In an MTN shelf registration, the issuer can release the bonds at its discretion.

Retail note issuers commit to releasing a set number of bonds each week during the life of the registration. The issuer does have discretion to adjust the coupon rate, call features, and maturities in response to market fluctuations. The company might offer the same kind of bonds week to week, or change the type or maturity of the offerings. It might offer monthly pay or semiannual pay bonds, interest-bearing bonds or zero coupons, and callable or noncallable bonds.

General Motors Acceptance Corporation (GMAC), the financial arm of General Motors, was a pioneer in issuing corporate retail notes and used the moniker of SmartNotes to make them particularly attractive. The GMAC prospectus dated June 1, 2001, for example, is a shelf registration for the issuance of $8 billion. They are unsecured and unsubordinated debt. These bonds were rated below investment grade in 2006.

Americans love brand names, and retail note issuers have capitalized on this, with many creating their own logos. Caterpillar Financial Services Corporation has PowerNotes; Tennessee Valley Authority, Electronotes; United Parcel Services, UPS Notes; and Freddie Mac, FreddieNotes. The bond-rating agencies give each of these issuers high ratings although that is no criterion for issuing these notes.

Corporate retail notes are usually offered on a Friday, and the prices are good until the next Thursday although the days of the open order period may vary from one issuer to another.

In 2003, Household Finance Corporation was the first corporate issuer of the inflation-protected corporate bond, modeled after the government's TIPS and sold through brokers. It was launched by Incapital LLC and Bank of America Corporation in the Inflation-Protected InterNotes program.[10] Corporate inflation-protected notes pay out the inflation adjustment monthly rather than having you wait until the bonds mature like the TIPS. This payout eliminates the phantom income problem that TIPS have. However, if inflation is low, you will not have much cash flow because the base rate is between 1 percent and 2 percent. The resale market is negligible, and the coupon payments are subject to state and local taxes, as are all corporate bonds.

ADVANTAGES

Simplicity is the hallmark of corporate retail notes. You do not have to understand bond basics to purchase one. Because they're always issued at par, you do not have to understand the differences between premium, discount, and par bonds. Nor do you have to understand accrued interest. Large, highly rated corporations usually issue them. They are convenient, come in a variety of maturities and payment options, and are sold in small lots.

You do not have to decide quickly if you want to purchase them because the offering remains stable for five business days despite market fluctuations. And, there's always next week because new issue corporate retail notes are frequently available and always sell at the same price at every selling broker.

RISKS

You can lose money on the sale of corporate retail notes. Their price and yield bounce around just like that of any fixed-income investment. They also may have lower yields than institutional corporate notes due to features geared to attract the retail market. This is a buy-and-hold investment because the spreads may be quite wide on the sale although they are negotiable, as with any other bond.

Always ask if the bonds have a senior lien or a subordinated lien on assets before you buy. In the event of a failure to pay in a timely fashion, holders of senior lien bonds can demand accelerated repayment, whereas holders of subordinated lien bonds must wait until an actual bankruptcy filing for assets to be allocated to creditors.

Corporate retail notes provide liquidity for the company when the commercial markets may be closed to them. For company survival, liquidity is always good, although it may not be good for you if they are piling on the debt.

PRICING INFORMATION

Corporate retail notes are priced at or near par, which is usually $1,000. That is also the minimum purchase amount. They have no accrued interest when first issued. Corporate retail notes do not trade well in the used bond market so make sure you can hold them to maturity before you buy. Diversify among industries because if there is a change in the outlook for an industry or a change in the way the rating agencies look at the ratings, you may have many bonds downgraded at one time.

INFORMATION SOURCES

For information on corporate retail notes look at Direct Access Notes (DANs) through LaSalle ABN AMRO Financial Services at www.directnotes.com and Internotes from Incapital LLC at www.internotes.com. There have been new entrants into the field, with Merrill Lynch issuing CoreNotes, as well as many others. You can get a prospectus from any participating broker/dealer listed on either Web site, or you can visit the Web site of the individual issuers.[11]

SPECIAL FEATURES AND TIPS

With the introduction of online information, it is easy to check out corporate retail notes offerings each week. The offering sites can e-mail you information on new offerings as they're formulated.

If you purchase monthly pay bonds, they have a slightly higher yield than equivalent semiannual bonds because you receive cash sooner. Not all issuers of these notes will necessarily be identified by a brand name when the notes are sold so inquire about whether you're purchasing a bond, an MTN, a direct access note, or an internote. Most corporate retail notes contain a survivor's option, or death put, permitting the estate of the beneficial owner the right to put (that is, sell) the note back to the issuer at face value, as described in chapter 19.

Corporate High-Yield Junk Bonds

A junk bond is often equated with a high-yield bond. Although there are bond merchants who prefer that no distinction be made between the terms, the two are not synonymous. A bond may be high yielding without being junk, and a junk bond may not be high yielding.

A ROSE BY ANY OTHER NAME

A high-yield bond is simply one that currently yields more than other available bonds. It does so for any number of reasons, including (1) it's perceived as riskier than other bonds and so must offer a higher return to attract investors; (2) it has an early call date and must offer a higher return to compensate investors for the short amount of time the bond will be held.

Junk bonds are the debris of failing or distressed companies. In 2007, an astounding 71 percent of U.S. industrial corporations tracked by Standard & Poor's fell into this category.[12] Often paying no interest income because their coupon payments have been abandoned, the bonds are frequently the playthings of speculators. Those who buy these bonds are betting that they will eventually be sold for more than their current market price. Thus, unlike all other bonds, junk bonds are bought more for their capital appreciation potential than for their interest payouts. "Thar's gold in that thar junk!" as the saying goes. However, in 2005, James Grant, editor of *Grant's Interest Rate Observer,* had a different perspective. "Never before have junk-bond investors been paid so little for risking so much," said Grant.[13]

The term *junk* also covers the bonds of rising stars, new start-up companies turning to the bond markets for additional capital. Although the majority of these start-ups have no (or only the most speculative) risk rating, some are promising enough to be in the double-B category and have what the investment community considers interesting possibilities. These bonds can be called junk or, as some prefer, "businessman's risk" bonds.

Finally, some corporate managements deliberately create junk bonds as a protection against hostile takeovers. They make themselves unattractive by saddling themselves with debt from bond offerings and using the resulting funds to pay out high dividends to stockholders, thus, depleting company assets. Suddenly, highly rated bonds become junk bonds, much to the dismay of the bondholders. Who wants to buy a debt-ridden company? The answer is no one if the acquiring company cannot ascertain the depth of the problem. AIG, the world's largest insurer, was ready to sign on for an $833 million foreign investment in Hyundai

Group, but Korean regulators refused to provide protection in the event hidden debt bombs exploded.[14] The deal fell apart.

THE TRACK RECORD

Junk bonds have had a long, if not always honorable, history in American financial markets. The term first appeared sometime in the 1920s and was used to describe bonds that few would touch because they were below investment grade. Such bonds were also known as fallen angels, a term reflecting the fact that the bonds had once been respectable, investment-grade instruments and then had lost that designation when the issuing companies encountered extreme financial difficulties. Both analysts and investors avoided junk bonds not only because of the likelihood of their defaulting but also because the investment policies of many financial institutions excluded the bonds from their approved lists.

Since the 1980s, however, the application of the term *junk bond* has broadened. It now applies to bonds issued by established companies undergoing restructurings or LBOs. An LBO is the purchase of a controlling interest in a company through the use of borrowed money. Sometimes, a company will buy itself, changing from a publicly owned to a privately owned entity. When that happens, the once publicly traded bonds are no longer traded and become illiquid; holders then have to wait until the bonds mature to obtain the principal. When Seagate Technology Inc., the world's biggest manufacturer of computer disk drives, announced it would go private in 2001, for example, the trading price of its bonds fell by half.

In the 1980s, two developments had a significant effect on this market. First, the concept of modern portfolio theory became widely embedded in financial planning. In very broad terms, this approach holds that diversification smoothes out risks. In practical terms, it made holding junk bonds more attractive because it meant that the portfolio could capture the high yield of the bonds while reducing the risk of holding them through diversification.

Second, there was Michael Milken. He was, as the well-known quote explains, in the right place at the right time: junk bonds were acceptable portfolio components, and many companies were ripe for hostile takeovers and dismemberment. From his bastion at Drexel Burnham Lambert, Milken saw to it that high-yielding bond issues became the hottest items in town. They financed merger and acquisition activities that were used to take over companies and milk them dry or, as others preferred to describe it, to unlock their unrecognized values.

At the time, Milken was at his high-flying prime. Junk bonds were considered good investments not only for their money-making potential but also because their default rate was quite low. They were so good, in fact, that there was a narrowing in the difference between their yields and that of Treasuries. With the scandal surrounding the collapse of Drexel Burnham Lambert and the onset of the recession in 1990 to 1991, investors fled from junk bonds, selling them for whatever price they could get. The spread between junk bonds and Treasuries, which had once been about 200 basis points, ballooned to 1,200 basis points in November 1990.

Modern portfolio theory, however, remained unaffected. Throughout the 1990s, increasing amounts of high-yield bonds were bought for mutual funds. The attractiveness of their yields was such that even staid investment institutions, such as Vanguard and TIAA-CREF, introduced funds consisting solely of these bonds. Not all such funds are equal because many carry a high-yield name but have numerous investment-grade bonds to cushion the possibility of default.

BRAVE BUYERS

Junk bonds attract a unique clientele and require analysis that differs from that used for investment-grade bonds. As well-known investment-grade bonds began to slide (including those of Dole Food Company; Hasbro; and AMR, the corporate parent of American Airlines) and with the default rate calculated by Fitch Ratings at 12.9 percent in 2001, up from 5.1 percent in 2000, ten analysts who formerly focused only on either high-grade or high-yield bonds began to cover both types. In 2001, Moody's Investors Service downgraded the ratings of forty-nine such companies as the country slid into a recession.[15] With telecom companies, investors were lucky to get the quoted price of 14 percent to 20 percent of face value.[16] By 2006, many telecoms had defaulted. The default rate in 2006 was only 1.3 percent, but that is attributed to low interest rates.[17]

Bondholders who hear bad news and do not sell their holdings may inadvertently find themselves owners of high-yield paper. When the American automotive industry was unable to effectively compete in the world markets, holders of General Motors, Ford Motor Company, and Chrysler Corporation saw the ratings on their bonds sink below investment grade. The owners of telecoms suffered a similar fate. If you're concerned about a company, suspecting it may be the next Enron or WorldCom, and the media is not proclaiming its demise, ask your broker to call the credit-derivatives desk to ask about the activity for credit-default swaps for the company about which you're concerned. These swaps are basic insurance for big guys if they fear a default or price devaluation, and the activity trend might give you some information.

ADVANTAGES

For knowledgeable players, junk bonds can be very lucrative. In addition to their high yields, they also offer the potential for substantial capital appreciation if you happen to purchase a "rising star" instead of a "falling angel." Under the banner of diversification, investors purchase foreign stock and now high-yield foreign bonds. They are usually sold under the headings of emerging markets, global bonds, or foreign bonds and are usually purchased through mutual funds.

RISKS

Junk bonds carry the same risks as all other bonds, and then some. Interest rates may rise, depressing the prices at which the bonds are sold. Downturns in the economy affect all businesses, but the weakest companies suffer the most. Liquidity dries up just when you really need it.

The special risk for junk bonds is the heightened possibility of default and further rating downgrades. Credit watch or actual downgrades mean that the value of your bonds declines and their salability diminishes. Default may lead to your losing every dime of your investment. More frequently, you will have some recovery of assets that are paid in cash and securities. A Standard & Poor's study sampling 120 B-rated companies that tapped the debt market in 1996 found that by 2006, 6 percent had paid off their debt, a third defaulted, and a third were acquired.[18] The overall recovery rate on defaulted corporate bonds "remained well above their 36 percent historical average for 2005,"[19] although the huge spike in defaults in 2001 and 2002 may have weeded out many of the more vulnerable companies. If you were to hold only a few junk bonds—something few professionals would recommend—what would you expect your experience to be?

PRICING INFORMATION

Credit issues mainly affect the yield on junk bonds. The price of junk bonds generally does not respond to the movement of interest rates in the same way as better credits do. Treasury yields might change, but yields on junk bonds may not move or will move only fractionally. Traders value junk bonds principally on price discovery: as the prospects of the company improve and the risk of default is reduced, the value of its bonds will increase.

The thin market for these bonds makes them expensive to trade. Junk bonds are difficult to price unless they're actively traded. Their prices are set based on a total return approach, taking into account likely interest payments and return on capital invested. If your bonds are investment grade, and you fear they may be downgraded to junk, it might be advisable to sell before that happens. Trust companies and mutual funds mandated to hold high-grade bonds must sell bonds once they no longer have an investment-grade rating, thus, driving the price of the bonds down.

SPECIAL FEATURES AND TIPS

Some investors make a lot of money trading junk bonds. Generally, these individuals are retired and have time to closely follow bankruptcy proceedings. They make a bet on the reorganization of the company. A lot of bonds trade at the bottom of a bankruptcy when many holders want to get out and are willing to sell at $0.10 to $0.15 on the dollar. If the bet pays off, the return could be $0.40 to $0.50 on the dollar. This type of trading, however, is not for the faint of heart.

Defaulted bonds generally trade flat, that is, without accrued interest. If the bond is heading for default, you might be able to negotiate a sale with a due bill. A due bill is attached if a seller sold securities with interest due that the trustee identifies as belonging to the seller rather than the buyer. If a due bill is attached, the buyer's broker can claim the interest. You get a proportionate share of the next interest payment, if there is one, if you have a due-bill designation. If the buyer's purpose is to become a player in the restructuring by amassing a large block of bonds, he won't care about the interest.

Bond covenants, the written statement regarding the rights of bondholders, are not everyday reading. To give buyers of low-grade debt some hints about what kind of protections might be built into the covenant, in 2006 Moody's Investors Service began analyzing these securities and assigning ratings to them before they're sold. The ratings range from CQ-1, the strongest, to CQ-3, the weakest. One covenant the analysts particularly like is a change-of-control provision, which allows the buyer to give back the bonds at par if the borrower is acquired.[20]

If you want to purchase junk bonds, consider purchasing them through a mutual fund. Don't forget, however, that junk bonds are especially risky when the economy is heading into a recession.

CORPORATE CONVERTIBLE BONDS

Ah, convertibles! Back in our dating days, we loved riding along with the top down and the wind blowing through our hair while we debated whether that big black cloud up ahead really meant rain. If you like that kind of racy feeling, then convertibles are for you. They start off as simple, interest-paying bonds that yield less than the market rate, but they may wind up as dividend-paying stocks.

The fun part comes when you get to convert bonds into equity for a fixed number of common stock shares. For example, your

$1,000 face value convertible bond might become ten shares of common stock. Alternatively, your convertible bond might specify a conversion price rather than a number of shares. If the price is $100, then the security can be exchanged for ten shares. The term *parity price* is used to describe the price at which the shares are convertible. In this example, the parity price is $100. There may be a step-up feature that increases the price of conversion after a specified amount of time.

The majority of convertible issuers are below investment grade. Convertibles represent one of the few remaining funding sources available to companies saddled with large debt loads or with very volatile earnings. Management is reluctant to raise new funds by issuing stock because this would dilute and, thus, lower per-share value. By issuing convertibles, a company can have its cake and eat it, too. Often, a convertible bond carries a stipulation that it can be called if the stock appreciates significantly, a process called forced conversion. This provision gives the company leeway to issue either new convertible bonds or new equity shares based on the higher stock price.

ADVANTAGES

Convertibles offer a combination of good interest income and the potential return of a stock. They feature interest payments, which provide a stream of income, and a maturity date when the principal will be returned. In the event of bankruptcy, convertible bonds have senior status over preferred and common stock. If the stock drops, the bonds will theoretically cushion the fall for the convertible holder, while allowing an upside participation if the stock soars.

RISKS

If a company is increasingly looking like a candidate for bankruptcy, you will find its bonds will not hold their value. And, in the event of bankruptcy or a sinking share price, you will have given up a substantial yield for the benefit of an unattractive conversion feature.

If a company is doing well and the indenture provides that the bonds are callable, you can be sure that a call will happen if the stock price begins to recover. Depending on the price you paid for the bonds, you may suffer a loss and miss an opportunity for a big upside as well.

If you purchase an individual convertible bond and decide: "Now is the time to get out," you might have difficulty finding a buyer. This market is primarily institutional, populated by fund managers and insurance companies. You probably do not have a block of bonds that is attractively sized for them. Who is going to buy ten apples when they're looking for a truckload?

PRICING INFORMATION

Although the face value for corporate convertibles is generally $1,000, the price you pay for such a bond is based on valuation factors that are considered complex even by sophisticated investors. The purchase price is affected not only by call and put options but also by stock splits and dividend payouts that reduce the value of the stock. There may or may not be antidilution provisions in the bond indenture.

SPECIAL FEATURES AND TIPS

Convertibles behave more like a bond if the bond price is above par, which happens if the bond has a high coupon rate or is a zero-coupon bond selling at a premium to its current value. The bonds may be putable (that is, salable back to the issuer), which is good for you, or callable, which is not because it takes away your options. If you want to purchase convertible securities, you may want to consider buying them through a mutual fund, whose management has done all the work in assessing what is and what is not a good valuation.

Some convertibles have features that permit the issuer to decide when to raise the roof by allowing the company to dictate the timing of the bond conversion to stock. Although rating agencies like a debt conversion based on what is best for the company, it's better for the bondholder to be able to decide when and if to convert.

A conversion price is frequently 20 percent to 35 percent above the share price at the time of issue. For that price to be appealing, you must believe that the stock has good upside potential. Investors eagerly purchased technology convertibles in the 1990s in anticipation of rapid stock appreciation. The "tech wreck" in 2000 derailed windfalls from bond conversions and left many with neither income nor a full return of principal.

Price-Checking Corporate Bonds

Corporate bonds are traded in one of two ways: either on the New York Stock Exchange (NYSE) or in the over-the-counter (OTC) market. Almost all bonds were traded in the OTC market until late 2006, when the NYSE launched a new bond-trading system dubbed the NYSE Bonds. This new vehicle will potentially increase the number of issues at the NYSE.

The Web site www.investinginbonds.com through the Trade Reporting and Compliance Engine (or TRACE), gives you access to the latest trade prices for all corporate bonds. If you're using www.investinginbonds.com, go to "Bond Market and Prices" at the top toolbar and choose corporate bonds. Your first choice is to view the most active bonds traded. Seeing the bonds that are most actively traded might tell you what bonds to stay away from, or at least raise the question as to why they are most actively traded. The

FIGURE 11.1

Information from www.investinginbonds.com

Ratings ins.	Issuer CUSIP	Coupon Maturity	Call dates
A S	**BELLSOUTH CORP**	6.000	
A2 M	079860AK8	11/15/2034	
A F	Utilities/Telecommunication		

Source: www.investinginbonds.com. Courtesy of SIFMA.

site also offers pertinent headline news and commentary analysis you might find interesting. This site lists the ratings as S for Standard & Poor's, M for Moody's Investors Service, and F for Fitch Ratings. It also lists calls and gives the yield-to-worst or yield-to-maturity high and low for the day (see **Figure 11.1**).

If you're constructing a portfolio of corporate bonds, www.nasdbondinfo.com is the place to look. It uses the same TRACE engine as www.investinginbonds.com. It's best if you have a CUSIP number, the bond's fingerprint. We've tried using bond symbols, but the database was unresponsive. If you type in the company name instead, you might limit the number of responses by choosing a limited date range, coupon rate, or rating.

Once your bond shows up, click on the "Time and Sales" tab and you can choose information for the day or for a specific date range. By clicking on the "Descriptive Data" tab, you'll see a full description of your bonds. This site allows you to build a portfolio to track specific bonds. Such tracking is particularly helpful if you're swimming with the sharks in the high-yield markets. You can access corporate bond indexes for investment-grade and high-yield bonds by clicking on the "Time and Sales" tab at the top of the page as well as lists of most actively traded bonds. The tab "Membership Details" specifies which bonds are included in the index, and some trade information for each of those bonds.

Call prices	Price: High Low	Yield: High Low	Volume # of trades
	100.740 94.820	5.945 6.400	8,233K 159 trades Full history

Key Questions to Ask When You're Buying Corporate Bonds

◆ What are the CUSIP and trading symbol of these bonds?
◆ What is the rating for these bonds?
◆ How do these bonds compare to similarly rated bonds? If there's a difference, what accounts for it?
◆ What is the rating outlook for these bonds? Stable, negative, or positive?
◆ How many basis points over the equivalent Treasury bonds is this offering?
◆ How does this bond compare to similarly rated bonds in other market sectors?
◆ What are the fixed and extraordinary calls on this bond?
◆ When do these bonds pay interest?
◆ Is this bond listed on any exchange?

Chapter Notes

1. Jeff Somer, "And Then There Were 9: A Shrinking Credit Club," *New York Times*, July 29, 2001, C1.

2. Deborah Solomon, "Under Rising Pressure AT&T's CEO Tries to Hold On to an Icon," *Wall Street Journal*, November 16, 2001, A6 (A1).

3. Nouriel Roubini, "Sovereign Defaults on the Rise?" Nouriel Roubini's Blog. Retrieved from http://RGEmonitor.com/blog/rubini/91152.

4. Mary Anastasia O'Grady, "Argentina's Lessons for Global Creditors," *Wall Street Journal*, March 4, 2005, A15.

5. Christopher B. Steward, "International Bond Markets and Instruments," in *The Handbook of Fixed Income Securities*, ed. Frank J. Fabozzi (New York: McGraw-Hill, 2000), 369.

6. Frank J. Fabozzi, Richard S. Wilson, and Richard Todd, "Corporate Bonds," *The Handbook of Fixed Income Securities*, ed. Frank J. Fabozzi (New York: McGraw-Hill, 2000), 275.

7. "Corporate Bonds: Debt Delirium," *The Economist*, May 20, 2000, 90.

8. Gregory Zuckerman, "AT&T Sells $10.09 Billion of Corporate Bonds as Investors Line Up, Lured by Enticing Yields," *Wall Street Journal*, November 16, 2001, C13.

9. Don Kirk, "Concerns Over Hidden Debt Led to End of Hyundai Deal," *New York Times,* January 19, 2001, C2.

10. "Incapital LLC Launches New Corporate Bond Offering to Protect Individual Investors from Inflation," Yahoo! Finance, September 22, 2003.

11. For information about all corporate bonds, you can visit the SEC Web site at www.sec.gov/edgar/quickedgar.htm. Alternatively, you can call (800) SEC-0330 to receive documents or visit public reference rooms at SEC offices in Washington, DC; Chicago; and New York.

12. Serena Ng, "Junk Turns Golden, but May Be Laced with Tinsel," *Wall Street Journal,* January 4, 2007, C1.

13. Floyd Norris, "Best of All Possible Worlds? Bond Buyers Crave Yield but Show No Fear," *New York Times,* January 21, 2005, BU 5.

14. Abby Schultz, "Some Municipal Bonds Leave a Corporate Taste," *New York Times,* February 10, 2002, BU 9.

15. Phyllis Berman, "In Their Debt," *Forbes,* November 12, 2001, 138.

16. Fabozzi, Wilson, and Todd, 281.

17. Ng, C2.

18. Ibid., quotes a study by Nicholas Riccio, a Standard & Poor's credit analyst and author of the report, *The Rise of B-Rated Companies and their Staying Power as an Asset Class.*

19. Moody's Investors Service, "Default and Recovery Rates of Corporate Bond Issuers, 1920–2005." Released January 2006, Revised March 2006, 1.

20. Marine Cole, "Moody's to Expand Debt Evaluation," *Wall Street Journal,* September 13, 2006, C5.

CHAPTER 12

BOND LOOK-ALIKES

THEY LOOK LIKE bonds, and they often act like bonds, but they are not bonds. They are the financial instruments that compete with bonds and sometimes complement bond portfolios. Investors might become interested in these alternatives when they're seeking more cash flow or a different kind of cash flow to satisfy their financial needs. The spectrum of risks may be different from those associated with bonds, although that may be overlooked in the search for income.

And when investors are interested, financial firms and brokerage houses are quick to rush in with fancy-sounding products geared to those interests. Two of the many offerings go by the names of principal-protected securities (a great name in a sliding stock market) and equity-linked CDs (not so great in a sliding stock market). No matter what the name, we believe that many of these financial products are designed to appeal to investors known as "yield hogs." Typically, yield hogs consider only yield in examining investments and ignore other issues such as safety, liquidity, and tax implications.

Let's consider five classic look-alike bond alternatives and present the uses, advantages, and disadvantages of each: CDs, both direct sale and broker-sold; single-premium immediate fixed annuities and deferred fixed annuities; nonconvertible fixed-rate preferred stock; and dividend-paying common stock.

Certificates of Deposit

RATINGS

There are a number of rating systems for CDs. You may find one rating system in the newspaper for local bank CDs and other ratings used for brokered CDs. When you're considering purchasing a CD, be clear what the rating is supposed to indicate.

YIELDS

There are two key acronyms associated with CDs: APR and APY. When bank announcements refer to a "CD rate," they're referring to the annual percentage rate (APR). The APR is a measure of the simple interest return on your CD. The annual percentage yield (APY) is a measure of compound interest. Banks usually say that they compound interest daily. You would use this measure to compare a bank CD to other interest-paying investments.

If the APR is 5 percent on a CD, the APY would compute to a 5.10 to 5.15 APY when the bank compounds the interest if you leave the money with the bank. For example, if you invested $1,200 in a 12-month CD and the APR was 5 percent, the interest on your CD would be $60 per year. This is simple interest at a 5 percent rate. If you elected to receive your income monthly, you would receive $5 each month. It would be up to you to reinvest the $5 in order to get compound interest. Alternatively, assume that the APY was 5.15 percent and you take no distributions from the bank with respect to your CD until twelve months have passed and then you cash in your CD. In this case you would receive your $1,200 back plus $61.80 interest from the bank when your CD came due at the end of the 12-month period ($.0515 \times 1{,}200 = 61.8$).

BANK CERTIFICATES OF DEPOSIT

Bank CDs are time deposits, one of the simplest and most common investments. You deposit cash with a bank for a stated time period and earn a stated rate of interest. When you buy a $100, 12-month bank CD with a 5 percent interest rate, for example, you will receive all your principal plus $5 in interest for a total of $105 at the end of twelve months when the CD comes due. Interest is credited using the "simple compounding" method, which is not directly comparable to the yield-to-maturity on bonds.

Bank CDs offer a variety of interest payment options, including monthly, quarterly, semiannually, and yearly. The simplest way to know which type will yield more is to ask how much money you will receive in total over the life of this CD.

Bank CDs are generally nonnegotiable, which means that you can't sell them to a third party. You must wait until the CD comes due. If you need liquidity prior to maturity, you may return the CD to the issuing bank and pay a penalty for early redemption. The bank CD will not pay off automatically at the due date. If you do not request the bank to pay off the CD, the proceeds of the old CD will roll over automatically into a new CD of the same maturity, but at the bank's current interest rate. If you're seeking the highest rate within your time frame, ask the bank what CD "specials" they have.

To make the CDs more attractive than Treasury securities, banks may offer them at a higher interest rate than that paid on comparable Treasuries. Keep in mind that you do not pay state and local taxes on the interest earned from Treasuries whereas you do on the CDs, so the rates are not directly comparable.

Advantages. Bank CDs are one of the safest investments to be found if your principal is protected by the Federal Deposit Insurance Corporation (FDIC). The FDIC insures up to $100,000 of principal and interest per ownership category per bank for deposits in an account at an insured savings institution. CDs held in "self-directed" retirement accounts are insured for $250,000. Banks that display the FDIC or eagle sign at each teller window are FDIC insured. You can calculate insurance coverage using the FDIC's online estimator at www2.fdic.gov/edie.

Risks. Many financial institutions that sell CDs are not insured by the FDIC. These institutions often offer higher rates, but their CDs come with the risk that if the institution was to fail, you would lose some or all of your investment. At an FDIC-insured bank, if the face amount of the CD plus accrued interest exceeds $100,000 in all taxable accounts in your name ($250,000 in a self-directed retirement account), the excess is not FDIC insured.

Although you can generally withdraw cash from a bank CD before it matures, there is a penalty. Typical bank penalties for early withdrawals may be as follows:

- Maturity of 7 to 90 days: often all interest earned.
- Maturity of 91 to 364 days: often equal to 90 days' interest.
- Maturity of 365 days or greater: often equal to 180 days' interest.

These penalties may be large enough to reduce your principal. For example, suppose you bought a 24-month CD at a bank and needed to cash it in after three months. In this case you might pay a six-month interest penalty even though you earned only three months of interest. Carefully check the penalties before you buy because they will reduce your yield and can be quite onerous.

Tax implications. Interest from CDs is subject to federal, state, and local income taxes if applicable unless the CD is held in a tax-sheltered retirement account: In addition, there is a tax disadvantage to long-term (more than 12-month) bank CDs that pay interest at maturity rather than annually. You must report the interest earned each year on your federal income tax return, even if you don't receive the interest until a later year, unless the CD is held in a tax-sheltered retirement account.

Early withdrawal penalties are deductible whether you itemize your deductions or not. Withdrawal penalties for a CD held within a tax-sheltered retirement account are not deductible.

Pricing information. Newly issued CDs are purchased at face value. Banks may offer specials for particular maturities and quantities. If you simply roll over your CD without asking about specials, you may miss a more attractive rate.

Information sources. Good sources of information on current CD rates throughout the country and a CD calculator can be found at www.bankrate.com and www.bankrater.com. The latter is sponsored by Bauer Financial, which also publishes *Jumbo Rate News*, a magazine that covers 1,300 CD rates.

Special features and tips. Unless you give the bank instructions to redeem a CD when it comes due, the bank will reinvest your money automatically. There is often a ten-day window between the maturity of the last CD and the start of a new one; this interval gives you time to shop around to see if there are better returns elsewhere. Keep in mind that each financial institution is allowed to determine its own penalty provisions, and you should ask about the penalty for early withdrawals.

Although no one can predict the future of interest rates, if you believe interest rates will fall, a bank CD allows you to lock in a fixed rate. If you are investing $1,000 or more, compare CD rates with Treasury offerings before making your decision to invest. Be aware that some bank CDs are callable. This is important if you think you are locking in a high rate. Callable CDs are attractive only if their rates are significantly higher than those at prevailing levels.

BROKER-SOLD BANK CERTIFICATES OF DEPOSIT

In the 1980s, major brokerage firms began to sell bank CDs to their customers. It has proven to be a beneficial arrangement for all parties. Small banks are able to tap into a larger market by having a national firm sell their CDs, and the brokerage firms receive a fee from the banks for doing so. When you purchase a broker-sold CD, you are purchasing a share in a high dollar amount certificate, instead of purchasing the CD directly for the amount you're paying.

Let's see what a typical broker CD looks like and compare it to a typical bank CD.

◆ **Insurance.** Brokers will generally sell CDs from banks that are FDIC insured. However, the onus is on you to make sure that the bank issuing the CD has FDIC insurance.

◆ **Maturity.** Broker CDs have maturities that generally range between one month and twelve years. In comparison, many bank

CDs have lives of only five years or less. A broker CD automatically turns into cash at its due date. A bank CD automatically rolls over into another bank CD unless you instruct the bank to cash it in.

◆ **Maximum amount.** The face amount of many broker CDs should not exceed $90,000—to make sure that the principal and interest do not exceed the $100,000 insurance limit. Many banks will sell you a $100,000 CD, called a "jumbo," with a higher rate of interest.

◆ **Interest payout.** Brokered CDs generally pay semiannual interest, as do bonds. Some banks will pay you interest monthly, semiannually, yearly, or when the CD comes due. You must ask the bank what its payout possibilities are.

◆ **Resale.** The key difference between a bank and a broker CD is that the broker CD is negotiable. This means that you can generally sell the broker CD before its due date without paying a penalty. However, the market price you receive on the sale may be higher or lower than the CD's face value. If interest rates decline after you buy the broker CD, you may be able to sell your CD back to your broker at a gain. If interest rates have gone up over your holding period, you can hold the broker CD until it comes due and receive its face value or sell the CD to the broker at a loss.

◆ **Fees and commissions.** There is generally no stated commission charged to the broker's customers on the sale of a CD. The broker earns its fee from the bank, unless you purchase a secondary market CD, in which case there is a bid/ask spread.

When you purchase CDs, you may notice names of familiar companies showing up, like Target, GMAC, and General Electric banks. These institutions are not banks in the true sense of the word but are instead industrial loan companies (ILC). The Federal Reserve does not oversee the ILCs; that is done by the states. Don't worry; the ILCs do have FDIC insurance.

Advantages. When you buy a broker CD from a large firm, you have a veritable shopping mall of offerings. The firm can locate advantageous prices and a variety of CD offerings that you would be hard put to find on your own. This can lead to excellent buying opportunities. For example, compare the interest rate on a typical 5-year broker CD sold in October 2006 (5 percent) to the yield on a 5-year Treasury bond (4.56 percent). Although the choice of which to purchase may seem obvious, it is not. If you live in Florida, where there is no state income tax, the CD is the better choice. However, if you live in a high-tax state like California, you might be better off with the Treasury bond because the after-tax return may be higher.

Risks. As discussed previously, broker CDs are subject to market risk if sold before their due date. Do not confuse a bank CD with a CD-type annuity. The bank CD gives you the same tax deferral as the annuity if you purchase it for your retirement account. The bank CD guarantees the rate for the life of your CD, whereas the annuity may give you a higher rate the first year but a lower rate in the remaining years. Although there may be a penalty for withdrawing funds from a bank CD, the penalties for withdrawing funds from the CD-type annuity are much more severe and may amount to one and one-half years' interest the first year, declining very gradually from there.

Tax implications. Interest income from broker CDs is subject to federal income tax and state and local income tax if applicable, unless it's held in a tax-deferred retirement account. When they are sold early, however, the difference between the sale price and the purchase price is treated as either a long-term or short-term capital gain or loss unless it's held in a tax-deferred retirement account.

Pricing information. New-issue broker CDs can generally be purchased at face value, for a minimum of $1,000.

Special features and tips. There are many varieties of broker CDs, including zero-coupon CDs that pay no interest until maturity. Unless you purchase the CD in a retirement account, you have to pay taxes on the phantom interest. On a $50,000 investment yielding 5 percent, the first year's interest would be $2,500, and each year it would be more. Make sure you have enough money to pay the taxes.

Step-rate CDs. "Step-rate" CDs may "step down" or "step up." A step-down CD will generally pay an above-market interest rate for a stated period and then pay a lower, stated rate until it comes due. A step-up CD, also referred to as a "bump up" CD, will generally pay a below-market interest rate for a stated period and then pay a higher, stated rate until it comes due. Investors in step-rate CDs might wind up with more or less interest than a CD without these features, and the CDs may also be callable. As with all broker CDs, if you sell them before their due date, you may have a gain or a loss. It's important to get the buy-back terms from the broker in advance. Ask for a complete description as well as the offering memoranda, where the fine print might contain critical information.

Callable CDs. Some CDs are callable. CDs with a short call should have a higher yield-to-maturity than a bond with no call at all. For example, a 10-year noncallable bond might be yielding 5.05 percent, while a 10-year CD with a six-month call might be yielding 6 percent. If your bond is called away, you may have to reinvest at a lower rate. Sometimes a broker may say that the CDs are "one-year noncallable." That might lead you to believe that the CD comes due in one year. In fact, it means that the CD can be called after one year.

There are also inflation-protected CDs, similar to the TIPS described in chapter 6. Aside from the difference in issuer, the TIPS are exempt from state and local taxes, whereas the CDs are not. This distinction fades in importance if the CDs are purchased for a retirement account.

For risk takers, there are CDs linked to foreign currencies. For more information, visit www.everbank.com. If you want to bet on currency movements, and against the dollar, this is an easy way to do it. You can purchase a CD representing a basket of currencies. Although the yields may be higher than on FDIC-insured CDs, you can still have losses if the currencies fall against the dollar. This investment is not for the faint of heart. In addition, you have transaction fees to convert from the dollar to your currency choice and back again.

Key Questions You Should Ask When Buying a Certificate of Deposit

- What is the exact title of the CD?
- When does the CD mature?
- What is my interest rate?

◆ When the CD is cashed in on its redemption date, how much money will I have above my principal?
◆ Does the CD have any calls?
◆ Is the CD brokered?
◆ Do I have FDIC insurance with this CD?
◆ What am I giving up for the added features of extra liquidity, call protection, inflation protection, and survivor's option?
◆ If it has a survivor's option, what are the penalties or cost of terminating the CD early?

Single-Premium Immediate Fixed Annuities

A single-premium immediate fixed annuity (SPIA) is an annuity contract between you and an insurance company, in which you give the company a lump-sum cash payment in exchange for an agreed-upon monthly fixed amount that begins immediately. Depending on the terms of the annuity contract, the fixed monthly amount may be received for a fixed number of years, for life, or until a fixed total amount of money is paid.

Think of the immediate annuity as a fixed cash flow guaranteed by the insurance company. When you purchase an immediate annuity there will be no money to return to you when the policy terminates because the money will have been spent on the purchase of an insurance benefit: the scheduled stream of fixed payments to you. There is no fluctuation in the value of the principal because you have turned that money over to the insurance company and you don't have a principal amount anymore.

Each insurance company has its own variations on the following four distribution options. The most common options are the first two.

1 Life only. Payments are made for as long as you live. Your annuity contract can also provide for a joint and survivor annuity. If you elect this distribution option, payments will be made for your life and the life of your spouse or another named person. Typically a single-life annuity provides the greatest cash flow because it's based on one life span and may terminate in the shortest amount of time. A joint-and-survivor annuity will provide a lesser cash flow because it will generally pay out for a longer period of time (two life spans). If both beneficiaries die prematurely, the annuity does not pass to their heirs.

2 Life with period certain. You or your beneficiary will receive payments for the longer of (a) your life (or lives) or (b) a stated minimum number of years even if you die prematurely. Under such a policy, the beneficiary would inherit the remaining amount of the policy if you die before the stated number of years.

3 Period certain but not life. This guarantees payments for only a specified number of years, but not for life. Shorter guaranteed periods provide greater payments than longer periods.

4 Accumulated amount only. This option provides for payment of a specified amount per month until the annuity account is exhausted.

ADVANTAGES

An immediate fixed annuity provides you with a guaranteed stream of income for life (assuming you select one of the first two options), no matter how long you live. No other investment is so well constructed for this purpose. An annuity is a kind of longevity insurance. The purpose of a fixed annuity is to shift the risk of outliving your money to the insurance company, although you also lose access to extra cash you might need when you're older.

Although you might purchase a laddered portfolio of noncallable bonds as a substitute, if your life span is longer than expected and your assets are limited, you might run out of money. One advantage of bonds is that unexpended funds can be reinvested at higher rates if there is inflation, possibly increasing your cash flow if you have enough assets.

The payments from an immediate annuity are fixed and unaffected by financial market gyrations or interest rate fluctuations. If your immediate annuity provides for a payout of $1,000 per month for life, that is what you will get no matter what is happening in the financial markets.

Unlike many other investments, the stated returns on immediate annuities are net of any fees. What you see is what you get.

Fidelity and Vanguard, the mutual fund companies, have entered the field as low-cost providers of this type of annuity.

RISKS

Immediate annuities are irrevocable and, thus, worse than illiquid. Once you buy an immediate annuity for, say, $100,000, you have completely lost control of that $100,000 unless there is a thirty-day free-look period. You have exchanged your $100,000 for a stream of payments, and your deal is done. Before you buy an immediate fixed annuity, you should read the annuity contract to determine if you can get a prepayment for medical emergencies or for some other purpose. If there are no such provisions, assume your money is locked up for good. This is a reason to commit no more than a portion of your capital to an immediate annuity.

There is a risk that the insurance company could go broke and default on your annuity contract. This risk can be reduced if you buy only annuities of highly rated insurance companies. As we know, a high rating at purchase does not mean a high rating forever. Insurance companies can and do fail. However, there are generally state guarantee laws that may protect the annuity holder. The amount of the guarantee varies by state. Ask your agent, the insurance company, or the Department of Insurance in your state what the protection provisions are. The guarantee is based on insurance companies pooling resources in the event that one of them defaults. Even if there is a state guarantee, payments may be delayed for many years and there is a possibility that the claim may never be paid.

Most important, there is inflation risk. This is associated with all long-term fixed-income investments, and it can be a serious one when your payments are fixed but your purchasing power is declining drastically. Unlike Social Security, which is adjusted annually, a fixed annuity is static. Inflation erodes your buying power. For example, in the 1960s you could buy an ice cream cone for a dime. Today, a similar ice cream cone may cost $3. If you purchased an annuity in the 1960s that appeared adequate to your needs, today's prices would devastate you.

TAX IMPLICATIONS

Although most deferred annuities provide a tax deferral, that is not true of immediate annuities because you receive a stream of cash from their inception, and there is no accumulation phase. Part of the cash you receive is considered taxable income, and the remainder is a nontaxable return of your principal. The IRS provides tables that tell you how much of an immediate annuity is subject to federal income tax. See IRS Publication 939, *General Rules for Pensions and Annuities,* at www.irs.gov. Since the taxation of annuities is complicated, we advise you to seek professional tax and independent financial advice when purchasing them.

Many charities tout the tax advantages of buying annuities known as charitable gift annuities. With these instruments, you buy the annuity contract from the charity and the charity promises to pay you a stream of fixed payments for life, starting either immediately or when you reach a certain age. With this investment, you might receive a tax deduction as well as a stream of fixed payments. Keep in mind that you are counting on the charity remaining solvent.

PRICING INFORMATION

The cost of an immediate annuity ranges from $1,000 to generally as much as you want. The rate you receive will depend on the insurance company's expectation of your mortality and the current interest rates. Understand that the shorter your life expectancy, the higher the rate the company should offer you.

INFORMATION SOURCES

Be careful when you review Web sites for information on annuities because under the rubric of "fixed-income annuity," the sites sell tax-deferred variable annuities. Variable fixed annuities may give you a fixed interest rate for a year or more. However, it eventually becomes variable. These products are too complex for the typical investor to evaluate. Your best bet is to talk to a few insurance agents to get a sense of the alternatives available, or hire a fee-only adviser from the National Association of Personal Financial Advisors (NAPFA) at www.napfa.org, who can help you objectively evaluate whatever insurance contracts you are offered.

SPECIAL FEATURES AND TIPS

Immediate fixed annuities are the wallflowers of the insurance world. Although widely recognized as bond alternatives because they offer a fixed rate of return on a cash investment, their charms are rarely touted. Why? Because salespeople receive much higher commissions for selling variable annuities, and you'll find that, not surprisingly, where there are large fees to be made, there are many salespeople praising the product. We recommend immediate fixed annuities. Consider using an immediate fixed annuity to supplement your income when your earned income is falling because you're working part time or are nearing retirement.

Look at insurers who've earned the highest ratings for at least ten years and compare their quoted monthly distributions per $1,000 purchase. You can check the ratings of insurance companies by contacting A.M. Best at www.ambest.com (908-439-2200) and Weiss Research, now owned by TheStreet.com, at www.thestreet .com/ratings (800-289-9222). A.M. Best is paid by insurance companies for its ratings. Weiss Research is paid by consumers and is a more stringent evaluator. To get a final check on ratings, you might visit Moody's Investors Service at www.moodys.com (212-553-0377) and Standard & Poor's at www.standardandpoors .com (877-481-8724). You might also check the Insurance News Network Web site, www.insure.com. We find Fidelity, Vanguard, and TIAA-CREF (800-842-2252 or www.tiaa-cref.org) to be good companies with competitive rates.

If you have a significant health problem, ask about impaired risk annuities. Impaired risk underwriting is a process by which physicians or underwriters evaluate your life expectancy based on your health. If it is projected that you will not live as long as your life expectancy, you may get a higher payout.

Instead of buying one large, lump-sum immediate annuity, consider buying several with smaller amounts at different time periods. This allows you to capture any rising interest rates, and may add further protection against company defaults. Finally, buy the immediate annuity when you're older. The older you are when you buy an immediate annuity, the shorter your life expectancy and the higher the payout and rate of return. Since part of this income is deemed a return of principal, it will not be taxed. Consider buying an immediate fixed annuity after age seventy.

Key Questions You Should Ask About an Immediate Fixed Annuity

- Is there a thirty-day return policy on this insurance contract in case I change my mind?
- How much money will I get when I annuitize?
- What is the guarantee limit in my state?
- What is the rating of the annuity company?
- What are all the fees and expenses?

Deferred Fixed Annuities

Whereas the immediate fixed annuity premise is simple, the deferred fixed annuity is not. The "deferred" in the name is what makes it attractive to many investors because the tax on its income is deferred. The "fixed" refers to a fixed rate of return on the cash investment during the accumulation phase. Unfortunately, this investment is no longer what the title indicates because the underlying rate is subject to change and is not fixed. Finally, this instrument may never become an annuity if you so choose. However, there may be very steep surrender charges in the range of 7 percent to 12 percent if you wish to exit this investment within a year. Significant surrender charges may last for six years or more.

We suggest you think of deferred fixed annuities in terms of four phases: investment, accumulation, nonfixed distribution, and fixed distribution.

INVESTMENT PHASE

In this phase, you generally sign an annuity contract with an insurance company. The contract specifies that you make either a lump-sum payment or a number of payments over time.

ACCUMULATION PHASE

The terms of this phase are stipulated in your annuity contract and state the fixed rate of return on the cash that you invest for a fixed number of years. The contractual term may vary from one to many years. This is similar to the contractual return you would get on a CD from a bank for a fixed number of years. At the end of the contractual term, the insurance company will make another offer in which the fixed return will remain the same or be adjusted upward or downward. At this point, and at the end of any further contractual terms, you have three choices:

1 **Cash out your deferred fixed annuity.** If you cash out, you may be subject to insurance company penalties and federal income tax penalties. In addition, the entire gain is taxed as ordinary income in the year of the distribution.

2 **Transfer your deferred fixed annuity to another annuity company.** If you do so, you may trigger an early withdrawal penalty clause in your annuity contract. (Some annuity companies do not levy withdrawal penalties.) However, there would be no federal taxable income generated or tax penalties if you follow the tax rules for a tax-free exchange.

3 **Extend the term of your current deferred fixed annuity.** You may get a higher or lower interest rate on the extension.

NONFIXED DISTRIBUTION PHASE

Many annuity contracts allow you to make systematic or possibly irregular withdrawals from your contract. You can receive regular payments based on a variety of factors, including a fixed dollar amount, a percent of your account value, or your life expectancy. You can also change how the payments are made or stop the payments altogether.

If you make systematic withdrawals before your fixed distribution date, keep two points in mind. First, if you take too much cash out of your contract, you may not have enough to meet your distribution goals in the future. Second, withdrawals from your deferred fixed annuity might trigger penalties from the annuity company as well as federal income tax and tax penalties. Understand that once you purchase an annuity, the money belongs to the insurance company until you ransom it back.

FIXED DISTRIBUTION PHASE

In insurance language, this is known as annuitization, the time when you and the company agree on a permanent payment option. As with immediate annuities, the options include life-only, life with period certain, period certain but not life, and accumulated amount only.

Deferred fixed annuities are most suitable for individuals who wish to increase tax deferral above that offered through qualified plans, such as 401(k)s and IRAs, and who are not concerned that their heirs may not inherit any of the proceeds. See "Tax Implications" for additional information.

ADVANTAGES

The only advantage to a deferred fixed annuity is that the income accumulates tax-deferred. Since you are paying for the tax-deferred status of the annuity, it should *not* be purchased from your retirement account funds.

Although some states have a guaranteed minimum rate of 3 percent on deferred fixed annuities, in 2003 the state insurance commissioners adopted revisions that recommended that the fixed rate be replaced with a rate that floats as the yield of a 5-year constant maturity Treasury changes. Since state legislatures craft insurance law, the minimum rate rulings may be different from one state to anther. A state can choose to adopt this provision or not. Thus, you might get a guaranteed rate for a set number of years, or the rate may vary between 1 and 3 percent depending on where you purchase your contract. If you're receiving 1 percent on your investment, how much do you think will be left over after insurance company fees?

In general, a company paying higher interest will have lower fees. While you're looking at the attractive interest rate, be sure to look at the surrender charges in case you change your mind. In September 2006, Vanguard, which is known as a low-cost provider of these policies, was offering a 4.8 percent yield that could change at any time. The surrender charges begin at 6 percent in year one and decline over five years. You may not see the fees, but they are there.

RISKS

The rate, particularly the renewal rate, may not be competitive with other suitable investments. This is a particular problem if you invest at one rate (sometimes called a teaser rate because it is above a market rate) and it's followed by a renewal rate that's clearly below market. In this case, you're faced with the choice of switching to another annuity company, taking a below-market rate of return, possibly having to pay annuity company penalties, and possible tax penalties if you want to take a cash distribution.

Deferred annuity contracts are difficult to evaluate because they are so complicated. The underlying values are not fixed. You cannot get a clear indication of your return although you can be sure the insurance company is making money.

If the annuity company becomes financially troubled, you may lose some principal or your money may be tied up for a period of years. Because of this possibility, you should consider investing a portion of your cash with two or more companies to spread the risk of default.

Penalty payments for early withdrawals can be substantial in the early years of an annuity contract. A typical penalty schedule starts at 7 percent the first year, dropping 1 percent each year until there is no penalty in the eighth year.

Another risk is that the high yearly fees often result in lower returns.

Finally, beware of the bait and switch. You may start out looking for a deferred fixed annuity and be lured to a seemingly higher-paying variable annuity. As the Delaware Insurance Commissioner, Matthew Denn stated, "For seniors who are considering purchasing annuities, the first and most important tip is that in most cases, variable annuities are bad deals for senior citizens."[1]

TAX IMPLICATIONS

If the value of the annuity is paid out as a lump-sum distribution, all the earnings are subject to federal income tax as ordinary income in the year of the distribution. Thus, if you invest $50,000 in the annuity and there is a lump sum distribution of $70,000, $20,000 will be taxed as ordinary income in the year of the distribution. The remaining $50,000 is considered a tax-free return of principal. Historically, more than 50 percent of all deferred annuities have been liquidated by heirs. The heirs will pay ordinary income tax on any gains and possibly estate taxes on the value of the annuity.

If there are partial withdrawals before the annuity date, taxable earnings are paid first so that payment of taxes will be accelerated. If the deferred fixed annuity is annuitized and is paid out as a series of payments, the tax result is the same as for the immediate annuity. It consists of a combination of taxable earnings and return of principal. If you are younger than fifity-nine and one-half years at the withdrawal date, you will be subject to a 10 percent IRS penalty. There is no tax penalty if you are fifty-nine and one-half years or older at the date of distribution.

For the tax implications of annuity income, see IRS Publication 939, *General Rules for Pensions and Annuities.* You can find this publication and all other IRS publications on the IRS Web site, www.irs.gov.

PRICING INFORMATION

Minimum purchase is usually $1,000. There is usually no upper limit to the amount purchased although it is best to purchase more than one annuity if the amount of your contract is above the state guaranty level.

SPECIAL FEATURES AND TIPS

Deferred fixed annuities are most suitable for individuals who meet one or more of the following guidelines:

- They have contributed the maximum to their qualified plans, such as 401(k)s and IRAs before seeking a further tax-deferred investment.

◆ They will keep the deferred fixed annuity for at least fifteen years, and at that time they will be at least fifty-nine and one-half.
◆ They are not concerned that their heirs may not inherit any of the proceeds from the deferred fixed annuity.
◆ They expect to be in a lower tax bracket at the time they draw on the deferred fixed annuity.

Some annuity contracts provide for a free withdrawal privilege. The privilege is usually for only a certain fraction of the annuity's total value and it's offered only once per year. Check to determine how much of your cash may be withdrawn without paying a penalty to the annuity company each year; some allow you to take out 10 percent each year without a penalty. However, taxable income will still be generated as well as a possible tax penalty. Even if capital gains were recognized in your annuity, when there is a distribution, all of it is taxed as ordinary income. Thus, an annuity converts capital gains into ordinary income.

Jeff Broadhurst of Broadhurst Financial Advisors, a fee-only financial advisory firm, has these suggestions for alternatives to annuities: A possible alternative is to purchase municipal bonds for greater flexibility and retention of principal. Another option is to purchase Treasury strips of varying maturities to create a bond ladder. Still another alternative to annuities is to use low-cost index funds and create your own cash flow by automatic withdrawals of 4 percent or less per year.

Key Questions to Ask About a Deferred Annuity

◆ How long does the bonus rate last?
◆ After the bonus rate year, what is the rate of return and how long will it last?
◆ What is the interest-rate range for this annuity?
◆ How fixed is the "fixed rate"?
◆ What is the penalty per year for early redemption?
◆ Under what circumstances will the withdrawal charges be waived?

Nonconvertible Fixed-Rate Preferred Stock

Preferred stock comes in many shapes and forms: convertible; nonconvertible; variable rate; and numerous kinds of fixed-rate, including fixed-dividend, auction market, and remarketed preferred stocks. There are also complex preferred stock packages created by large brokerage firms. With billions of dollars in these instruments outstanding, they are not small players in the overall markets.

Of the many preferred stock variations, the one known as a nonconvertible fixed-rate preferred stock is most like a bond and is often sold as a bond alternative. For brevity's sake, we refer to this investment simply as "the preferred," which beats the acronym NFRPS any day.

Although the preferred has a number of bond-like features, it is legally a form of equity. Some preferreds have no due date on which the preferred must be paid off, and these are called perpetual preferreds. Many preferreds have a due date, but they're usually so far in the future as to be irrelevant. For example, in 2006, Citigroup issued a 6.5 percent preferred stock maturing in 2056, with five-year call protection. There is no contractual legal obligation on the issuer to pay dividends on the preferred. If the issuer misses a payment, it's not considered a legal default, but such an action would constitute a default if it were a bond.

The preferred pays dividends at a fixed rate per share each year. For example, if the par value of your preferred is $50 per share and the dividend rate is 8 percent per share, you would receive a dividend of $4 per year ($50 × 8%). Because preferred dividends are generally paid quarterly, you would receive $1 per quarter. This dividend is fixed and will never be increased, even if the earnings of the company grow. By comparison, the dividends on common stock may grow as the company becomes more profitable.

Although a preferred generally pays its dividends in cash, there are certain kinds of preferreds called payment-in-kinds (PIKs) in which the investor receives additional shares of preferred stock, rather than cash dividends.

Many issues of preferred are what are known as cumulative preferred. This means that if the issuer does not pay the preferred dividend when it's due, the amount of the dividend accumulates and will be paid if and when the issuer is financially able to do so. Thus, if the preferred is an 8 percent cumulative preferred with a par value of $50 per share and if dividends are not paid for a year on the preferred, the $4 dividend is accrued and will be paid in the next year, together with the usual $4 dividend for the second year, if the company is financially able to do so. Some issues reserve the right not to pay dividends for a specified number of years without consequence. If there is a failure to pay interest or principal on a bond, that failure is considered a default and a bankruptcy or reorganization may result. By contrast, if a dividend is not paid on the preferred, no such serious consequences ensue. The following, however, may be triggered if a preferred dividend is not paid on schedule:

1 The preferred may immediately be given priority over common stock dividends, and none of the latter will be paid until all unpaid dividends on the preferreds are paid in full.

2 There may be a restriction such that the corporation can't use corporate funds to buy back common stock. The point is to conserve cash for the payment of dividends on the preferreds.

3 Sinking fund payments to cover future debt obligations may be halted. The point here again is to conserve cash for the payment of dividends on the preferreds.

4 The preferred shareholders may receive voting rights that they did not have before.

Some preferred stocks are designated as noncumulative preferred. This kind of preferred allows management to skip a dividend and never make it up. Noncumulative preferreds have often come about as a result of a corporate reorganization or bankruptcy, where debt holders are given this kind of stock in exchange for their debt securities. If you own this kind of security and it stops making payments, the value of the preferred usually falls dramatically.

If there is a bankruptcy, liquidation, or other financial failure of the corporation, the preferred shareholders will be paid before there is any payment to the common shareholders. However, in this case the debtholders will be paid before there is any payment to the preferred shareholders.

Almost all preferred issues are callable at some time at a set price often after only five years. The price might be the issue price or could be a higher price that declines over the years to provide some protection from an early call. Many preferred issues include some call protection for the investor. Before you buy a preferred, you should examine closely when the preferred is callable and what specific protection you might have against an early call.

Generally, calls occur when interest rates have dropped, and there is an advantage to the issuer in calling in the preferred. If interest rates are falling, you don't want to have a call because you will have to reinvest at a lower rate. Calls may also occur if the issuer's credit rating has improved significantly and it can reissue at a lower cost of capital. If the issue has no call provision, the preferred will generally provide for a sinking fund. The sinking fund is used to redeem a certain number of preferred shares annually until all shares are retired.

Three nationally recognized rating organizations rate preferreds: Moody's Investors Service, Standard & Poor's Rating Group, and Fitch Ratings. These ratings are useful in comparing one preferred to another but not in comparing preferreds to bonds.

PREFERRED HYBRIDS

Trust preferreds are sold by companies that fund the trusts with their own long-term bonds. The company sells the preferred stock and then uses the money to purchase the bonds to fund the trust. The advantage to the issuing company is that the interest paid on the debt securities is deductible from its taxable income whereas normal preferred dividends would not be deductible. In the event of a change in the tax law that will prohibit this, expect that the preferred stock will be called.

Third-party trusts are created when brokerage houses purchase bonds in the open market, put them in a trust, and pay a set amount to preferred owners. Some of their acronyms are TOPrS

(Merrill Lynch), CorTS (Lehman Brothers), TIERS (Morgan Stanley), SATURN (Citigroup), and QUIPS (Goldman Sachs); each name is proprietary to the issuing firm. These trusts usually pay dividends semiannually. What they have in common is an underlying issuer flexibility, which means that all you really know is that you have a stream of income, but you do not know for how long. Since the quality of the bonds may be poor or the embedded options risky, you may lose your principal.

ADVANTAGES

Many preferreds offer a higher rate of current return than the return from highly rated corporate bonds and considerably higher than dividends from common stocks. There is a low minimum investment since many preferreds are issued in face amounts of $25 per share or lower. Most bonds are issued in minimum amounts of $1,000 per bond. Many preferred stocks are listed on the New York or American Stock Exchanges, making them easy to track and trade, while other preferreds trade in the over-the-counter market and are more difficult to follow.

RISKS

With the higher return on the preferred comes a greater risk. If the issuer defaults, there may be little or nothing left for preferred shareholders after all the issuer's debt is paid. There is a similar but smaller risk if the issuer is downgraded by one of the rating services, driving the market price down until the company regains its health and the change is recognized by the rating agencies.

Since the preferreds generally never come due or have very long maturity dates (thirty to sixty years), the price for preferreds will drop quickly if interest rates are rising. Many inexperienced owners panic when they see the value of their shares plummet, whereas experienced traders put in low bids waiting for the expected fearful to sell.

The five-year call provision on new-issue preferreds makes them vulnerable to reinvestment risk, which is serious when interest rates are falling. Remember, it is because of the higher current return that you made the decision to invest in the preferred in the first place. Once the call protection passes, the preferreds usually do not rise above their $25 face value because they may be called at any time.

Some preferreds reserve the right to defer quarterly payments for ten years. If a noncumulative preferred stops paying, the value of your preferred will drop like a stone.

PRICING

Preferred stock is quoted on a current-yield basis, which reflects only the amount of current cash you're receiving. There is no compounding in the preferred yield computation. Moreover, preferreds "trade flat," meaning that each quarterly period the interest builds up and is included in the share price. This is different from bond interest because accrued interest is not included in the bond's price.

To find out the current yield without the accrued dividend, ask the broker to strip out the dividend from the price and figure the current yield on that basis. Although the price of the preferred should drop by the amount of the dividend, this does not always happen. You must own the preferred one week before the dividend is paid to qualify for payment. Some brokers tell buyers that they can get five quarterly payments in fifty-three weeks, which is literally true, but the first dividend is included in the price. When preferreds are priced above par, it is usually an indication that a dividend payment is pending.

TAX IMPLICATIONS

You report the dividends from some preferred stock as ordinary income on your federal income tax return. The dividends from other preferred stock are taxed at a 15 percent rate in 2006; that rate may expire in 2008.

INFORMATION SOURCES

The best information source on preferreds is the prospectus published at the time of issue. You can phone the issuing company to get a prospectus by mail or get the prospectus from the SEC's Web site at www.sec.gov/edgar/quickedgar.htm. A useful Web site with comprehensive lists of available preferred shares is www .quantumonline.com, a financial services Web site.

SPECIAL FEATURES AND TIPS

Be careful what kind of preferred you buy. For example, some preferred shares automatically convert into the common stock of the issuer after a number of years. Avoid such preferred stock because there may be an automatic conversion at a time when the price is unfavorable to you.

Under certain conditions, such as tax law changes or securities law changes, the issuer may redeem the preferred. You must check the prospectus to find out about special redemptions, calls, or sinking funds. Some preferred issues are traded on an exchange and may be very liquid. However, other issues are not listed and may be very thinly traded, creating a liquidity risk if you wish to sell.

When analysts review preferred issues, one of their main tests is to determine the company's ability to meet fixed dividend payments. They compare issues using the "coverage ratio," which measures the degree to which a company's cash flow covers its interest and dividend payments. A ratio of two to one or better is considered comfortable.

Be especially careful of the possibility of an early call if you purchase the preferred at an amount in excess of its par or call price. For example, assume that the par value of the preferred is $25 per share, and you buy the preferred for $30 per share. If the preferred is called after one year for its par value of $25 per share, you will have lost $5 per share, a significant reduction of your principal. You would be subject to a similar risk if the preferred has a sinking fund and as a result the preferred is redeemed.

Unless you're purchasing preferreds into your retirement account, look at the after-tax yield and compare it to that of municipal bonds. You may find that the return on the preferred is not worth the added risk.

We do not recommend preferreds to our clients because of the combination of short calls and very long maturities, which may result in substantial losses if interest rates go up.

Key Questions to Ask About Preferred Stock

◆ How much free cash flow of the company is available to pay dividends on the preferred?
◆ Is the security cumulative preferred?
◆ What is its rating?
◆ Will earnings be subject to ordinary income or a 15 percent tax rate? What is your proof?
◆ What is the fixed call, sinking fund, or other call options?
◆ Is the preferred selling at a premium? If so, how much will I lose if it is called?
◆ Has this issuer ever deferred payment of the dividend? If so, for how long?

Dividend-Paying Common Stock

If you're looking for income, dividend-paying stock is a current choice as weary investors battered by stock losses consider jumping ship. Mind you, brokers emphasize dividends when they're no longer banking on big market moves in the foreseeable future. After the 1929 crash, the perception of risk drove dividends higher on stocks, which continued to pay high rates until the 1950s, when stocks began to be purchased for capital gains and bonds were purchased for income. Did stocks become less risky, or did marketing of stocks change?

Many stocks pay regular dividends, although a one-time dividend may also be declared. Good earnings are not required for dividends.

ADVANTAGES

Generally, people who purchase stocks because of their dividends seek a cash flow and a possible upside in the appreciation of the stock.

RISKS

Betting on stock dividends for your cash flow is risky. One reason is that companies paying high dividends tend to be in the same struggling market sectors. The highest yields in 2006 were in the automotive industry, with the financials and utilities following. As we've seen in the automotive industry, an entire sector can falter, putting in danger stock prices as well as dividend flow. In 2006, when Ford Motor Company announced that it would stop paying dividends in the fourth quarter on its common and class B stock, the share value dropped 12 percent on the day of the announcement.[2] Ford was paying a dividend of $0.50 in 2000, but with the drop in interest rates, the dividend stabilized at $0.10 in 2002. The dividend yield on the Standard & Poor's 500 index was 1.8 percent in 2006. General Motors, a company that halved its dividend, was still paying 3 percent in 2006 as talks of restructuring and bankruptcy continued. DaimlerChrysler, which was in similar economic straights, was paying a dividend of 3.4 percent.[3] Just as in bond investing, in common stock investments, if you reach for yield, you risk losing your principal.

Interest on bonds and dividends on preferred stock must legally be paid before a common stock dividend. Common stock dividends may be paid in shares instead of cash.

SPECIAL FEATURES AND TIPS

Companies are not required to pay out dividends on their stock. They may choose to retain the cash in order to grow the company or use the cash for stock buybacks. They may also pay out dividends, even if their earnings and cash flow do not support them, because it bolsters the share price. Although some companies pay dividends quarterly, the dividend payments cannot be assured until the dividend is actually declared by the company's board of directors. Dividends may not be even or regular. They may follow the cash flows that companies generate, which may be seasonal or cyclical.

You can purchase the individual stock of one or more companies, or you can buy a portfolio of stock through a mutual fund specializing in stock dividends. Banking on stock dividends from funds will tend to disappoint because funds are required to use them first to pay expenses, and there may not be much left to pay investors.

Chapter Notes

1. Commissioner Matt Denn, "List of Questions Seniors Should Ask When Purchasing Annuities," October 19, 2005. Retrieved from http://www.de.us/inscom, click on "annuities."

2. Tara Siegel Bernard and Jilian Mincer, "With Ford's Dividend Out of Gas, Investors May Seek Other Models," *Wall Street Journal*, September 19, 2006, D2.

3. Ibid.

PART FOUR

OPTIONS FOR PURCHASING BONDS

ONCE YOU'VE LEARNED about bond basics and reviewed the vast number of bond choices, you're ready to make decisions on how to invest your funds in bonds. Basically, you have two choices: you can purchase individual bonds or buy them packaged together as funds.

When you purchase individual bonds, you get to select the specific characteristics of the bonds that you wish to own. The question, of course, is how do you, buy them? You can purchase Treasury debt and U.S. savings bonds directly from www.treasurydirect.com or from many commercial banks. Or you can check out sources of information on the Internet for municipal and corporate bonds before talking to brokers.

We describe the ins and outs of buying bonds through the Internet, purchasing them newly issued or previously owned. When they come due, they will automatically come due at their face value. Pay once to buy them and enjoy them until they reach maturity. We suggest Web sites to look at and ways to deal with brokers so you can get the best bang for the buck.

Alternatively, you can purchase bonds that are packaged together in a variety of forms. Funds provide safety through diversity in riskier market segments but never come due. Open-end mutual funds are the most generic type, with a variety of closed-end funds carving out market niches of which the exchange-traded fund (ETF) is the new kid on the block. There are a lot of bond funds out there, and their price quotations fill columns of small type in newspapers across the country and are updated daily on the Internet. Many are hard to find because they are listed among fund families that include stock funds as well. And once you find a bond fund, it's often difficult to understand exactly what it invests in. This section of the book clears the information fog surrounding these financial instruments and describes the composition of more than twenty different types of funds.

We explain the advantages of funds, when to use them, how to evaluate them, and how to size up their fees. Find out how the concept of yield for funds differs from yield-to-maturity used for individual bonds. Learn about duration, total return, and other measures of the payout from funds. See how open-end mutual funds compare to closed-end funds (including ETFs) and individual bonds in ways that might matter to you. We explain all this and more in this section.

Learn how to find great bond funds by using mutual fund selectors, and use calculators provided by Web sites to compare returns on different funds. Discover the advantages and disadvantages of all the different bond funds. Find out where to locate offering statements and more. You can profit in the bond markets, and we provide you with the tools and information you need to do so.

CHAPTER 13

HOW TO BUY INDIVIDUAL BONDS

A Tool Kit

THE MOST COMPELLING reason to buy individual bonds is that bonds come due at a defined time. Unlike bond mutual funds of any kind, individual bonds pay their face value in cash at maturity. This distinguishing characteristic is a key ingredient in many aspects of financial planning. Need a large chunk of cash for a tuition payment on December 15 ten years from now? Buy a bond that matures on December 1, 2017. Planning to retire? Buy a continuing series of bonds that come due when needed. The list is almost endless.

A frequent question investors ask is how do you choose between buying bonds and bond funds? There are a number of issues to consider. Diversification is a key one. Advisers suggest that if you have $50,000 to invest, you can purchase a sufficient range of high-quality securities to adequately diversify credit quality. If you can hold your bonds for five years, you are better off purchasing individual bonds. If you need liquidity or do not have enough assets to diversify your purchases, then it is better to purchase a fund. Also, some types of securities are simply better held through funds, including Ginnie Maes, junk bonds, and certain types of foreign bonds. Keep in mind that funds usually hold either stocks or bonds, and virtues attributed to funds are actually the result of the nature of the securities that are in the portfolio, as we will discuss in chapter 14.

Although the case for buying individual bonds is a simple one to make, trying to put a bond portfolio together is a bit more complicated. This chapter gives you guidelines for evaluating Web sites and for locating a bond broker. For specific questions about buying particular bonds, look at the end of each chapter that details a particular class of bonds.

Buying Online

The federal government offers the only unfettered bond-purchasing avenue open to you as an individual investor. Created in August 1986 by the U.S. Bureau of the Public Debt, TreasuryDirect (www.treasurydirect.com) is a book-entry securities system that allows you to maintain accounts directly with the U.S. Treasury (see chapter 6). This system lets you purchase all newly issued Treasury bills, notes, and bonds at auction without paying a commission. Also available at TreasuryDirect are EE and I savings bonds and TIPS.

With the growing popularity of the Internet, TreasuryDirect has become even more accessible and friendly. You can open your TreasuryDirect account online by filling in an account form on the spot. When your bonds come due, you can automatically reinvest your principal if you have given written instructions to do so. Interest flows to the account you designate. When you order bonds online, cash will be withdrawn from your bank or brokerage account to pay for them. You can also sell your bonds through this account.

With the successful implementation of TreasuryDirect and the advent of day-trading stock buyers, it was widely assumed that buying bonds online would also evolve into a simple matter of a single click. As it turns out, that assumption was wrong. Individual retail clients don't have free access to purchase bonds online. Without a broker, individuals can purchase only new-issue Treasuries. Thus, while the Web allows you to check sites and view bond prices and offerings, in most cases you still have to use a broker to finalize your trade.

Pricing Information

Price transparency in the bond markets gained momentum from the House of Representatives' Bond Price Competition Improvement Act of 1999 (H.R. 1400). Responding to this new law, the site www.investinginbonds.com was established. This site provides current prices on bonds that traded more than four times the previous day. Keep in mind that for bonds to do this, there must be quite a large supply of them available. This limits the number of postings because most bonds trade infrequently. The site also allows you to track the history of specific bond issues to see how they performed and how their prices compare to similar securities. The database does not allow you to check for daily price swings in the broad marketplace.

The Municipal Securities Rulemaking Board (MSRB), which was established by Congress in 1976, has stipulated that before making the purchase, bond purchasers have the right to receive "all material" information about a security available to brokerage firms. A material event might be notice of a pending downgrade resulting from economic weakness in a source of revenue that might negatively impact your bonds. This kind of information does not fit into the formats currently used on Web sites dedicated to bond offerings. For example, only a few sites give access to an offering statement.

Although Web sites have become more sophisticated, the problem remains that the obligatory material to be posted on them is not easily understood. Bonds, as must be evident by this point, are complicated. In a hypothetical example, let's say that you were offered Smallville USA GO muni bonds, of which 80 percent are escrowed to their April 1, 2013, maturity, and the remainder are not. Would you know how to interpret this information? Since you are reading our book, we hope the answer is yes, or you know how to find the answer here. For most people, however, the answer is a resounding no. And what is really distressing is that many financial advisers cannot correctly interpret this information because they don't know much about bonds either.

The MSRB further stipulates that brokers must recommend bonds to you that are "suitable" to your needs. There is some question as to whether or not posting bonds on the Internet is, for all intents and purposes, an offering to sell, thus, sidestepping the suitability issue. Although some argue that stock buyers have successfully mastered buying stock online from financial professionals, it is still the MSRB's position that trading in the electronic marketplace be limited to those who can make informed investment decisions without the services of a broker. It is not enough to declare yourself "informed" and say that you're willing to take on the risks. The Web site needs to verify that you will meet your obligations as its host company defines them: that you understand what you're buying and are able to pay for the bonds. With each transaction, they must also verify that you chose "suitable" bonds.

"Wait a minute," some might protest, "It is possible to buy bonds online. I just bought some last week." Well, yes, you may think you have, but what you actually did was to tell a clearing broker to buy the chosen bonds for you. This is an expensive process because you now have two middlemen instead of one: the broker and the Web site managers. The Web sites charge fees similar to those of discount brokers. More traditional bond brokers charge only a spread. In addition, the Web sites must verify that you chose suitable bonds; if they're deemed unsuitable, the trade has to be unwound—somehow.

In the event that the MSRB reverses its position and allows you to trade online without dealing with a middleman, you should know that most of the trading sites do not own the bonds that they trade and that the bonds are screened and priced for retail trade. Individual brokers are beginning to show their inventory online, but the only way you will know whether you're getting a good deal is to shop around. Do not assume that just because the trading platform you're using shows bonds from many dealers, you are getting the best buy. Also, the Web sites do not allow you to bid for the bonds at a lower price. That right is reserved for brokers. Visiting a Web site offering bonds, however, can help you clarify your thinking. Remember, despite what brokers may say, all of them sell bonds to make money. It's your job to figure out how they do it and to decide whether you're okay with their share.

Brokers who charge a flat fee for service are probably also making a "spread," the difference between the current market price and the cost of purchase. Other brokers charge only a spread, although they sometimes tack on a service charge that is not figured into the yield. (Remember, bonds are bought and sold on yield.) The only way you can know if you're getting a good price is to compare the offerings of a few different brokers, whether you view the bonds online or talk to a broker in person. If you do not see what you want to purchase, your broker might be able to check the "pick list," which is a trading platform dealers use to trade among themselves.

REAL-TIME PRICES

Although sites that post offerings for sale may be helpful with regard to pricing, they may also be quite misleading. The offering levels will not automatically change with the fluctuation of interest rates. Just like the offering sheets that were mailed out weekly, the posted prices of the bonds given on the site might be out of date. When you click to purchase the bond, the bond might not be there anymore, or the price might have changed. The broker might be just testing the waters to see what kinds of offers are made for the bonds.

Even dealers have problems with bond purchases on the Internet. If there is an offering of 100 bonds, and someone sells 50 bonds on the telephone in the office, there are now only 50 bonds left. Before the broker can update the screen, someone else is clicking on the 100-bond offering online. The selling broker is now "short 50 bonds." They can either cancel the trade in the office, try to find the bonds somewhere else, or tell the wire service: "I am such an idiot! I have only 50 bonds to sell." Customers and the wire service are not happy when the broker tells them that they have to break the trade. They can do that only so often.

Although you may have access to online trading, it is best if you find your bonds online but talk to a broker to purchase them. A broker might be able to offer you a discounted price or a better deal on bonds owned by the firm. Particularly attractive deals may never be posted online because they can be easily sold, thus, saving the broker the cost of posting the item. Some firms charge extra to talk to a broker. You will have to decide what is in your best interest.

The best online databases allow you to set the criteria and limit the number of offerings that pop up. For municipals, for example, you might want to choose a state and a maturity and yield range, AMT or not, and so on. The more restrictive your criteria, the fewer offerings you will see. At www.fidelity.com, you can access screens of all the major bond categories. You can check their offerings even if you are not an account holder there. Go to Research, Fixed Income, and then pick the individual bond type you want to review. Set your criteria, and away you go.

A good online service will give you detailed call information, including sinking funds and extraordinary calls. If a corporate bond has a make-whole call or a survivor option, that information should also be listed. However, no matter how good the Web site, there may be details that you are missing that a broker can tell you.

Key Questions to Ask About Buying Bonds Online

◆ What happens if there is a "fail" (the term used when a broker on the other side of the trade doesn't deliver)?

◆ What happens if the bonds that are delivered are not what you thought were described, or include an undisclosed call?

◆ If there is a material event you were not aware of because you lack access to the information sources that brokers have, do you have any recourse to return the bonds? In other words, to whom do you turn if you have a problem?

Choosing a Broker

Although being unable to trade online is a disappointment for consumers who are active traders, there are certain comforts in talking to a knowledgeable person about your investments. Not surprisingly, professional traders often find value in talking to one another as well. If they put in a trade electronically, they may follow it up with a phone call to discuss specific issues presented by the purchase. Relationships among brokers are especially important when they need to work out problems with a trade.

Given that the opportunities for unlicensed investors to trade bonds on an Internet exchange are quite limited, it behooves bond buyers to select a broker to do so. "It vexes me to choose another guide," the writer Emily Brontë once wrote. Although it might vex you too, it could translate into extra money and profits if you do it right.

THE RIGHT BROKERAGE FIRM

How do you find a good bond brokerage firm? You can check with friends and family to find out if they have a firm they like working with. Firms advertise on the Bond Market Association Web site at www.bondmarkets.com; click on the type of bond you're seeking to buy and you'll see a listing of the members and their specialties in that category. Ask if the brokerage firm is a member of the Securities Investor Protection Corporation (SIPC). This member-supported insurance company provides limited customer protection in case of bankruptcy, although it does not protect against trading losses. The brokerage firm may also have additional insurance, adding protection above the levels provided by SIPC.

It is probably not a surprise to hear that all brokerage firms are not alike. As in every other field, there are specialists, in this case, those who deal in particular kinds of bonds. While any broker can purchase bonds on your behalf, not all can execute the purchase or sale at the same price. Remember, most bonds trade in an over-the-counter market.

CRITERIA TO CONSIDER

Seek a brokerage firm that trades the kinds of bonds you want to buy and is willing to accommodate your investing style. You need to shop around in order to determine which firm has the kind of inventory you require. Some brokerage firms make the retail municipal market their specialty, though they may also offer other kinds of securities. They may have a specific regional orientation, specialize in national market bonds, or specialize in lower-quality bonds. Retail firms deal in smaller lots of bonds, and their salespeople are usually quite knowledgeable. The brokerage firm may tell you that it handles all kinds of securities, but once you see the firm's offerings you will know whether it provides the kinds of bonds you want along with good service and prices. The firm may not be able to offer you new issues if it does not participate in the selling syndicate.

Final steps in a thorough due diligence might be to ask for a description of the broker's typical client and then ask to talk to some of the broker's longer-term clients. The SEC provides a toll-free hotline operated by the National Association of Securities Dealers (NASD) for a background check of the broker or sales representative (800-289-9999), or visit their Web site.

The broker can screen bonds to meet your specifications. If you are in a high-tax state, for example, you may want to see bonds only from that state. You might have a particular maturity or rating in mind. Similarly, you would customize your search on the Web by selecting the criteria that match the kind of bond you seek. The broker will help you think through your options and then will show you the offerings that might match.

Once you've gathered a list of potential candidates, begin thinking in terms of the relationship. A brokerage firm may be outstanding, but it is a flesh and blood person with whom you will be dealing. To find a good individual broker, speak to the sales manager and ask for a recommendation. Then ask about the broker's experience with and amount of time allocated to bond trades. That experience is important because when choosing a broker, you are seeking to establish a mutually profitable, long-term relationship. And because this relationship is founded on money (your principal and their income) it's worth taking some time to make sure it's a solid one.

ESTABLISHING A RELATIONSHIP

The first step in establishing such a relationship is gathering information. What you learn will let you know if you can develop a rapport with the broker or whether there is a complete absence of chemistry between the two of you. Tell the broker what your goals are and ask how he or she thinks you might best achieve them. Do this long before you're prepared to make an investment so you can consider the recommendations. Ask what kinds of investments other clients have been purchasing. How does the broker evaluate those investments? Does the broker see a place for those investments for you? You do not wish to be hurried into taking actions that do not support your goals.

Find a broker whose basic philosophy aligns with yours or one who at least respects your perspective. The broker should inform you when bonds come due, or when there are substantial amounts of cash in your account. The broker should keep you up-to-date on marketplace swings and have the patience to answer your questions. Remember, there is no such thing as a dumb question, and you should not feel that your questions are out of place. The suggested securities should support your investment objectives. We recommend that you purchase plain-vanilla bonds. When you're offered an intricate investment and your eyes glaze over, don't stick around to try to understand it. If you're in a casino, the cards are stacked in favor of the house. Despite the deal's seeming attractiveness, you're likely to come out the loser. It is okay if you miss an opportunity; there is always another.

USING A STOCKBROKER

Just because you purchase stocks from a particular broker, don't assume that broker is the wisest choice for purchasing your bonds. Many stockbrokers do not know about or have little interest in bonds. Stock buyers who use discount stockbrokers believe that they can also purchase bonds at a discount from the same source as well. Unfortunately, there are no discount bond brokers. Bond brokers generally act as principal in a sale, which means that they buy the bonds for their own account and then sell them for a profit. Contrast that procedure with the purchase of stock, in which the broker acts as an agent, bringing together the buyer and seller for a disclosed fee, called a commission.

If you're convinced that you want to purchase individual bonds, be wary of any broker who tries to shift you into stocks or who strongly suggests packaged investments like mutual funds, unit investment trusts, and exchange-traded funds. This kind of recommendation indicates that the broker is not really interested in bonds, either from a lack of expertise or a belief that bonds don't generate enough money to warrant attention. However, as we explained, mutual funds do make sense if you're buying certain securities such as junk bonds, Ginnie Mae mortgage securities, or TIPS for some income as well as inflation protection.

THE MANAGED ACCOUNT

The deterioration in profits among major brokerage firms in the early 2000s has led to a change in the way brokerage firms sell bonds to individuals. Some firms now penalize brokers for trading individual bonds by either charging them a fee or not compensating them for certain types of trades. Instead, brokers are encouraged to have their customers move their assets into fee-based accounts. One such account is called a "wrap" account. It is managed by your broker for an annual fee that is equal to a fixed percentage of assets and is unaffected by the number of trading transactions. Alternatively, your broker might suggest what is commonly called a managed account if you have at least $500,000 in assets. This is an account managed by an outside adviser.

If you are a buy-and-hold investor doing limited transactions, these accounts are not a plus for you. The incentive for the broker is that he or she personally earns more. The reality is that the firm management has substantially reduced a broker's incentive to sell you bonds on a per-transaction basis. Despite all the yachts the brokers are supposed to have, many of them still need income to pay off their mortgages. Ask for a copy of the firm's commission and compensation schedule if you're curious about how the firm's policy affects your broker. As one broker said of fee-based accounts, "One of my clients said to me that they have been dealing with me for years on a transaction basis, and they see no reason why they should increase their expenses and pay me a fee. I can't even talk to them about it."

This emphasis on fee-based accounts is in part the result of the success of the National Association of Personal Financial Advisors (NAPFA). That organization's advertising pointed out the conflict of interest that commission-based advisers have. The ads ask whether advisers are doing what is in the best interest of the client or instead giving advice that generates the most personal revenue. The media gave great press coverage to NAPFA, and the public responded by seeking those advisers.

The big investment houses were caught on the wrong side of the issue and moved to co-opt the fee-only position by creating the wrap account. However, correctly applied, fee-only service means providing for the client what is in the client's best interest by charging a fee for advice and letting the client decide what is best.

The brokerage firms prefer that new clients pay a fixed annual fee instead of paying per transaction for bond purchases. The minimum account size is usually $100,000. The annual payment may be collected at the beginning of the year or quarterly. There are two types of accounts: one in which the in-house broker makes the investment decisions either independently or in conjunction with the investor; the other is the so-called discretionary managed accounts, for which outside money managers make all the decisions. Although a fee account might make sense for the active trader, it extracts a heavy price from the people who want to purchase a few medium-term bonds and let their funds accumulate.

An advantage of a managed account is that you might receive a bond allocation from a new issue that you might otherwise not have gotten. A possible disadvantage is that you will get small pieces of many issues, which will make selling more expensive. Remember, the firm is creating a mini–mutual fund just for you. Some broker or dealer is also making a spread when the bonds are traded, in addition to the up-front annual fee that's charged. There may also be penalties if you decide to leave the managed account.

If you think a managed account would be a good idea because you do not have the time to do the work, you might ask what happens if it doesn't work out. For example, some brokerage houses impose exit fees on in-house accounts, and these often include a closing fee that will not be more than the annual fee plus 1 percent of various eligible assets. In addition, they will not waive certain fees on mutual funds or closed-end funds.

To assess how well your investments in a managed account are doing, look at how much money you put in and how much is there at the end of a year rather than focusing on the benchmarks and other razzle-dazzle numbers and percentages. And be sure to ask your accountant how the account activity has affected your taxes.

Evaluating Bond Prices

Trading bonds is not like trading stocks. Stocks can be bought at uniform prices and are traded through exchanges. Most bonds trade over the counter, and individual brokers price them. For example, since the vast number of municipal bonds trade infrequently, you will probably never find three or more dealers offering the same bonds. This can make it difficult to compare prices, not only for municipals but also for other market sectors. However, with the advent of Investinginbonds.com and almost real-time reporting of trades, investors are well on their way to such transparency. It also helps that Fidelity Investments has chosen to disclose its fee structure for bonds, making it clear what it will cost you per trade. ShopforBonds.com has chosen to quote its fee in basis points instead of dollars. Ten to twenty basis points translates into $1 to $2 per $1,000 bond. Fidelity charges $1 to $4 per bond. Some online brokers charge a flat fee, ranging from $10.95 at Zions Direct to $45 at Ameritrade. Depending on the number of bonds trading, one may be more favorable than another.

The fee disclosures, however, do not reveal the spreads between the buy and sell price embedded in the transaction that some dealer is making in the pipeline. Keep in mind that only by comparison shopping can you find the best deal, after all fees are taken into account. Other sites may not charge any fee but rather embed their profit in the spread. Does this take time and energy? Yes. Making money takes time. One way to make money is not to spend it. You will have to decide if learning the ropes and doing due diligence is worth your time.

NATURE OF THE MARKETPLACE

The bond market is a dealer-to-dealer market, one in which firms hire traders to deal in specific types of bonds. A brokerage firm might have Treasury, corporate, and municipal bond desks. The desk is a euphemism for a group of traders sitting in a room in front of computer monitors, who specialize and trade in a particular portfolio sector of bonds. The broker, often referred to as the account manager, discusses the bonds with you, and the trader is the person who actually buys and sells the bonds. When the account manager wants to give you a price break, he consults with the trader who is the one who must agree to it.

When the broker owns the bonds being sold to you, there can be some flexibility in the price, depending on the price the trader paid and the current market direction. For example, if a broker owns thirty-five bonds and you want only twenty-five ($25,000), he might give you a price break if you bought all thirty-five instead of leaving him with an odd lot of ten. If the broker owns twenty-five bonds, they might be sold all or nothing (AON). If you're shown equally interesting bonds from different dealers, one of them might be willing to give you a break on the price. Remember that brokers want to sell you bonds, but they need to make a living, too. They won't work for nothing, no matter how nice a person you are.

If a trade is "done away," meaning that the broker has to purchase the bonds from another brokerage firm, you will pay two spreads in the transaction instead of one. Discount brokerage firms tack on a fee in addition to the spread because they purchase most of their bonds from other firms.

WHOLESALE VERSUS RETAIL

The bond marketplace is divided into wholesale or institutional markets and retail markets. In the wholesale market, corporate, agency, and Treasury bonds trade in million-dollar blocks, with $100 million blocks not infrequent. Municipal bonds trade in $100,000 blocks by comparison.

In an odd twist, bigger is not necessarily better when it comes to buying bonds. In buying small odd lots of an issue, individual buyers often get a better price than institutional traders buying large blocks. That's especially true for municipal bonds. As the broker Stoever Glass announces on its Web site, www.StoeverGlass.com, "Rather than focusing on larger lots, you should consider smaller lot sizes where you can get higher yields." At the same time, do not assume that you're getting a better deal just because it's an odd lot. Volume discounts do not apply to municipal bonds when you're buying, but if you're selling, size does matter. Larger lots fetch a much better price.

You can do better purchasing off-the-run Treasuries, the older issues that trade less frequently than new-issue Treasuries in the secondary market. That's because newly issued Treasuries are used as trading vehicles because of their large lot size and liquidity. Your best Treasury deal, however, is the new issue, if you can time your purchase with the auction. If your broker charges you a fee, you can always go to TreasuryDirect and purchase your bonds there if it is worth your time and effort.

New-issue municipal bonds may also be well priced because often, though not always, you're getting an institutional price and structure. A bond structure refers to the coupon size, (for example, 4 percent or 5 percent) and whether the bonds are selling at par or a premium. Institutions prefer premium bonds because they have better trading value. Premium bonds are priced to the worst-call yield, often resulting in a higher yield-to-maturity than discount bonds. Individuals tend to like par bonds selling close to face value because they like to know their semiannual interest payments are just that—all interest—instead of a mix of interest and return of principal. New-issue bonds may also have longer call protection than secondary market offerings.

Bonds of similar quality and maturity will trade in the same range. If you don't like the yield on the AAA-insured bonds, maybe you'll prefer lower-quality bonds with higher yields. Ask yourself if the added risk is worth the return. For example, assume two bonds are selling at par, one rated AAA and the other BBB. Although one has a higher yield, its interest payments are only $25 more per year, or $250 for the ten-year holding period. Is that worth the risk and any subsequent loss of sleep?

NEW-ISSUE ORDER AND CONFIRMATION DETAILS

You can tell how any market is doing by watching the spreads. Are they widening or shrinking? Although there is much greater yield in junk than in higher-rated bonds, the downside risk of losing your principal is also much greater. If your broker tells you that the spread between the plain-vanilla bond and the junk bond is historically low, you know that you're not being paid much for the higher risk. If the spreads are really wide, then you know the market believes the bonds are very risky right now. When the market speaks, listen! Then decide how to act.

When you put in an order to buy bonds of a new issue, which is called an expression of interest, you legally commit to buy the bonds if they're issued as described. Should interest rates rise between your order date and the bond's issue date, you're still expected to accept them. If the bond offering changes in any way, the broker will come back to you to describe the terms of the deal. If you like the new terms, you buy the bonds. If not, you're no longer obligated to purchase them.

Once you've made your bond selection, you'll receive a confirmation in the mail. Although each broker confirmation is slightly different, they all contain the same information. The bond description includes the amount purchased, trade and settlement dates, the unit price, accrued interest, total cost, and whether the bond is callable or not. Treasury bonds settle the next day, whereas corporate and municipal bonds settle three days after the trade, although the broker may be able to arrange for extra days to settlement if you ask. All bond issues are assigned a CUSIP number, the equivalent of a Social Security number for the bonds. Your account number printed at the top of the slip should be put on your check if the cash is not already in your account.

Key Information at the Point of Purchase

Figure 13.1 contains definitions of key terms as well as suggested questions to ask when you discuss these issues with your broker. Ask each of these questions, and you will have the basic information you need for a bond purchase. Keep in mind that the broker has a conflict of interest because the broker is not only your adviser in the transaction but also a principal to it. The broker owns the bond that he sells you and earns a fee called a "spread," the difference between the broker's cost and the price at which he sells to you.

FIGURE 13.1

Terms and Questions for a Purchase

Issuer	The entity that issues the bond.	*Who is the issuer? Who is responsible for the payment of interest and the repayment of the principal?*
Basis points	There are 100 bps in 1 percentage point. The difference between a 5 percent yield and a 6 percent yield is 100 bps.	*What is the difference in basis points between bond X and bond Y?*
Call	The right of the issuer to redeem the bond prior to maturity.	*Is this bond subject to any calls?*

Coupon	The contractual interest obligation that the bond issuer agrees to pay to the bondholder annually. If the coupon is 5 percent and the face amount of the bond is $1,000, then the interest payment for the year is $\$1{,}000 \times .05 = \$50$.	*What is the coupon amount?*
CUSIP	The fingerprint of the bond, your key to knowing all bond details, including pricing.	*What is the bond's CUSIP?*
Dated date	The issue date of the bond and the date when the bonds start paying interest.	*What is the dated date of the bond?*
Face amount	The dollar amount of the bond payable at the due date.	*What is the face amount of the bond?*
Insurance	Support for creditworthiness if the issuer cannot pay.	*Who is the insurer, and what is the insurer's rating?*
Maturity	Ending date of the bond, the due date.	*What is the maturity date of the bond?*

(continued on the following page)

Terms and Questions for a Purchase *(continued)*

Price	How much you pay for the bond. The price is set in relation to the yield.	*Is the bond priced to the call or to maturity?*
Rating	Issued by bond-rating institutions; estimates the bond's level of risk, indicating how likely the issuer is to pay the interest and face value of the bond when due.	*What is the bond's rating outlook?*
Yield-to-Maturity; Yield-to-Worst call	A percentage that measures how much the bond will return, assuming you hold it to maturity. It is the basis of comparison of all bonds to each other. **The yield sets the price.** You pay the price associated with the worst yield possible if the bond is called.	*What is the yield of the bond? To what date is it priced?*
Unit cost	Another way to describe the price, as if the bond had a face value of $100 instead of $1,000.	*What is the unit cost of the bond?*

CHAPTER 14

BOND FUNDS

The Good, the Bad, and the Worst

LET'S FACE IT. The easiest way to invest in bonds is to buy a bond mutual fund. Financial firms have catered to this strategy by creating almost 3,000 such funds and packaging them in a variety of shapes, structures, and contents. But holding an individual bond differs greatly from owning a bond fund because the fund has no due date. "A bond mutual fund is not by definition a fixed-income product," says Cort Smith, senior editor of *Investment Adviser.*

As we described in chapter 5, fixed-income investments calculate the compounding yield-to-maturity and worst-call yield, referred to as "yield." Funds cannot use those yield calculations so the meaning of the word *yield* is different when it's applied to them. Fund yields are a good measure of their income-generating potential, more like a current yield for individual bonds.

Although many view competition as a good thing (actually, we do, too), when it comes to funds, it isn't. The tremendous number of funds competing for your attention and dollars has created a severe case of obfuscation. Until 2002, this situation was further compounded by the fact that only 65 percent of a bond fund had to consist of the kind of bonds described in the title of the fund. That changed when the SEC mandated that 80 percent of the securities in a fund must be within the parameters set by the fund name as of July 31, 2002. That still leaves 20 percent of fund assets to be invested either in cash for redemptions or in more lucrative and risky securities in an attempt to goose up yields. In other words, if it says it's a Treasury bond fund, it must be a Treasury bond fund, mostly.

Common Ground

What remains unchanged is that trying to classify and categorize bond funds is a daunting task. Let's first review the characteristics common to all funds. No matter what the size or purpose, every bond fund has a per-share net asset value (NAV). This is the measure by which funds are valued daily. It is calculated by dividing the sum of the values, reduced by any liabilities, of all the bonds in a portfolio by the number of shares outstanding. All funds also provide a figure known as total return. This consists of a fund's cash distributions, plus or minus any change in share price during a specified period.

The NAV drops after a fund pays out the required 90 percent or more of its realized capital gains and dividends, usually in December, to reflect the lower fund value. You pay taxes on the distribution whether you owned the fund one day or one year. Before you invest, it's a good idea to find out when the fund generally makes this distribution.

Since funds are pass-through entities for tax purposes, if you hold shares of a taxable bond fund outside of a retirement account, you must report your share of the fund's interest income minus the fund's expenses. In addition, if the fund has realized capital gains, you must report your share of capital gains annually, whether the fund pays it out to you or reinvests it. If the fund has losses, they will offset the gains recognized by the fund. However, for tax purposes, if a fund has net capital losses, these capital losses may not pass through to its shareholders.

MATURITY

Unlike bonds, which have specific due dates, bond funds are described, as required by the SEC, in terms of their approximate maturity. All funds have dollar-weighted averages that reflect their stated maturities. Money market funds, which are almost cash equivalents, have maturities of one year or less. Funds with maturities of less than three years are short term. Although the SEC does not define the word "limited," it is usually applied to funds with maturities that fall between short and intermediate, generally less than five years. Intermediate funds are those with average maturities of three to ten years, and long-term funds are all those with maturities of ten or more years. The majority of bond funds are long term. *Because there is no fixed maturity date for bond funds, they are missing the key characteristic that distinguishes an individual bond. Bonds come due, bond funds do not, although the bonds within the fund do come due. If you purchase a bond maturing in three years, you know you will get the face value of the bond back in three years. If you purchase a short-term bond fund, you don't know what your shares will be worth in three years. They may be worth more or they may be worth less.*

A general rule is that the longer the maturity, the higher the yield and the greater the fund's price fluctuation. That's not to say that short-term rates don't fluctuate. The Federal Reserve Board cut short-term rates eleven times between 1999 and 2002, and raised them fourteen times between May 2005 and December 2006. The difference is that the bonds in short-term funds come due quickly, and new ones are bought at the prevailing rates. If new money is flooding into a fund, it helps a fund mirror the going rate for bonds so the yield adjusts rather quickly on the upside or downside.

YIELD

Because bonds in a fund do not all mature at the same time and bonds in many funds are replaced when they no longer are within the fund's investment parameters, the concept of yield-to-maturity is not applicable. Instead, the SEC has mandated a seven-day yield calculation specifically for money market funds in addition to a thirty-day yield calculation required for all funds, including money market funds. The SEC-mandated yields are standardized calculations that are the same for all funds. They allow you to compare returns after fees and expenses. These yields are not comparable to the compound yields on individual bonds.

In addition, an SEC rule that took effect in February 2002 requires all mutual funds, bond and stock alike, to calculate their returns on an after-tax basis. Because so many factors go into an after-tax calculation, the SEC mandated a uniform approach that uses the highest federal tax bracket (35 percent in 2006). The SEC rule also requires that any loads be subtracted from the after-tax return. This calculation is a useful tool for comparing one fund to another. It appears in each fund's prospectus and advertising material that touts tax efficiency.

The advertised yield on a bond fund can and will change over time. The yield you expect to get will not necessarily be sustained. You can get some indication of how much money your fund will earn over the course of a year by looking at the twelve-month distribution yield. This yield is the sum of all dividends paid over a period of time divided by the ending price. This return is comparable to a current yield on bonds and includes a payout of both principal and interest. There are likely to be disparities between the thirty-day and twelve-month yield calculation because of changes in the composition of the fund over time, and the distribution yield does not back out expenses.

DURATION

To supplement the notion of maturity, an often-used indicator in fund analysis for bonds is duration, a predictor of the volatility of a fund's NAV that reflects the bond's sensitivity to interest-rate changes. In the event that interest rates rise, duration gives a measure of how much the fund will lose in value. The fund's duration is usually permitted to fluctuate between 95 percent and 105 percent of the duration of its benchmark, as the manager makes adjustments to the portfolio.

The longer the average maturity of a bond fund; the greater the price sensitivity it will have to interest-rate shifts. However, in general, the more extended the maturities, the greater the interest payments into the fund, which cushions the market fluctuations.

Unlike individual bonds, funds do not have a maturity. For that reason, the concept of duration is used instead to compare funds. You might be asked: "Do you want to purchase a fund with a longer duration with a higher yield or one with a shorter duration and less volatility?"

The problem with using duration as a measure to compare funds of similar maturities is that each individual bond has its own duration and will act slightly differently when interest rates change, whereas the fund has a composite duration. Funds that appear to have comparable durations will suddenly start behaving differently when interest rates shift. Thus, sometimes people purchase ultrashort bond funds that have very short durations when the money market yields are low, only to find that they have much more market volatility than a money market fund because of a different portfolio construction. For this reason, investing in an ultrashort bond fund is not as useful a tool as it might appear.

DERIVATIVES

Derivatives are becoming more commonplace in the bond fund world. They're used to manage all kinds of risks and sometimes to speculate as well. A derivative is an investment that is based on, or derived from, some underlying security, currency, or index. One example of a derivative transaction is an agreement between two parties to exchange a fixed-rate security for a variable-rate security within a set period of time, based on an agreed formula. Derivatives may be used as a hedge against interest-rate fluctuations, to protect against credit erosion, or to make a bet in order to increase the returns of the fund. Examine the prospectus or the statement of additional information to learn about a fund's use of this tool.

ADVANTAGES

Bond funds tend to offer the following advantages:

◆ **Income.** Regular monthly income with interest and principal payments made as dividend distributions. Individual bonds usually offer semiannual payments, though some pay monthly.

◆ **Reinvestment.** Automatic reinvestment of income. Be aware, however, that this advantage is reduced if the fund charges a fee for the reinvestment.

◆ **Diversification.** Should one bond in a fund default, the others will supposedly smooth out any disaster ripples. You can choose to purchase bonds of the highest credit quality, like a Treasury bond, with minimum diversification required, or purchase more investment-grade bonds of lower quality in smaller amounts. If you invest in high-yielding bonds with poor credit quality, purchase them through a fund.

◆ **Daily liquidity.** A simple phone call translates into a sale posted at day's end; some funds offer free check writing on the accounts.

◆ **Bookkeeping services.** Funds keep track of all your purchases and redemptions and report to you and to the Internal Revenue Service.

◆ **Professional management.** Many bonds are difficult to evaluate. Foreign bonds and complex mortgage securities are best purchased through a fund.

DISADVANTAGES

Bond funds generally feature the following disadvantages:

◆ **Lack of fixed maturity date.** An individual bond always provides a due date on which you will receive all your money back, but a bond fund almost never does; in other words, bonds come due, bond funds don't.

◆ **Lack of income guarantee.** With an individual bond, the payment schedule is fixed, whereas payments from the various bonds in a fund can vary.

◆ **Capital gains tax.** You have to pay tax on capital gains realized by the fund. Funds generate capital gains when they sell bonds to raise cash for redemptions or trade securities. Funds that have a high turnover rate, a measure of annual portfolio change, are said to be tax inefficient when they generate capital gains, because the gains are passed through to the shareholders. Funds can't pass through tax losses.

◆ **Susceptibility to market risk.** Even conservative Treasury bond funds are subject to market risk. For example, *BusinessWeek* warns:

"If the yield on a 10-year Treasury jumps by half a percentage point from 5 percent now, it will lose about 10 percent of its market value."[1] That means that even the bond fund holding the safest securities could still experience a market decline that may continue for many years.

Checking the Costs: Hidden and Unhidden

Management and other fees are another constant among all bond funds. After all, these funds are created for management's benefit and not necessarily for yours. Therefore, it's important for investors to review this feature of bond funds thoroughly.

LOAD

The largest and most blatant cost is referred to as the load. In effect, this is the sales commission earned by the person who sells you the fund. Funds that have such sales commissions are known as load funds. With these funds, you generally lose money right from the start because the load is deducted from the amount of money you initially invest. Critical comments about front-end loads, as they're called, have led fund companies sometimes to allocate the loads over a number of years or to tack them on at the end. Go to www.sec.gov/answers/mffees.htm for a complete discussion of fees.

Fierce competition among funds has reduced load amounts over the years. Whereas once they were frequently as high as 8 percent, 4 percent to 5 percent figures are more typical now. In an effort to reap commission riches and still be competitive, some funds have introduced smaller loads, with assessments ranging from 1.5 percent to 3.5 percent of the initial investment. These funds are known as low-load funds.

And then there are the funds known as no-load funds, which are without commission charges. Because there are no commissions involved with their sale, these funds must be bought. That is, you must seek them out rather than expecting a salesperson to offer them to you. Fortunately, they are easy to find because they advertise extensively.

OTHER CHARGES

Other costs, decidedly camouflaged, include back-end loads (yup—some funds charge you to get out of them); annual management fees to cover administrative expenses; advertising fees on the no-load and load funds (they're officially designated as 12b-1 fees); plus all the transaction fees that the fund pays when it buys and sells the bonds in its portfolio. And there are more: some funds have loads on reinvested dividends, exchange fees if you want to transfer from one fund to another, frequent transaction charges, and shareholder accounting costs.

These fees add up. Vanguard, the giant mutual funds organization and pioneer in no-load funds, capitalized on this in one of its ads. The headline stated: "This is the story of the investor who lost $31,701 and didn't even know it." The copy went on to show how management fees ate up that much in the potential income from an initial $25,000 investment over a twenty-year period.

When financial services firms sell funds without front-or back-end loads, they may have a very high annual fee called a "12b-1 fee," as noted previously. A fund from a no-load fund family sold by a broker might have a small load attached to it to compensate the broker for making the sale.

Both load and no-load funds are beginning to group buyers according to the amount of their investments. They do this by creating classes of shares for the same fund, generally labeling them by letters of the alphabet. As you might expect, fees on larger deposits are lower. This information is all spelled out in a fund's prospectus.

Here are some rules for understanding fees and share classes on funds sold by brokers. Always review the prospectus so that you will know the exact terms of the shares you're buying.

- Consider Class A shares if you're planning to stay in the fund. They have a high initial charge (front-end load), but long term the 12b-1 fees have been low.
- Consider B-shares only if you plan to stay for the long term because there is a load, like those for annuities, which generally declines over a six-year period. Early exit triggers a nasty back-end

load. Eventually, the high 12b-1 fee declines. There is a longer lock-up period on B-shares than on C-shares.

◆ C-shares, like B-shares, have no up-front load and they have a lower back-end load if you exit the fund before one year. The 12b-1 fee has traditionally been 1 percent.

◆ D-shares are for do-it-yourself investors and may have the lowest fees.

If you are a do-it-yourself investor and looking to keep your costs down, you may purchase no-load funds. Fund families like Vanguard and Fidelity have no-load funds and even lower-cost funds if you have substantial assets to invest. Some funds have instituted retirement shares for 401(k)s and IRAs, which over the long term may have the highest fees of all and are designated by a different letter. Other fund families skip the alphabet soup and have specially designated funds for high-net-worth individuals that have the lowest cost. For example, Vanguard has Admiral Funds, T. Rowe Price has Summit Funds, and Fidelity has Spartan Funds for substantial depositors.

High fees associated with the purchase of funds are there to compensate the broker for the time spent with you. High fees hobble the fund manager in the race to produce good performance results. To compensate for the higher expenses, these funds are more likely to swell the yield by purchasing nonrated, longer-term, and lower-rated bonds.

When you reach for the highest-yielding, best-performing mutual fund, stop for a moment and consider this: a manager took risks to achieve it. Next year the fund could tank even if the strategy remains the same because of changing economic conditions. Strategies that reach for above-average yields are a necessity for funds with substantial fees. To use the stock phrase: past performance does not predict future returns.

We're biased in favor of funds with the lowest costs. We were, therefore, quite pleased to read about work undertaken by Morningstar, the fund tracking and rating company. As reported in November 2001, funds with the lowest fees performed the best overall: "In areas ranging from ultrashort bond funds to the multisector and intermediate-term bond categories, we found that the lowest-cost quartile of funds posted total returns over the year through October 31 that were better than those of the high-expense offerings."[2]

What's more, Morningstar found that the higher-cost funds took on added risk in order to boost the yield and compensate for the added fund costs. The article concludes by pointing out, "If you pay less, you're likely to get better returns and lower risk. That's not a bad combination."[3]

SEC POINTERS

To aid investors, the SEC introduced a free online service in 1999 to help investors calculate mutual fund fees described in an offering statement (the prospectus), accessed via www.sec.gov/edgar/searchedgar/prospectus.htm. The prospectus details the charges levied by your fund and will detail past performance.

The SEC points out that everyone purchasing a fund should read the prospectus, and it recommends the following steps for doing so:

- Note the date of issue of the prospectus that appears on the front cover. The date should be within the year of your receipt of the prospectus.
- Look at the chart showing the fund's annual total returns and at the total returns compared to industry benchmarks, as well as shareholder fees and shareholder expenses.

MORE ABOUT FEES

To analyze fees and expenses for mutual funds and exchange-traded funds (ETFs), go to the NASD Web site at www.nasd.com/index.htm; choose the "Investor Information" tab at the top of the page and then choose "Tools & Calculators," then "Analyze Mutual Fund and ETF Fees and Expenses," for an evaluation or comparison of three mutual fund companies.

To analyze mutual fund fee breakpoints, go to the NASD Web site and follow the first two steps above; then choose "Look Up Mutual Fund Breakpoint Information." This tool will enable you to check out what discounts and sales charge waivers are available on funds you're considering. This is a complicated tool that comes with a wonderful tutorial to explain how to use it.

Buying for Total Return

Bond traders all look at their bond returns in terms of total return. Because we recommend a buy-and-hold approach for individual investors, we do not look at bonds in this way. Total return takes into account the interest you earn plus the increase and decrease in the value of the bonds. In addition, any transaction costs, fees, and taxes you might have to pay reduces your total return.

Total return for individual bonds is the same concept that's applied to the return on stock or any other investment. The total return concept should not be applied to individual bonds if bonds are to be held to maturity. By marking-to-market the value of your bonds every day, brokerage houses encourage you to evaluate the performance of your bonds based on total return. In this way, they hope that you will be motivated to sell your bonds when you have a gain or a loss without thinking through the advantages of the buy-and-hold strategy. In showing the market movement, they do not trace the tax effects of the transaction or show you the fees and costs of trading.

Bond funds always use the concept of total return because the funds keep the duration of the fund in the same range, selling securities that have a shorter duration and purchasing ones that fit the fund profile. If you place a little bet on market movements, win or lose, the result is not very significant. If you place a big bet, the results can pack quite a wallop. To cite a well-known epigram, "The market may stay irrational longer than you can stay solvent."

Fund Categories

In choosing funds, an investor needs to be familiar with the U.S. fund industry's terminology for fund categories. Here, we'll designate four types, with the order ranging from the most closed to the most open. They are unit investment trusts (UITs), closed-end funds, ETFs, and open-end mutual funds. According to the Investment Company Act of 1940, only open-end investment companies may be called mutual funds.

UNIT INVESTMENT TRUSTS

Also known as defined portfolios, UITs are the purest form of a closed-end fund. Once a trust is created and beneficial interests in the trust are sold, it's considered closed with regard to the creation of further shares. Bond portfolios in UITs consist of ten or more securities that are packaged together and sold as a fixed number of shares. The portfolio frequently contains high-coupon bonds balanced by long-term zeros. Once these bonds are selected, the portfolio never changes until the high-coupon bonds are called. When that happens, the income from the UIT, which is why you purchased it in the first place, gradually diminishes until all you're left with are a few interest-paying bonds and a portfolio of zero-coupon bonds producing no income. This happens long before the shares are to be redeemed at the specified date by the originator of the UIT. Faced with the loss of your income, you may sell the UIT back to the originator at a generally unfavorable price. Check Part B of the prospectus to find out about the early redemption provisions on the bonds.

UITs carry high front-end loads or back-end loads (sales charges up to 8.5 percent are permissible, though they are usually between 4 percent and 5.5 percent). The effect of the load is to reduce your return as well as the actual amount of money that you have to invest by the cost of the load. If you consider purchasing them, ask what kind of return it would take to recover your load expenses as well as to make a good profit.

UITs came into vogue in the 1950s, when municipal bond mutual funds were not permitted to pass through tax-free income, but UITs were. It was not until 1976 that the tax laws changed and allowed open-end mutual funds to do the same. Although they no longer serve the alternative, money-saving purpose for which they were conceived, UITs persist as an investment vehicle because their high loads have made them a very lucrative broker product. They're touted as an easy way to obtain diversification without having to pay high management fees. The load fees are always in very small type. We don't recommend UITs.

CLOSED-END FUNDS

A closed-end bond fund consists of an asset pool of fixed-income securities. Once the fund is created, the investor trades ownership shares in the fund as stock. When you wish to sell a share, you're subject to the vagaries of the marketplace and how much other investors deem your shares are worth. The value of your shares could be higher or lower than the fund's underlying NAV. In addition, you have to pay a commission to a broker to buy or sell.

Closed-end bond funds, like UITs, have a fixed number of shares, but they differ from UITs in every other respect. Closed-end funds are managed, and the managers have great latitude in their investment practices. Although 80 percent of the bonds in the portfolio must match the description of the fund, the managers may use derivatives to make interest-rate plays, use repurchase agreements, buy zero-coupon bonds, and invest in floating- and variable-rate debt. The managers can and do leverage the bond portfolios by creating and selling auction-rate preferred stock (ARP). The management uses the proceeds from the sale of the preferred stock to buy additional long-term bonds, which may result in higher returns. These activities also give the share price of these funds greater volatility. Closed-end bond funds do not have specified redemption dates and are traded on exchanges like stocks after they're issued. The new-issue investors pay an embedded commission, guaranteeing a decline from the original issue price once they begin to trade.

When the closed-end fund is trading on the exchange, there are two values to watch: the fund's NAV and the market price of the fund's shares. Often prospective investors are not willing to pay the full NAV of the fund, and the shares trade at a discount to the NAV. This happens with such frequency, it seems logical to wait until new issues drop in price before buying. It makes sense to look for those funds that are more deeply discounted than others if the cash flow is the same. A general rule of thumb is that a closed-end bond fund may be an attractive buy when its discount to NAV is significantly greater than its average discount over the previous five years. The thinking is that the share price of the fund is likely to rise as the discount narrows to its normal range. Thumbs come in many different sizes, and so do the discounts that may never disappear even when the NAV is much higher. At such times, investors in these closed-end funds demand that the funds be transformed into open-end funds. Sometimes this happens, and a quick profit is made. More often than not, the investor is stuck with a poorly priced investment.

Closed-end bond funds selling at a discount to their NAV are popular when interest rates are declining. At such times, the yield on the bonds in the portfolio is attractive because it's higher than current market rates. This yield advantage is further enhanced if the price of the fund is at a discount to its NAV. During 2001, when the Federal Reserve reduced interest rates eleven times, investors clamored for the posted yields on closed-end bond funds, so much so that several of the funds were selling at more than 130 percent of their NAV. Other firms, sizing up the profit potential in the situation, scrambled to introduce new closed-end funds. New is better, for the broker, that is, because new funds generate commissions more easily. Nuveen Investments, for example, the most prolific issuer of closed-end muni funds, brought forth twenty new funds in 2001, raising more than $4 billion in the process.

Do closed-end funds yield more than just plain boring individual bonds? With 33 percent leverage, you bet they do. They also have substantially more risk of loss of principal. When the yield curve is flat or inverted, the storm clouds appear on the horizon. Leverage becomes less profitable, and your total return will fall. Although leverage increases your cash flow, it also hastens a decline in fund value when interest rates rise. However, you cannot compare the yield-to-maturity on a bond to the so-called yield on a closed-end fund. Like all mutual funds, closed-end funds pay out any capital gains that might be generated from the sale of an investment. If the bonds in the portfolio are callable and interest rates are falling, so will your dividend returns as the high-coupon bonds are called and replaced with bonds with lower coupons. Furthermore, to maintain the dividend, management may keep liquid assets in case the income is insufficient to generate an even payment stream. Thus, your "income" may be made up of interest, capital gains (on which you pay taxes), and distributions of paid-in capital (your money returned to you). This is a far cry from straight interest paid on a bond, and that's why the two are not comparable. While you enjoy your income stream, you might not realize the differences in income sources until you receive a tax statement at the end of the year.

Management, as well as market condition, counts when it comes to the performance of closed-end bond funds, and the result is a tremendous variation in returns. In 2001, for example, the one-year NAV return among high-yield closed-end bond funds varied from +13.2 percent to −33.1 percent. Even among the more conservative closed-end, national muni funds, the returns varied from a high of +8.1 percent to a low of −0.9 percent. If interest rates increase after you purchase a closed-end fund, you can have the worst of two worlds: declining income and declining market value. For more information on closed-end funds, visit the official Web site of closed-end funds, www.cefa.com.

EXCHANGE-TRADED BOND FUNDS

An ETF containing a bond portfolio is a relatively new concept. It is a closed-end fund that is sold on an exchange. Investors pay brokers for the purchase and sale of the ETF instead of the broker receiving a commission from the issuer. The ETF is pegged to an index, such as the Lehman Brothers Aggregate Bond Index, which means that there is minimal internal trading activity.

The difference between an ETF and a mutual fund is significant. With mutual funds, the cash comes in first and then the bonds are purchased. With ETFs, the creators put the bonds in first and take back "creation units." When you buy stock of an ETF, you're purchasing a piece of a creation unit. Those units remain outstanding until the original creator decides to swap back units for underlying shares in the ETF. The value of the ETF is based on quotes for the underlying stock, because new shares can be created or redeemed almost instantaneously.

There are three advantages commonly attributed to ETFs: (1) you can sell them any time the exchanges are open, as opposed to mutual funds in which you receive the NAV at the end of the trading day; (2) because they are passive portfolios following an index, the management fees are minimal; and (3) the funds are supposed to be tax efficient. Through complicated structures, they may be able to avoid making yearly capital gains distributions.

ETFs also have some disadvantages. They can sell at a discount to their NAV, but the discounts on these funds historically have been less than those on typical closed-end funds. You have to pay a management fee when you own an ETF, as well as a commission to either buy or sell it. There are also trading costs incurred by the ETF because bonds mature and need to be replaced. The ETF management fee does not cover future distribution fees, although they do not assess a 12b-1 fee. These charges add up and could well wipe out any tax advantages in an ETF when compared to those of a no-load index mutual fund. Also, you must determine what the payout schedule might be. ETFs may pay monthly dividends like bond funds, or they may pay quarterly, semiannual, or annual dividends.

Importantly, ETF managers have not invested in their own funds. In a 2006 review of their regulatory findings, Dan Culloton, a senior fund analyst at Morningstar, reported, "Exchange-traded fund families urge you to join the ETF revolution, but many of the people managing their own funds are sitting the uprising out."[4] Visit www.quantumonline.com and www.vanguard.com/ETFs for more information.

OPEN-END MUTUAL FUNDS

An open-end bond fund also consists of an asset pool of fixed-income securities. In this case, the number of ownership shares is not limited. Rather, the fund is inaugurated with an initial number of shares. The total value of the asset pool is divided by the number of shares to come up with the NAV. Because the pool is open, investors can buy additional shares. The buyer is charged the existing NAV, plus any loads, and then the fund manager uses that money to go out and buy more assets. In an open-ended bond fund, you buy a pro rata share of the fund's value. When you wish to exit, or cash out, you're given the NAV of your shares, minus any fees, at the end of the trading day on which you exit. When funds are very popular, they may be closed to new investors.

Open-end funds are just that: the number of outstanding shares changes constantly as investors buy or redeem them from the fund. The fund's bond investments also change as managers readjust the maturities of the bonds, take advantage of favorable market conditions, meet redemptions, or invest new funds.

Unlike closed-end funds, open-end funds are not traded. They are bought either directly from the fund family or from a broker who is an agent for the fund company. Their NAV at the end of the trading day is always the price at which they are bought or redeemed.

A great variety of funds is offered in this format. Information about them is widely published and easily obtained in the media and on the Internet. Prices are quoted daily. Newsletters track funds, giving buy/sell recommendations. Most funds discourage active trading because it requires a portfolio readjustment if cash needs to be raised to pay for the redeemed shares.

Of all types of funds, open-end mutual funds have the most variable fee schedule, depending on whether they're sold by a broker who charges a load or bought directly from the fund company. **Figure 14.1** is a table that compares the features of individual bonds to open- and closed-end bond funds.

NOTES TO FIGURE 14.1

◆ **Cash flow certainty.** Individual bonds provide the anticipated income. Open-end funds and closed-end funds will have variable income.

FIGURE 14.1

Comparison of High-Quality Individual Bonds, Open-End Bond Mutual Funds, and Closed-End Funds Including ETFs

Taxable Bonds	Individual Bond Ladder With Plain-Vanilla Bonds	Open-End Bond Funds	Closed-End Funds (CEFs) and Bond ETFs
Reportable capital gains	Under your control	Yes, uncertain	Yes, uncertain
Cash flow certainty	Certain	Uncertain	Uncertain
Principal at risk	Not if held to due date	Yes	Yes
Leverage	You decide	No	For CEFs and ETFs maybe
Initial transaction costs	Spread to purchase the bonds	For no-load funds, no; for load funds, yes	Commission to buy and sell funds
Final transaction costs	None, if not sold	For no-load funds, no; for load funds, maybe	Commissions and possible loads
Shares trade at NAV	Not applicable	Yes	Maybe
Ongoing fees	None	Yes	Yes
Duration decline	Yes	No	No
Credit diversification	Not required	Yes	Yes
Credit risk	Minimal	Yes	Yes
Interest risk	Interest paid on schedule	Uncertain	Uncertain

◆ **Trading costs.** Individual bonds have one transaction cost. Open-end funds are bought and sold at the NAV at the close of the date of sale. All funds pay price spreads (the difference between the buy and sell) to trade bonds, which are passed on to fund holders. Closed-end funds, including ETFs, must be purchased and sold through a broker. Closed-end funds may or may not trade at their NAV.

◆ **Diversification.** You don't need diversification with individual plain-vanilla bonds because the bonds have high credit ratings, and the default rate is so low. The funds' diversification is so great that it increases the operating and management costs of the funds.

◆ **Interest-rate risk.** You receive a predictable rate of return on your individual bonds but not with the other vehicles. Even if the fund provides a consistent cash flow, some of that cash flow may be a return of your principal. Funds will lose value if interest rates rise. Their duration usually remains within a specified range. For this reason, we can say that funds, even though they hold bonds, do not provide the same benefits as individual securities.

◆ **Principal at risk.** Unless there is a bond default, there will be no realized loss of principal if individual bonds are held until they come due. If interest rates rise, you can sell your short-term bonds without much loss and reinvest at the higher rates. Remember, the duration of individual bonds gets shorter year after year. The duration of a fund stays within a range because shorter-maturity bonds are sold and replaced with longer-maturity bonds. Closed-end funds and some open-end bond funds may use leverage, which heightens the risk to your principal while possibly increasing your cash flow. If interest rates have risen from the time of purchase, you will have a greater loss if your fund has leverage. Some funds may also include catastrophe (cat) bonds, which are insurance-linked bonds that translate natural or man-made disasters into credit risks. This high-yield investment pays high returns, making a fund's yield look very attractive. In the event of a disaster linked to the cat bonds in your fund, you may lose part or all of their future interest payments and principal.

Chapter Notes

1. Paul B. Farrell, "Bond Funds Offer 'Danger Zone' Shield." Retrieved January 29, 2002, from www.cbs.marketwatch.com.

2. Scott Cooley, "High-Cost Bond Funds Are for the Birds," *Morningstar FundInvestor*, November 30, 2001.

3. Ibid.

4. Dan Culloton, "Do ETF Managers Eat Their Own Cooking?" Morningstar .com, September 12, 2006.

CHAPTER 15

BONDS FUNDS

A Taxing Matter

IN THIS CHAPTER, we'll look at bond funds from the point of view of their taxable status and, within that status, consider the different portfolio types. When comparing the returns on bond funds, it's very important to examine their portfolios to understand why the returns are different. As you'll see, types of bond portfolios may be presented in more than one format, which we'll point out as we describe each one. The fund types are presented in alphabetical order.

Tax-Exempt Funds

There are fewer varieties of tax-exempt funds than there are taxable funds. We describe four here. Just as you would for individual municipal bonds, compare the after-tax return on a taxable bond fund with a tax-exempt fund to determine which would give you a better return. Between October 2005 and October 2006, municipal bond funds returned 4.22 percent compared to taxable bond funds, which returned 4.16 percent, according to Morningstar.[1] Furthermore, Peter J. DeGroot, vice president and head of municipal strategies at Lehman Brothers, reported that in August 2006 the tax-adjusted returns on municipal bonds for those in the highest tax bracket were 9.63 percent during the previous ten years, compared to 6.88 percent for taxable bonds.[2] Past performance is no predictor of future returns, but if we can reduce expenses, we have a better chance of coming out ahead.

Check out the yields on the state-specific funds compared to the national funds to see if you can avoid paying state taxes as well, while helping to support the state economy by being a lender. Although you may think you should buy a fund with the name of your state on it, there are times when a national muni fund would be more advantageous. Funds may purchase bonds subject to the AMT in order to boost yields. If you're subject to this tax, you might want to check into the fund's policy and review its portfolio before you buy. You might earn more, on an after-tax basis, in a fund that holds no AMT bonds than you would in a fund that holds only bonds of your state of residence.

MUNICIPAL BOND FUNDS: HIGH YIELD (JUNK BONDS)

As described in chapter 10, the credit quality of municipal bonds varies tremendously. Bonds at the lower end of the spectrum are forced to offer a higher yield to attract investors. Some financial institutions buy these up and package them as high-yield municipal bond funds. These funds suffered great setbacks in 1999 and 2000 as a result of the credit crunch following the bankruptcy of Orange County, California. Investors in a Heartland Advisers fund, for example, saw the fund's value decline by more than 70 percent in one day.[3] These losses were the result of illiquidity in the high-yield market, which limited the ability of the pricing services to adequately value the bonds. The fund manager decided to retain higher values than were justified. Heartland management repriced the funds when they learned about the problem.

Although Heartland got caught in the crunch, other high-yield funds suffered as well. When the savings and loans stopped lending because of their own credit crisis, municipalities opened the spigots to let industrial-development bonds flow. Generally backed by the revenue generated from the projects, many failed to reach their revenue targets. Although municipal bonds are generally considered a credit snooze, industrial-development bonds were racking up defaults.

In short, high-yield municipal bond funds are every bit as risky as corporate high-yield bond funds. Buyers of these funds must be ever vigilant. The funds are available as open-end mutual funds and as closed-end funds.

MUNICIPAL BOND FUNDS: MONEY MARKET MUTUAL FUNDS

These funds offer all the convenience of traditional taxable money market funds plus their income is tax exempt. The trade-off is a smaller pretax yield than that offered by traditional taxable funds. These funds are divided into national and state-specific funds. National funds generally provide higher yields than state-specific funds as well as greater diversity. However, someone in a high-tax state, such as California, might choose a state-specific money market mutual fund to receive income that is exempt from local, state, and federal taxes. You won't find this type of fund at banks, which currently offer taxable FDIC-insured money market accounts.

Containing short-term notes with a maximum maturity of thirteen months with an average maturity of ninety days, the bonds in the fund are named for the source of the funding that will repay them. Thus, a Treasury money market will hold Treasury bonds, and a cash-management account will hold a variety of instruments that are more risky. A muni money market fund will hold munis and may contain bonds subject to the AMT unless otherwise specified. State-specific muni money market funds appeal to those in a high tax bracket in a high-tax state. These funds also buy tax-free commercial paper issued by municipalities and variable-rate debt to satisfy the demand for product, as well as auction-rate securities or variable-rate demand obligations, long bonds sold with short puts of seven days or a month or more.

There have been no losses in money market funds so far even when a security defaulted. We don't worry about money markets from big mutual fund companies. Historically, if a security defaulted, the mutual fund companies purchased the defaulted security from the money market fund at its face value to maintain its dollar-per-share price. Sellers of money market funds chose to reduce their fees to avoid "breaking the buck," which occurs when the management fees and expenses exceed the income of the fund.

Unfortunately, those who invested in money market subaccounts through their variable annuity found that they got a negative return when the fees exceeded earnings, while surrender charges prevented them from switching to another fund. In the annuity world, a negative return "is just not as visible," according to Brian Nestor, head of Vanguard Group's annuity and insurance services unit, "because you don't have a buck going down to 99 cents or 98 cents, [and without that high visibility] I don't think our providers feel the need to waive fees."[4]

MUNICIPAL BOND FUNDS: NATIONAL

These funds come in two varieties: investment grade and high yield (junk). The title of the fund will tell you which variety it is. Included in these funds are bonds from all states.

Investment-grade funds, like their corporate cousins, come in short-, intermediate-, and long-term varieties. Some bond funds contain only insured bonds, which pay a lower yield in exchange for the added protection. Because of the broad diversity of these funds, many believe that the extra protection is not necessary.

If your state charges income tax on out-of-state bonds, the fund management will provide you with an end-of-the-year statement that will outline what percentage of bonds it holds from all states as well as the taxable income that results from bonds subject to the AMT. If 10 percent of the bonds were from your state, for example, you would not pay any state income tax on that income. Both investment-grade funds and high-yield funds are available as UITs, closed-end funds, and open-end mutual funds.

MUNICIPAL BOND FUNDS: STATE SPECIFIC

If you have to pay high state taxes on bonds issued by other states, you should invest in state-specific funds. These funds provide income that is free of all income taxes. The funds may be more volatile than national market funds if state-specific credit quality issues arise. Always compare the returns on state-specific funds with the national counterpart. Buy the national funds whenever your tax situation permits. These state funds always contain the name of the state in the title. They are available in UIT, closed-end, and open-end mutual fund formats and may contain bonds whose income is subject to the AMT.

Taxable Funds

From 2000 to 2002, billions of dollars were pumped into taxable bond funds as investors fled the falling stock market. These investors were seeking an easy way to capture the safety and promised return of bonds. Although investors have drifted to gold, real estate, and the stock market, in 2007 money continues to pour into bonds both nationally and from overseas investors who are "hungry for yield."

The moral of bond fund performance is that the funds run the gamut of the risk spectrum, although the spreads on high-yield versus investment-grade bonds are still quite narrow. The fund categories that follow are arranged in alphabetical order. We considered putting the safest and most conservative first, and the riskiest, most volatile, and potentially most lucrative last, but that would have been misleading. Some kinds of bonds in funds are intrinsically safer than others, but there is always the 20 percent of a fund's assets that managers may invest at their discretion. That may make a bond fund less safe than it appears.

BUY-WRITE FUNDS

If you're searching for added return, sellers of these covered-call funds hope you will choose them. The funds get their name from the fact that they buy stocks and then write call options on them. The options generate cash but limit the upside potential of the investment. If the price of a stock in the fund rises above the call price, the stock is called away. However, there is no limit to the downside movement of the stock. Mushrooming with the low interest rate in 2006, this fund category was created twenty years ago, but fell into disfavor as performance lagged. To support this fund, a BuyWrite Benchmark Index was created by the Chicago Board Options Exchange. The index tracks the movement of the

S&P 500 and the call options sold against it. These funds have an expense ratio greater than 1 percent. They are closed-end funds, sold as bond alternatives.

CONVERTIBLE BOND FUNDS

Convertible bond funds behave more like stocks than bonds and are a steamy addition to any portfolio. Read all about the underlying components of convertible bonds in chapter 11 and note in particular that the majority of convertible bonds are below investment grade. These funds perform best when the stock market is on a roll and interest rates are rising. If you're looking for safe income, it's best to look elsewhere.

Compared to losing stock market returns, convertible bond funds posted gains between 1999 and 2001. Since then they have been weak performers. If you're looking for gains to top stocks, check out convertibles when stock market volatility is subdued. Investing in the lowest-grade bonds is not always a walk in the park. In February 2002, for example, Lipper and Company's convertible hedge fund slashed its value by 40 percent. This dramatic one-time repricing reflects a fund manager's desperate attempt to cover losses in the hope that better times are imminent. Hedge funds are attracted to the potential outsized returns of convertible bonds. Between 2002 and 2006, these funds have been weak performers. They are available as open-end funds.

CORPORATE BOND FUNDS: HIGH YIELD (JUNK)

Funds in this category will vary greatly in their holdings and in their returns as well. They can contain almost any kind of investments in widely different proportions, as long as the prospectus discloses the information. The yearly turnover of a portfolio can be as low as 20 percent or as high as 80 percent. The fund can be dedicated to providing high income or total return but not to both simultaneously. Probably more so than for any other fund category, it's important to know the investment philosophy of the sponsoring firm. The Vanguard High-Yield Corporate Fund, for example, consists principally of cash-paying bonds that carry credit ratings of B or better, which means that some of the bonds in the portfolio are investment grade. This mix lowers the fund's yield, but reduces exposure to bond defaults and losses of capital.

Other high-yield funds contain predominately C-rated bonds, which could send shivers of despair through some investors and trigger dreams of lucrative glory in others. Try to uncover why the fund you're considering offers a higher yield. To estimate the risk of a higher-yield bond fund, before investing you should find out the breakdown of its credit quality, sector allocation, and average maturity and compare them to those of similar funds.

The perceived wisdom on the Street is that the best time to buy these funds is after there has been a shakeout in the corporate market, with lots of defaults. The thinking behind this is that when the recession is over, it's likely that the survivors will be able to regroup and sustain themselves until the next downturn and credit squeeze.

Because this book is intended for use in both good times and bad, we must remind you that during the period before a recession is actually announced, these funds can get dicey. Between 1999 and 2000, for example, there were $11 billion of redemptions in junk bond funds, leaving the valuation of the underlying bond portfolios in question. One analyst reckoned that some managers were overstating the value of their bonds by 10 percentage points or more. That was partly because the market became so thin that they were hard to price, but also, presumably, because their true values were so frightening.[5] You can compare your fund performance to an NASD-Bloomberg Active U.S. Corporate High Yield Index at www.investinginbonds.com. There are both closed- and open-end varieties of corporate high-yield bond funds, as well as exchange-traded funds.

CORPORATE BOND FUNDS: INVESTMENT GRADE

Containing bonds in the top four rating categories, investment-grade corporate bond funds are grouped into those with short-, medium-, and long-term maturities. It is important to consider these maturity distinctions because long-term corporates are extremely sensitive to changes in interest yields.

From 2000 to 2006, investment-grade corporate bonds have been very popular with overseas investors. For example, in 2001, these investors purchased almost half of all new corporate bonds. In 2007, the media is still waiting for the moment when these bonds fall out of favor with foreign investors, anticipating that there could be a value decline in funds holding these bonds. Before buying such a fund, ask if junk bonds are included in the mix to spruce up the yield. These funds are good to park in your retirement accounts because you can defer paying taxes on their income. Investment-grade corporate bonds are available as either closed-end funds, open-end funds, or ETFs. Check out your fund against the NASD-Bloomberg Active U.S. Corporate Investment Grade Index at www.investinginbonds.com.

DIVIDEND-PAYING STOCK FUNDS

If you choose to purchase stock through a mutual fund emphasizing dividends, keep in mind that in 2006, "the average equity-income offering in Morningstar's mutual fund database has a net expense ratio of 1.40 percent. The average 12-month dividend yield—which is paid after management and administrative fees—is only 1.63 percent,"[6] reported Josh Peters, the author of the *Morningstar DividendInvestor.* The managers of these funds need to show that their stock picks outperformed those in other funds so the turnover rate is 51 percent annually, according to Peters, which further generates transaction costs and taxes on capital gain. If you purchased the S&P 500 in 2006, the average dividend yield was below 2 percent.[7] These yields are very low compared to bond yields, but then you're always hoping for stocks to appreciate. This category is considered a bond alternative. It is sold in closed-end fund, ETF, and open-end mutual fund format. Sometimes municipal bonds are mixed in.

FOREIGN BOND FUNDS

International bond funds invest only in foreign bonds. Global bond funds may hold U.S. corporate bonds in addition to the bonds of foreign issuers. There are also funds that hold bonds of emerging markets or sectors of those markets. Multisector and balanced funds may contain a mix of foreign and U.S. securities. These funds have higher fees and greater risk than U.S. bond funds. Currency fluctuations present a unique risk to this bond sector no matter what the maturity structure. Ask yourself if you're prepared to bet against the U.S. dollar. Some people do, but timing is everything. The funds are available in closed-end, open-end, and ETF formats.

GOVERNMENT BOND FUNDS

This is a catchall category, but it is not a one-size-fits-all category, despite its benign title. These funds can contain a variety of securities. Some are plain-vanilla funds having a mixture of Treasuries and agency securities and mortgages. Some of the mortgage debt might not be issued through government agencies. Others may allow the trading of futures and options, which increases potential profit and multiplies the risk. Some funds are managed for total return and include the separate trading of STRIPS. Look in the prospectus to find out what securities are in the fund portfolio and review chapters 6 through 9 to understand what you're purchasing. They are available in closed-end and open-end formats.

GNMA FUNDS

The GNMA funds are popular. The funds invest in mortgage-backed securities guaranteed by Ginnie Mae, an agency of the U.S. government (see chapter 9). These funds are very liquid and of high quality. Here is an example where bigger is better, and Vanguard takes the prize, though Fidelity, USAA, and Payden-funds GNMA funds are good performers, too. The largest funds have usually enough diversity to cushion market fluctuations from principal prepayments while providing very attractive risk-adjusted returns. When the rate of mortgage refinancings increases rapidly because of declining interest rates, this fund does not perform as well as funds with noncallable bonds. However, this kind of fund handles moderate ups and downs well, especially if the fund is very large. Size matters here because mortgage securities are always being called and new ones purchased to replace them. We recommend that your GNMA purchases be through a fund because of the unpredictability of the calls and pricing opaqueness. They are available through open-end mutual funds.

INDEX FUNDS

Like stock index funds, bond funds that are indexed invest in a broad array of bonds that represent a sampling of the bond index rather than all the issues in the index. Currently, the index of choice is the Lehman Brothers Aggregate Index for investment-grade bonds, though some index funds use different standards of measurement. Thus, while the Lehman Brothers Aggregate contains more than 5,000 issues, a fund may hold only a fraction of them. Fund managers have considerable flexibility in what they choose to buy, and bonds may be traded more than you would expect.

Bonds incorporated in the index must come from sizable issues. Government and corporate bonds make up 70 percent of the index, but mortgage-backed and asset-backed securities and Yankee bonds are also included. When a bond's maturity falls below one year, it is dropped from the index and from these portfolios. Although the bonds in the funds do not precisely mirror the index, management attempts to match the duration and yield profile of the index so that the fund returns will be comparable. Led by Vanguard, other index fund providers have lowered their fees to remain competitive.

Index funds come in short, intermediate, long, and total market formats. As a policy, they tend to steer away from low-grade bonds. Those who believe in indexing make a powerful case for bond index funds. Standard & Poor's in 2006 reported in its S&P Indices Versus Active Funds (SPIVA) quarterly: "[Bond] Indices outperformed in six of eleven styles [of funds] over the past three years. Indices outperformed in ten of eleven styles over the past five years."[8] In the second quarter, 2006, "only long-term government and short-term general [bond] funds outperformed their indices."[9] Furthermore, John Bogle, founder of the Vanguard Group of mutual funds, states that in "the mutual fund field, risk and reward go hand in hand only if *cost is held constant.*"[10] In 2006, Fidelity Investments lowered the costs of its index funds below those of Vanguard to become the industry leader.[11]

Until recently, bond index funds were offered only in the open-end format. The introduction of exchange-traded bond funds has changed that. The ETFs also mirror indexes and are purported to have the additional advantage of not passing through capital gains although as of 2006 there had not been a significant difference. Information about index funds is posted on the Internet at www.indexfunds.com. Bond index funds are available in open-end and ETF formats.

INFLATION-PROTECTED SECURITIES FUNDS

These funds are relative newcomers to the mutual fund family, with asset pools primarily consisting of TIPS issued by the Treasury (see chapter 6). Although these funds are thought of as conservative investments for individuals fearful of inflation, at times they have delivered very handsome returns. However, they do not fare as well in a low inflation scenario.

TIPS are a type of bond that is advantageous to own through a fund. When owned individually, some of the return is added to the principal amount but is not realized until the bond matures. Nevertheless, if you own the bond outside of a tax-sheltered retirement account, you will have to pay tax on the phantom income you receive annually. However, when TIPS are purchased through a fund, you receive not only the current income but the increase from the inflation accrual as well.[12] Bond managers pass on this benefit to you by selling the fraction of the face value of their bond holdings corresponding to the inflation accrual. Inflation-protected bonds are available in open-end and ETF formats.

LOAN-PARTICIPATION FUNDS

This type of fund consists primarily of repackaged bank loans and contains risky credits made to finance many financial activities, including highly leveraged buyouts, mergers, and acquisitions. When the economy is troubled, the liquidity of these securities evaporates.

The purpose of the fund is to provide income. Preservation of capital is secondary. If the notion of higher-than-average income flow excites you, consider what would happen if there were defaults and the principal was no longer there to generate that income. The loans are usually B-rated paper—that's junk bond quality. Low interest rates have nurtured troubled companies, making these funds appear safe, but an upturn in rates will trigger defaults. A flagging economy increases the risk that you will lose money invested in a loan-participation fund. Expect a 30 percent loss if the fund is not leveraged. If it is leveraged, you will lose more. If you are getting a rate of return of 8 percent or better, the fund is leveraged.[13]

Similar funds are sold with names such as "floating rate" or "prime rate" in their titles, although they are hardly prime. Because the loans held by the fund are short term, these funds are often sold as higher-yielding alternatives to money market funds. Banks are now delighted to have a way to shift the risk of widespread loan defaults to investors. Substantial fees further cut down the attraction of these funds so they often are leveraged to goose up the yield. Loan-participation funds frequently return cash when the loans are prepaid, triggering some capital gains that are passed on to the shareholder. They have the same pricing difficulties as high-yield bonds. Expect the market liquidity of these funds to dry up oncc defaults are reported. The nail-biting quality of these investments increases when you see both your principal and income disappear as companies fail to meet their debt obligations. To maintain liquidity, the funds must keep a substantial sum in cash and liquid securities. Originally appearing in the closed-end format in 1988, they are still sold that way.

STABLE-VALUE FUNDS

Stable-value funds and individual guaranteed investment contracts made up 21.3 percent of the assets in 401(k) plans in 2006.[14] These funds often have the word *preservation* in their title because of the SEC's restriction on the use of the term *stable.* They're composed primarily of new age guaranteed investment contracts (GICs), asset-backed securities, and corporate bonds. Banks or insurance companies provide a "wrapper," or insurance policy, that cloaks the assets and insulates them from market swings. Like any other investment, the quality of these funds will vary depending on the asset mix. To compete in the market when interest rates are rising, some of these funds are apt to adopt riskier strategies like investing in non-U.S.-dollar bonds hedged against currency risk and using nondollar, fixed-income futures.

These wrappers may not prevent a default because you're relying on an insurance company to protect you. Trust Advisers Stable Value Plus Fund declared bankruptcy in 2005 as a result of imprudent investments. As a result of a settlement with Circle Trust, the adviser to the fund, the 1,500 pension plans invested in the now $200 million fund will receive all principal plus a little interest. This was not a mutual fund but rather a collective trust. These entities do not have to provide daily pricing and detailed prospectuses to the SEC because the SEC does not regulate the trust.[15] GICs also ran into trouble in the 1990s when Executive Life and Mutual Benefit Life failed.

Stable-value funds were investigated by the SEC in 2004 because their underlying investments fluctuated in value yet the NAVs always remained stable.[16] As a result of the SEC's activities, many funds closed. Those remaining have had to adjust their portfolio content and oversight to meet the SEC's objections.

Penalties established either by the fund or by the retirement account regulations may be imposed for early withdrawal or for withdrawal whenever the ninety-day commercial paper rises to a level above a fund's payout. To find these funds, visit www.stablevalue.org. They are sold as a bond alternative.

STRATEGIC OR MULTISECTOR BOND FUNDS

Players seeking high total returns in the high-yield, foreign, and U.S. bond markets gravitate to this type of fund. Relatively new to the game, the portfolio managers can shift their assets to the sectors they view as most rewarding. It's very difficult to evaluate these funds because there is no benchmark against which to measure them. They're considered to be very high risk. They are available as closed-end and open-end funds.

TARGET-DATE FUNDS: ZERO COUPON

These funds hold bonds that pay no current interest. Unless held in a tax-sheltered retirement account, you must report the imputed interest every year, that is, the interest they would have paid if they were paying interest. The title of the fund states a targeted maturity, but what is referred to is really a targeted duration. The entire bond portfolio does not come due at the same time; however, bonds that do not mature with the majority of the securities are sold at the fund maturity target. Composed mostly of Treasury and agency bond strips (see chapters 6 and 8), the funds pose no default risk. Although they may be purchased to buy and hold, more often they are bought to make an interest-rate play. In a declining interest-rate market, these bonds appreciate rapidly. Longer-term funds are extremely volatile. For example, a 1 percent decline in interest rates on a portfolio of zero-coupon bonds with a ten-year duration will result in a 10 percent gain, whereas a corresponding 1 percent increase in interest rates will provide a corresponding 10 percent decline in fund value. In addition to price swings, especially on long-maturity funds, these funds may have restrictions on selling large positions in order to limit trading. Read the portfolio carefully before buying. Adding these funds to a prospectus is not for the timid. Find them among closed-end and open-end funds.

TARGET-DATE FUNDS: LIFE CYCLE, OR ASSET-ALLOCATION, FUNDS

Like their zero-coupon relative, these funds target the date of your retirement. Unlike the straight target bond fund, the fund is a "fund of funds." It's a wrapper containing bond, stock, real estate, or other types of funds. The fund presumably starts out with a high percentage of stocks, which gradually are replaced with bonds over the years. You pay two levels of fees: one for the underlying fund and another for the wrapper. This type of fund surged in 2003, becoming the most popular new type of fund for retirement accounts when it became apparent that most individuals ignore retirement planning and do not rebalance their portfolios. Mostly managed by Fidelity Investments, Vanguard Group, and T. Rowe Price Group in

2006, they are not all structured the same. Although each manager has a similar variety of investments, they are held in different proportions. They increase their bond holdings on a variety of schedules as retirement approaches. Unfortunately, holding your assets in bond funds will not protect your principal the way individual bonds do if interest rates rise. It's important to read the prospectuses if you choose this type of investment, and to reevaluate your decision periodically. They are found among open-end funds.

TREASURY BOND FUNDS

Plain-vanilla Treasury bonds fill these funds in short-, medium-, and long-term maturities. Paying the lowest yields, their claim to fame is safety and state tax exemption. We cannot understand why anyone would buy these funds when they could buy the Treasuries in minimum amounts of $1,000, for no transaction or management fees through TreasuryDirect or through your broker for a one-time fee (see chapter 6 for details). Treasury bond funds are available in closed-end, open-end, and exchange-traded funds.

ULTRASHORT BOND FUNDS

These funds invest in floating-rate securities, whose interest rates are periodically reset. The definition of ultrashort varies from one-year to five-year maturities. Likewise, the mix of securities and the use of derivatives differ from one portfolio to another. The fund's purpose may be high current income only, or it may also aim for capital preservation and liquidity. The fund may be called adjustable rate, variable rate, short term, capital preservation, or have ultrashort in the name.

Ultrashort bond funds have high expense ratios. They do best in a down market and may not earn enough to cover their expenses when interest rates are falling and bond prices are rising, as was the case for the Strong Advantage (STADX) in 2001, even though it had a duration of 0.75 years. It was not the worst performer in this category. Since they are not money market funds, there is no commitment to maintain an even share price of $1 per share as does a money market although some funds in this category do so. An alternative to this kind of fund might be a short corporate bond fund or short corporate bonds themselves. Open-end mutual funds are the place to look for them.

Chapter Notes

1. Virginia Munger Kahn, "Mutual Funds Report; Good Times Keep Rolling for Municipal Bonds," *New York Times* online, October 8, 2006.

2. Ibid.

3. Joe Mysak, "Events at Heartland Are Only the Beginning," Bloomberg.com, October 25, 2000.

4. Karen Damato, "Money Funds Offered by Annuity Firms Break Below $1 Net Asset Value Level," *Wall Street Journal*, November 8, 2002, C1, C13.

5. "Corporate Bonds: Debt Delirium," *Economist*, May 20, 2001, 90.

6. Josh Peters, "The Case for Income from Individual Stocks," Morningstar online, September 8, 2006.

7. www.indexarb.com, September 12, 2006.

8. Standard & Poor's, *Indices Versus Active Funds Scorecard, Second Quarter 2006*, July 19, 2006, 3.

9. Standard & Poor's, 1.

10. John Bogle, *Bogle on Mutual Funds* (New York: Richard D. Irwin, 1994).

11. Jim Lowell, "In Pictures: Five Hidden Gems among Fidelity Index Funds," *Forbes* online, September 13, 2006.

12. Frances Denmark, "Safe Harbor," *Bloomberg Wealth Manager*, December 2000/January 2001, 88.

13. Don Martin, "High-Yield Bank Loan Mutual Funds May Offer Hidden Risk," *Los Altos* online, September 20, 2006.

14. Jan M. Rosen, "Just How Stable Is 'Stable Value?'" *New York Times*, October 8, 2006, BU 28.

15. Ibid.

16. Eric Jacobson, "Is This the Death of Stable-Value Funds?" Morningstar online, August 18, 2004.

CHAPTER 16

CHOOSING A BOND FUND

THE INFORMATION RESOURCES on the Internet are a great boon to investors seeking to narrow down their fund choices. Before undertaking a search, however, it's important to determine what kind of investor you are or want to be. Do you want to engage in the thrills of trading, always hoping to be one profitable step ahead of the market, or do you want to simply buy and hold bond funds and get on with the rest of your life? We call the former an active investor and the latter a passive investor. An active investor seeks out actively managed total-return funds or no-load funds. The pitfalls of this strategy are potential loss of capital, higher expenses, and short-term capital gains that may be taxed as ordinary income. The passive investor seeks out and holds no-load index funds in order to pay minimal fees and negligible taxes.

You also need to consider your tax status. If you're in a high tax bracket and want to generate tax-free interest income, you may want to have municipal bond funds in your portfolio. If you're subject to the AMT, check out whether the funds buy municipal bonds subject to the AMT. If a fund holds taxable bonds, your income will be currently taxable, unless the funds are held in a tax-sheltered retirement account. Income dividends from non-AMT municipal bond funds will be exempt from federal tax but may be subject to state and local income taxes, depending on the laws of your state affecting income from municipal bonds.

In choosing the specific type of fund, you need to determine your level of credit risk tolerance and then match that with the fund categories we've described. You also need to determine the level of interest-rate risk you can tolerate. Finally, you should also review whether you need income for a short period, an income stream for many years, or just the knowledge that you'll be reaping income in the future.

The Search Begins

There are various criteria you can use on Web sites to narrow your fund selection. Let's say, for example, that you would like to receive a safe, steady stream of taxable income that's slightly higher than that of a broad-market bond index. After reading the descriptions of the funds in chapters 14 and 15, you settle on a long-term, investment-grade corporate bond fund.

Your next step is to go on the Web and type www.yahoo.com, for example, or to your local library to find Morningstar reports. On Yahoo!, click on "Finance," then scroll down to find "Mutual Funds," then the mutual fund screener. You can then click on a number of settings to narrow your search. But the more specific you are, the less likely you'll be satisfied with the results.

We recommend choosing between taxable and tax free and focusing on fees. See what comes up. Then go back and experiment by narrowing your search criteria. We suggest that you always click on "No Load." We also strongly recommend that you buy only highly rated funds with low expense ratios. These funds, however, are not always easy to find.

Following the instructions in our example, we set the following parameters for our search:

- **Type:** Bond, long term
- **Morningstar rating:** Five stars
- **Load:** None
- **Expense ratio:** Less than 0.5 percent
- **Minimum investment:** Less than $1,000

We then clicked on the "Find Funds" button and, to our dismay, learned that not a single fund fit our criteria. We then started to change the parameters here and there. Finally, when we reduced the rating to four stars, increased the minimum investment to less than $2,500, and increased the expense ratio to less than 1 percent, we located four funds that filled the bill. For each one of them, we could obtain a current quote, a chart, a profile, a performance review, a listing of the holdings, and a comparison with all others in its category. We could also choose to review some prospectuses. We did note, however, that there was no bond index fund listed in the group; for lower cost and higher yield, you could put on your Sherlock Holmes cap and sleuth the financial press. As an alternative to the global search, you might want to just check out the Web sites of the large and well-regarded fund families such as Fidelity, PIMCO, Vanguard, TIAA-CREF, T. Rowe Price, and American Century Funds. See the Appendix for Web addresses.

Yahoo! presents a wealth of information to help you make a knowledgeable decision about which bond fund to buy. Other helpful information sources that can augment your search are the Morningstar Web site, www.morningstar.com; the magazine and news sites of *Forbes,* www.forbes.com, (try Annual Fund Screen for best-performing funds); *BusinessWeek* at www.businessweek.com (Under Investor, go to Economy and Bonds); *SmartMoney* at www.smartmoney.com; *Money Magazine* at www.money.cnn.com/magazines, *Kiplinger's Personal Finance* at www.kiplinger.com, the *Wall Street Journal* at www.wsj.com, *Barron's* at www.barrons.com, and http://moneycentral.msn.com for investor information and fund research. The *Wall Street Journal* and *Barron's* sites are not free.

Why visit more than one site? Some of them have very annoying advertising that becomes nearly torturous after only a few minutes so you might want to vary the kind of headaches you'll experience. Also, the Web sites do not all profile the same funds or profile them in exactly the same way. The *Forbes* site, for example, tells how the funds perform in up and down interest-rate markets. It also assigns grades for tax and cost efficiency, and then gives an overall risk-adjusted rating, with number 1 being the best. This Web site also relays the Lipper Leader Scorecard, with a checkmark for the best score, replacing the number 1. The Lipper Leader Scorecard includes ratings for total return, consistent return, preservation, tax efficiency, and expense. This is very useful information to keep in mind so that there won't be any surprises. Some sites have a bond calculator, chat rooms, informative articles, and a variety of other interesting features.

MORNINGSTAR

We've mentioned Morningstar a number of times. Morningstar is a financial information company that analyzes funds and provides comprehensive data in an easily accessible format. Many online sites purchase their information from Morningstar although the data are not as complete as the data found on its own Web site. Formerly available only in libraries, Morningstar now offers its services online for an affordable price.

What Morningstar online gives you that the printed library version does not, is easy access from anywhere and the ability to sort the information based on your individual preferences. The first sort is based on the Morningstar star ranking. To be rated at all, a fund must be in existence for three years. Funds are rated against other funds in focused comparison groups. Within the group, there may be as many five-star as one-star funds because they will be arrayed along a bell curve. The ratings are adjusted for fund "loads," or sales charges. There are no guarantees, though, that a precipitous event might not catch the firm off guard, or that a fund that performed well in the past will continue to do so. However, Morningstar has changed its risk measure to reward consistent performance over a number of years rather than fiery flashes of brilliant returns.

In the free online version of Morningstar, the list of funds does not include all the funds it tracks. Also, exchange-traded closed-end funds and open-end mutual funds are mixed together. It's easy to be overwhelmed by the sheer amount of information presented. However, if you keep your perspective, you'll find your way. Most important are the fund fees, the kinds of bonds included in the fund, the duration of the fund assets, credit quality, and the table of annual returns. In addition to providing comprehensive information, Morningstar online also has some smart tools to enable you to compare your fund to other funds in the same category.

A feature added in 2006 provides dollar-weighted returns. It calculates a return based on cash flows in and out of a fund as opposed to the usual time-weighted returns, which show how a fund performed on an absolute basis. Thus, times when the fund has more money will get a heavier weight than the times it has less money. This measure was constructed in response to the growing understanding of how often individual investors have bad timing, going into a fund when its yields are peaking and pulling out when the yields drop. Timing is especially poor for the riskiest types of investments. In addition to the dollar-weighted return, each fund will have a "success ratio," which will represent the percentage of total returns captured by the dollar-weighted average.[1]

"Best Buy Funds are not only stingy with overhead costs, but also have done a decent job in delivering risk-adjusted returns over the long haul," *Forbes* tells investors on its Web site.[2] Found most frequently on the *Forbes* list, Fidelity and Vanguard funds are the persistent top performers in most bond fund families. Other top-performing bond funds include, American Century, Payden, TCW, T. Rowe Price, USAA, Bernstein, and Dodge and Cox. In the junk category, the top players are Westcore, Buffalo, Neuberger Berman, and Fidelity. For long-term total return, the PIMCO Total Return bond fund (PTTDX), run by Bill Gross, beat the Lehman Aggregate Bond Index in nine of the ten years ending calendar year 2005.

Whoever said fund picking was quick and easy? It can, however, be both fun and profitable.

Chapter Notes

1. Raymond Fazzi, "Fund Returns: Theory Versus Experience," *Financial Adviser*, August 2006, 66.

2. Forbes.com, January 11, 2007.

PART FIVE

BOND INVESTMENT STRATEGIES

"IF YOU DON'T know where you are going, you will end up somewhere else," said Yogi Berra, manager of the New York Yankees. In this section, we'll help you get to where you would want to go, if you knew where that was. In chapter 17, we outline four steps you might take to design and execute your personal bond-investment strategy. Before making any investment, you should update your life objectives and financial needs. After you've considered your future, divide your investment funds into two pots: secure and risk taking. Having done that, consider what the after-tax consequences of your investment choices might be and how the results might modify the working model of your proposal. Finally, purchase plain-vanilla bonds that meet your financial objectives.

We offer a variety of financial-planning stories in chapter 18. These stories will give you a sense of how you might use bonds to design your own bond portfolio. One of our examples is a socially conscious investor who takes the unusual step of using bonds as her investment vehicle. Other investors deal with life-planning issues of achieving financial security, saving for college, and preparing for life's transitions.

In chapter 19, we present the concept of the yield curve, a plotted snapshot of interest rates, and how to adjust your investment strategies to maximize your return. We show you how to construct a bond ladder tailored to your own personal needs within the context of market fluctuations, tax consequences, concerns for safety and yield, and a variety of other factors.

Throughout our many years as financial advisers, we have followed a basic set of rules that have stood the test of time and have served our clients well. We call them the "Richelson Investment Rules" and share them with you here. They are conservative in that they are designed both to protect and to enhance the value of your investments. The 100 percent bond portfolio fully complies with these rules.

Rule 1. Precisely define all your objectives. List your financial objectives, life objectives, and values as specifically as you can. These objectives should determine the type of investments you choose.

Rule 2. If you can't afford the risk, don't play. The potential return from an investment is generally proportional to its risk. Determine what percent of your investment portfolio you will put at risk and what percent you will keep safe in plain-vanilla bonds.

Rule 3. Don't lose money. We do not say this in jest. People talk only about their winners, whether at the racetrack or in the stock market. You rarely hear about the money they lost. Compared to investors who win some and lose some, you'll come out way ahead if you never lose money. In Part One, we explain how the 100 percent bond portfolio can keep your money safe.

Rule 4. Evaluate the return on all investments on a risk-adjusted, after-tax basis. Our investment philosophy is that an investment should generate the largest after-tax economic return with the least risk of losing capital, the smallest investment costs, and the least aggravation. To compare apples to apples, always look at each investment on a risk-adjusted, after-tax basis. Risk adjusted means that in comparing one investment to another, you evaluate the likelihood of losing money. No investment made solely for tax purposes is a good investment.

Rule 5. Understand the investment. Don't invest in anything unless you understand its function as an investment vehicle and its tax consequences. When you experience MEGO (my eyes glaze over), consider it a warning flag. Promoters of investment products love to tell you about the front-end tax benefits of an investment and the gains that will surely be yours. However, they often don't mention what the downside may look like, how difficult it might be to sell the investment product, who will buy it, what the spreads might be, and whether there are adverse tax consequences when the investment terminates.

Rule 6. Understand the investment's liquidity. Be in control of the investment. Liquidity and flexibility are as important as yield, particularly if you need or want to sell the investment product before its due date.

Rule 7. Check for the seller's conflicts of interest before you buy. Always look for the seller's potential conflicts of interest and try to determine whether they may affect the description you've been given of the investment. Brokers, for example, often get larger commissions for trading stocks and complex financial products than they do for bonds bought and held for many years.

With these rules in mind, let's review investment planning strategies for how to increase your returns with bonds.

CHAPTER 17

INVESTMENT PLANNING WITH BONDS

How to Design Your Bond Portfolio

There are two times in a man's life when he should not speculate: When he can't afford it, and when he can.

—MARK TWAIN

LIKE RODNEY DANGERFIELD, bonds get no respect. Their advantages are woefully underappreciated. We believe that bonds are the best investments available, and we wholeheartedly agree with Andrew Mellon's prescient late-1920s observation that "gentlemen prefer bonds." We believe that ladies should, too.

Mellon's statement was memorable, although a bit too pithy. Bonds are an extremely diverse financial category. They come in all denominations and maturities, from ultrasafe Treasury bills to risky junk bonds and unfathomable CMOs, and they serve a variety of needs and purposes. You don't simply buy "a bond" just as you don't simply buy "a car." There are important choices involved, and you need to understand the specific reasons for your intended purchase, what you're going to use it for, and how long you intend to keep it.

Investors tend to buy bonds with different strategies in mind. The 100 percent bond portfolio is a strategy for investing in very conservative, plain-vanilla bonds to preserve principal and receive a steady stream of income to support the life objectives and financial needs of the investor. This is in accord with *Richelson Investment Rule 1: Define your objectives* and *Richelson Investment Rule 3: Don't lose money.*

Designing a Bond Portfolio

We recommend following four steps in designing your bond portfolio:

1 Determine your life objectives and financial needs.

2 Divide your investment portfolio into two parts:

◆ **Bonds.** We consider plain-vanilla bonds to be the best and most predictable investments because we can determine their future value and their rate of return (the yield-to-maturity).

◆ **All other investments.** We consider all other investments to be speculative because we can't determine their future value or their rate of return.

3 Perform a tax-planning review of your investments to maximize your after-tax returns.

4 Purchase the bonds that meet your needs in each of the following three categories:

◆ Need for a cash reserve or lines of credit for emergencies.

◆ Identifiable needs, objectives, and anticipated life transitions, for example, retirement, the cost of your children's education, weddings, expensive vacation trips, and purchase of a house. For some of you there is a desire for financial independence.

◆ Unanticipated life transitions that may profoundly change your life, such as a critical illness, disability, death of a spouse, divorce, job change, and job loss. We advise all our clients to plan to accumulate at least enough plain-vanilla bonds to deal with the possible unanticipated transitions and bumps in the road that come to us all.

Reviewing your life objectives and financial needs is challenging, sometimes unpleasant, and always time consuming. It can become a more attractive process, however, if you think of it in terms of the big payoff it provides (a secure financial future and peace of mind). If you were our client, we would ask you to do the hardest part of the work first, articulating your life objectives and financial needs, uncovering the most important eventualities, including the possibility of unanticipated transitions that may profoundly change your life. We would then ask you to decide how much of your money you want to keep safe in plain-vanilla bonds and how much of it you want to use to speculate. After a review of your tax situation, we would then align your bond and other investment choices with your life objectives and financial needs.

STEP 1. DETERMINE YOUR LIFE OBJECTIVES AND FINANCIAL NEEDS

RICHELSON INVESTMENT RULE 1

Identify Your Financial Goals and Life Objectives Before Making Investment Decisions

"Prediction is very difficult," observed Nobel physics laureate Niels Bohr, "especially if it's about the future." So it's not surprising that predicting the course of your life is quite a challenge. We are not cookie-cutter people but rather individuals with complex personal and investment needs compounded by life in a multifaceted world that's changing at an accelerating pace.

Predicting the financial future is impossible because the basic questions are too complex to solve with any degree of consistency or certainty. The culture of the financial world is like any other culture. It's about intangible, ambiguous, unstable, and often-contradictory stories that people tell each other as they try to make sense of the actions of the marketplace.

Since we don't know what the future holds for you or for the investment markets, your investment strategy should consist of aligning your investments with your life objectives and financial needs rather than trying to guess what asset class will outperform in the future. The 100 percent bond portfolio makes it possible to execute this investment strategy.

The first step in our process of investment planning is to have you define your life objectives and values that reflect who you are now and the lifestyle that you would like to enjoy in the future. Your age, health, and family situation influence your life objectives and your values. Once you define these, the key question in your investment-planning process is what combination of bonds will best support your objectives and values with the least amount of risk? Note that the key question is not which investments will perform best next year or in the next ten years. No one knows the answer to that question. We advise clients to match their objectives and their values with the investments that have the least amount of risk, rather than trying to find the next "hot" investment area that will double their money in a year or two. That is why we like plain-vanilla bonds.

Your present and future life objectives, values, and financial needs depend on many factors that are specific to you and your family. Looking at some basic categories of goals may help you formulate and define your own life objectives and financial needs. We believe that there are three levels of goals and financial needs:

1 **Basic security and unstated goals.** Planning is required to deal with possible disasters. You might be in an auto accident, you might be suddenly unable to work, or a fire might destroy your home. Different types of insurance can help protect you from the consequences of these types of events.

2 **Intermediate goals and obligations.** These goals are consciously anticipated, finite in time, and saved for and generally completed before retirement. Examples are weddings, second homes, boats, and trips around the world. Consider also the need for financial

reserves that will enable you or your children to attend college or professional school, enter a new business, or take advantage of an opportunity.

3 Lifetime goals. These are your long-term financial goals, such as retirement, career change, or financial independence. You're financially independent when your cash flow from investments exceeds the expenses needed to maintain your current standard of living. Achieving financial independence is so powerful for some individuals that they will purposely reduce their current standard of living to achieve this goal in future years.

STEP 2. DIVIDE YOUR INVESTMENT PORTFOLIO INTO TWO CATEGORIES

RICHELSON INVESTMENT RULE 2

If You Can't Afford the Risk, Don't Play

Divide your portfolio into two categories:

1 Determine how much of your investment portfolio you want to keep safe in plain-vanilla bonds.

2 Determine the amount of money you will use to speculate on other investments. This will be your play money.

Plain-vanilla bonds are predictable. For example, assume you buy a $100,000 bond that has a coupon rate of 5 percent and comes due in ten years. If you reinvested the coupon interest at the rate of 5 percent, you would have about $163,000 at the end of the ten-year period. To make this calculation on a business or financial calculator do the following:

- Enter the 100,000 for present value (*PV*).
- Enter the interest rate as 5 for interest (*i*).
- Enter the ten-year life as 10 (*n*).
- Press future value (*FV*).

In addition to providing you with coupon interest semiannually, bonds automatically turn into cash in the amount of their face value at their due dates. The future value of investments other than bonds is indeterminable. They may appreciate a great deal in value or they may decline precipitously. That's why we recommend that you support your financial plan with plain-vanilla bonds. We understand that you may wish to speculate. We just want you to carefully decide how much of your money you will put at risk.

STEP 3. PLAN FOR TAXES

RICHELSON INVESTMENT RULE 4

Evaluate the Return on Investments on an After-Tax Basis

The only way to understand the real value of an investment is to determine its return after you pay your taxes. Uncle Sam and some states will take their share. You can't spend what you pay in taxes. There are a few tax guidelines that you should follow to maximize your after-tax return with respect to bonds.

Determine your marginal tax bracket. You need to know your marginal federal, state, and local income tax brackets. In other words, at what rate do you pay income tax to each of these taxing authorities on the interest income you earn? You can find this out from the relevant tax tables of each taxing authority or from your tax preparer if you have one. The question to ask your tax preparer is, "What is my marginal income tax bracket for interest income?"

Let's simplify this discussion by saying that we define a high federal income tax bracket as 25 percent or higher. In 2006, you reach the 25 percent federal tax bracket if your taxable income exceeds $29,700 if you're single and $61,300 if you're married and file a joint return.

State income taxes. You should consider state and local income taxes very carefully because they vary greatly. Some states such as Florida and Texas have no state income tax and some high-tax states, such as California, have a top state income tax rate that exceeds 9 percent. If you live in a high-tax state like New York and in a high-tax city like New York, your tax bracket may be very high once you combine your federal, state, and local tax brackets.

Before you make an investment, consider the total amount of taxes you would pay. For example, which bonds will give you the highest after-tax returns? You can get a rough idea of the impact of taxes if you compare tax-exempt bond yields to taxable bond yields with the calculator found at www.investinginbonds.com. Or you can use the simple formula found in chapter 19, relating to bond strategies. It makes sense to consider the tax consequences of other nonbond investments as well. However, you should always consult your tax adviser before you invest because the Web site calculator doesn't take into account your particular tax situation, including whether you're subject to the AMT.

If you live in a high-tax state and need a cash-equivalent investment, consider a money market bond fund that holds state-specific bonds. For example, if you live in California, you might invest in a money market fund that holds only California tax-free municipal bonds so that your interest income would be free of federal and California income taxes. However, if you are subject to the AMT, it might be more important to fund a money market fund that doesn't own AMT bonds.

Selection of investment accounts. See *Richelson Investment Rule 7: Check for the seller's conflict of interest.* Focus on the distinction between the two kinds of accounts available to individual investors: taxable accounts and tax-sheltered retirement accounts. Tax-sheltered retirement accounts include IRAs, 401(k) plans, 403(b) plans, and other pension accounts. For simplicity's sake, we'll refer to all these accounts as pension accounts. The key question is which of your investments should be in a taxable account and which should be in a pension account.

You should keep after-tax investments in your taxable account. The interest income recognized in your taxable account is subject to federal income tax, except for interest income earned from tax-free municipal bonds. That means that if you're in the 25 percent tax bracket or higher, you should consider buying tax-free municipal bonds in your taxable account. If you're in a lower tax bracket, you might consider buying taxable bonds in your taxable account because taxable bonds generally yield more interest income than tax-free municipal bonds of the same rating and maturity, even on an after-tax basis.

All income and capital gains recognized in your pension account each year are tax-deferred and not subject to tax in the current tax year. However, money and securities paid to you from your pension account (except for Roth IRAs) are generally taxed at your ordinary income tax rate in the year they're distributed to you no matter what investments your pension account holds. Therefore, if you generate capital gains in your pension account, you will have converted lightly taxed capital gains into ordinary income when these gains are distributed to you. That's why some tax advisers counsel that you hold your stocks in your taxable account.

If you can get a deduction for a contribution you make to your pension account, you should seriously consider doing so. If an employer will match some or all of your contribution to a 401(k) account, prudence dictates that you should make your contribution and get the financial and tax benefits. Unfortunately, 401(k) plans generally offer a menu of mutual funds and are not self-directed. This means that participants can't buy individual bonds in a company-sponsored 401(k) plan. Our recommendations for a 401(k) plan are as follows: buy bond index funds, money market funds, short-term bond funds, GNMA funds, and high dividend-paying stock funds such as a value stock index fund. If you purchase a fund with dividend-paying stocks and bond funds, you will guarantee a flow of income that can compound. However, there will be no shelter from market fluctuations.

Although deferred-income annuities are often recommended for pension accounts, they should be purchased only in your taxable account because their main selling point is that they provide a tax-deferral. There is no need to pay the costs of an annuity to get a tax deferral when you already get a tax deferral in your pension account. Annuities may be suggested for your retirement account because that may be where your money is, but generally that choice is not in your best interest.

If you invest in U.S. savings bonds, you receive a tax deferral, as discussed in chapter 7. In addition, there are major tax opportunities available for certain taxpayers to fund education expenses with U.S. savings bonds. See the "Special Features" section of chapter 7, relating to U.S. savings bonds.

STEP 4. SELECT BONDS TO SUPPORT YOUR LIFE OBJECTIVES AND FINANCIAL NEEDS

RICHELSON INVESTMENT RULE 5
Understand the Investment

The purpose of Step 4 is to match bond investments to the three general types of financial needs: emergencies, identifiable needs, and unanticipated transitions.

A cash reserve for emergencies. How much ready cash do you need to set aside for emergencies, such as a job loss or an illness? The traditional advice is that you should have somewhere between three months and one year's worth of readily available cash and cash equivalents to weather these storms. The answer will be specific to you and your family situation and should take into account whether you and/or your spouse have adequate insurance coverage (which you should consider having) in the following areas:

- Medical insurance
- Disability insurance
- Life insurance
- Long-term care insurance
- Property and casualty and umbrella insurance to cover your home, office, cars, boats, and so forth.

If you take the planning steps set forth below, you may need to keep much less in cash. The calculation should also take into account the probability of finding satisfactory new employment during the next year. There may be other employment opportunities available, but in today's economic climate, finding a job that's the right fit for you might take longer. Therefore, be prepared by considering our recommendation to set up the following lines of credit before an emergency occurs:

◆ A line of credit to borrow against your home (if you have one). This is called an equity line of credit, which should cost you nothing to set up and ideally you will never use it.

◆ An extra credit card or two with a high line of credit to be used only in an emergency.

◆ A line of credit with your bank that costs nothing to set up and keep in place.

If you have a portfolio of bonds or stocks in a brokerage account, you will be able to take a margin loan for personal expenses against the value of your portfolio in your brokerage account. If you are not currently taking a loan against your securities, all your bonds and stocks should be in a so-called cash account at your brokerage firm. That way, in the event of a bankruptcy of your broker or custodian, your securities will be legally more secure.

If you need to borrow against your securities, you can quickly switch some or all your securities from the cash account to a so-called margin account. You can borrow between 50 percent and 90 percent of the value of your securities in your margin account, depending on which securities you hold and the custodian that holds them. Thus, if you have a short-term need for cash, you don't have to sell your bonds to get it. With a margin account loan, the interest rate you pay for the loan generally declines as the amount of the loan increases. Keep in mind that if you need to sell your plain-vanilla bonds, they are very liquid and can be easily sold at a small cost.

As you can see from the number of uncertainties and possible emergencies mentioned earlier, if you have good insurance coverage and good lines of credit, the amount of cash and cash equivalents you need keep on hand to fund emergencies may be very small. If you have a substantial bond ladder, you might have a quantity of bonds coming due each year. In that case, no special planning is necessary, other than to have adequate insurance and good lines of credit.

To the extent that you wish to have cash equivalents to fund any emergencies, they would be among the following:

◆ Money market accounts, both taxable and tax free.
◆ Treasury bills.
◆ Agency debt coming due in less than one year.
◆ Brokered CDs that can be sold back to your broker at any time without a penalty.
◆ EE or I savings bonds if they have been held for more than one year.
◆ Any other plain-vanilla bonds that are coming due in less than one year because with such a short maturity they will be selling close to their face value.

Funding identifiable needs, objectives, and anticipated transitions. As part of your financial-planning process, you should identify those needs, life objectives, and anticipated transitions that you believe will occur during your lifetime. You would then match these specific items with bonds that come due when you believe you will need the cash. Bonds are perfect for this matching process because you can buy bonds coming due in any year you need the money. All your identifiable needs should be taken into account when you plan your bond ladder.

Suppose you're saving for a custom addition to your house, an expensive vacation trip to Africa in three years, or college in ten years. In these examples, your needs dictate investments in bonds that will come due when you need the cash. For example, the date when money will be needed for college tuition is predictable. You can fund college tuition by buying bonds that come due when your child will be eighteen, nineteen, twenty, and twenty-one. If you are in a high tax bracket, you would buy tax-free municipal bonds to come due in each of the required years rather than taxable bonds.

An excellent choice to fund college tuition for high tax-bracket individuals is deferred-interest, zero-coupon, tax-free municipal bonds because they often pay more interest than coupon municipal bonds. In addition, zero-coupon bonds save you the trouble of reinvesting the interest as it comes due. Another possibility to fund college tuition expenses are EE and I savings bonds. See the discussion in chapter 7 on how to use these bonds to fund education tax free if your income doesn't exceed certain limits.

The ideal bonds to use to fund your identifiable needs and specific objectives would be our old friends the plain-vanilla bonds listed below:

- Treasury bonds, both coupon and zero-coupon
- TIPS bonds and I savings bonds if you are concerned about inflation
- EE savings bonds
- Agency bonds, both coupon and zero-coupon, but not mortgage bonds
- FDIC-insured CDs, brokered and bank issued
- Highly rated and insured municipal bonds, both taxable and tax free, both coupon and zero-coupon
- Highly rated corporate bonds
- Highly rated Yankee bonds

These plain-vanilla bonds provide the ultimate in security. There is little possibility of a default, and market risk is reduced if you create a custom bond ladder. Longer-term, plain-vanilla bonds will not default, but they do have market risk (inflation risk) because of their longer maturities. The longer-term investments we suggest generally provide a higher yield than the shorter-term investments without any more default risk. However, market risk increases if the long-term bonds must be sold before they come due, whether you purchase individual bonds or a bond fund.

Your specific selection of bonds should depend on your tax status. For example, if you are seeking tax-free income, you would concentrate on highly rated tax-exempt municipal bonds. If you are looking to defer tax payments, you would choose series EE and I U.S. savings bonds. If you are in a high tax bracket, you would not want to purchase zero-coupon taxable bonds or TIPS bonds in your taxable account because if you do, you would pay current taxes on imputed interest income and you don't receive the cash until maturity. Zero-coupon bonds and TIPS are excellent choices if they're held in a pension account.

If you live in a high-tax state, you might find Treasuries and certain agency bonds attractive because they are not subject to state and local income tax. (See chapter 8.) If you are concerned that your portfolio may be eroded by inflation, invest in TIPS and I U.S. savings bonds.

Funding unanticipated transitions. When we provide a financial plan for a client, we always consider unanticipated transitions and bumps in the road, such as a critical illness, disability, death of a spouse, divorce, job change, and job loss. Fortunately, many of these adverse events can be covered by insurance. However, having a significant portfolio of plain-vanilla bonds arrayed in a bond ladder provides additional protection against the fallout from these events. For investors concerned about unanticipated transitions, we can't stress enough the protection and peace of mind that a significant portfolio of plain-vanilla bonds provides.

Many investors dream of having financial independence, but most people do not want to make the sacrifices required to achieve it. They seek, at best, to accumulate enough investment assets to deal with the unanticipated transitions and bumps in the road. For those hardy souls who seek financial independence, there is no better solution than the 100 percent bond portfolio producing more interest income than your cost of living. Remember that there are two ways to get to financial independence: generate more interest income, or reduce your expenses. Downshifting to reduce expenses could put many investors on the road to financial independence.

If you need reliable income as you get older, when you have fewer years to make earned income, you should create a program to save more money. If you have earned income that is high one year and low the next, a stream of income from your bonds that smoothes out your cash flow's ups and downs would be very desirable.

Starting out with less than $25,000 to invest. If you have less than $25,000 to invest, buy short-term or intermediate-term bonds. Don't buy long-term bonds because you can't afford the market risk if you need your funds. You don't need to diversify when you buy the plain-vanilla bonds listed below because they are so safe:

- Treasury bonds

- TIPS bonds
- Agency bonds
- CDs
- EE and I savings bonds
- Highly rated municipal bonds (if you're in a high tax bracket)

If you invest in bonds early in your life, the income will be able to compound, exponentially multiplying many times in your life.

Evaluating Risk

RICHELSON INVESTMENT RULE 3
Don't Lose Money

There is no place in the 100 percent bond portfolio for risky, aggressive, expensive, and complicated investments. These risky investments can be part of a portfolio you reserve for speculative investments, rather than sound investments as we define them. The key is to understand the nature and degree of risk you're taking on and to make sure that it's appropriate to your situation.

Make speculative investments only when you understand the nature of the investment and have the capacity to deal with a possible loss. Remember, there is a direct correlation between risk and reward. Although you have a chance to make a lot of money with speculative investments, you also have a chance to lose a lot of money. Investments we consider speculative might not seem very risky to some, but we have an aversion to losing money.

The securities we call speculative and recommend against including in your 100 percent bond portfolio include:

- Collateralized mortage obligations(CMOs) and individual mortgage securities
- Nonrated or poorly rated corporate and municipal bonds
- Emerging-market bonds
- Bonds denominated in a foreign currency
- All long-term bonds that come due in more than twenty-five years, except as an integral part of a bond ladder
- All common and preferred stock

For investors in a high tax bracket, the highest returns are often found with the longest-term municipals and with municipals with very short calls. However, each of these bonds has a different kind of market risk. High-yield municipal funds are available, as are leveraged closed-end municipal funds, but both increase the risk of municipals up a few notches to an unacceptable level.

Also available are mutual funds called "government bond" or "mortgage bond" funds. Although these sound safe enough, they may be risky if they contain a significant amount of nonagency mortgage securities including CMOs and high leverage. Investigate the mix of investments to see what the funds contain to make a determination if it suits your needs and risk tolerance. Foreign bond funds, including global, multisector, and balanced bond funds, offer potentially high returns and definitely carry high risk. Long-term target bond funds containing zero-coupon bonds have considerable market risk despite their containing Treasuries as well as long-term corporate bonds.

In terms of risk, all aggressive bond investments are not created equal. Long-term municipal bonds and municipal bond funds have less risk than similar high-yield corporate funds and funds holding foreign bonds. Corporate bonds are generally more risky than municipals. A long-term zero-coupon bond has very high interest-rate risk if you need to sell it before its due date even if the default risk is minimal. Buying zero-coupon Treasuries in a closed-end fund creates market risk because the investment is long term as well as zero-coupon. There is also the risk that the price of the fund may fall below its NAV (for example, the underlying value is worth $1.00 per share, but it is selling at $0.90).

A closed-end leveraged bond fund will also increase a portfolio's potential return as well as its actual risk. Closed-end municipal bond funds are often leveraged because the municipal yield curve is generally steeper than the interest paid on short-term taxable bonds. The combination of leverage and higher long-term interest rates creates a better cash flow for the fund but increases the volatility of the price swings. Consider *Richelson Investment Rule 6: Understand the investment's liquidity.*

All professional bond traders speculate with bonds and so do many individual investors. Traders place bets on the direction of interest rates. For example, if they believe that interest rates will decline, they buy long-term bonds; the bond purchased might be very conservative Treasury bonds or corporate bonds. If they're right, they can make a bundle. To increase the size of their bets, they might buy the bonds on margin and use leverage to increase their return. When they buy on margin, their broker lends them part of the purchase price. For Treasury bonds, the margin might be as much as 96 percent of the purchase price. In this case, they will lose all their investment if interest rates go up instead of down and the price of their Treasuries declines by more than 4 percent.

Income buyers (investors who are concerned only with monthly income) should keep in mind that if the yield on a bond is much more than that of a plain-vanilla bond, the risk of loss is much greater. Reaching for current yield may delay the problem of inadequate income. However, when considering speculative investments, remember *Richelson Investment Rule 7: Check for the seller's conflicts of interest before you buy.*

Reevaluating Your Portfolio

An investment-planning exercise is not a once-in-a-lifetime event. It should be done periodically to reflect the changes in your needs, lifestyle, and income. When you're young, you should review your financial plan with each major change in your life, such as getting married or becoming a parent. As you get older, you should review your financial plan with regard to the needs of your dependents. Finally, long before retirement looms, you should review what income you will need and how best you can achieve that objective. It sounds like work, and it is, but it's worth the trouble.

CHAPTER 18

FINANCIAL PLANNING WITH BONDS

Case Studies

CHAPTER 17 DESCRIBES how an investor might use bonds in the investment-planning process. But let's put these theories to the test now and see how they pan out when the rubber meets the road. For most people, that happens when they realize they must plan for a life transition or when they suddenly find themselves faced with one. These events require decisions about how to proceed. Here, we'll present a number of case studies to illustrate the practical uses of bonds in planning for life transitions.

Critical Choices: Easing Life's Transitions

Each of the following case studies presents challenges and changes the person must confront. There are many ways to solve a problem. Here, we offer some possible solutions to coping with and smoothing out life's unexpected turns.

CHANGING COURSE

Earl, a lawyer, graduated from Columbia Law School and practiced as a corporate attorney at C & M, a large and prominent Wall Street law firm in New York. Earl learned a great deal in his first three years at the firm by working long hours on challenging legal matters. He also earned a great deal of money. Although his life at C & M was as he had expected, by the end of his third year, Earl came to understand that something was missing. He wanted to have more control of his own life, and he saw that this would not be possible if he continued to work at a large law firm.

To create better balance in his life, Earl visualized a plan to create a new law firm together with a few other attorneys, a plan that would allow them to reduce their work hours, enjoy their work more, and have the type of camaraderie that was missing at C & M. Earl also came to understand, with some help from us, that he would need substantial savings before he would truly feel that he had some control over his future.

To make his plan for a new law firm a reality, Earl began to save with the goal of financial independence. He had heard about the 100 percent bond portfolio in his first meeting with us. Although he liked the concept, he didn't have a need for it at that time. Now, because of Earl's desired goal, he was ready to implement a new financial plan supported entirely by bonds.

We told Earl that launching his new plan would require substantial changes in his lavish lifestyle. His first step would be to sell his New York co-op and rent a small apartment in which to live. If he was serious about his plan, Earl would have to save $500,000 by reducing his expenditures and saving a large part of his high income for the next ten years. We knew that he was very cautious and would not actually quit his job to launch his plan unless he had $500,000 to deal with the uncertainties of his newly planned life. Earl was a realist and understood that as with any new business there would be good years and bad years, and he would need a cash fund to protect himself from an early failure.

Since Earl was single and living in New York, a high-tax jurisdiction, we suggested that he use New York State tax-free municipal bonds as his savings vehicle. These bonds would be free of federal,

New York State, and New York City taxes, a huge plus for a New York resident.

The plan was simply stated but hard to carry out. It relied on three steps to achieve the $500,000 savings goal:

1 Earl must sell his co-op, which would net him $125,000 after he paid off his mortgage, taxes, and closing costs. We would invest the $125,000 in a ladder of New York State tax-free municipal bonds. The bonds would have a minimum life of ten years, be noncallable, and return 4 percent interest tax free. These bonds would be worth about $185,000 at the end of the ten-year period if all the income was reinvested in additional New York State municipal bonds yielding 4 percent.

2 Earl would save $25,000 each year for ten years, and we would purchase additional New York State tax-free municipal bonds at 4 percent interest. If Earl made these lifestyle changes, he would be living well below his means. Thus, he should be able to save $25,000 per year. These savings each year would enable him to accumulate about $312,000. The $312,000 plus the $185,000 would get him to his $500,000 goal.

3 We made sure that Earl had sufficient disability insurance, medical insurance, auto insurance, and an umbrella policy sufficient to protect him against as many risks as possible.

To carry out his plan, we helped Earl create a custom bond ladder composed of tax-free municipal bonds from only New York State issuers, which came due between five and fifteen years. If Earl is serious about his planned transition, he will save his money; this will enable him to escape from the "golden handcuffs" of corporate America and begin his new life. His financial plan is sound and attainable.

MEETING A NEED FOR SAFETY

Sean left a large corporate employer to become an independent consultant. At the time he was setting up his new business, his investment portfolio was completely in stocks, with most in the high-tech sector. When Sean came to us for financial advice, we advised him to sell all of them. When he asked whether we were making a market call that stocks were going to decline substantially in value we said we were not. The reason for our advising him to sell was that his finances could not sustain the downside risk of a stock decline. He was creating a new business and it was not clear how long it would take to launch it and make it profitable. It was also uncertain how much cash Sean would need to fund his new venture. If his new venture needed cash, it could not financially survive a serious stock market decline.

The next day Sean sold all his stock and kept all his money in cash equivalents, such as Treasury bills and money market accounts, which have no market risk and could be easily turned into cash for his business needs. As it turned out, we unknowingly had made a prudent decision because over the next nine months in 2001, the stock market declined drastically in value; Sean did need to call upon his savings to support his business.

After eighteen months, however, Sean's business became profitable, and it's now sustaining itself. Although his economic situation is better, Sean's income is still somewhat unpredictable. He needs to build up his cash flow. He has added municipal bonds to his mix to reduce his taxes as well as to provide for a good current income. Because Sean lives in Texas, which has no state income tax, he can buy municipal bond issues from any state, which will also increase his portfolio's diversity. He decided to keep some of his funds in cash equivalents, and with the rest he created a five-year bond ladder to increase his return and still provide for liquidity.

PLANNING FOR COLLEGE EXPENSES

Mr. and Mrs. Suburban, a young couple living in California, earn enough money to be in at least the 25 percent federal income tax bracket and a 9 percent California income tax bracket. The Suburbans have a newborn daughter named Maya. One of their financial objectives is to begin to save enough to finance at least part of Maya's college education.

The couple explored four choices for how to fund Maya's college expenses:

1 The Suburbans could set up a custodial account for Maya with a lump-sum contribution of $25,000. With these funds, they could buy noncallable Treasury bonds yielding 5 percent or $1,250 (25,000 × .05). Since the $1,250 of interest earned on the Treasury bonds is less than $1,700 for 2006, the interest income would be very lightly taxed because it would be taxed under Maya's Social Security number. In other words, because the $1,250 of interest income is below the dollar amount specified by the IRS ($1,700 for 2006), the so-called kiddie tax would not apply. If the kiddie tax did apply, some of Maya's taxable income would be taxed to Mr. and Mrs. Suburban in their federal income tax return. However, putting money into a custodial account has disadvantages. The money in the account may be used only for Maya's needs and expenses and may not be used for the Suburbans' personal use. Also, colleges may provide less financial aid to students who have money in their own names.

2 The Suburbans could buy EE or I U.S. savings bonds in their own name. If the Suburbans earned less than a certain amount of income in the year they cash in the savings bonds and use the money for Maya's college tuition, then some or all of the interest income earned on the savings bonds might be tax free. (See chapter 7 for a fuller description of all the technical requirements that must be met to take advantage of this tax-saving opportunity.) The Suburbans were distressed about the many qualifications required for this tax break. Because of the many uncertainties, the Suburbans decided not to buy savings bonds to fund Maya's education.

3 We did not recommend a Section 529 plan to save for college because the money in these plans is locked up in mutual fund-type investments with annual fees. In addition, these funds are exclusively for college expenses. Unless they paid a penalty, the Suburbans would not be allowed to access this money if they had unanticipated emergencies or transitions. This is another reason to keep the money in their name rather than in Maya's name.

4 The Suburbans decided to purchase zero-coupon tax-free California municipal bonds yielding about 4 percent and coming due when Maya starts college at eighteen. If they are successful in investing $5,000 per year for fifteen years and can earn an average of 4 percent on their bonds, they will have about $100,000 in their college fund. In their tax bracket, a 4 percent tax-free rate is equivalent to a taxable return of more than 6 percent so the municipal bonds are a better deal for them from every perspective. All the earnings on these California municipal bonds will be free of federal and California state income tax. If they need the money themselves, they could sell one or more of the bonds to raise cash.

AN UNANTICIPATED TRANSITION

Barbara and her husband, Jim, lived in New York. They worked long hours, she as an investment banker and Jim as a writer. They loved their work so much that they gave it priority in their lives. The result was an unanticipated transition, a divorce. Barbara won custody of Bobby, their only child, who was twelve years old. In the property settlement, Barbara thought she did well because she received assets worth $2 million consisting of their Manhattan co-op residence ($1 million after paying off the mortgage); their beach house, which she loved, ($500,000); and her IRA, which was fully invested in stock ($500,000). It is not unusual in a divorce for women to take the house or houses and let their ex-husbands take much of the financial assets. Although Barbara received more than half of the assets, she didn't do as well as she thought because she didn't take into account the taxes that would be payable on the sale of the real estate.

After the divorce, Barbara discovered that her financial world had changed drastically because she was going into debt even though she made a handsome living. Barbara could not continue her predivorce lifestyle in Manhattan and at the beach. Without both her income and Jim's, she could not cover all of her co-op and other living expenses including Bobby's private school expenses.

Barbara was worried and came to us for advice after her divorce. Barbara's financial needs were clear:

- ◆ Meet her current living expenses.
- ◆ Provide for her retirement.
- ◆ Have the option to downshift in the future to a less stressful job that pays less.

◆ Take care of Bobby's needs, including education expenses.
◆ Provide an investment fund to protect her and her son against unforeseen difficulties.

Barbara needed a financial makeover to accommodate her new situation. We quickly determined that Barbara's major problem was that the bulk of her assets were in very valuable but non-income-producing real estate. Not only did the houses not provide a current stream of income but they also ate up a significant amount of her cash every month. The real estate might appreciate in value in the future, but that didn't help her current cash flow problems. Barbara also knew that her real estate might drop in value even after many years of appreciation.

Barbara loved living in Manhattan, where she worked, but it was no longer a feasible option because of the high costs including private school tuition for Bobby. If she continued to live in Manhattan, she would be unable to meet her new financial objectives. Barbara's financial plan involved the following steps:

◆ Find a rental apartment in New Jersey that has access to a train to Manhattan and a good public school system for Bobby.

◆ Sell her Manhattan co-op and the beach house. Take the after-tax proceeds from the sales and use the money to fund a custom bond ladder composed of tax-free New Jersey municipal bonds since Barbara was now a New Jersey resident. We recommended that Barbara have a plan to accumulate $2 million in her custom bond ladder. At a 4 percent tax-free return, this $2 million fund would provide $80,000 in tax-free income. Once Barbara had a cash flow of $80,000 per year of tax-free income, she could consider taking a less-stressful but lower-paying job because her tax-free income would be enough to supplement her earned income.

◆ Sell the stock in her IRA and buy short-term agency bonds and longer-term TIPS bonds to protect against inflation and to have a secure retirement account.

◆ Have some bonds come due in six to nine years to fund Bobby's college tuition, beginning at age eighteen. Though Barbara was told that it's likely it will take Bobby five or six years to graduate, she is hoping she will have the financial resources at that time to move back to Manhattan or buy a house in New Jersey.

SOCIALLY CONSCIOUS INVESTING

Mikala had always struggled with the idea of investing her money. For her, money had been associated with capitalists and avarice. She had been a member of an entire community built around the idea of voluntary poverty. Her needs were met by community-owned food co-ops, clinics, and housing. Her community had everything it needed except money, the filthy lucre. She had been comfortable in her position until she suddenly found herself the heir to her aunt's rather tidy fortune.

Mikala was feeling flustered and uneasy about her task. Money is not concrete, something you can hug, like a tree, or smell, like a flower. It is an abstract idea that's tangled up with issues like love, power, and greed. How we view money is tied up with our childhood and with our deepest fears. Mikala had grown up in a poor family, feeling that there never would be enough. She could not understand how her rich friends would just give money away. She believed that they were suffering from the guilt of having too much. They believed that if they gave their money away, people would love them, and they would then be entitled to enjoy the money. However, the guilt was never assuaged. Some of her poor friends in the co-op thought that since money was dirty, anyone associated with money must necessarily be a bad person. On the other hand, Mikala had read that some rich people believe it is their responsibility to continue the family money-making tradition so as not to let themselves and the family down. They used their position and assets to help find solutions to the world's problems, sometimes just one person at a time.

Faced with her newfound wealth, Mikala had to decide what to do. Should she give it away, earning that glowing feeling when everyone tells you how wonderful it is that you've donated your funds? Or should she hold onto the money? Mikala knew that many people generously donated funds for all sorts of projects. She tried donating some funds and giving money to friends and family. Though the money was gratefully received, it became an invitation for everyone to just ask for more. Also, she then had no control over how the money was spent once it was gone.

Mikala realized that she was not willing to part with her money although she felt guilty about having it. The money was causing a feeling of low-grade terror complicated by ignorance of how to manage it and the shame of not knowing how. She was smart enough to know that she did not know. She decided her slogan would be: "End poverty: learn about money!"

In Mikala's parents' generation, all people had to do was save money and have a little fiscal restraint. As the philosopher Jacob Needleman explains, "Earlier generations placed considerable moral value on an individual's ability to 'make his own way,' to 'stand on his own feet,' almost without regard to what sort of work one did."[1] Now, complained Mikala, we're supposed to find "meaningful work," and know how to invest money. It is assumed that money-management skills blossom along with adulthood, yet most of our parents and our teachers are deficient. Investing money was not an issue for past generations because they did not live long after retirement.

The question of how to invest brought memories of Mikala's childhood; she remembered betting one dime at a time at the county fair until she lost her dollar. She recalled how her father used to go into a car dealership with the $3,000 to buy that new car he needed and then convince himself he really didn't want it anyway. She remembered Christmas Clubs that let you deposit your money in the bank but did not pay you any interest.

Mikala's parents purchased a $25 U.S. savings bond for $15 every month so they would have enough money to retire. They had never borrowed money until they decided to take a loan to help purchase a business that her mother wanted to start. Taking a mortgage in the 1930s was very risky because banks offered only three-year balloon mortgages. That means you pay only the interest on your loan for three years and at the end of that period, the entire principal is due. If you couldn't pay off the principal at that time, you forfeited your collateral. People did not borrow without careful consideration. Only the advent of government-sponsored agencies that purchased mortgages from banks made the mortgage market so liquid.

Ill-advised advisers. Initially, Mikala's money was in the hands of her cousin, a stockbroker, who put her money in a managed account. After a couple of years of paying a fee of 1.25 percent of her principal per year for the privilege of losing money there, she decided she needed a change.

She sought out financial advisers but was wary of their advice. One adviser encouraged her to purchase life insurance policies and annuities, telling her that her money would grow inside the insurance policies and the annuities would provide her income for life. Since she had no children, Mikala was not concerned about leaving money to heirs. Life insurance is supposed to insure you against a risk you cannot cover. This insurance policy seemed to her a very expensive "savings plan." If she were to purchase a policy, the money would belong to the insurance company. She could borrow the money out of the plan, but she would have to pay interest on the loan. If the loan was not repaid, it would reduce the value of the policy. This did not make any sense to Mikala. Why give your money to someone else so that you could borrow it back? As for the annuities, Mikala looked at the fees and the lock-up of her funds and decided that it was an expensive way of getting an income stream. She did not view the insurance company as her friend because her parents had had such trouble collecting on a policy they owned.

There were lots of other advisers willing to serve. Since they gave advice *and* sold products, Mikala was wary of them. She saw that as a conflict of interest. Mikala remembered reading about it:

> Ignorance and shame about money creates the tsunami of revenues that washes through the financial service industry. Money in motion generates fees; managed money generates more fees; advice on how to manage or move money generates yet more fees. The public's lack of financial education is startling.[2]

From her reading, Mikala knew that she could invest in mutual funds that would place the money in stocks of companies that were considered socially responsible. However, she did not like the ups and downs of the stock market. In addition, Mikala was told that the average earnings of equity funds that employ some sort of "socially responsible investing" approach is routinely about 2.7 percent behind the average for all equity funds.[3] Those funds primarily screen out, somewhat arbitrarily, investments in the following major areas: alcohol, tobacco, defense, pornography, and gambling.

Mikala wanted to be conscious of where her money was going and what effect it was having on the world. She did not want to spend her life looking at the market wondering what she should do next. She did not like the idea of putting her money into a retirement fund that was a blind pool of money. Nor did she see how a managed account differed substantially from a mutual fund. Mikala believed that it was better to take the time to understand the alternatives than to thoughtlessly rely on someone else.

Mikala appreciated how sensitively her parents considered life's alternatives. That memory led Mikala to consider investing in bonds in honor of her mother and father who struggled hard to improve their children's lot in life and their own.

Mikala's bond portfolio. Mikala's friend recommended that she read our book *The Money-Making Guide to Bonds.* Once she did, she decided to call us and see if she could retain us as her advisers. At her first consultation, Mikala discovered that if she purchased individual bonds, she would have very low expenses on her investments and there was a huge selection. Essential to choosing the right bonds was to determine:

- How to allow for cash to be available for planned and unplanned life events and transitions
- What percentage of assets to put at risk
- How Mikala's tax position affects her portfolio
- Which bonds would fit best in her financial plan

Mikala decided that she generally did not want to put her funds at risk. She anticipated having little earned income so she would be in a low tax bracket. She had a need for some cash income and for ongoing income. However, she did not have any specific milestones that had to be met.

We advised her to purchase some taxable bonds to boost her marginal income tax rate into the 25 percent bracket. Taxable bonds she could consider included U.S. Treasury bonds, corporate bonds, agency bonds, and CDs. Mikala considered investing some of her funds in bonds of corporations that supported her beliefs. After investigating the possibilities, she realized that no corporation would exactly meet her criteria. Dig deep enough and you can always find problems. Mikala knew that leaving the money in the bank was not an alternative because the bank could turn around and lend the money for things she might find objectionable. Mikala realized she would have to compromise both to protect her assets and to be paid for the risk she was taking. As a result, Mikala decided to purchase agency bonds because she was willing to support the mortgage market and help people achieve their goal of home ownership. Some of the agency bonds were also exempt from state income taxes.

Once her federal marginal tax bracket was high enough, the majority of Mikala's funds should be invested in tax-free municipal bonds. Within that category, bonds are issued for all kinds of purposes. There are certain bonds that require voter approval (GO bonds). Voter approval means that the voters support the project and are willing to pay for it. All GO bonds would fit Mikala's criteria. Investing responsibly would not mean that she had to accept less return than other investors receive.

GO bonds are frequently issued for the support of schools. Since education was an essential value in her life, Mikala decided that she would use her money to invest in schools by purchasing school bonds, in effect, lending money to communities to help them build and equip schools.

Mikala also decided to purchase state-issued housing bonds since they provide below-market-rate mortgages to low-income families. These mortgages can be quite risky if they do not have strong financial guarantees. However, the ratings on Mikala's bonds were AA to AAA, depending on the strength of the guarantees.

Mikala also liked water and sewer bonds, which are also GO bonds, because they provide fresh water and maintain good hygiene for a community. Wastewater treatment plants were not her favorite investment, but she saw the need for those services. In this way, she was voting with her money for the establishment of services that provide for the health and well-being of the people around her.

All these bonds pay interest every six months. There is also no state or federal tax on the interest from the municipal bonds because she purchased them in her home state of Pennsylvania. Mikala made sure that all her bonds were insured to give her belt-and-suspenders protection. The default rate on the kinds of bonds she selected was very low. Because of the insurance, Mikala's portfolio had bonds with AAA ratings.

Mikala laddered her portfolio to minimize both the inflation risk and the reinvestment risk. Although there is no perfect investment that will protect against inflation, Mikala knew that she would always have some funds to reinvest in the event of higher rates, thus, mitigating to some extent the impact of inflation. Also, she knew that she could sell some of the bonds with short maturities to purchase bonds selling at higher rates. She could also choose to purchase inflation-protected bonds, but they would reduce her cash flow since they have low current-interest payments, and she would have to pay taxes on the imputed annual income.

Charitable lending and personal growth. Believing that it's better to teach someone how to fish than to give them a fish, Mikala decided that with the income from the bonds, she would set aside a portion for helping people who would ordinarily not qualify for loans from traditional lending institutions. She thought of Grameen Bank in Bangladesh, the first bank established to make low-cost, collateral-free loans, founded by Muhammad Yunus, the winner of the 2006 Nobel Peace Prize. As of 2006, the bank had 6.39 million borrowers, 96 percent of whom were women. The loans enable the borrowers to begin a simple business and earn a living. However, Mikala also wanted to support projects close to home.

There are many microlenders both in the United States and around the world to whom Mikala might donate. Also, she could deposit some funds in a community development credit union. Although receiving below-market rates, her money would be FDIC insured and the funds would be lent to low-income members. The devastation of Hurricane Katrina, for example, led the banks in New Orleans to call for funds needed for community redevelopment. There are many community development opportunities, including community development loans, venture capital, and microenterprise funds not far from where Mikala lives.

Once Mikala understood the concept of microlending, she realized that her own family could benefit from such funds. She was one of nine children, and she already had grandnieces and grandnephews who would soon be applying to college and needed help. To create an incentive for her relatives and protect herself from feeling like an ATM with arms, Mikala created a college fund. She offered to match any money contributed to the college fund dollar for dollar and offered an additional interest-free loan for four years for those who participated. With legal help, she created a contract for participants to sign. She wanted the relationship to be formal so the young college-bound participants and their families would appreciate the meaning of a contract and the importance of what she was offering. She planned to fund this account on a current basis so that every dollar she received she immediately matched. She planned to use deferred-interest-paying bonds for younger children so she could put less money into the fund and still meet her obligations. The magic of compound interest would do the rest.

Church bonds. Another opportunity for Mikala was church bonds. These bonds are issued by all religious denominations to support their missions and expansions, and are repaid from donations of the congregation. The bonds are not rated by the traditional bond-rating agencies. If the congregation stops paying, the bonds can and do default. Although Mikala had told us that she did not wish to risk her capital, she believed in this project and wanted to support it.

Mikala's church was seeking donations to build a residential retirement facility, especially for patients with Alzheimer's disease. Mikala was willing to give some funds, but there was another way to help that she preferred more. To begin construction on the facility as soon as possible, the church decided to float a bond issue that was not rated. A nonrated bond usually means that the project is very risky. In this case, the issue was very small, and it didn't make financial sense for the church to pay for a rating.

Mikala liked the notion of creating a special place for people suffering from this disease since her father had struggled with it before his death. She liked the leadership and felt that they had good intentions as well as financial savvy. She asked us to review the loan-offering documents and investigate the offering to see if it had reasonable prospects of paying interest and returning her capital. Satisfied by our response that the documents were properly drawn, she purchased the bonds for her portfolio. Although she knew that there was a risk that she might lose her money, she was glad that she had the financial wherewithal to help. Mikala believed in the words of Bob Mandel in *Wake Up to Wealth*: "Surely poverty is not the soil of the good life any more than money is the root of all evil."[4]

Mikala's life plan. Mikala feels very comfortable with her life plan. She found a way to make her money grow that didn't require endless attention on her part. She can use the revenue to help change lives and at the same time continue to support herself. Although she still finds money an uneasy friend, she realizes that it is giving her opportunities that she never dreamed about. In addition, the income from her bonds gives her the chance to further her pursuit of truth and inner development recommended by philosopher Jacob Needleman, when he wrote:

> To those who wish to put their dollars to good use in the world, I would suggest they consider seeking out the help that would enable them to work at becoming within themselves men and women who actually can see reality and understand the Good. It is not easy; it takes a great hunger, and the freedom that money brings can be a tremendous help in finding the guidance that is necessary.[5]

Some common threads run through all these case studies.

◆ First, we are often faced with daunting life challenges. If you deal wisely with your financial resources, your money can help.

For this reason, start early to save your money to increase your resources so they will be there when you need them.

◆ Second, it is not written in stone that the lifestyle you're currently living will be yours for the rest of your life. Life's circumstances may require you to change. You are not alone, though it may feel that way. Reach out and you will find others on your path as well.

◆ Third, your goals should drive your choice of investments, not the hoped-for returns from the current hot investment idea of the month. Aligning your investments with your goals will enhance your personal well-being.

◆ Fourth, look for conflicts of interest when reviewing advice and financial offerings. If your interests and your adviser's interests are not aligned, seek another opinion.

◆ Finally, if you wish to use your money to help others, you can do so in a way that will not undermine your own financial position. You must take care of yourself first if you wish to help others. Remember that when you fly in an airplane and the oxygen masks fall, the recommended procedure is to put your own mask on first before you try to help someone else.

Chapter Notes

1. Jacob Needleman, *Money and the Meaning of Life* (New York; Currency Doubleday, 1994), 270.

2. Perry Glasser, "The Last Shame in America: Why Is Everyone So Squeamish About Money?" *Utne*, July–August 2003, 64–65.

3. "SmartMoney Fund Screen/Socially Responsible Funds," *Wall Street Journal*, September 12, 2006, D2.

4. Bob Mandel, *Wake Up to Wealth* (Celestial Arts: Berkeley, CA, 1994).

5. "Bucking Economic Greed: Even Tiny Sums Can Help Build a Better World," *Utne*, July–August, 2003, 62.

CHAPTER 19

MAXIMIZING PROFITS

How to Make the Most Money From Bonds

LET'S GET DOWN TO the nitty-gritty: making money from bonds. In this chapter, we review a variety of techniques and strategies that will help you determine when to buy and sell bonds, how to take advantage of tax benefits, how to minimize the risks to your capital, and how to increase your returns. In short, we'll offer practical and profitable ways to use all the previous information presented in this book.

Knowing When to Buy and Sell

There are two types of bond buyers: those who engage in a buy-and-hold strategy and those who try to time the market. We view the former as investors and the latter as speculators. Those in the first group buy bonds and, in the absence of personal financial or strategic reasons to sell, hold them until they come due. The market timers in the second group, however, seek to anticipate interest-rate movements and then capitalize on short-term market swings by a strategy of in-and-out trading.

There is little evidence that even the top economists can consistently predict the health of next year's economy much less the direction of interest rates. If the world of finance has yet to produce a professional who can accurately and consistently predict the future, what is the likelihood that you or your broker can? Even if, through sheer random luck, you properly guess the direction of interest rates, you still might not make money unless you overcome the dual costs of trading spreads and taxes on the gain.

We endorse a buy-and-hold strategy because you only need to make one right decision: when to buy. The variations in a bond's price while you hold it are not a serious concern because you will be paid both your scheduled interest and the face value of the bond at its due date. Therefore, unless you hold long-term bonds, the ups and downs of a bond's price should not matter to you if you can hold the bond until it comes due at face value. When you trade bonds, however, you must make two right decisions to be successful: when to buy and when to sell. We recommend to our clients that they avoid market timing and leave this activity to traders who move big positions and watch the trading action all day every day. Making one right decision of this nature is hard enough; making two is a risky choice.

THE YIELD CURVE

There are certain times when it may be financially necessary or strategically advantageous for you to buy or sell bonds. Although it's not easy to spot buying opportunities in the bond market, there is a tool, known as the yield curve, that's widely used to discover such opportunities. The yield curve can also help you decide which specific maturities, among the many alternatives available in the market, make sense for you to buy.

A yield curve is the name given to a chart that plots the interest rates being paid by bonds of the same *credit quality* but different maturities. In the chart, the interest rate is found on the vertical axis and the maturity on the horizontal axis. Short-term rates are controlled by the Federal Reserve (the Fed) by changing the federal funds rate, the rate at which banks borrow and lend to each other.

That, in turn, affects the rates banks pay depositors and charge for loans. These rates affect all short-term rates, which, in turn, affect economic activity and inflation. Investors' expectations control long-term rates. The yield curve is a graphic description of borrowers' and lenders' actions in response to the changes in the costs of doing business.

Experts invariably disagree on which way interest rates will go next or on what the shape of the yield curve means for interest rates in the future. Although this is disappointing, you will still get significant information from studying the yield curve because it can tell you when to be careful and when an advantage may appear. The yield curve will help you decide how to maximize your return within the context of your own personal investment plan.

The yield curve has three classic shapes: ascending, flat, and inverted. Each, as depicted in the examples that follow, tells a different story.

Ascending yield curve. In a tranquil world, all yield curves would look like the one that appears in **Figure 19.1**. Bonds with the

FIGURE 19.1

Ascending Yield Curve

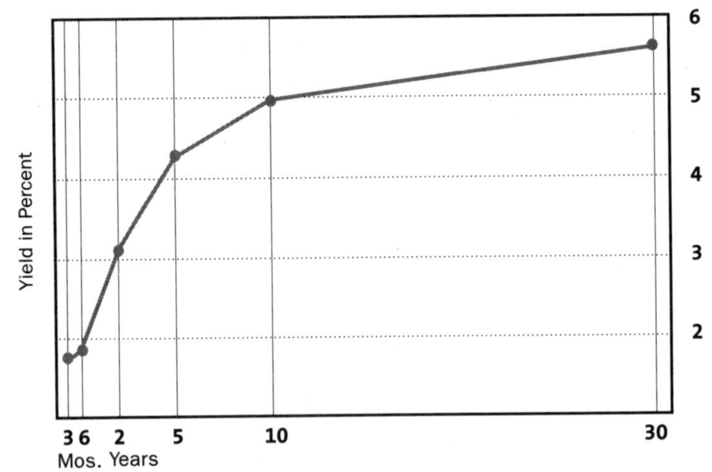

shortest maturities (those on the bottom left) would have the lowest yield (also on the bottom left) because there is less risk associated with holding them. For bonds that won't mature for many years, there is more uncertainty and additional risk. It's not unusual for there to be an ascending yield curve for, say, the first ten years of the period plotted on the curve and then a flatter curve from year ten to year thirty.

The greater risk of long-term bonds comes from their greater volatility, inflation risk, and default risk. Bondholders who take on that extra risk are paid back in the form of higher interest rates. The additional return on longer-term bonds is called the risk premium and is shown in the upper-right part of Figure 19.1. A spread of about 3 percent between the 3-month Treasury bill and the 30-year Treasury bond would not be unusual in an ascending yield curve. At times when the yield curve is ascending, consider buying longer-term bonds to capture the additional yield while staying within the parameters of your bond ladder, which is discussed later in this chapter under "Strategies for Reducing Market Risk."

Flat yield curve. When the yield curve is flat, you receive more or less the same interest rate whether you buy a short-, intermediate-, or long-term bond (see **Figure 19.2**). At these times, we generally advise our clients, within the context of their financial plan, to stay in the intermediate range because of greater market uncertainty about long-term bonds and the possibility of declining short-term rates. In that case, it usually makes sense to buy bonds with maturities only as far out on the yield curve as is comfortable until it flattens. This is called the "peak" of the yield curve. For the longer-term bonds, with maturities after that point, you may not be paid enough for the risk.

Inverted yield curve. If there is an inverted yield curve, bonds with a short maturity have a higher yield than long-term bonds (see **Figure 19.3**). An inverted yield curve is infrequent and sometimes indicates that a significant economic change is coming, such as a recession. In 2006, many pundits argued that the inverted curve did not indicate a recession because the demand of foreign buyers and hedge funds exceeded the supply of bonds, thus, driving long-term interest rates down.

FIGURE 19.2

Flat Yield Curve

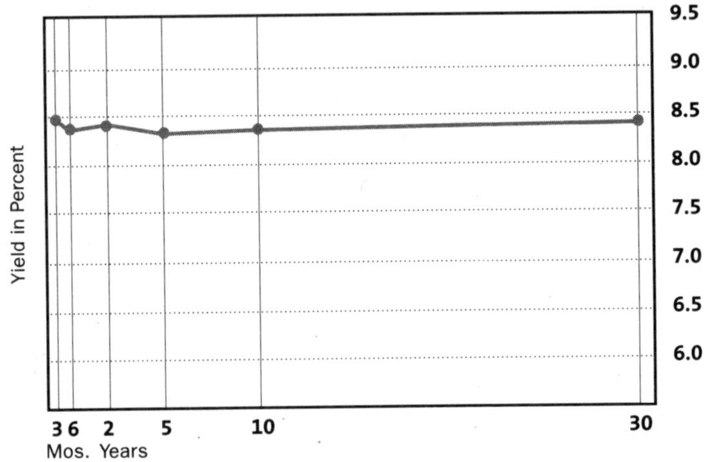

FIGURE 19.3

Inverted Yield Curve

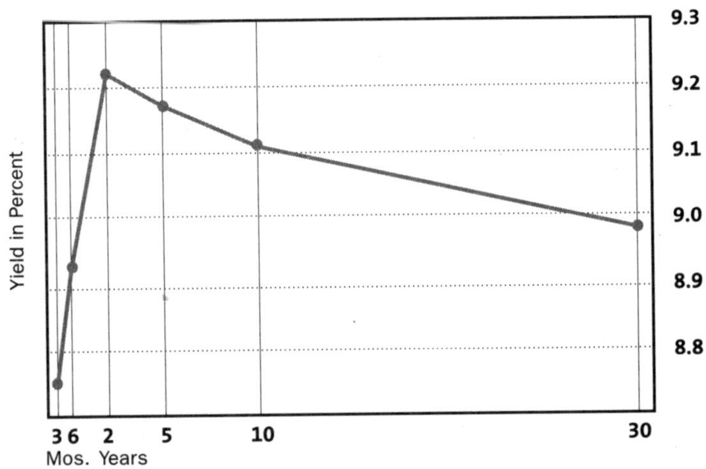

Bond-buying decisions are more difficult under these conditions. If you buy longer-term bonds, you're not being paid for the risk. You can get the highest yield by taking what appears to be the safest path, buying short-term bonds. However, this strategy might have an unfortunate outcome because the inverted yield curve does not usually last for long. Short-term yields may rapidly decline, leaving you averaging down to ever-lower yields. You also miss the opportunity to lock in the yields available in longer maturities, which may look very appealing in hindsight.

The threat that you will have to average down (get a lower interest rate) when your bonds come due is what's called reinvestment risk. In the early 1980s, for example, all interest rates were sky high and the yield curve was steeply inverted. During this period, many very conservative CD buyers bought six-month CDs and kept rolling them over every six months as they came due at lower and lower rates as the years went by. Unfortunately for them, they missed a huge buying opportunity to lock in long-term Treasury bonds yielding 15 percent in the early 1980s. In the early 2000s, the yield curve flattened and then inverted with the same result: high short-term CD rates attracted the individual investor, while professional investors scrambled to lock in longer-term rates in anticipation of the decline in rates overall.

For an excellent presentation and discussion of the yield curve, visit SmartMoney's Web site at www.smartmoney.com. Follow the path to "Economy and Bonds" and then to "The Living Yield Curve" found in the Bond Toolbox area. There, you can see for yourself how the yield curve has changed from 1978 to the present.

Strategies for Deciding When to Sell

We do not recommend market timing, but there are many times when it's appropriate to restructure your bond portfolio and sell bonds before they come due. Using the following strategies should help you decide when to take action.

◆ **Monitor the changes that may occur in your federal tax bracket.** A substantial increase or decrease in your federal income tax bracket might lead you to a decision to sell municipal bonds and purchase taxable bonds, or vice versa. For example, your federal tax bracket might decrease as a result of your retirement, large business losses, substantial charitable contributions, or other deductions, or increase due to a big promotion, a great business opportunity, or an inheritance.

◆ **Check state tax rates if you move from one state to another.** A change in your residence from one high-tax state to another high-tax state or from a low-tax state to a high-tax state can trigger a need for portfolio change to minimize your taxes. In each of these cases, you might sell the municipal bonds issued by one state and buy municipal bonds issued by the other state. For example, if you move from New York to California, you might want to sell your New York municipal bonds and buy California municipal bonds to take advantage of the California state tax exemption for in-state bonds. California would tax your New York municipal bond interest.

◆ **Follow changes in the federal tax code.** Some tax-free municipal bonds, for example, are subject to the AMT. They're called AMT bonds. Discussion continues in Congress about modifying or abolishing the AMT; any tinkering with it could affect the desirability of owning or selling AMT bonds.

◆ **Profit from price gains.** Consider selling if you have a substantial gain on your bonds and you have a noninvestment use for the money or wish to invest in another asset class.

Strategies for Finding Bargain Bonds

When the general level of interest rates moves up or down, most bond sectors (for example, long-term bonds) usually follow. However, a bond sector may become relatively cheap compared to others as a result of the supply and demand for that sector.

◆ **Study the Treasury bond yield curve.** Determine the most desirable maturity range based on your needs. Suppose you were considering the purchase of a bond with a five-year maturity. You might find that purchasing a bond in a longer or shorter maturity might provide a better return as well as support your particular situation. Also, compare the yields on outstanding Treasury bills, notes, and bonds in the same maturity. The off-the-run securities might yield a little extra because there is less demand for them. Maybe you wanted to purchase a longer-term bond. The large projected federal government surplus and the government buyback of 30-year Treasuries in the 1990s resulted in a sharp decrease in the yield of long-term Treasuries in 2000. However, when the projected surplus significantly diminished in 2001, the yield increased because the potential supply of Treasuries going forward seemed ready to increase.

◆ **Compare the Treasury yields to tax-exempt municipal bond yields.** Even if you're in a lower tax bracket, municipal bonds might make sense for you if their yields approach those of Treasuries. There's a lot of historical data supporting the premise that on average the yields on highly rated, tax-free municipal bonds are normally 80 percent to 90 percent of Treasury bonds for similarly dated maturities. If yields on tax-free municipal bonds are greater than 90 percent of Treasuries, as they were for a time in 2000 and 2003, the municipals would be a good buy because they yield almost as much as Treasuries, and the income is tax free. In this situation, even the taxpayers in the lowest tax bracket benefit from munis.

◆ **When buying corporate bonds, compare the returns of subsectors in the same maturities.** All corporate bonds do not move in unison. By comparing the yields of automobile companies to rail companies, for example, you will understand that there is a yield differential for similarly rated bonds in different market sectors. Junk bonds became relatively cheap in 1989, 1990, and 2001 because of the large number of defaults and the threat of more of the same caused by the recessions in those years. Thirty percent of the junk bonds defaulted in the early 1990s, although they became a buy after the yields had increased significantly and the threat of default had diminished. In 2007, junk bonds were very expensive; consequently, they should be avoided.

◆ **Consider investing in bonds that have had many rating downgrades but may appear promising to you because you believe there will be an upgrade.** In 2006, for example, New York City bond ratings were upgraded, signaling that these bonds were becoming safer. This perception of safety was a consequence of New York's improved fiscal health, a credit rating upgrade, and investors' growing confidence in Mayor Michael Bloomberg. It helps if the bonds are insured, just in case your best guess turns out to be wrong.

Strategies for Staying Away From Overvalued Bonds

Just as there are periodic bond-buying opportunities, there are also bond-avoidance situations, times when one or more sectors may be relatively expensive.

◆ **Compare the Treasury yield curve to the yield curve of other taxable market sectors.** Professional bond traders always speak of the yield above Treasuries as a way to describe how a bond is priced. If you're not getting a satisfactory risk premium above the Treasury yield, don't take the risk. Buy the Treasury. The Treasury bond yield curve can be found on the Web at www.bloomberg.com. See also http://finance.yahoo.com/bonds for interesting online displays that list the yields and spreads between maturities of Treasuries.

◆ **Watch out for junk bonds.** When the yield spread between Treasuries and junk bonds moves to within 200 basis points (2 percent), as it did in 2007, it's an indication that junk bonds are comparatively expensive.

◆ **Compare maturities.** If the yield curve is relatively flat, there is little or no risk premium being offered for buying longer-term bonds. As a general rule, you want to be in short- or medium-term maturities if you are not getting enough interest to warrant longer-term bonds.

◆ **Compare asset classes among corporate bonds.** Some sectors are often cheaper as a result of market news, but they may not have been repriced yet to reflect the increased risk. When a sector is being flailed by the media, prices drop substantially.

◆ **Ask questions about corporate bond yield spreads over Treasuries.** The yield spreads indicate the market's perception of corporate strength, and they fluctuate based on rumor and market news. If a yield looks too good to be true, it probably is.

Strategies for When Interest Rates Are High or Rising

When interest rates go up, there is a hue and cry that bond investors will take serious losses. But we always love it when interest rates are rising because it creates wonderful opportunities for investing money at higher rates and increasing our income. For example, if interest rates go up from 4 percent to 6 percent per year over a period of time, an investor can increase cash flow by 50 percent. Remember, when the commentators say it is a bad time for bonds because rates are rising and prices are falling, you can say, let the bad times roll.

WHEN INTEREST RATES ARE RISING

◆ **Quickly invest your cash.** If you hold cash or cash equivalents, you can now invest the cash in intermediate-term bonds at a more favorable rate of return than when rates were lower. This can only be good news. Intermediate Treasury bond investments should be in the two- to ten-year range if the yield curve is fairly flat. Intermediate municipal bonds should be in the seven- to fifteen-year range if they have a steeper yield curve.

◆ **Consider cashing in your bank CDs.** This strategy holds true only for a bank CD purchased from a bank and not for a CD purchased from a broker, a so-called brokered CD. (See chapter 12 for more on CDs.) If you hold a CD purchased directly from a bank, take advantage of the fact that the principal of the CD never goes down. If interest rates have risen significantly, you might cash in your bank CD, pay the penalty, and then reinvest your cash in a higher-yielding and equally safe investment, such as an intermediate-term Treasury, agency bond, or even another 5-year CD. To discourage this strategy, some banks charge one year's interest or more. The penalty might be higher than the interest that you earned and, thus, will reduce your principal. Other banks charge between a three-month and six-month interest penalty. Check with your bank on the withdrawal penalties before you invest. On the other hand, if interest rates are low, you can use bank CDs as a place to keep your principal safe until rates move up.

◆ **Cash in U.S. savings bonds that have been held for twelve months or more.** If you hold EE or I savings bonds, you can cash them in after you hold them for twelve months or more. If you hold them for less than five years, you will pay a penalty equal to three months' interest, but if you hold them for more than five years, there is no penalty. The key point here is that you never lose any of the amount you invested or the accrued interest with a savings bond (except possibly the three-month interest penalty). If interest rates have risen significantly, you can cash in your savings bonds and earn even more income by reinvesting in safe but higher-yielding bonds. Keep in mind that if you cash in your EE or I bonds, you must pay federal income tax on the accrued interest.

◆ **Buy premium bonds.** If you might sell bonds before maturity, premium bonds will hold their value longer in a rising interest-rate market. But keep in mind that if you spend all your interest income, you will be spending some of your principal as well.

◆ **Buy new issues.** When rates are rising, you might consider buying new issues because new issues are price leaders. The brokers are hoping they will not have to take a loss on their existing inventory and do not mark down their prices quickly. New issues are priced at the current market value.

◆ **Hold on to inflation-protected bonds.** Inflation-protected bonds such as TIPS and I savings bonds are a good hedge if interest rates are rising as a result of inflation. In that case, the principal of your TIPS and I savings bonds will increase in value if you hold them until their due date.

◆ **Swap your bonds.** There are many opportunities to swap your bonds, although it's better to sell twenty-five bonds or more to get a better price. Three kinds of swaps are suggested:

1 **Swap short-term bonds for intermediate- or long-term bonds.** A swap will allow you to lock in higher returns if longer-term bonds are yielding significantly more than short-term bonds. In this case, you may either take a gain or sell at a small loss. While selling at a loss might not initially seem like a great idea, keep in mind that your loss will be small if the bonds that you are selling will come due within two years, because in this case they should be priced close to their face value.

2 Do a tax swap and take a tax loss. This is a trading strategy that one-ups the tax collector. It involves selling any low-interest coupon bonds you own that are selling below their purchase price. This generates a tax loss. Simultaneously, you buy new bonds to lock in the same or a higher return. In the 1970s, when interest rates were constantly rising, tax swaps were considered every year. The last quarter of the year was called the tax-swapping season.

3 Upgrade your credit quality. Swaps can be done to upgrade the credit quality of your portfolio by swapping a weaker credit for a stronger one at a time when the spread between better credits and weaker credits has narrowed.

Strategies for When Interest Rates Are Low or Falling

Again, we love it when interest rates are rising. However, there is also money to be made when rates are falling as long as you think strategically. Here are some suggestions:

◆ **Don't stay in cash.** When interest rates are low, you may believe that it will be best to keep your money in a low-yielding money market fund and wait for interest rates to rise. Although this strategy may work out well, many other times staying in cash may prove costly because the longer you wait for rates to go up, the higher the rates must go to compensate you for waiting and earning lower returns. For example, if money market rates are 2 percent and 5-year bond rates are 4 percent, if rates stay the same, you have lost 2 percent per year for the period involved. Even if rates do move up later, they must move up enough not only to make up for the lost interest but also to make up for the risk that the rates may not rise. Staying in cash is a type of market timing and is unlikely to work out favorably over the long term.

◆ **Buy EE bonds.** EE savings bonds allow you to lock in the current return being paid by the Treasury for at least twenty years without losing any principal or accrued interest. If interest rates kick up in the future, you can redeem your EE bonds, take your gain, and then buy higher-yielding bonds.

◆ **Take a capital gain.** When interest rates are low or falling, consider selling some of your bonds to take a capital gain. However, this strategy makes sense only if you intend to invest the proceeds in another asset class, such as equities or real estate, or have a need for cash for a personal expenditure, such as buying or improving your home. There is little or no advantage in taking a capital gain and then investing in similar bonds once you pay transaction costs related to selling and buying and taxes on the gain.

◆ **Consider the secondary market.** Investigate the secondary bond market for previously owned bonds. When interest rates are falling, you might consider buying bonds in the secondary market rather than new issues. New issues, being price leaders, may have lower yields at these times.

◆ **Consider constructing a barbell portfolio.** When interest rates are low, investors flock to intermediate-term bonds, pushing the yields of these bonds down. In this situation, you might increase the yield of your bond portfolio by using a barbell structure (see Figure 19.6). In this structure, you split your portfolio between long- and short-term bonds (each constituting one part of the barbell). In doing so, you capture the higher returns of 20- to 30-year long-term bonds and their gains if interest rates decline, while having ready access to the cash in short-term bonds that have maturities of two years or less. The combination of long-term and short-term bonds provides an intermediate-term average maturity and portfolio duration, which may be higher than the return on the intermediate-term bonds.

If you're a trader, a barbell will provide gains if long-term yields decline and you can sell your long-term bonds at a gain. If the long-term interest rates go up, the substantial short-term bond position would cushion the decline in the value of your portfolio. However, keep in mind that if you guess wrong, you may take substantial losses.

◆ **Buy bond funds with longer-term maturities.** When interest rates are falling, longer-term bond funds will give you the highest total return. If you're adventurous, consider target maturity funds and long-term corporate bond funds. If you're more conservative, consider long-term Treasury or municipal bond funds.

Investing for Tax Advantages

Always view purchases of bonds and other investments in terms of their after-tax returns. To do so, you must first determine your highest federal income tax bracket. You then compare the return you would get on an investment that's taxable with the return on one that's not. The result is called the taxable equivalent yield. The following simple formula makes this comparison:

$$\text{Taxable bond rate} \times (1 - \text{Your top marginal tax bracket}) = \text{Tax-free bond rate}$$

For example, assume that the taxable bond rate is 7 percent and your top federal income tax bracket is 28 percent. The computation would be made as follows: $.07 \times (1 - .28) = (.07 \times 0.72) = .0504$ or 5.04 percent. In this example, a taxable yield of 7 percent is equivalent to a tax-free yield of 5.04 percent if you're in the 28 percent federal marginal tax bracket. Thus, if you can get more than 5.04 percent on a tax-free bond, the tax-free bond would give you a higher after-tax return than a 7 percent taxable bond. This computation doesn't take into account state income taxes. The bond calculator at www.investinginbonds.com does take state taxes into account.

A REMINDER ABOUT TAXES

This is as good a place as any to review the tax implications of the bond investments discussed in this book. Keep these distinctions in mind when you compare yields and risks and decide on your asset mix.

◆ **Income exempt from federal income tax.** Interest from tax-exempt municipal bonds and dividends from tax-exempt municipal bond funds, but not interest from taxable municipal bonds and taxable municipal bond funds. For some taxpayers, interest from AMT municipal bonds are subject to the AMT.

◆ **Income exempt from state income tax but not federal income tax.** Interest from Treasury bonds, notes, bills, STRIPS, TIPS, savings bonds, and certain agency bonds as well as dividends from certain taxable municipal bonds and bond funds that hold these securities.

◆ **Income deferred from current federal and state income tax but ultimately subject to tax.** Interest from EE and I savings bonds until you redeem them. Even when you redeem them, they are not subject to state income tax. In addition, interest from EE and I savings bonds may be tax-free if used for education expenses by qualifying taxpayers (see chapter 7). Fixed deferred annuities are tax deferred until payout begins and then fully taxable. All interest from any bonds in a tax-sheltered retirement account is tax deferred until it is distributed and then the income is subject to federal income tax at ordinary income tax rates no matter what the source of the interest income. State taxation of these distributions varies from state to state.

◆ **Income subject to federal income tax immediately.** Unless in a tax-sheltered retirement account, income from all taxable zero-coupon bonds, taxable municipal bonds, and AMT bond income for some taxpayers.

STRATEGIES FOR PLACING BONDS IN TAX-EFFECTIVE ACCOUNTS

One subject often raised by our clients is how to place bonds in their accounts to minimize taxes most effectively. Which bonds should be placed in a taxable account and which should be placed in a tax-sheltered retirement account, such as an IRA or 401(k)? Although the answers are not black and white, here are some suggestions that may help.

◆ **Always place all tax-exempt municipal bonds in taxable accounts.** These bonds should never be placed in tax-sheltered retirement accounts (unless the yield on tax-exempt municipal bonds is higher than taxable bonds) because distributions from these accounts are always treated as ordinary income for federal income tax purposes even if they result from tax-exempt municipal bonds.

◆ **Place EE and I savings bonds in taxable accounts.** The tax deferral is wasted in a tax-sheltered retirement account, even assuming you can get a trustee to hold them.

◆ **Hold taxable STRIPS and TIPS in tax-sheltered retirement accounts.** Some of the interest from these securities results in imputed or phantom income that is currently subject to tax if held in taxable accounts but creates no current tax liability if the securities are held in tax-sheltered retirement accounts.

◆ **If you place taxable bonds and bond funds in tax-sheltered retirement accounts, the advantage is that the taxable interest and capital gains are deferred and not subject to current tax.** The disadvantage is that long-term capital gains generated in these accounts are treated as ordinary income when they are distributed. Thus, if a bond is held for more than one year, you have converted long-term capital gains, which are lightly taxed, into ordinary income, which may be heavily taxed. In addition, there is no tax benefit for losses realized in a tax-sheltered retirement account. Note that there is a 10 percent tax penalty on an early withdrawal before age 59½ from a tax-sheltered retirement account.

◆ **If you place bonds that are infrequently traded in taxable accounts, any long-term capital gains are lightly taxed in 2007 at a 15 percent federal income tax rate.**

STRATEGIES FOR INDIVIDUALS IN HIGH TAX BRACKETS

Tax-exempt municipal bonds are the best and last great tax shelter for individual investors. Individuals who are in high tax brackets benefit most from an investment in tax-exempt municipal bonds. However, even taxpayers in the 25 percent tax bracket generally can benefit from an investment in these bonds because the interest income is not subject to federal income tax. In 2007, a single taxpayer reached the 25 percent federal income tax bracket when the taxpayer's taxable income exceeded $31,850; married taxpayers reached the 25 percent federal tax bracket when their taxable income exceeded $63,700.

However, there are two other categories of municipal bonds to watch out for: one category is municipal bonds subject to the AMT. They're called AMT bonds because their interest income is subject to the federal AMT for certain individuals. The AMT keeps changing, and it is unclear who will be hit by this tax in any year.

The other bond category is called taxable municipal bonds. The interest income from these bonds is subject to federal income tax but not subject to the AMT. Taxable municipal bonds provide a higher interest rate than tax-exempt municipal bonds, and many are insured; some are zero-coupon bonds. Highly rated taxable municipal bonds are excellent investments for your tax-sheltered retirement accounts.

STRATEGIES FOR TAX-SHELTERED RETIREMENT ACCOUNTS AND INDIVIDUALS IN LOW TAX BRACKETS

Generally, bonds that are good for individuals in low tax brackets are also good for tax-sheltered retirement accounts because in both cases interest income is either not subject to tax currently or is taxed at a low rate. Some individuals in high tax brackets will be in a lower tax bracket after they retire from their full-time job and their earned income terminates along with their job. Should this be the case for you, review your bond portfolio carefully. You may be in a position to take advantage of your new lower tax bracket and increase your after-tax income.

For tax-sheltered retirement accounts and low-tax-bracket individuals:

◆ **Consider STRIPS, TIPS, Treasuries, agencies, taxable muni bonds, and highly rated corporate bonds.** They are safe. The adverse tax consequences of STRIPS and TIPS (because they generate phantom income) will not result in a significant amount of tax if the low-bracket taxpayer has little or no other taxable income.

◆ **Check out AMT bonds.** If it's clear that you will not be subject to the AMT currently or in the future, buying AMT bonds may be an opportunity for you. They often provide 20 to 30 basis points more yield than non-AMT bonds, frequently without any sacrifice of credit quality. However, keep in mind that AMT bonds may be difficult to sell at a good price. In addition, even if you are not subject to the AMT today, you might be subject to it in the future. Some muni funds may hold a high proportion of these bonds to boost their yield. Always investigate what percent of a bond fund is held in AMT bonds to maximize your return after tax. The fund company can give you this information.

◆ **Consider selling your tax-free municipal bonds.** If you are no longer in a high-enough tax bracket to benefit from the tax exemption, you may do better on an after-tax basis by selling your municipal bonds and buying higher-yielding taxable securities including taxable municipal bonds and AMT bonds. This may also be the time to buy a fixed immediate annuity.

◆ **Redeem your EE and I savings bonds and buy safe plain-vanilla bonds, such as Treasury bonds, to generate current cash flow.** However, the redemption will be a taxable event unless the income from such bonds can be used for educational purposes by qualifying taxpayers.

◆ **Buy TIPS and I savings bonds for safety and to provide protection against inflation.**

Investing and Risk Tolerance

Investors must walk the line between fear and greed. We want to have as much as we can and often feel envious when our peers are doing better with their investments than we are. The reality is that the return on an investment is generally proportional to the degree of its risk. Your peers, for the most part, have simply taken on more risk if their returns are better than yours or they have a selective memory of only the good times. There is no free lunch. However, there is this book, and the following information provides guidelines on how to reduce risk while still getting a good return.

PRACTICAL CONSIDERATIONS FOR ASSESSING RISK TOLERANCE

If you've read this far, you've probably already assessed your need for income, the level of risk you're willing to assume with your bond investments, and your capacity to actually sustain losses. Now consider the following questions:

◆ **If your bond portfolio declined in value would you panic and sell your bonds?** If so, you probably have a low risk tolerance and failed to keep in mind that your bonds will come due at their face value. To be at peace with your bond investments, you should consider buying only short- and intermediate-term bonds that you can hold until they come due. If you can hold bonds until they come due, you will have no reason to panic or sell your bonds prematurely.

◆ **Would you engage in an interest-rate play by buying 30-year bonds with an eye toward selling for a significant gain if interest rates decline? Would you buy a bond with a 12 percent yield and take the risk of losing a significant amount of your capital?** If so, you are a speculator and should have a high capacity for loss.

◆ **Is your portfolio heavily weighted in equities and illiquid investments such as real estate?** If so, a conservative bond portfolio will provide a safe foundation enabling you to take on more risk with other investments and business ventures.

STRATEGIES FOR REDUCING THE RISK OF DEFAULT

When bond investors think of risk, the main risk that many consider is default risk, the risk of an issuer going bankrupt and bondholders losing their investment. Bad times in an industry or problems that are specific to the issuer might cause a default. Here's how to stay away from such risk.

◆ Buy the plain-vanilla bonds described in chapter 2, and in any case buy only bonds rated at least A or better for municipal bonds and AA or better for corporate bonds. When you're looking at ratings, it's important to determine when the bond was last rated by the rating agency. In general, ratings by the major rating agencies are often good predictors of the likelihood of a default. However, if the rating was done years ago, it may not reflect the current financial position of the issuer. Ask your broker not only for the rating of the bond, but also for the date the bond was last rated and by which rating agencies; then hope for the best because we all know that the rating agencies sometimes make big mistakes, as they did in rating Enron.

◆ Purchase bonds that are insured by a highly rated insurer or have some other credit enhancement that you can understand. Bond insurers are only as good as their asset base and can get overextended. If a credit agency downgrades a bond insurer, all the bonds it insures will be downgraded as well. If you buy a portfolio of insured municipal bonds, vary your holdings so that different municipal insurance companies are represented, thereby providing diversity.

- Diversification of bond issuers and due dates is a good way to minimize the risk to your bond portfolio. Diversify your holdings by issuer and, where applicable, by geographic region and market sector. If you don't have the minimum $50,000 we consider adequate to buy a sufficiently diversified bond portfolio, buy bond funds. There are many to choose from, including bond index funds, corporate and junk bond funds, and mortgage bond funds, including GNMA funds and municipal bond funds. Bond funds consisting of bonds issued by less-developed countries or denominated in a foreign currency are "high risk/high reward" investments. These bonds are exceptionally risky and could be subject to losses due to currency fluctuations as well as country defaults, as evidenced by the defaults in Russia and Argentina. However, keep in mind that even if your bond portfolio is less than $50,000, diversification is not required if you buy only plain-vanilla bonds, such as Treasuries, agencies, savings bonds, or similarly rated bonds, as described in chapter 2.
- Consider including different geographic regions in your municipal bond portfolio, even if you are in a high-tax state. Although you may pay some extra taxes, this practice protects you from the economic impact of regional downturns, particularly if you hold some lower-rated muni bonds. However, diversification may not be required if you buy insured muni bonds that are insured by different highly rated insurance companies.
- Diversify your corporate holdings by purchasing bonds from different market sectors. In this way, you can obtain the higher yield offered on corporate bonds while protecting yourself from the impact of an economic decline affecting one sector. One corporate bond fund would provide you with enough diversity.
- Purchase plain-vanilla bonds that are simple to describe and understand. Although stories about stocks might help you to find an undervalued stock, stories about bonds are usually bad news.

If the features of the bond are complex, remember that they were constructed for the issuer's benefit, not yours. Simple is good.

◆ Think twice about an investment in a sector, market, or region that is getting bad press. Take some time to consider if the extra yield is worth the extra risk. You should spend more time picking out a bond than a shirt. Purchase bonds in thriving areas and growing sectors of the economy.

Strategies for Safe Investing

In bad times, not only do interest rates often go down, but also the spread between the interest rates payable by solid issuers and weak issuers widens to reflect the higher chance of default of the weak issuers. The opposite happens in good times when the spread between solid issuers and weak issuers lessens, and you are not paid for the risk you take by buying the weaker issues.

◆ When spreads lessen across the rating spectrum, buy the good credits. Don't reach for extra yield in good times, when you're not being paid enough to take the risk. Even when spreads widen out between low- and high-grade credits, purchase only weak credits if you feel confident in your judgment. If not, keep your assets in higher-rated bonds.

◆ Buy prerefunded munis. They are the safest financial instruments in the municipal bond area because they're backed by assets placed into an escrow account. Ask what the prerefunded assets are, especially if the bonds have not been rerated. The best case is when the munis are prerefunded with Treasuries.

◆ Purchase Treasuries and agencies instead of corporates. You don't need to diversify when you purchase Treasuries so a Treasury fund is overkill unless you want the check-writing privileges. Some agency funds may contain leverage and derivatives and may not be as safe as you think. Pure GNMA funds are safe and worthy of your consideration.

STRATEGIES FOR REDUCING MARKET RISK

With the exception of money market funds, CDs, and savings bonds, all bonds are subject to market risk, whether they are

Treasury bonds or junk bonds. The principal cause of a price decline caused by market risk is generally a rise in interest rates. There are steps you can take to protect yourself against this risk.

◆ Use a bond ladder to reduce market risk and reinvestment risk. A bond ladder is a powerful risk-reduction technique that will smooth out the interest rate you earn and thus reduce reinvestment risk. Laddering a portfolio means you buy and hold a number of bonds that will come due over a period of years. The period might range from five to twenty years. When the first bond comes due, it's replaced with a bond of an equal amount at the longer end of the maturity ladder. For example, if you want to invest $100,000 in a bond ladder over a five-year period, you would buy $20,000 of bonds coming due in each year (see **Figure 19.4**). When the first $20,000 bond came due, you would buy another 5-year $20,000 bond, thus, extending your ladder by one year.

The bond ladder is a flexible tool that takes into account both the structure of the yield curve and your own particular needs. If

FIGURE 19.4

Five-Year Bond Ladder

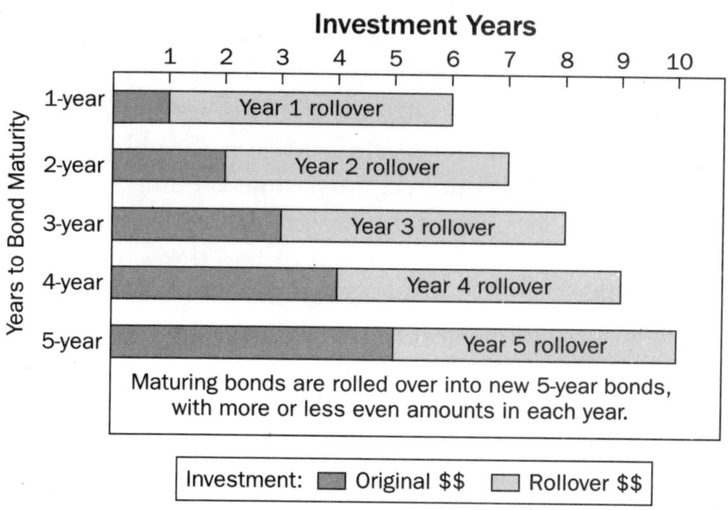

the yield curve is flat, you might want to keep your ladder from one to ten years. If the yield curve is ascending and steep, you might prefer a five to twenty-year ladder. If you have a particular expense, such as college tuition, you can modify your ladder to target particular years so that the required tuition money would be available for each year. This is called "income matching."

A laddered portfolio has several advantages. It averages the rates of interest that you earn over a period of years. A ladder provides more overall return in a rising interest rate market because if interest rates are rising, you will replace lower-yielding bonds that come due with higher-yielding longer-term bonds. A ladder results in less market risk than investing only in longer-term bonds. It provides flexibility by giving you access to your funds, because some bonds will come due each year or so, without the cost of selling a longer-term bond. It allows you to buy some longer-term bonds without undue market risk. Laddering is a strategy for individual investors who know that they can't predict where interest rates may go. It produces a steady, predictable stream of interest income that pays more than a strategy based on short-term investments only and reduces interest-rate risk and reinvestment risk.

When constructing a ladder, take into account all your investments in all your accounts, including money market funds, bank CDs, and savings bonds. Don't make the mistake of having a separate ladder in your taxable account and another similar ladder in your tax-sheltered retirement account. You should plan on one ladder that reflects all your accounts, while keeping in mind your cash flow needs. Once you have your ladder, don't worry about the current value of your bonds in good or bad times, unless you're looking for signs of quality deterioration. Unless you're going to sell, market fluctuations don't matter if you can hold your bonds until their due dates. In a so-called bear market for bonds (when interest rates are going up and the price of bonds is going down), you can reinvest at higher rates. In a bull market (when the price of bonds is going up), you can take capital gains.

We take laddering one step further and recommend that clients use a custom bond ladder so that bonds are purchased to come

FIGURE 19.5

Bond Ladder When the Yield Curve Is Steep

Year	Cash amount
Less than 1 year	$220,000
5	30,000
6	40,000
7	50,000
8	75,000
9	85,000
10	100,000
11	
12	
13	
14	

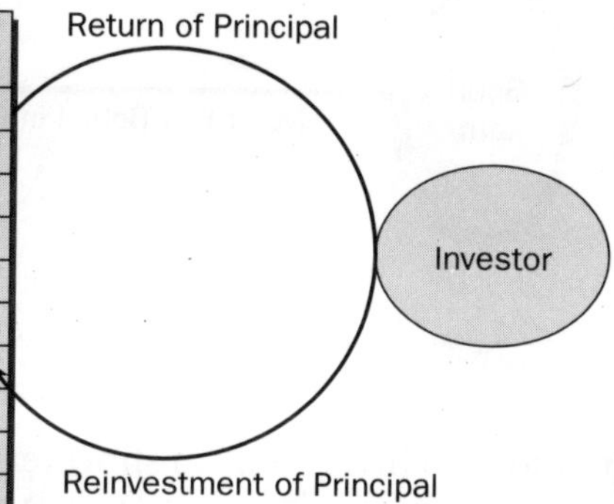

due over a period of years, with the amounts of bonds coming due in different years set to match the amounts needed to meet the client's financial objectives and needs. **Figure 19.5** is an example of a custom bond ladder we designed for Peter, whom you met in chapter 3. The ladder has $220,000 in money market funds and Treasury bills all coming due in less than one year so that Peter has access to enough cash to start up his new business. Because Peter is rewarded by higher interest rates for each year in the ladder, he decided to put increasing amounts into those later years. He plans to reinvest the cash available when a bond comes due or when his new business turns profitable. To whatever extent they don't need their annual interest income for Peter's new business or to support their family, Peter and Jane plan to reinvest it in another bond so that their portfolio will grow.

A custom bond ladder can be modified over the years as your needs and family situation change and as the returns on short-term and long-term bonds change. For example, at some point, there may be very high short-term rates and long-term interest rates. If you were financially flexible enough, you might modify

FIGURE 19.6

Barbell Approach to Bond Investing

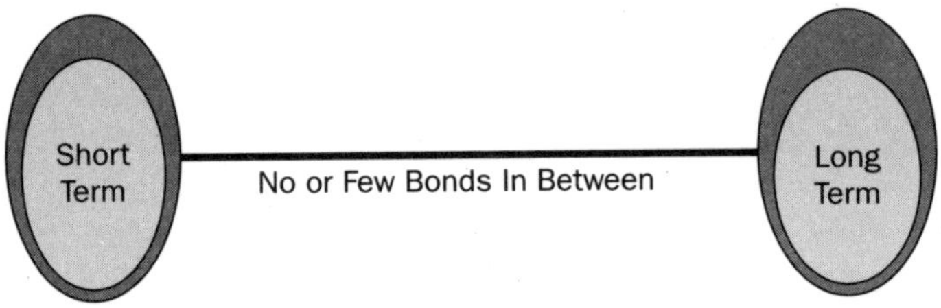

your ladder to invest only in short-term and long-term bonds, with nothing in between. Instead of a ladder, you might construct what is called a "barbell," as shown in **Figure 19.6**.

A barbell may be visualized as a ladder with a few or many rungs missing in the middle. The barbell strategy is often used by traders because the short and long bonds are the most volatile, and the market swings will produce the greatest possibilities for gains and losses.

Once you become comfortable with the idea of a bond ladder, you should create a custom ladder to suit your particular needs, taking into account the investment climate in which you find yourself. Your decisions about how to structure your ladder should blend your personal needs and where the yield curve indicates you can get the highest yield.

In summary, a well constructed bond ladder will often produce a portfolio with returns close to the return on long-term bonds, but with substantially less risk.

◆ **Purchase bonds that you can hold to their due date.** If you buy short- and intermediate-term bonds, your market risk will be significantly reduced because it's more likely that you can hold them until they come due. If there is inflation and interest rates go up, that's good news because when your bond comes due, you can reinvest at a higher rate.

◆ **Buy individual bonds rather than bond funds.** Remember that bond funds never come due. If interest rates go up and stay up for many years, which they have done in the past, you might have the equivalent of a permanent loss. Individual bonds come due at their face value. However, we do recommend bond funds for junk bonds and mortgage securities. If you wish to speculate with a portion of your portfolio, you might use bond funds to invest in foreign bonds, convertible bonds, and other off-the-beaten-path investments.

STRATEGIES FOR REDUCING LIQUIDITY RISK

Liquidity risk is the risk that you may not be able to sell your bonds quickly at an attractive price if you can't hold them until they come due. Listed next are strategies on how to reduce the liquidity risk.

◆ **Buy bonds in minimum blocks of $25,000.** If not, consider open-end bond funds for great liquidity.

◆ **Purchase bonds that will come due when you need the cash.** This reduces transaction fees and provides security knowing the money will be there when you need it.

◆ **Select bonds with good credit ratings that have wide market appeal.** Look for ratings from well-known issuers or bonds supported by insurance or other credit enhancements that are in stable market sectors, both regional and industrial. Highly rated bonds will sell more easily and at smaller spreads.

STRATEGIES FOR REDUCING CALL RISK

A call is not favorable to an investor because issuers generally call bonds when interest rates have declined. A call may result in reinvestment risk because the money returned from a called bond may have to be reinvested at a lower interest rate. Here are ways to protect yourself from call risk:

◆ **Before you buy a bond, ask your broker for a statement of all calls, not just the fixed calls.** Request a copy of the bond description from one of the information agencies, such as Bloomberg. They have a listing of all the calls.

◆ **Buy bonds that are not callable for at least five years.** If bonds are callable in less than five years, you should get a higher interest rate than for noncallable bonds.

◆ **Buy low-coupon bonds.** Low-coupon bonds are less likely to be called. However, low-coupon municipal bonds bought at a discount may result in adverse tax consequences. Check with your tax adviser before you buy bonds selling at a deep discount.

◆ **Request a listing of a fund's holdings.** Before you buy a fund, request a complete listing of its holdings to see if they consist primarily of premium bonds. If they do and the bonds are called away, it will reduce the fund's NAV.

Investing for Income Needs and Financial Goals

Bonds are all about generating income to satisfy your financial needs. In this section, we consider strategies you might use to satisfy short- and long-term goals and, finally, strategies we've developed over the years to generate additional income.

STRATEGIES FOR SHORT-TERM GOALS

You may want to invest at least some money in short-term bonds to create a readily available source of funds that will take care of you if you lose your job or have some other emergency needs. See chapter 17 for suggestions on how to fund emergencies without buying cash equivalents.

You may want to save for other short-term goals, such as education expenses or the down payment on a house, car, or boat. The following strategies will help you accomplish these objectives.

◆ **Buy bonds that come due when you need the money.** That way you can minimize the amount of money that you need to keep in short-term investments.

◆ **Buy Treasury bills, Treasury notes, STRIPS, and CDs.** You can buy them to match your maturity needs. You would hold them until they come due or roll them over at maturity into other Treasuries. If you use TreasuryDirect to buy them, you pay no transaction costs.

◆ **Buy money market funds.**

◆ **Use bank money market accounts for small sums of money.** They provide limited checking privileges but yield more than a traditional checking account.

◆ **Use money market funds tied to your checking account.** Most or all your cash will earn interest if the funds do.

◆ **Use a stand-alone money market mutual fund for excess short-term funds if they yield more than funds tied to your checking account.**

◆ **Use cash-management accounts for added yield and somewhat more risk.** Invest with a strong sponsor for added safety. Whether interest rates go up or down while you're saving, your principal will be protected. However, distinguish between cash-management accounts, money market mutual funds, and tax-exempt money market accounts. (See chapter 15 for descriptions of each.)

◆ **Buy short-term bonds.** Consider agency bonds, highly rated corporate bonds and corporate retail notes, and municipal bonds that all come due within five years. If you can hold them until they come due in five years or less, there would be no market risk and no loss of principal unless there is a default. These short-term bonds are also available in a variety of mutual funds. There are short-term corporate and muni bond funds. For the more adventurous, there are riskier funds, such as loan participation funds, municipal preferred stock, and ultrashort bond funds.

◆ **Check out the advantages of EE or I savings bonds.** Although you can't cash them for twelve months, your principal is completely protected, and the interest earned is tax deferred until you cash them, subject to a three-month interest penalty if you redeem them within five years.

◆ **Buy callable bonds.** If you can accept that they might be called, you may receive a higher yield-to-call and yield-to-maturity. Only purchase them if the calls and the maturity work with the rest of your portfolio. Do not overload your portfolio with bonds all maturing or callable in the same years.

◆ **Buy death put bonds if you are anticipating a death in your family.** These are corporate retail notes and some certificates of deposit that you can sell back to the issuer if the bond owner dies. This will enable you to fund final expenses and estate taxes.

STRATEGIES FOR LONG-TERM GOALS

Sometimes your strategy will be to invest for the long term in order to create a fund for retirement and for significant family needs, such as paying for education expenses in ten to fifteen or more years. In this case, consider using the following kinds of bonds to accomplish these objectives.

◆ **Buy intermediate- or long-term Treasury bonds, STRIPS, and agency bonds for safety.** These bonds are among the safest you can buy. The Treasuries and certain agency bonds are exempt from state income tax.

◆ **Buy certain federal mortgage securities through funds.** Ginnie Mae funds provide safe investments that will not default.

◆ **Buy EE and I savings bonds to let your savings grow tax deferred.** Savings bonds can be held for as long as thirty years without market risk or the risk of loss of any principal. EE and I savings bonds also provide a tax deferral, and if they can be used for education, a tax-exempt return for certain qualifying individuals.

◆ **Use I savings bonds and intermediate- or long-term TIPS as hedges against inflation.**

◆ **Check out intermediate- and long-term highly rated corporates and highly rated municipal bonds.** Corporates and taxable municipal bonds will provide a higher rate of return than Treasuries and agencies. However, tax-free municipal bonds may provide a higher return after taxes. If the highly rated corporate and municipal bonds are selected carefully, they should prove to be good investments for the long term. They can also be purchased through bond index funds, targeted maturity funds, and municipal bond funds.

STRATEGIES FOR INCREASING INCOME

Certain bonds and securities will enable you to increase the return from your bond portfolio if you are prepared to take on additional risk. Here are some suggestions:

◆ **Consider fixed immediate annuities.** They might be good investments if used as income replacement for earned income when you retire (see chapter 12).

◆ **Buy highly rated taxable bonds.** If you are retired and in a low enough tax bracket, consider selling your tax-free municipal bonds and buying higher-yielding corporate bonds and retail notes, corporate bond funds, and bond index funds. Keep in mind that highly rated corporate bonds are riskier than similarly rated muni bonds.

◆ **Buy junk bond funds.** Consider junk bonds only for the speculative part of your portfolio and only if you can earn substantially more as compared to safer taxable bonds to compensate you for a great deal more risk. The amount of additional return will depend on how dicey the market is. Although you may buy them in good times, you need to be compensated for the losses you may experience in bad times. Remember that junk bonds trade more like stocks than bonds. Two well-regarded junk bond funds are Vanguard High-Yield Corporate, and Fidelity Capital & Income Fund. The Vanguard fund is conservative and as a consequence the yield is not as high as those of some other junk bond funds (see chapter 15).

◆ **Buy long-term bonds.** Although we have cautioned against buying long-term bonds, they have their advantages. They generally yield more than shorter-term bonds, and they appreciate more in declining interest-rate markets. If a higher current return is important to you and you can afford to risk some of your principal, consider buying long-term bonds in the following situations:

—There is a steep yield curve so that long-term bonds yield considerably more than short- and intermediate-term bonds, and you have more than a ten-year period during which you can hold these bonds.

—Long-term bonds are yielding more than intermediate-term bonds, but you do not have a ten-year holding period. However, you're prepared to take a market risk because of the high current return and the possibility of a significant capital gain. In other words, you are knowingly speculating on the direction of interest rates.

—Long-term bonds are yielding considerably more than intermediate-term bonds, and you have a substantial portfolio of bonds that are short term and intermediate term, so that you can hold the long-term bond forever as part of your permanent portfolio. In this case, adding long-term bonds to your bond ladder to get the extra yield is not a risky strategy, and we recommend it.

You may also want to buy long-term bonds if you have a substantial portfolio and are concerned with reinvestment risk.

◆ **Use premium bonds to get more current income.** Why would you pay $1,200 for a bond that comes due at its face value of $1,000? As one investor said, "I didn't build my capital by paying premiums for anything!" The impression is that you're paying more than you should. This reluctance on the part of some investors may provide you with an opportunity to get the following possible benefits from premium bonds: a higher yield-to-maturity than a par or discount bond, a higher cash flow, and a cushion in the face of increasing interest rates.

◆ **Use discount bonds and zero-coupon bonds to grow your portfolio.** Consider buying discount bonds and zero-coupon bonds, such as Treasuries, STRIPS, and zero-coupon municipal bonds, if your income is high and you want them to serve as a savings-and-growth portfolio. Consider buying discount bonds in the following situations:

—They are yielding more than par and premium bonds after taxes. Take into consideration that the discount may be subject to tax each year or when the bond comes due. Check with your tax adviser.

—You're concerned that currently high interest rates will decline significantly in the future. In this case, the appreciation of the discount bond as it approaches its face value will help maintain the bond's yield-to-maturity. If you buy a zero-coupon bond, you will get the stated yield-to-maturity because there is no income from the bond that you need to reinvest. In addition, if interest rates do decline, discount bonds will appreciate in value more than par or premium bonds.

—Because of its lower coupon, there is less chance of a discount bond being called than a par or a premium bond.

◆ **Reread this book.** It's all here: descriptions of specific bonds, information on how to find a bond broker, details on many different funds, and numerous strategies on how to make and save money. Enjoy and profit from the efforts of our labors to make yourself wealthier and wiser.

If You're Starting Out With Less Than $25,000 to Invest

If you have less than $25,000 to invest, buy short-term or intermediate-term bonds. Don't buy long-term bonds, because you can't afford the market risk if you need your funds. You might not need credit diversification, but you might need maturity diversification. How would you deal with that? Buy the following short- or intermediate-term bonds:

- Treasury bonds
- TIPS
- Agency bonds
- CDs
- EE and I savings bonds
- Highly rated muni bonds (if you are in a high tax bracket)

APPENDIX

USEFUL WEB SITES

www.americancentury.com A no-load bond mutual fund company.

www.annuity.net A site that focuses on fixed annuities. It provides a simple calculator, and offers a variety of fixed annuities.

www.bankrate.com A good place to search for all kinds of interest rates for loans and deposits offered by the nation's banks.

www.bankrater.com A simple, easy-to-use site for CD rates and bank ratings.

www.barrons.com A good source of information about corporate bonds. Subscription required.

http://blog.bondbuyer.com A free site that generates commentary and discussion about issues relating to municipal bonds. Michael Stanton, the publisher of the *Bond Buyer*, and his business staff write the *Bond Blogger* daily.

www.bloomberg.com A multipurpose site that provides current Treasury bond, TIPS, and muni bond yields; includes a fund selector, a calculator, and more.

www.bondhead.com A site with previews and reviews of credit markets and their related economies, including links to articles.

www.businessweek.com The Web site of the business news weekly magazine. Look under "Investing" on the top tabs for information affecting the markets. There is also a "Scorecard" for mutual funds.

www.buybonds.com A site that provides California bond offerings, weekly bond updates, preliminary offering statements, and other bond information.

www.buycaliforniabonds.com This new Web site will make it easier for individual investors to learn about California bonds and buy them on the same terms as institutional investors.

www.cefa.com A Web site devoted to closed-end funds.

www.circlelending.com A service site "for families and friends" that can help you structure private loans.

www.CNN.com The Web site of the cable news network. Click on "Business" then "Markets and Stock" if you want to check bond rates and read bond news or "Mutual Funds" for fund information, plus extras. You can also use http://money.cnn.com to access this site.

www.dbrs.com The home page of the Dominion Bank Rating Service.

www.directnotes.com A source of weekly corporate retail note rates called Direct Access Notes (DANS) from some high-quality issuers. The notes can be purchased through one of the affiliated brokers.

www.dodgeandcox.com A no-load bond mutual fund company.

www.emuni.com A site established by Standard & Poor's, J. J. Kenny Drake, and E-Muni, containing prospectuses of new and recently issued revenue bonds.

www.fanniemae.com The Fannie Mae home page, offering the latest news about Fannie Mae and information about the housing market. Click on "Debt Securities" in the left column.

www.farmcredit-ffcb.com The Web site of the Federal Farm Credit Banks Funding Corporation, a federal agency that describes the type of bonds offered.

www.federalreserve.gov The main site for the Federal Reserve, which contains news articles and allows you to sign up for notices of upcoming events.

www.fhlbanks.com The Web site of the Federal Home Loan Bank, a federal agency.

www.fidelity.com. A very user-friendly site for bonds specializing in no-load bond funds.

www.finance.state.ut.us The state of Utah home page, which posts the most recent prospectuses, as well as annual reports under "Financial Reporting," then "State Bonds."

www.firstgov.gov A site that provides a connection to the home pages of all states and tribal governments in the United States.

www.fitchratings.com The Fitch Ratings home page, on which you can read rating actions.

www.forbes.com A good source of articles and information about personal finance, including a fund screener and top fund picks.

www.freddiemac.com The Freddie Mac home page, with information about Freddie Mac's program to issue debt, new mortgage issues, and the good works of the company to further affordable housing.

www.ginniemae.gov A site on which you can gain a general education about these pass-through securities and view prospectuses.

www.immediateannuities.com A very effective calculator showing the costs of a variety of benefit combinations. It also has a table showing state guarantees.

www.imoneynet.com A good source of information about money market rates.

www.internotes.com A site on which you can view current offerings of corporate retail notes called "InterNotes" and prospectuses of selected corporations issuing them.

www.investinginbonds.com A site with reports of bonds traded four or more times on the previous day and trading histories of individual bonds. Decide whether to purchase taxable or tax-exempt securities using the updated tax calculator, plus a wealth of information.

www.irs.gov The Internal Revenue Service home page, which can assist you with your tax questions.

www.kennyweb.com A site giving you the municipal bond indexes from Standard & Poor's.

www.kiplinger.com A personal finance magazine with good fund information.

http://moneycentral.msn.com A site that provides fund research and investor information.

www.money.cnn.com/magazines A site providing fund information and personal finance articles.

www.moodys.com A site on which you can search for bond ratings by CUSIP or name of issuer.

www.morningstar.com A premier site for mutual fund information of every sort, with many tools.

www.munifilings.com A site on which you can access brief material event notices by CUSIP, state, or through a more specific request. Click on the left-hand button "Material Events Online," and tab to find information about bond calls and other events.

www.muninetguide.com A user-friendly hub for municipal bond research created by the National Federation of Municipal Analysts (NFMA) and MuniNet.com.

www.muniOS.com A site that provides new-issue offering statements on selected competitive deals.

www.napfa.com The home page of fixed-income advisers.

www.nasd.com/index.htm The home page of the National Association of Securities Dealers. Go to "Investor Information" where you can choose excellent tools for mutual fund fee and mutual fund fee breakpoint analyses. Provides corporate bond pricing information that can also be found at www.investinginbonds.com.

www.pimco.com A bond fund family Web site noted for Bill Gross's commentary on the markets.

www.personalfund.com One interesting tool that evaluates fund costs and the effect of taxes on your mutual fund choice.

www.quantumonline.com A site on which you can search for information about closed-end funds, preferred stock, and exchange-traded securities.

www.sec.gov The home page for the Securities and Exchange Commission and a good source of investor information. There are tools for analyzing fund fees and expenses, as well as other interesting tools. Look for "Investor Information," then "Publications." Under "Search" type what you are looking for.

www.sifma.org The home page of the Securities Industry and Financial Markets Association.

www.smartmoney.com A good site for personal finance information. Look for their mutual fund screeners.

www.stablevalue.org A site dedicated to educating the public about stable value funds. Check out the glossary to review terms that show how these funds can be made risky.

www.standardandpoors.com Standard and Poor's home page, which posts interesting articles about bond ratings.

www.stoeverglass.com A provider of bonds in the secondary, used bond market.

www.treasurydirect.gov The only financial services Web site that allows you to purchase Treasury bills, notes, bonds, and TIPS at the Federal Reserve auctions. You can also purchase savings bonds.

www.troweprice.com A no-load bond fund company.

www.tva.com The Web site of the Tennessee Valley Authority, a federal agency.

www.vanguard.com The home of the first low-cost bond funds.

www.westcore.com A no-load bond fund company.

www.wsj.com The *Wall Street Journal* home page. Mostly for subscribers, though under "Free Content" there are prospectuses and annual reports for viewing.

www.yahoo.com An excellent finance megasite and search engine.

INDEX

About the Authors

Dr. Hildy Richelson is president of the Scarsdale Investment Group, Ltd., a registered investment adviser. She restricts her practice to the design and management of bond portfolios. Dr. Richelson is quoted as a bond expert in the *Wall Street Journal, Money,* and other publications. She and Stan Richelson have authored three other books on bonds including *The Money-Making Guide to Bonds* (Bloomberg Press). They've been interviewed by Bill Griffith on CNBC's *Power Lunch* and by Mary Fay on CN8's *Money Matters.* Dr. Richelson received her PhD from Syracuse University.

Stan Richelson is a NAPFA-registered comprehensive fee-only financial adviser, and a life-planning coach. Before becoming a financial adviser, he practiced law for a major Wall Street law firm, as well as for major corporations. Stan received a JD from Columbia Law School and an LLM (in taxation) from New York University Law School. He is a member of the Pennsylvania and New York bars. With Dr. Richelson, he coauthored *Venture Capital: The Definitive Guide for Entrepreneurs, Investors and Practitioners* (John Wiley & Sons). The Richelsons practice in Blue Bell, Pennsylvania.

You may contact the authors with questions and comments at:

hildyrichelson@comcast.net
stan.richelson@comcast.net